THE VORTICISTS

THE VOR

TICISTS

MANIFESTO FOR A MODERN WORLD

Edited by Mark Antliff and Vivien Greene

With contributions by
Paul Edwards
Anna Gruetzner Robins
Robert Hewison
Tom Normand
Philip Rylands
Robert Upstone

Tate Publishing

First published 2010 by order
of the Tate Trustees
by Tate Publishing, a division
of Tate Enterprises Ltd,
Millbank, London SW1P 4RG
www.tate.org.uk/publishing

on the occasion of the exhibition
The Vorticists organized by
The Nasher Museum of Art at Duke University
Peggy Guggenheim Collection
Tate Britain

The Nasher Museum of Art at Duke University,
Durham, North Carolina
30 September 2010 – 2 January 2011

Peggy Guggenheim Collection, Venice
29 January – 15 May 2011

Tate Britain, London
14 June – 4 September 2011

Exhibition at Tate Britain supported by
ART MENTOR FOUNDATION LUCERNE

A catalogue record for this book is available
from the British Library

ISBN 978 1 85437 885 9

Distributed in the United States and Canada
by Harry N. Abrams, Inc., New York

Library of Congress Control Number:
2010924785

Designed by Rose
Colour reproduction by Alta Image, London
Printed and bound in Belgium by Die Keure

Front cover: Edward Wadsworth, *Rotterdam*
1914 (detail, no.38)

Measurements of artworks
are given in centimetres

FSC
Mixed Sources
Product group from well-managed forests
and other controlled sources
www.fsc.org Cert no. SGS-COC-004433
©1996 Forest Stewardship Council

CONTENTS

FOREWORD

This exhibition looks both forward and backward. It is the first exhibition of Vorticism to be held in Italy, only the second in continental Europe (after Hanover and Munich in 1996–7), and the first to be held in the United States since 1917. For new audiences in North America and Italy, it offers retrospective insights into a little-known British avant-garde, and reveals an episode that, though short-lived, was of electrifying force and vitality. For an audience in Britain familiar with Vorticism and its artists this exhibition contributes new accents through its focus on the exhibition at the Doré Galleries in 1915, on the New York reception of the movement in 1917, and on the Vortographs of Alvin Langdon Coburn, as well as wider-ranging themes explored in the essays in this catalogue.

Vorticism was, as Paul Edwards has remarked, 'a high-water mark of modernism in England at least until the 1930s'. Yet even in Britain it was for decades overlooked in the history of art; it did not resurface until 1951, when it featured in the publication *Contemporary British Art* by Herbert Read, whose perception of the movement as a one-man phenomenon later underlay the exhibition *Wyndham Lewis and Vorticism* that opened at the Tate Gallery in 1956. An astonishing exhibition at the d'Offay Couper gallery in London in 1969, *Abstract Art in England 1913–1915*, brought the movement to the art market. At the same time a brilliant student at Cambridge University, Richard Cork, gave Vorticism the full art-historical treatment it deserved: first in an undergraduate thesis, then in an exhibition at the Hayward Gallery, *Vorticism and its Allies*, and subsequently in a two-volume history, *Vorticism and Abstract Art in the First Machine Age* (1976), a magnum opus that still today is the platform for all research. Meanwhile, William C. Wees had already published a survey that placed Vorticism in the wider intellectual and literary milieu of London before the First World War: *Vorticism and the English Avant-Garde* (1972).

Vorticism had closer affinities with Futurism than other avant-gardes of its time, yet despite this the movement has remained largely unknown in Italy except to a subset of twentieth-century art historians, some scholars of modern literature, and a tiny circle of amateurs. In the United States, Vorticism is unknown to the general public, but thanks perhaps to the dispersal of John Quinn's collection there, to Ezra Pound's celebrity, as well as to a cultural partiality towards modern British art, university libraries, museums, and private collectors have continued to seek out the work and even the ephemera of Vorticist artists.

The story is a fascinating one: it tells of England's efforts to overcome the cultural inertia of the Edwardian period (the reign of Edward VII, 1901–10). Specifically it took place in the years from 1910 to 1914, during which Londoners – artists, critics, the general public – came to terms with continental modern art: Post-Impressionism, Fauvism, Cubism, Futurism, even the art of Kandinsky. Rebellion and change in art can be set against the broader social and political background of imperial Britain in a period of dramatic, often violent change: the birth of social welfare, the end of aristocratic rule and the weakening of the House of Lords, the militancy of the suffragettes, Home Rule for Ireland, growth in the power of labour unions, miners' strikes, and the gathering international storm that erupted into the First World War.

The presentation of this exhibition in Durham, North Carolina, Venice, Italy, and London, England, is perfectly appropriate: Vorticism's roots in London, its connections to contemporary Italian art of the period, and its exportation to New York are all captured in this partnership of three museums – the Nasher Museum of Art at Duke University, the Peggy Guggenheim Collection, and Tate Britain. We would like to express our gratitude to all the many institutions and private individuals who have lent their works of art for this enterprise and who are mentioned individually on p.8. We thank Mark Antliff, Professor of Art History and Visual Studies at Duke University, and Vivien Greene, Curator of 19th- and Early 20th-Century Art at the Solomon R. Guggenheim Museum, New York, for their pivotal roles as both the originators and the curators of this exhibition. At the Nasher Museum of Art, we also thank the exhibitions staff and especially Sarah Schroth, Nancy Hanks Senior Curator. In London Robert Upstone, Chris Stephens, and Tim Batchelor, supported by Gillian Buttimer and Andy Shiel, have been in charge of bringing the exhibition 'home'.

Finally it is a great pleasure to thank those whose funding has made this exhibition possible. At the Nasher Museum of Art, support has been provided by the Mary Duke Biddle Foundation, Marilyn M. Arthur, Trent and Susan Carmichael, the Graduate Liberal Studies Program at Duke University, Pepper and Donald Fluke, James and Laura Ladd, Olympia Stone and Sims Preston, and Nancy Palmer Wardropper, with assistance from the British Council. Exhibitions at the Peggy Guggenheim Collection are made possible by Intrapresæ Collezione Guggenheim. The support of a number of important donors has been critical to the successful realization of *The Vorticists* at Tate Britain: we are especially indebted to the Art Mentor Foundation Lucerne. We should also like to thank Oliver Prenn for his generous commitment towards the exhibition in London.

Kimerly Rorschach
Mary D.B.T. and James H. Semans Director
Nasher Museum of Art at Duke University

Philip Rylands
Director, Peggy Guggenheim Collection

Penelope Curtis
Director, Tate Britain

ACKNOWLEDGEMENTS

The genesis of this exhibition goes back almost four years, when we realized that a presentation on Vorticism had never been done in the United States or in Italy. From the moment we embarked upon the rewarding and exigent journey that brought this project to fruition, we have benefited from the collaboration, generosity, and support of many individuals and institutions.

First and foremost, *The Vorticists* is made up of magnificent loans from Europe and America. We are deeply grateful to the munificent lenders who have allowed their prized works to be part of this exhibition and to tour to three countries. We thank: Matthew Teitelbaum, Michael Parke Taylor, Art Gallery of Ontario, Toronto; Anne Jones, Arts Council Collection, Southbank Centre, London; Rita McLean, Birmingham Museums and Art Gallery; Ivor Braka; Andrea Rose, Diane Eccles, The British Council, London; Neil MacGregor, Antony Griffiths, Stephen Coppel, British Museum, London; Michael Basinski, James Maynard, Poetry Collection, State University of New York at Buffalo; John Moore, Cecil Higgins Art Gallery, Bedford; Pasquale Gagliardi, Giuseppe Pavanello, Fondazione Giorgio Cini onlus, Venice; Katherine Reagan, Division of Rare Books and Manuscripts Collections, Cornell University Library; Deborah Swallow, Barnaby Wright, The Courtauld Gallery, London; Deborah Jakubs, Archive of Documentary Arts, Rare Book, Manuscript, and Special Collections Library, Duke University Libraries, Durham, NC; Anthony Bannon, George Eastman House, Rochester, NY; Susanna White, Fred L. Emerson Gallery, Hamilton College, Clinton, NY; Richard S. Frary; Johanna and Leslie Garfield; Diane Lees, Imperial War Museum, London; Michael Harrison, Sebastiano Barassi, Kettle's Yard, University of Cambridge; Virginia Tandy, Moira Stevenson, Manchester City Art Galleries; Thomas Campbell, Gary Tinterow, Samantha Rippner, The Metropolitan Museum of Art, New York; Kaywin Feldman, The Minneapolis Institute of Arts; Earl A. Powell III, Dodge Thompson, Harry Cooper, National Gallery of Art, Washington, DC; Claudia Funke, Rare Books Collection, University of North Carolina at Chapel Hill; Anthony G. Hirschel, Richard Born, The David and Alfred Smart Museum of Art, The University of Chicago; John Smith, Walt Kuhn, Walt Kuhn family papers, and Armory Show records, Archives of American Art, Smithsonian Institution, Washington, DC; Nicholas Serota, Penelope Curtis, Caroline Collier, Tate, London; Mark Jones, Juliet Ceresole, Ruth Hibbard, Victoria and Albert Museum, London; Maria Balshaw, The Whitworth Art Gallery, University of Manchester; The Wyndham Lewis Memorial Trust; Amy Myers, Scott Wilcox, Yale Center for British Art, and Jock Reynolds, Yale University Art Gallery, New Haven, CT; as well as private collectors who wish to remain anonymous.

At the Nasher Museum of Art we are forever indebted to Sarah Schroth, Nancy Hanks Senior Curator, who masterfully guided this project from its inception, managed the intricacies of the loan process, and the many aspects of implementing the exhibition from fundraising to installation. Kristen Greenaway, Director of Development, also worked tirelessly to secure funding. Wendy Livingston successfully marketed the show to American audiences. We laud Charles J. Carroll, Registrar, as well as Carolina Cordova, former Coordinator of Exhibitions and Publications, and Myra Scott, former Registrar, for the key roles they assumed in assembling the exhibition at its inaugural venue. We also thank Juline Chevalier, Curator of Education, who created the audio guide and Brad Johnson and his preparatory staff for realizing a stunning installation.

At the Peggy Guggenheim Collection in Venice we extend our heartfelt thanks to Chiara Barbieri, Director of Publications and Special Projects, for managing the Italian edition of this book in all its complexities. Grazina Subelyte, Registrar, is to be commended for orchestrating the transport of these works to and from Venice. We also appreciate the contributions of Alexia Boro, Simone Bottazzin, Siro De Boni, Sophie Micol Fabiani, Giulia Mazzolani, Laura Micolucci, and Elena Minarelli. The impeccable exhibition design has been ingeniously done by Shraddha Aryal, Exhibition Design Coordinator, Solomon R. Guggenheim Museum. We salute the Guggenheim interns who have worked on various phases of this project: Katherine Boccard, Candida Clark, Emma Enderby, Natalia Lauricella, Roos van der Lint, Anna Musini, and Juliette Rizzi. Initial curatorial administrative assistance was provided by Kimberly Belmonte.

Our colleagues at Tate Britain have been great supporters of this project from its early days. We are very appreciative of their valuable collaboration. In particular, we thank Judith Nesbitt, Chief Curator, for deftly managing this project. We are extremely grateful to Chris Stephens, Head of Displays, and Robert Upstone, former Curator, Modern British Art, and Tim Batchelor, Assistant Curator, for their sensitive and indispensable curatorial oversight at the Tate. For the realization of the exhibition in London we are also indebted to Tate Britain's Registrars, Technicians, and colleagues in Tate's Development department, Tate Learning, and Tate Media.

This catalogue is the result of a fruitful cooperation between institutions. At the Solomon R. Guggenheim Museum, New York, the book was edited with care and attention by Kamilah Foreman, Associate Editor. Supervision of the project was initially undertaken by Elizabeth Levy, Director of Publications and Web site.

We also are grateful to Elizabeth Franzen, Associate Director of Publications, Editorial; Stephen Hoban, Managing Editor; and Melissa Secondino, Associate Director of Publications, Production for the important parts they played. At Tate Publishing we thank Roger Thorp, Publishing Director, for suggesting the Tate undertake this catalogue. Judith Severne, Project Editor, has our gratitude for her dedication to the many facets of this book, which she brought together and made cohere. We also thank Deborah Metherell, Picture Researcher, Roanne Marner, Production Controller, and Francesca Vinter, Sales and Rights Coordinator. The book's design – historically evocative and also contemporary – is due to the vision of Rose Design.

Very special thanks are owed to the authors who have contributed new scholarship of such depth and insight to this catalogue. We are honoured to share the pages of this book with Paul Edwards, Anna Gruetzner Robins, Robert Hewison, Tom Normand, Philip Rylands, and Robert Upstone. Their essays have greatly enriched the Vorticist landscape.

This exhibition has a significant archeological dimension to it, as we traced lost works shown in the Vorticists' three exhibitions and those illustrated in *Blast*. This process of 'excavation' would not have been possible without the kindness, generosity, and support of colleagues and friends to whom we are profoundly grateful. We acknowledge: Jonathan Black, Richard Cork, Paul Edwards, Matthew Gale, Sara Geelan, Andrew Gibbon-Williams, Alison De Lima Greene, Anna Gruetzner Robins, Kim Gibson Harman, Alexander Hollweg, Dick Humphreys, Jessica Iles, David N. Johnson, Janet Lehr, Patricia Leighten, Gillian Metcalfe, Brigid Peppin, Pamela Roberts, Nancy Spector, MaryAnne Stevens, Joe R. Struble, David Thomson, Robin Vousden, and Michael Wilsey.

Finally, we are tremendously thankful to the directors of the institutions who trusted in us and joined to organize this exhibition: Kimerly Rorschach, Mary D.B.T. and James H. Semans Director, Nasher Museum of Art at Duke University; Richard Armstrong, Director, Solomon R. Guggenheim Museum and Foundation, and Philip Rylands, Director, Peggy Guggenheim Collection; and Nicholas Serota, Director, Tate, and Stephen Deuchar, former Director, and Penelope Curtis, Director, Tate Britain.

Mark Antliff and **Vivien Greene**

ESSAYS

Note on the plates and essay illustrations

The works illustrated in the essays and plates are organized to evoke the three Vorticist exhibitions mounted by the group: the 1915 Doré Galleries show in London, the January 1917 Penguin Club exhibition in New York, and the February 1917 Camera Club exhibition of Vortographs in London. Since many of these works were subsequently lost, or are unavailable now, when necessary like works are included in their place. The work of the Vorticists was also disseminated in print and the catalogue includes a section focusing on the two issues of the Vorticist magazine *Blast* (1914–15), as well as the extensive ephemera produced by members of the group.

The following abbreviations are used to indicate which works were either in each show, or closely related to such work, or were illustrated in *Blast* (with overlap in some instances). Further supplementary information regarding these works can be found in the List of Works:

D	Doré Galleries
B	Blast
P, S	Penguin Club and Sunwise Turn (see p.149)
C	Camera Club

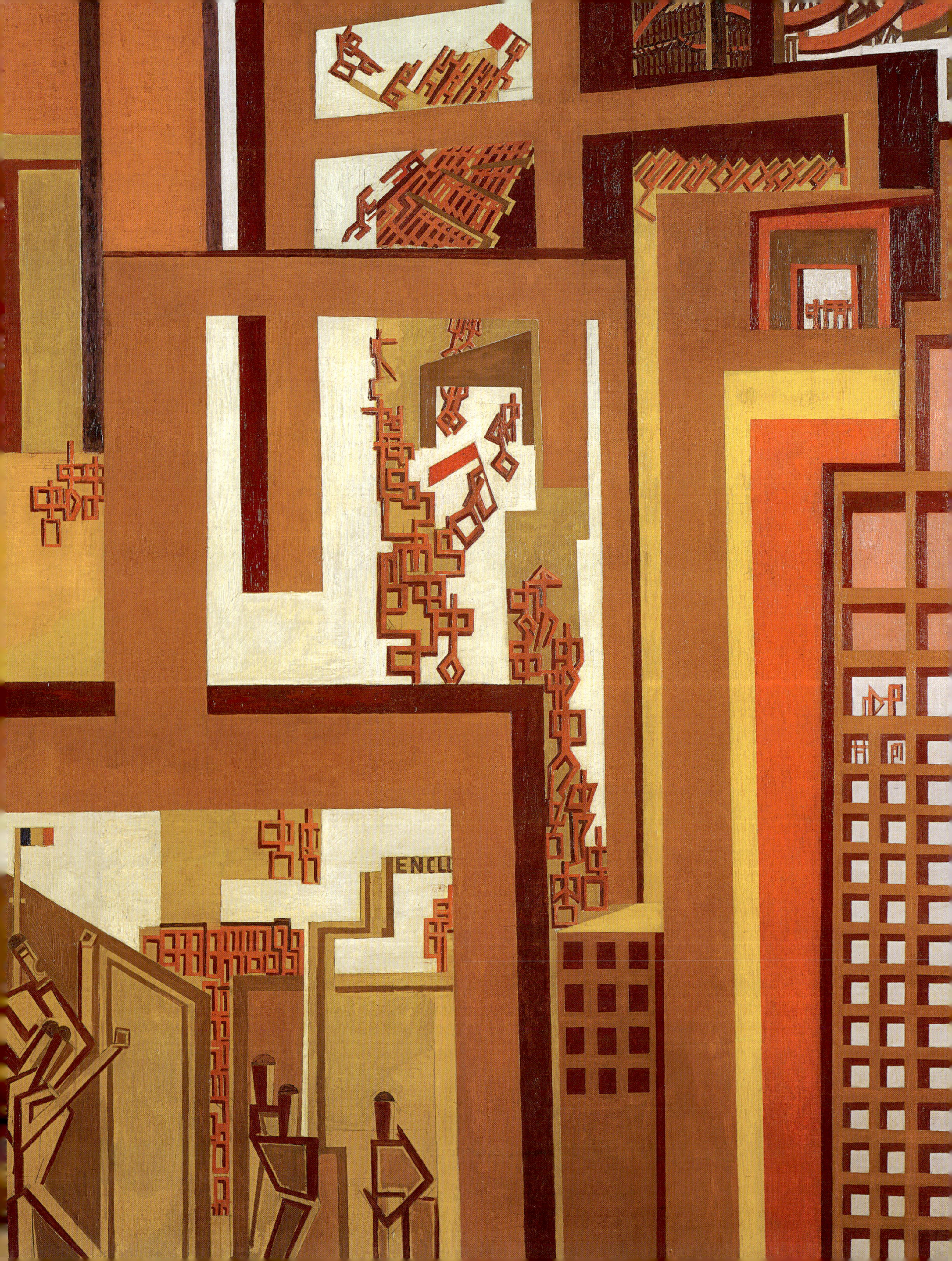
ENCL

INTRODUCTION

Philip Rylands

In the summer of 1914, at the time of the assassination of Archduke Franz Ferdinand in Sarajevo (28 June) and only weeks before Germany invaded Belgium (4 August), Vorticism blazed into existence in London. During the cataclysmic years of the First World War, its flames spluttered and eventually, in 1919, winked out. This response to French Cubism and Italian Futurism owed much to the energizing ego of the poet Ezra Pound (1885–1972) (fig.1), who gave the movement its name, to the leadership of the writer and painter Wyndham Lewis (1882–1957) (fig.3), and to the philosophy and criticism of T.E. Hulme (1883–1917). The Vorticists exhibited together in June 1915 at the Doré Galleries, London: they were Jessica Dismorr (1885–1939), Frederick Etchells (1886–1973), Henri Gaudier-Brzeska (1891–1915), Lewis, William Roberts (1895–1980), Helen Saunders (1885–1963), and Edward Wadsworth (1889–1949) (fig.4).[1] That same year the American patron John Quinn began amassing a collection of Vorticist works under Pound's guidance, and in January 1917 Quinn opened the only other major Vorticist exhibition, at the Penguin Club, New York. In February 1917 the American expatriate and Vorticist ally Alvin Langdon Coburn (1882–1966) showed his Vortographs – now celebrated as the first abstract photographs – at the Camera Club, London, with a catalogue preface by Pound. These exhibitions were complemented by the group's journal *Blast* (1914–15), which had a significant impact on avant-garde circles in London and New York as well as across Europe. Two major avant-gardists, David Bomberg (1890–1957) and the American expatriate Jacob Epstein (1880–1959) (fig.2), although they declined membership in the group, created paintings, sculptures, and drawings with clear affinities to Vorticist ideas and imagery.[2]

Vorticism is a story of the acceptance and transformation of contemporary European art by young artists working in London. It belongs to the larger history, from 1910 on, of the reception in Britain of French Post-Impressionism, Henri Matisse and the Fauves, the Ballets Russes, Cubism, Futurism, and Vasily Kandinsky. Vorticism was the most advanced, the most sharply characterized of the London-based avant-gardes: the Bloomsbury Group (Vanessa Bell, Duncan Grant, Roger Fry and the artists of the Omega Workshops), Augustus John (considered a genius and the first British artist to be tagged a Post-

Detail from Wyndham Lewis *The Crowd* 1914–15 (no.7)

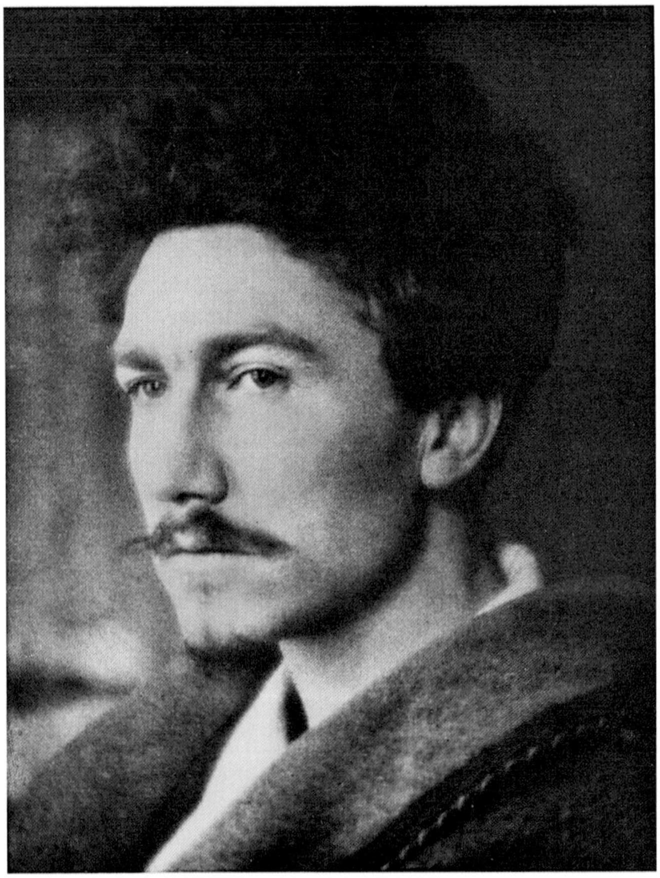

Fig.1
Alvin Langdon Coburn
Ezra Pound 1913
Photogravure
23.5 x 17.5 cm

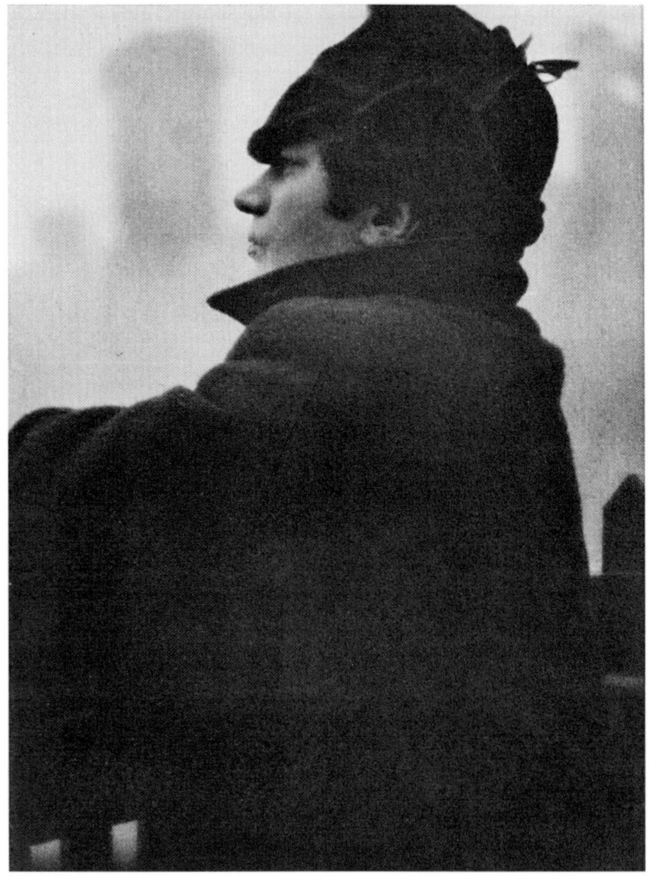

Fig.2
Alvin Langdon Coburn
Jacob Epstein 1914
Photogravure
23.5 x 17.5 cm

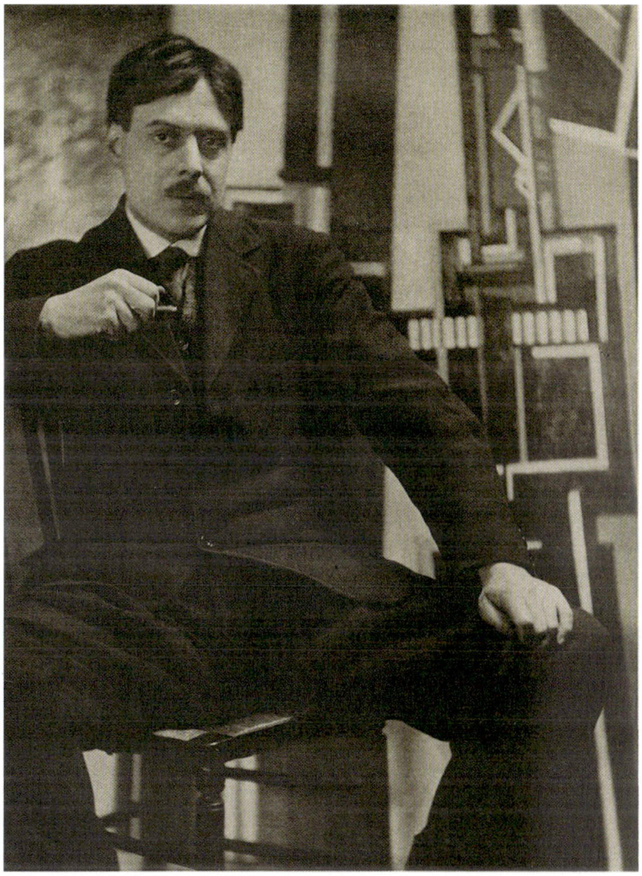

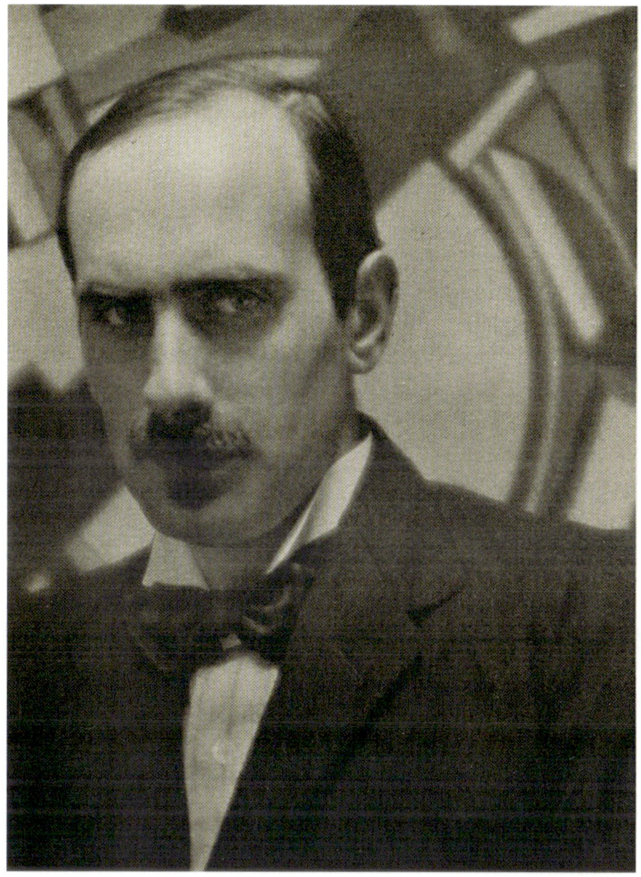

Fig.3
Alvin Langdon Coburn
Wyndham Lewis 1916
Photogravure
23.5 x 17. 5 cm

Fig.4
Alvin Langdon Coburn
Edward Wadsworth 1916
Photogravure
23.5 x 17.5 cm

Impressionist), the Rhythmists (John Duncan Fergusson, Anne Estelle Rice, and others), and the Camden Town Group led by Walter Sickert.

During the Edwardian period (1901–10), official British culture was vehemently isolationist. There was a nascent restlessness, however, among certain art critics, Frank Rutter and Fry among them, who felt that the best art was being produced outside the Royal Academy of Arts, by foreign artists, and by British artists open to foreign influence, such as the New English Art Club (NEAC) and James McNeill Whistler and his circle. Rutter, a campaigner for French art before Fry even discovered Paul Cézanne, organized in 1905 a comprehensive exhibition of 300 Impressionist paintings at the Durand-Ruel Gallery in London. Little sold, critics were disdainful, and, though Rutter raised the funds for a gift, the National Gallery would not accept anything more advanced than a painting by Eugène Boudin.

In the same year, Epstein, aged twenty-four, arrived in London via New York and Paris, Vanessa Stephen (later Bell) started the Friday Club, a painting circle that was the embryo of the Bloomsbury Group, and Sickert returned from France. Under Sickert's leadership, a group of pro-French painters formed, including Robert Bevan, Harold Gilman, Charles Ginner, and Spencer Gore, who later coalesced as the short-lived Camden Town Group in 1911. Early in 1908 Pound arrived in London from Venice. In June Epstein's first commission – statuary for the British Medical Association building in the Strand – was both the first occurrence in British art of non-classical, non-Christian art as a component of an avant-garde style, and the first of the new century's art scandals of public shock and dismay, including accusations of pornography.[3] Again in 1908, Rutter established the Allied Artists' Association (AAA), a non-juried summer exhibition that opened the door to European artists of the calibre of Constantin Brancusi and Kandinsky. In December Lewis's European *Wanderjahre* ended with his return to London. In 1909, Fry resigned his position as curator of European painting at the Metropolitan Museum of Art, New York, and returned full-time to England.

Between November 1910 and January 1911, the exhibition *Manet and the Post-Impressionists*, organized by Fry at the Grafton Galleries, both shocked its London audience and opened discussion among artists and the art establishment about the purposes and values of painting.[4] The critical mass of the exhibition consisted of paintings by Cézanne, Paul Gauguin, and Vincent van Gogh. Cézanne was the most controversial, with members of the NEAC, teachers at the Slade School of Fine Art, and followers of Sickert unable to see him as other than an incompetent draftsman. This exhibition and Fry's championship of Cézanne – his insistence on Cézanne's heroic application of his personal 'temperament' to formal values – established Fry's pre-eminence as a patron and arbiter of new talent, exhibition organizer, and agent for commissions.[5]

Two years later Fry organized the *Second Post-Impressionist Exhibition: British, French and Russian Artists*, again at the Grafton Galleries (October 1912–January 1913).[6] Cézanne was the only survivor from the first show. The emphasis shifted towards contemporary developments, primarily the painting of Matisse but also of Pablo Picasso (with a small number of Cubist works). This was not, however, a debut for Cubism in England. Roberts reported of the Slade School (where most of the Vorticists studied, the main exceptions being Etchells and Gaudier-Brzeska), 'we were all familiar with the work of the French Cubists'.[7] Etchells, Cuthbert Hamilton, Lewis, and Wadsworth were included in the English section of Fry's show.

The art historian Charles Harrison has written: 'the issues at stake in the years 1910–12 are not expressible simply in terms of the conflict between "progressives" and "reactionaries": the significant argument was between those like Fry and Bell who saw progress in art as involving the assertion of the autonomy of aesthetic experience, and those like Sickert who felt that art needed to be underwritten by the security of its reference to a world of gross material facts'.[8] The Vorticists were to reject both positions. How they could do so depended in part on the 'idiosyncratic pictorial project' of Lewis,[9] in part on the impact of Italian Futurism, and in part on the entry of Pound and Hulme into the field of art criticism in January 1914.

By the summer of 1912, Lewis, more cosmopolitan than his contemporaries, had developed an Expressionist treatment of the human figure in a Cubist web of arcs, angles, and planes. This was the style of his lost decorations for the Cave of the Golden Calf (1912) and of an almost nine-foot canvas titled *Kermesse* (also now lost; see no.60), shown at the summer 1912 AAA exhibition.[10] A *Mother and Child*, the most controversial of his submissions to the *Second Post-Impressionist Exhibition*,[11] and a series of illustrations (1912, nos.47–9, 58) for William Shakespeare's *The Life of Timon of Athens* indicate the maturity of this proto-Vorticist style. Lewis's emergence at the forefront of contemporary art was meteoric. He had returned to London in 1908 determined to be a writer (which he continued to be throughout his life). His first exhibited works (with the Camden Town Group in 1911) had been drawings of character types comparable to the protaganists in his first published short stories. According to Tom Normand, a literary and philosophical component separated Lewis's art from that of his colleagues, even Wadsworth, whose work was closest to his.[12]

In March 1912, the Sackville Gallery hosted the first exhibition of Futurist paintings by Umberto Boccioni, Carlo Carrà, Luigi Russolo, and Gino Severini.[13] The show was ridiculed in the press and did much to create the popular conviction that non-academic, modernist art of any kind could be classified as 'futurist' – if not insane. As a repertoire of visual sources, its impact was limited. In the second version of Boccioni's triptych *States of Mind* 1911, a Cubist-inspired treatment of the figures is comparable to the evolving figure style of Lewis. Severini's huge *The Pan-Pan Dance at the Monico* 1909–10/1959–60,[14] which dominated the show, impressed Bomberg who began abstracting his figures in a similar manner. A year later, in April 1913, Severini was given a solo show at the Marlborough Gallery. His work prompted transient Futurist trains and omnibuses in paintings by C.R.W. Nevinson (1889–1946) and Wadsworth. Nevinson, who met Severini at his show, was to become the best-known English Futurist.

However, Futurist painting was less influential than the rhetoric of its manifestos and of its founder F.T. Marinetti. From March 1910, Marinetti lectured in London frequently. His impassioned performances thrilled his London audiences with horror. The Sackville Gallery catalogue published three Futurist manifestos in which the language echoed his declamatory style. One of these claimed that 'there can be no modern painting without ... an absolutely modern sensation', but rejected comparison with 'the Post-impressionists, Synthetists and Cubists of France', indicating, to a combative intelligence such as Lewis's, a path for forging avant-garde identity: the refusal to be associated with other avant-gardes.[15] First among these, for Lewis, was Futurism, whose allegiance to an optimistic and vitalist interpretation of the philosophy of Henri Bergson he rejected. Meanwhile Fry was calling for a 'purely abstract language of form – a visual music', what Clive Bell in 1914 described as 'significant form'.[16] As Robert Upstone shows (pp.27–33), Lewis, in late 1913, countered Fry

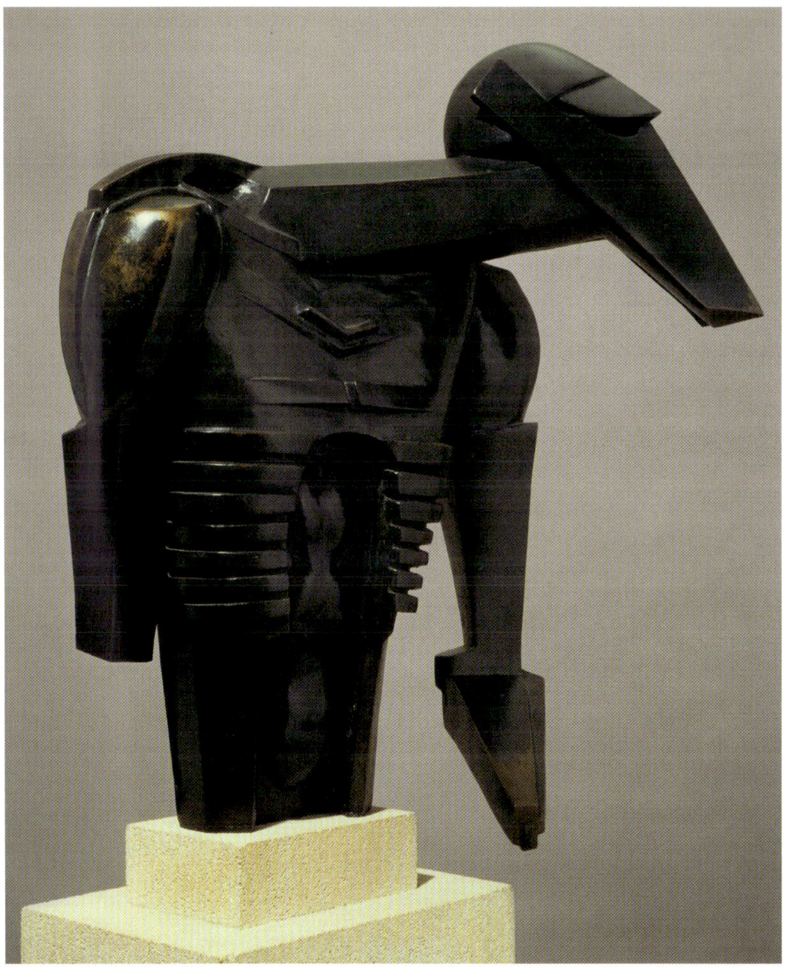

Fig.5
Jacob Epstein
Torso in Metal from the 'Rock Drill'
1913–16
Bronze
70.5 x 58.4 x 44.5 cm

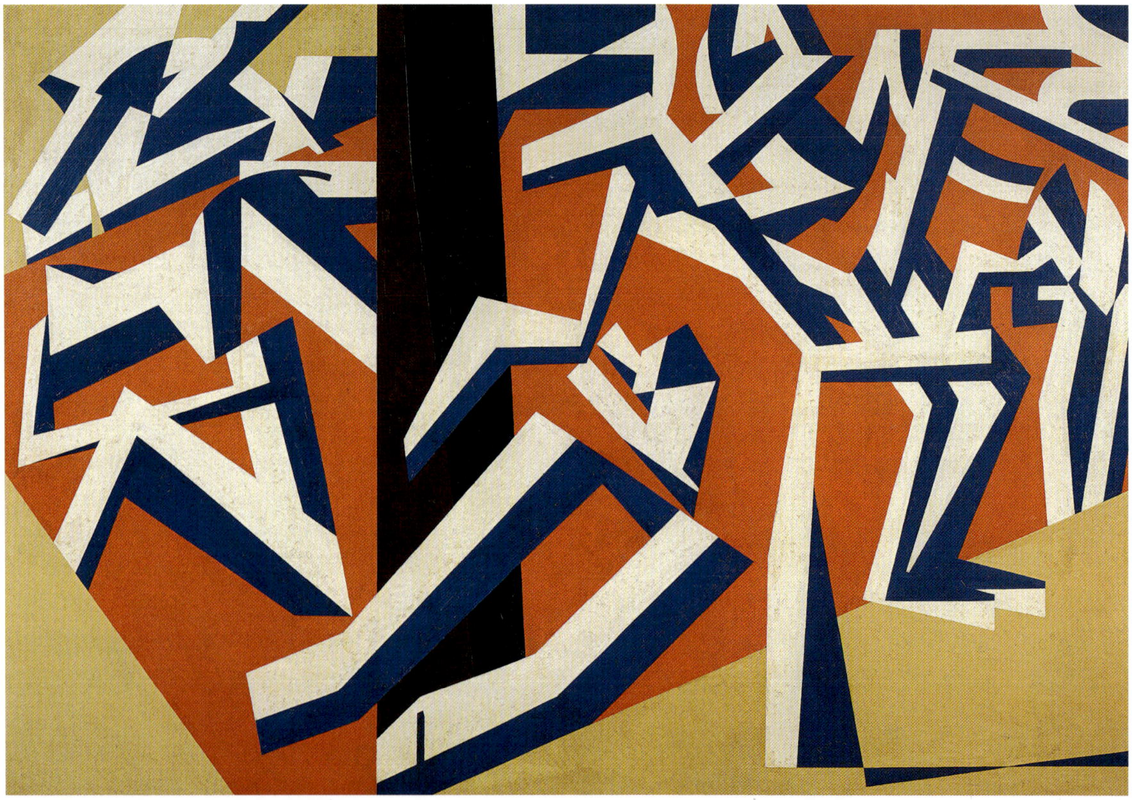

Fig.6
David Bomberg
The Mud Bath 1914
(no.6)

and Bell by deploying the synaesthetic metaphor to justify a hard-edged, staccato form of abstraction more akin to Futurism than the whimsical, decorative art Bloomsbury championed. For a rebellious spirit like Lewis's, the Bloomsbury aesthetic must have seemed insipid when compared to Futurism's call for 'aggressive movement, feverish insomnia, the double quick step, the somersault, the box on the ear, the fisticuff'.[17]

In the summer of 1913, Fry founded the Omega Workshops, with the intention of providing work for indigent artists and of introducing modern art to the British moneyed classes by applying it to household furnishings. Lewis worked there briefly before, by means of an apparently wilful misunderstanding, he precipitated a breach with Fry in what has been called 'The Ideal Home Rumpus' (see pp.27–8).[18] Together with Etchells (previously close to Fry and the Bells), Hamilton, and Wadsworth, he quit the workshops and circulated a savage denunciation of Fry. This ended both Fry's leadership and a period, since November 1910, of relative unity among all radical artists in London.

From October 1913 until June 1914, Marinetti seemed a plausible candidate for the mantle of leadership that had been stripped from Fry. On 18 November 1913, the Omega secessionists, plus Nevinson, arranged a dinner in Marinetti's honour. The proselytizing Marinetti would have been justified in seeing them as the nucleus of a London Futurist group.

Meanwhile, in October, Rutter had mounted the *Post-Impressionist and Futurist Exhibition* at the Doré Galleries, in which Epstein, Etchells, Hamilton, Lewis, Nevinson, and Wadsworth showed together. This exhibition confirmed the rupture with the amorphous Post-Impressionism of Bloomsbury (which was not represented) and the formation of a group of English artists reacting to Cubism and Futurism: Etchells with hesitant attempts to emulate Picasso and Lewis; Nevinson with a Futurist bias that was to distinguish him from the others; and Wadsworth with a group of Cézanne-inspired landscapes with Cubist facets. Lewis, who exhibited seven works, including *Kermesse*, was by then producing full-fledged Vorticist images such as *Composition* 1913 (no.64), in which the figure is subsumed almost out of recognition in a shallow congested relief of architectonic surfaces and pseudo-machinery.

The new avant-garde was confirmed in the Cubist Room of a mixed show in the Brighton Public Art Galleries called *An Exhibition of the Work of English Post-Impressionists, Cubists and others* (December 1913–January 1914), an uneasy alliance of the Lewis and Sickert groups (see pp.31–2, below). The magazine *Blast*, as a mouthpiece for this English Cubist group, was conceived at about this time (by Nevinson, who was to withdraw in February), though it was not published until July 1914.

In January 1914 Hulme delivered a lecture in which he discussed the aesthetics of Wilhelm Worringer, whom he had met the previous month. His intention was to explain the geometric and primitive components of the art of Epstein and Lewis.[19] Using Worringer's concepts of 'abstraction' and 'empathy', he distinguished between the 'vitalistic' art of the past (representational, organic) and a developing 'geometric' art of the future (abstract, mechanistic).[20] These were respectively safe, familiar, and loved on the one hand, and adventurous, dangerous, and shocking on the other. The new art was for him 'the precursor of the re-emergence of the corresponding attitude towards the world, and so the breakup of the Renaissance humanistic attitude'.[21] He associated 'rigid lines and dead crystalline forms' with 'a general process of adjustment between man and the outside world'.[22] Post-Impressionism, Futurism, and Cubism were dismissed as being irrelevant to this nascent art, but Hulme justified the need to draw from the past (archaism and primitivism). He wrote, 'the specific differentiating quality of the new art' will be 'the idea of machinery'.[23]

Hulme was an important force. His short career (he died in Nieuwpoort, Belgium, on the Western Front) was dedicated to rejecting the Victorian values that had lingered in Edwardian London. Yet he was by no means the anointed critical voice for Vorticism – Lewis would never have allowed this. Hulme himself had little sympathy for Lewis.[24] He was critical of Lewis's work in his review of the London Group exhibition in March 1914.[25] Lewis in turn rejected Hulme's correlation of Bergson's philosophy with empathetic humanism by recasting Bergsonian metaphysics in terms of a dramatic confrontation between human will and our material condition. Paul Edwards demonstrates that such thinking proved seminal to Lewis's Vorticist aesthetic (pp.35–45). His schism with Hulme was seconded by that of Pound, who published his own version of Vorticist aesthetics beginning in February 1914, one month after Hulme's first foray into art criticism. Pound was unique in adapting Bergsonian vitalism and the philosophical anarchism of the German thinker Max Stirner to a spirited defence of the primitivism and related recourse to 'direct carving' developed by Gaudier-Brzeska and Epstein, as Mark Antliff shows in his essay (pp.47–57). The rivalry between Hulme, Lewis, and Pound – both sexual and art-political in Lewis's case – perhaps contributed to the detached posture adopted by two artists who figure importantly in the Vorticist aesthetic but who nonetheless insisted on their independence: Epstein and Bomberg.

Hulme's first foray into art journalism was a defence of Epstein, with particular reference to Epstein's carvings in 'flenite' (no.34), one of which he himself owned.[26] In 1913 Epstein had been working on *Rock Drill* 1913–15 (no.3), an armoured figure mounted on a contraption for quarrying stone. It was a Vorticist sculpture *avant la lettre* and the epitome of Hulme's definition of the new art as geometric and machine-like. Hulme intended to publish a book about Epstein, although no manuscript survived his death in September 1917.

In July 1914 Hulme wrote the only review of Bomberg's first solo show, at the Chenil Gallery, which he opened acrimoniously by congratulating Bomberg on his independence from the 'English Cubists', 'for his work is certainly much more individual and less derivative'.[27] Hulme went on to discuss, based on his reading of the German thinker Johannes Volkelt, how aesthetic emotion is not autonomous – an attack on Clive Bell's theory of 'significant form', which Bell had published in *Art* four months earlier. Bomberg's precocious response to Cubism (as early as 1912) was second only to Lewis's. Between 1912 and 1914 he executed a series of outsize canvases that manifested Hulme's call for the dehumanization of the figure. These paintings, *Vision of Ezekiel* 1912 (fig.14 on p.32), *Ju-Jitsu* c.1913, *In the Hold* c.1913–14, climaxing in *The Mud Bath* 1914 (fig.6), the centrepiece of the Chenil show, were a personal variant of Cubism on a heroic scale and qualified him as the most advanced painter working in England at the time.

By spring 1914 Lewis and his circle had broken with both Sickert and Fry, Camden Town and Bloomsbury. In March he and his friend the artist Kate Lechmere registered an organization called the Cubist Art Centre, which opened a month later at 38 Great Ormond Street as the Rebel Art Centre. It was to be the locus of Lewis's new, fractious avant-garde, as a meeting place and venue for art classes, studios, and lectures.[28] Perhaps Lewis intended to replace the recently closed Cave of the Golden Calf as a bohemian hangout. It was more obviously a riposte to Fry's Omega Workshops (mocked by Lewis in *Blast* as 'Mr Fry's curtain and pincushion factory').[29] Its prospectus stated that 'the starting point and the alphabet of the teaching' would be 'the principles underlying the movements in Painting, known as Cubist, Futurist, and Expressionist'.[30] In late July the school foundered after only four months on the rocks of Lewis's jealousy, divisiveness, and even incompetence. Nevertheless, this was the crucible for Vorticism.

The 'Rebels' were Etchells, Hamilton, Nevinson, and Wadsworth, as well as Lewis and Lechmere. During its short life, the centre brought together other artists: Pound's wife Dorothy Shakespear (1886–1973); two former Fauves, Atkinson and Dismorr; Saunders, who like Dismorr had turned to Cubist-inspired painting in 1913; and Arbuthnot, an experimental photographer. Lewis co-opted the young Roberts by hanging drawings by him in the centre.[31] Gaudier-Brzeska also became an enthusiastic member.

Gaudier-Brzeska, a young Frenchman, had settled in London in January 1911. He rapidly entered avant-garde circles, publishing drawings in *Rhythm* magazine (1911–13) and becoming a friend of Hulme and Epstein. His portrait bust of Horace Brodzky, cast early in 1913, revealed the first intrusion of Cubist form into his work. Around the end of the year, he carved the *Red Stone Dancer* c.1913 (fig.7), which reflected Epstein's interest in non-western art from the British Museum, Pound's poetic theory of the Chinese ideograph, and Hulme's invocation of geometric form. Pound met Gaudier-Brzeska in the rooms of the 1913 AAA exhibition and became a generous patron, championing Gaudier-Brzeska's work in the avant-garde journals *The Egoist* (1914–19) and *The New Age* (1907–22), and buying work and commissioning portraits, including Gaudier-Brzeska's *Hieratic Head of Ezra Pound* (fig.8, and fig.25 on p.53), begun probably in January 1914 and exhibited in May at the Whitechapel Art Gallery. Together with Epstein's *Rock Drill*, this was Vorticism's most compelling image in sculpture.

A second and larger exhibition of Futurism opened at the Doré Galleries in April 1914, with considerable press coverage. Lewis and the other Rebel artists may have panicked as their identity seemed inexorably to be merging with Futurism in the public perception. Overconfident perhaps in the charisma of his leadership, on 7 June Marinetti, together with Nevinson, published a manifesto in the *Observer* newspaper entitled 'Vital English Art: Futurist Manifesto'. This listed the Rebel artists as Futurists and gave the Rebel Art Centre as its address. Lewis, Gaudier-Brezska, and others reacted swiftly, heckling Marinetti and Nevinson at a recital at the Doré Galleries (12 June) and issuing a letter to the daily press dissociating themselves and the Rebel Art Centre from Marinetti's manifesto. This flurry of activity, as described here by Robert Hewison, precipitated the emergence of the term 'Vorticism' as the group's name (pp.67–73). With his flair for cryptic and abusive language, Lewis vilified Futurism in the pages of *Blast* as Marinetti's 'Automobilism and Nietzsche stunt'.[32]

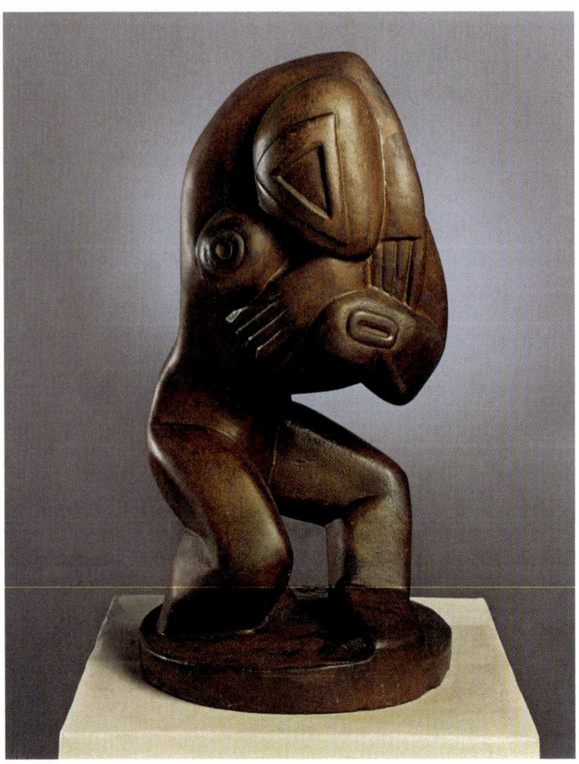

Fig.7
Henri Gaudier-Brzeska
Red Stone Dancer c.1913
(no.10)
[D]

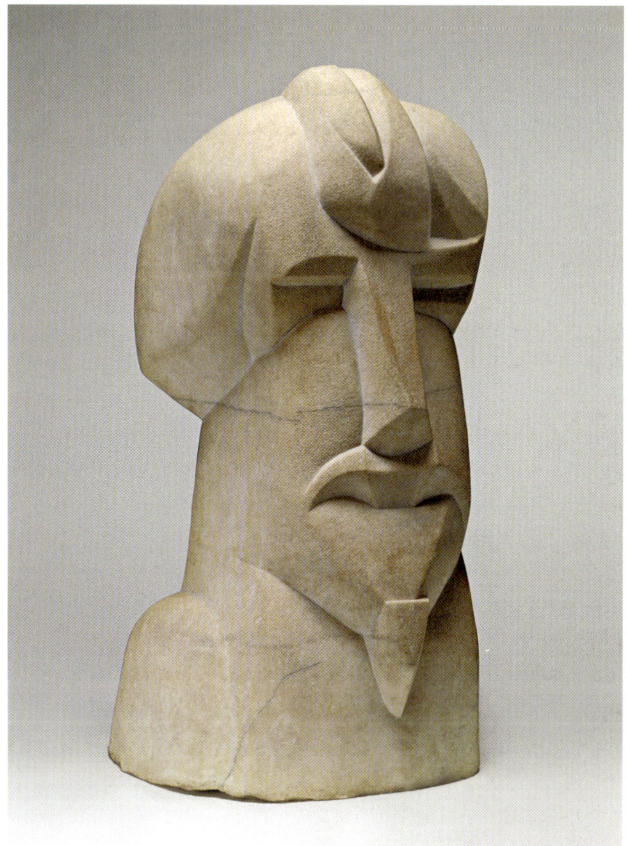

Fig.8
Henri Gaudier-Brzeska
Hieratic Head of Ezra Pound 1914
(no.1)
[B2]

The faceted angularity of Vorticist figuration was Cubist in origin, but its similarity stops there. The Cubist exploration of reconfigured form, with a narrow repertoire of subjects (the portrait, the disrobed seated model, or the table with still-life clutter), had little to do with Hulme's, Lewis's, and Pound's conviction that a new art signalled radical changes in the human condition. Paintings shown by the Vorticists at the Rebel Art Centre and at the AAA in June 1914 were abstract. They were contemporary with and sometimes arguably more advanced than comparable abstract experiments in Europe by Robert Delaunay, Kandinsky, František Kupka, the Rayonists, Synchromists, and others. Avant-garde art produced in London, by this measure, with the intellectual apparatus provided by Hulme, Lewis, and Pound, could hold its own against the Europeans – an unthinkable claim four years earlier.

Pound apparently used the term 'Vorticist' for the first time in April 1914.[33] Interviewed in 1915 for the Russian journal *Strelets* (*The Archer*) (1915), he defined the vortex as 'that point in the cyclone where energy cuts into space and imparts form to it ... the pattern of angles and geometric lines which is formed by our vortex in the existing chaos'.[34] In the first issue of *Blast*, he had written: 'The vortex is the point of maximum energy. It represents, in mechanics, the greatest efficiency'.[35] This degree of conceptual grounding in the spirit of a new age, comparable to but radically different from the Futurists' campaign, distinguishes Vorticism both from the elitist aestheticism of Bloomsbury and from the lower-middle-class realism of the Camden Town painters.

The second and last issue of *Blast*, the 'War Number', was published more than a year later, in July 1915, but by this time the 'vortex' – the concentration of energies in London – was no longer working. Lewis was struggling with debt (including moneys owed in the wake of *Blast* no.1's failure to sell) and busy painting, writing, and inventorying his work in advance of enlisting for the war, which he did in March 1916. Gaudier-Brezska, Roberts, and Wadsworth also signed up for military service. Art came to a halt in London, and the frenetic cultural politics that had galvanized it since 1910 were out of place by the spring of 1915 by which time it had become clear that the war was not going to end swiftly, and that it was not to be a traditional war of manoeuvring armies on the offensive, but a stalemate of lines of defence. The Vorticists nevertheless exhibited together as part of the

London Group at the Goupil Gallery in March 1915. This show included Lewis's *The Crowd* 1914–15 (fig.9) and Epstein's *Rock Drill* mounted on its tripod (no.3). In June–July, the *First Vorticist Exhibition* took place at the Doré Galleries – the subject of Anna Gruetzner Robins's essay (pp.59–65). Harsh criticism in the press for these exhibitions provoked waspish defences in Lewis's contributions to the War number of *Blast*. Perhaps more important was that the fulfilment of the Vorticist programme, coherently presented in the stylistically unified, rectilinear works in the Doré Galleries show, posed questions of what would follow, especially given the deepening drama of the war – a drama brought home by Gaudier-Brzeska's death at the Front, at age twenty-three, five days before the show opened on 10 June. *Blast*, no.2, revealed some hesitancy about the definition of Vorticism.

Yet there were silver linings: from the first month of the war Pound wrote tirelessly about Vorticism and its artists in the periodical press and in 1916 published his memoir of Gaudier-Brzeska. In 1915 he established relations with Quinn as both collector of Vorticist work and impresario for an exhibition at the Penguin Club, New York, in 1917 – an episode recounted here by Vivien Greene (pp.75–83). In 1916, as is discussed by Tom Normand (pp.85–91), Coburn developed the Vortograph and showed his experiments at the Camera Club, London, in February 1917.

However, when Lewis returned from duty as a Canadian Corps War Artist in 1919, he no longer had an appetite for group activities. Despite Pound's heroic efforts, the dissipation of Vorticism's energy was intrinsic to its incendiary character, with Lewis as the fuse and the dynamite. Vorticism was a victim of the First World War. The years prior had witnessed the beginnings of the welfare state, as well as the rise of organized labour, of severe industrial unrest, and of vexed political questions such as Suffragettism and Home Rule for Ireland. It was against this background that British artists came to terms with the avant-gardes in Europe. Vorticism, in the field of painting, sculpture, and even literature, was the modern movement that more than any other expressed the changing social, economic, and material conditions of life in England in the 1910s.

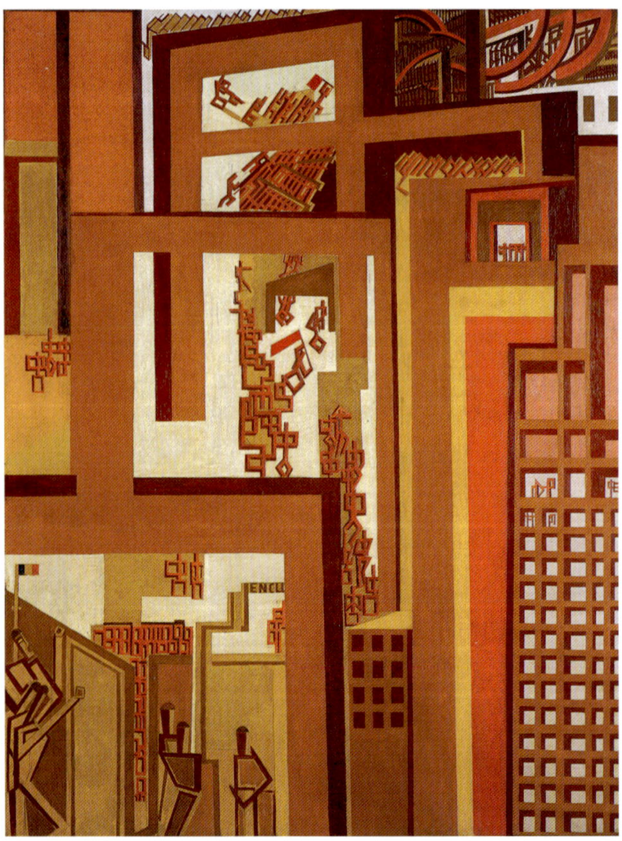

Fig.9
Wyndham Lewis
The Crowd 1914–15
(no.7)
[D]

NOTES

1 These artists, with the exception of Frederick Etchells, had previously signed a manifesto in *Blast*, no.1 (July 1914), p.43. The poet Richard Aldington (1892–1962), artists Malcolm Arbuthnot (1877–1967), Lawrence Atkinson (1873–1931), and Cuthbert Hamilton (1884–1959), as well as Ezra Pound also signed the manifesto. Atkinson showed at the Doré Galleries as an invitee.

2 The extensive bibliography of Vorticism is dominated by Richard Cork, *Vorticism and Abstract Art in the First Machine Age*, vol.1 (London: Gordon Fraser, 1976) and vol.2 (Berkeley: University of California Press, 1976). Volume 1 includes 'Biographical Outlines of the Artists Associated with Vorticism', pp.xvii–xxiii.

3 For the British Medical Association building, see Richard Cork, *Art beyond the Gallery in Early 20th Century England* (New Haven: Yale University Press, 1985), pp.9–60, and Rupert Richard Arrowsmith, 'Jacob Epstein: The Indian Connection', *Burlington Magazine*, vol.150, no.1268 (November 2008), pp.742–6.

4 For the exhibition and notes on the sporadic appearances of French modernist painting in London prior to 1910, see Anna Gruetzner Robins, *Modern Art in Britain, 1910–1914*, exh. cat. (London: Merrell Holberton in association with Barbican Art Gallery, 1997), pp.15–45, 186–8. Roger Fry, in giving the exhibition its title, introduced the term 'Post-Impressionist' to the lexicon of avant-garde painting.

5 See Richard Verdi, 'Art History Reviewed III: Roger Fry's "Cézanne, a study of his development", 1927', *Burlington Magazine*, vol.151, no.1277 (August 2009), pp.544–7. In 1911 Fry arranged for artists Bernard Adeney, Etchells, Max Gill, Duncan Grant, and Albert Rutherston to decorate the dining room of the Borough Polytechnic in London. In May 1912 he organized an exhibition at the Galerie Barbazanges, Paris, *Quelques Artistes Indépendants Anglais*, with paintings by Vanessa Bell, Etchells and his sister Jessie, Charles Ginner, Grant, Lewis, Helen Saunders, and himself. In 1912 he was acting as a mentor to Etchells, Grant, and Wyndham Lewis. In 1913, he commissioned work by Vanessa Bell, Henri Gaudier-Brzeska, and Grant for his house in Guildford. In March he organized a show of Bloomsbury painters, including Etchells, at the Alpine Club Gallery. The Omega Workshop project was the culmination of his efforts to nurture advanced British art.

6 See Gruetzner Robins 1997, pp.64–107, 190–1.

7 William Roberts, quoted in Cork 1976, vol.1, p.57.

8 Charles Harrison, *English Art and Modernism, 1900–1939* (London: Allen Lane; Bloomington: Indiana University Press, 1981), pp.45–74, especially p.48.

9 Lisa Tickner, 'A Lost Lewis: The *Mother and Child* of 1912', *Wyndham Lewis Annual*, vol.2 (1995), p.8.

10 The Cave of the Golden Calf, also known as the Cabaret Theatre Club, at 9 Heddon Street, was the creation of Frida Strindberg. During its brief existence (June 1912–February 1914), it was at the centre of bohemian life in London. Other artists made decorations (Gore, Epstein), all now lost except the Golden Calf itself, by Eric Gill. See Cork 1985, pp.61–115.

11 This now-lost work is illustrated in Gruetzner Robins 1997, p.97.

12 Tom Normand, *Wyndham Lewis the Artist: Holding the Mirror Up to Politics* (Cambridge: Cambridge University Press, 1992): 'Lewis's Vorticist paintings and drawings remained bound to the theory of the tragic and the comic' (p.51). Normand makes clear Lewis's unique (even among the Vorticists) intellectual position: 'Lewis attacked the fundamental romanticism upon which the modern movement was based' (p.52). Paul O'Keeffe has speculated that the 1910–11 exhibition *Manet and the Post-Impressionists* provoked Lewis, who had been expelled from the Slade School of Fine Art in 1901, into resuming seriously his activity as a painter. *Some Sort of Genius: A Life of Wyndham Lewis* (London: Jonathan Cape, 2000), p.104.

13 See Gruetzner Robins 1997, pp.56–63, 189.

14 A replica of the original work was painted by the artist in Rome in 1959–60.

15 'The Exhibitors to the Public', in *Futurist Manifestos*, ed. Umbro Apollonio, trans. Robert Brain, R.W. Flint, J.C. Higgitt, and Caroline Tisdall (New York: Viking, 1973), pp.45–50, especially pp.45, 46. See also Giovanni Cianci, 'Futurism and its Impact on Vorticism,' in Andrew Wilson (ed.), 'Vorticism', special issue, *ICSAC Cahier* (Brussels), no.8/9 (December 1988), pp.83–101.

16 See Andrew Wilson, 'Rebels and Vorticists: "Our Little Gang"', in Paul Edwards (ed.), *Blast: Vorticism, 1914–1918* (Aldershot: Ashgate, 2000), p.25.

17 Marinetti's 1909 founding Futurist manifesto, quoted in *Futurist Manifestos*. This contrast in tone between the critical subtleties of the one and the strident affirmations of the other is highlighted by Wilson, 'Rebels and Vorticists'.

18 Quentin Bell and Stephen Chaplin, 'The Ideal Home Rumpus: Wyndham Lewis and Roger Fry', *Apollo*, vol.80, no.32 (October 1964), pp.284–91.

19 Delivered on 22 January 1914 to the Quest Society, the lecture is published with the title 'Modern Art and its Philosophy' in Karen Csengeri (ed.), *The Collected Writings of T.E. Hulme* (Oxford: Oxford University Press, 1994), pp.268–85.

20 Wilhelm Worringer, *Abstraktion und Einfühlung* (Munich: R. Piper, 1908).

21 Csengeri 1994, p.269.

22 Ibid., p.274.

23 Ibid., p.282. Hulme used this moment to attack Fry, 'a mere verbose sentimentalist,' for his description of 'machinery as beautiful as a rose' (ibid.).

24 Lewis felt that his leadership of the avant-garde was threatened by Hulme and that Hulme, who was attractive to women, alienated the affections of Lewis's friend Kate Lechmere, who had funded the Rebel Art Centre and the first issue of *Blast*.

25 T.E. Hulme, 'Modern Art, III: The London Group', *The New Age* (26 March 1914), in Csengeri 1994, pp.294–8.

26 T.E. Hulme, 'Mr. Epstein and the Critics', *The New Age* (25 December 1913), in Csengeri 1994, pp.255–62.

27 T.E. Hulme, 'Modern Art, IV: Mr David Bomberg's Show', *The New Age* (9 July 1914), in Csengeri 1994, pp.302–9.

28 For the Rebel Art Centre, see Cork 1976, vol.1, pp.145–84.

29 Wyndham Lewis, 'A Review of Contemporary Art', *Blast*, no.2 (July 1915), p.41.

30 Cork 1976, vol.1, p.157.

31 Andrew Gibbon-Williams, *William Roberts: An English Cubist* (Aldershot: Lund Humphries, 2004), p.22.

32 Wyndham Lewis, 'The Melodrama of Modernity', *Blast*, no.1, p.143.

33 See Ezra Pound, *Gaudier-Brzeska: A Memoir* (London: John Lane, 1916), p.93, in which he states that his September 1914 essay on 'Vorticism' in the *Fortnightly Review* was 'for the most part a closer form of a rather informal lecture given at the Rebel Art Centre'. On 19 December 1913, Pound had used the term 'Vortex' in a letter to William Carlos Williams: see *The Letters of Ezra Pound, 1907–1941* (London: Faber and Faber, 1951), p.65. London at this time, for him, was 'a vortex' of intellectual and artistic activity. Cianci 1988, pp.86–9, refutes the notion that Pound's use of the vortex concept was rooted in Edwardian poetic and occult circles by pointing to its deployment by the Futurists in their paintings and manifestos, as 'a concrete symbol of urban life', which was the meaning Pound gave the term in the above-mentioned letter. Cianci convincingly attributes the strident and hyperbolic tone of Pound's pronouncements on art and poetry to Marinetti's inspiration.

34 Pound, quoted in Richard Humphreys, 'Demon Pantechnicon Driver: Pound in the London Vortex, 1908–1920', in *Pound's Artists: Ezra Pound and the Visual Arts in London, Paris and Italy* (London: Tate Gallery Publications, 1985), p.67.

35 'Vortex. Pound', *Blast*, no.1, p.153.

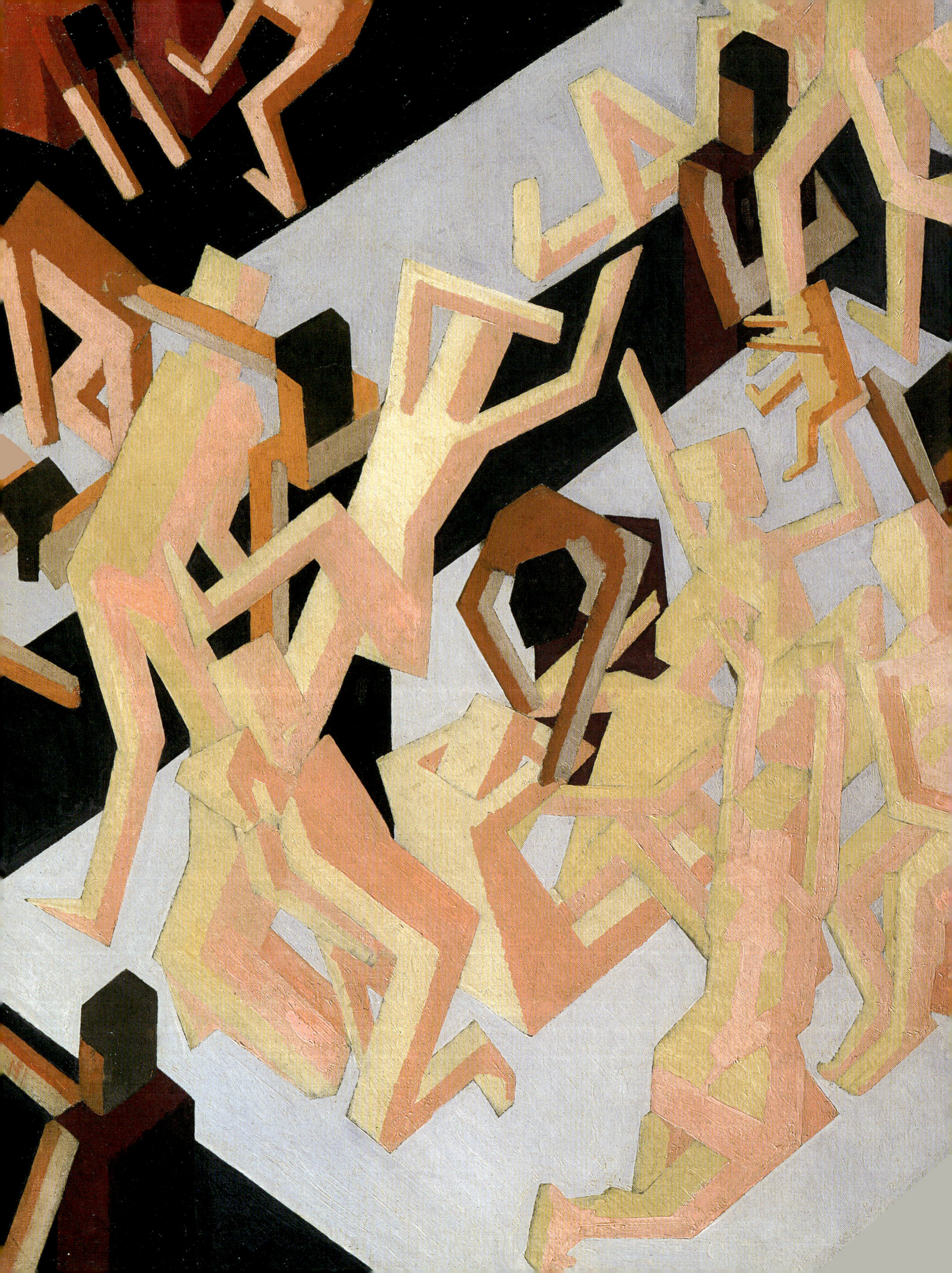

'THE CUBIST ROOM' AND THE ORIGINS OF VORTICISM AT BRIGHTON IN 1913

Robert Upstone

An important staging post in the emergence of Vorticism was the 'Cubist Room', organized by Wyndham Lewis, in *An Exhibition of the Work of English Post-Impressionists, Cubists and others* from December 1913 to January 1914 at the Brighton Public Art Galleries. Lewis's catalogue description of the motivation and agenda for the 'cubist' art in the show signifies his thinking just prior to the development of authentic Vorticism, and reveals how he began to define the group: who he included at this moment, and through which pictures their identity was expressed. In that sense the Cubist Room at Brighton was a rehearsal for the *First Vorticist Exhibition* at the Doré Galleries, which opened in June 1915 and showed some of the same works.

Selected by Spencer Gore and staged by the recently dissolved Camden Town Group, the Brighton show was a politically charged event, intended to unify the London avant-garde in an alliance between the Camden Town painters and other more advanced elements to be named the London Group. Gore's vision of creating peace and unity foundered at Brighton, and the show reinforced the growing fissure between Lewis and his allies and other British modernists. At Brighton Lewis secured a dedicated space for the first time, which he named the 'Cubist Room' and which gathered the most attention. The other two rooms contained Camden Town work and that of several women painters excluded from this men-only group, including Sylvia Gosse, Nan Hudson, and Ethel Sands, the Post-Impressionist friends of Walter Sickert, the leading French-informed artist of the day. The jarring stylistic differences between Lewis's 'Cubists' and the other artists demonstrated irreconcilable ideological differences, and the physical segregation further emphasized the polarity. Even the show's name struggled to blend the differing shades of art featured. Lewis deliberately set his group apart, setting a political tone in the catalogue by describing their contribution as 'revolutionary art'.[1]

Lewis's colleagues were Bernard Adeney, David Bomberg, Jacob Epstein, Jessie Etchells, Fanny Eveleigh, and C.R.W. Nevinson, along with the three painters with whom he had recently stormed out of the Omega Workshops, Frederick Etchells, Cuthbert Hamilton, and Edward Wadsworth. This bitter dispute already damned the alliance's chances, and the Bloomsbury artists – despite being Post-Impressionists – were deliberately left out. Both Lewis and Gore viewed them with utter contempt because of Roger

Detail from David Bomberg *Vision of Ezekiel* 1912 (fig.14)

Fry's apparent dishonesty over a commission from the *Daily Mail* to create a Post-Impressionist room at the annual Ideal Home exhibition. Instead of passing it on to Lewis as intended, Fry appropriated it for the Omega Workshops. When Lewis discovered the full facts from Gore, who had handled the initial contact from the newspaper, he resigned from the Workshops and took Hamilton, Etchells, and Wadsworth with him. He sent artists, patrons, and journalists a furious letter, the notorious 'Round Robin', written by Lewis but signed by all four, which laid bare the situation and heaped scorn on Fry and the Bloomsbury painters.[2] It also strongly distinguished between Bloomsbury and the art and ideology of the Lewis camp. Hitting at additional underlying class distinctions, Lewis wrote of Omega and Bloomsbury:

> As to its tendencies in Art, they alone would be sufficient to make it very difficult for any vigorous art-instinct to long remain under its roof. The Idol is still Prettiness, with its mid-Victorian languish of the neck, and its skin is 'greenery-yallery', despite the Post-What-Not fashionableness of its draperies. This family party of strayed and Dissenting Aesthetes, however, were compelled to call in as much modern talent as they could find, to do the rough and masculine work without which they knew their efforts would not rise above the level of a pleasant tea-party, or command more attention.[3]

Lewis consciously used Brighton as a platform for his group. He demanded a separate catalogue introduction, written by himself. This late addition was not written when the press view took place on 15 December,[4] suggesting likely disagreements over its inclusion and separatist tone. 'To be done with terms and tags', Lewis wrote, 'Post Impressionism is an insipid and pointless name invented by a journalist [Fry], which has been naturally ousted by the better word "Futurism" in public debate on modern art'.[5] This insult to Fry also dismissed the rest of the artists at Brighton, who had termed themselves 'English Post-Impressionists'. Lewis now hailed the birth of a new abstract British art, pioneered by himself, Etchells, Hamilton, Nevinson, and Wadsworth, who:

> are not accidentally associated here, but form a vertiginous, but not exotic, island in the placid and respectable archipelago of English art. The formation is undeniably of volcanic matter and even origin; for it appeared suddenly above the waves following certain seismic shakings beneath the surface. It is very closely knit and admirably adapted to withstand the imperturbable Britannic breakers which roll pleasantly against its sides.[6]

Such language emphasised the unified, rock-like strength of their revolutionary principles, while their being 'admirably adapted' suggested an evolutionary replacement of art that was 'placid and respectable'. Lewis then outlined his belief in the formative experience of modern city life – 'A man who passes his days amid the rigid lines of houses, a plague of cheap ornamentation, noisy street locomotion, the Bedlam of the press, will evidently possess a different habit of vision to a man living amongst the lines of a landscape' – and that these artists' work 'underlines such geometric bases and structure of life'.[7] The only appropriate artistic response to modern life, Lewis explained, was abstraction:

> All revolutionary painting to-day has in common the rigid reflections of steel and stone in the spirit of the artist; that desire for stability as though a machine were being built to fly or kill with; an alienation from the traditional photographer's trade and realisation of colour and form as such independently of what recognisable form it covers or encloses. People are invited, in short, to entirely change their idea of the painter's mission, and penetrate, deferentially, with him into a transposed universe, as abstract as, though different to, the musicians.[8]

Lewis pursued this musical analogy in a *Brighton Herald* interview. Under the heading 'Anarchic Art', the unidentified critic perceived the difference between Camden Town painting, which 'is advanced, but has a clear relationship with the more academic and popularly intelligible forms of painting', and works in the Cubist Room, which needed 'a new set of words, a new scale of values' to describe them. This largely sympathetic article was informed by the author encountering Lewis 'touching-up' one of his pictures and asking him to explain *L'Après-midi d'un Faune* (undated):[9]

> 'Could one suggest', the question was hazarded, 'that the picture represents the vision of amorous desire that was in the faun's dreaming consciousness?' The painter, with mental reservation, said it could.
>
> 'What does this represent?' pointing to a series of curves. The artist shrugged his shoulders. 'It is a suggestion of the recumbent female form projected from one plane to another. These lines are extensions of that idea. Those lines are processes evolved from it. To understand these things you require to understand the expression of rhythmic emotion.' ...
>
> 'Our painting', the artist pursued, 'does not set itself in rivalry with photography. Painting should be as much an abstract art as music.'

'You mean, do you, that painting which represents definite scenes and incidents is to be classed with the music that imitates the sound of the huntsman's horn and the galloping of the horses? You aim then to represent in painting what a movement in a symphony by Beethoven does in music?'

The artist assented, but added: 'Of course one must remember that painting, being a visible art, cannot be abstract in the same way as can music. There is always something which is not abstract in painting.'[10]

The article identified the work as based on the Stéphane Mallarmé poem and, like Lewis's analogy of abstraction and music, indicated an interesting synaesthetic agenda by translating the emotion of poetry into paint, a link with both Symbolism and the more recent ideas of Vasily Kandinsky. It also gives valuable, albeit somewhat critical, evidence of what the painting looked like: 'It seems a monstrous thing of blatant colour and meaningless curves. Here is a fragment of a rainbow; lower is a curious arrangement of curved lines and of seemingly unrelated colours which may symbolize the female form ... One half of the picture is occupied by a strange, incomplete shape. One has heard ladies declare it to be a new form of highly coloured shrimp!'[11]

Many of the critical responses to the Cubist Room were deeply hostile. Dubbing the artists 'revolutionaries', the *Observer* feared the contagion of the national school, describing them as 'significant specimens of various infantile maladies that threaten to undermine the robust constitution of British art', adopting the alien, foreign style of Cubism.[12] The *Sunday Times* was more sympathetic, noting 'they really shew an exhilarating eagerness to smash up all the cherished traditions of the old school. You cannot help being excited by this brain-whirling orgy'.[13]

While much of the work is now lost, it is evident there was a quite varying degree of cubism; the purer, harder abstraction of Vorticism had yet to develop. Lewis's six pictures (all now untraced) were perhaps the most advanced.[14] Sickert correctly perceived in *Creation* 1912 (fig.10) – the large, nine-foot-square painting that Lewis had

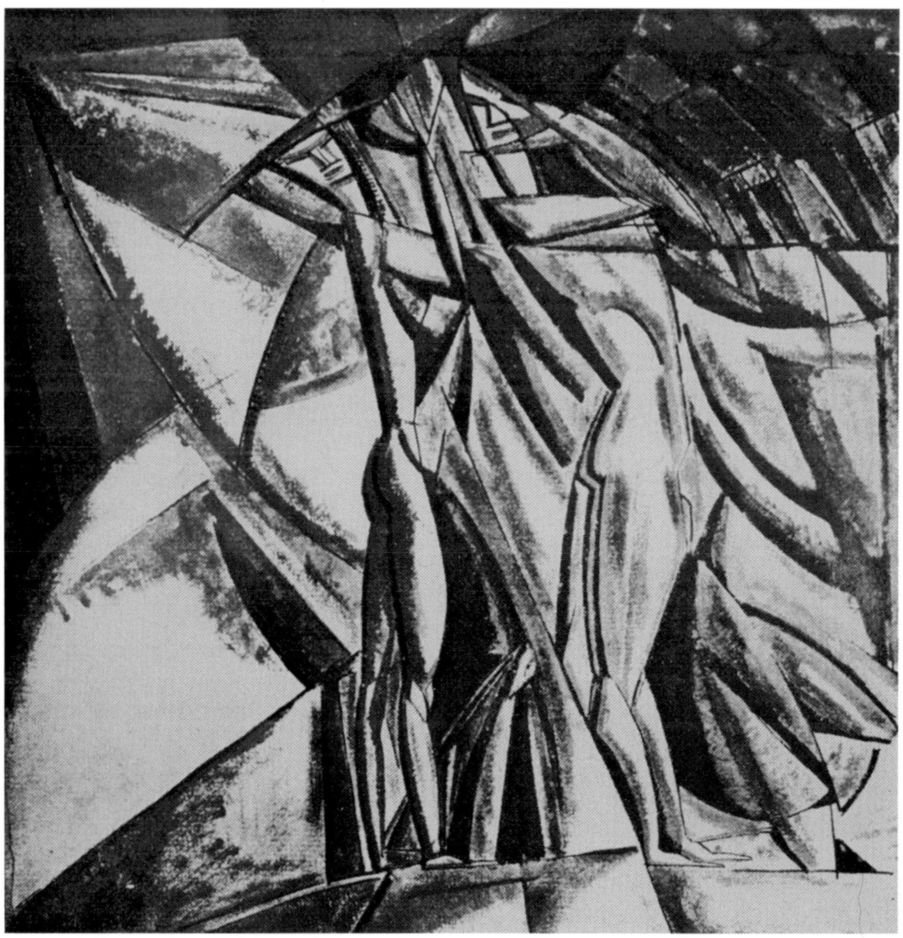

Fig.10
Wyndham Lewis
Creation 1912
Untraced; reproduced from a contemporary illustration for the *Second Post-Impressionist Exhibition* (1912–13)

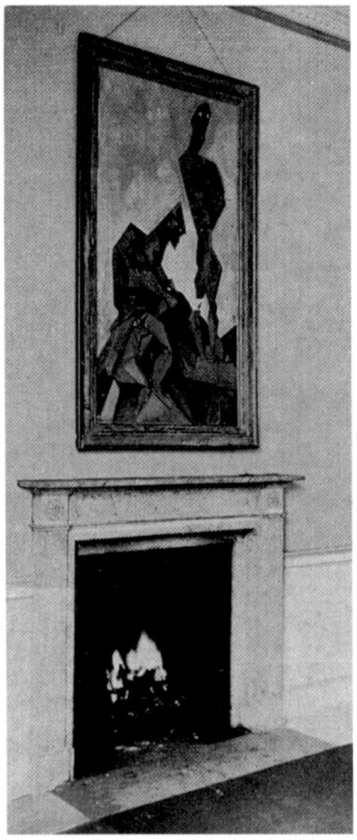

Fig.11
Wyndham Lewis
Possibly *Group*, shown above the fireplace at the Rebel Art Centre, *The Graphic*, 25 April 1914

shown at the *Second Post-Impressionist Exhibition: British, French, and Russian Artists* (1912–13) — some insistent sexual content in its naked, dancing Dionysian figures. Lewis refuted this in a letter to the *New Age*, a modernist journal.[15] But in its treatment of the female nude, *L'Après-midi d'un faune* also had a sensual, albeit more subtle, agenda.[16] Of Lewis's other pictures at Brighton, it is possible that *Group* was the oil painting of Cubist figures photographed above the fireplace in the Rebel Art Centre (fig.11).[17]

Epstein showed no sculpture at Brighton, sending three drawings instead, including a study for the *Rock Drill* 1913–15 (no.3) which may well have been fig.12. In the catalogue Lewis drew special attention to Epstein as 'the only great sculptor at present working in England', and noted: 'He finds in the machinery of procreation a dynamo to work the deep atavism of his spirit'.[18] This statement suggests the other two drawings were connected to sculptures and quite possibly studies for *Birth* 1913–14 (fig.13) or *Flenite Relief* 1913. The subject matter seems confirmed by Lewis's observation that 'symbolically strident above his work, or in the midst of it, is, like the Pathé cock, a new born baby, with a mystic but puissant crow'.[19] Elsewhere, defending the Cubist Room, he wrote of Epstein's 'heroic pre-occupation with Human Birth'.[20]

Among other paintings, Bomberg exhibited *Primeval Decoration* 1912, but his inclusion appears to have been fraught with dissent.[21] Lewis objected to him being elected to the London Group but was overruled by Harold Gilman. When Lewis left out Bomberg's *Vision of Ezekiel* 1912 (fig.14), Spencer Gore still sent it with the other pictures. Lewis hung it behind a door and omitted it from the catalogue, and finally Bomberg withdrew the work in disgust.[22] Nevinson showed what was probably a watercolour of *Waiting for the Robert E. Lee* c.1913 which essentially repeated the dense, overlapping figures of Gino Severini's Futurist painting *The Pan-Pan Dance at the Monico* 1909–10. He also included the oils *Dawn at Southwark*, *Gare St Lazare*, and *Camden Town*.[23] Wadsworth's contribution included a Cubist pair of local landscapes: *The Pells, Lewes* and *Sussex Farm*.[24] Some

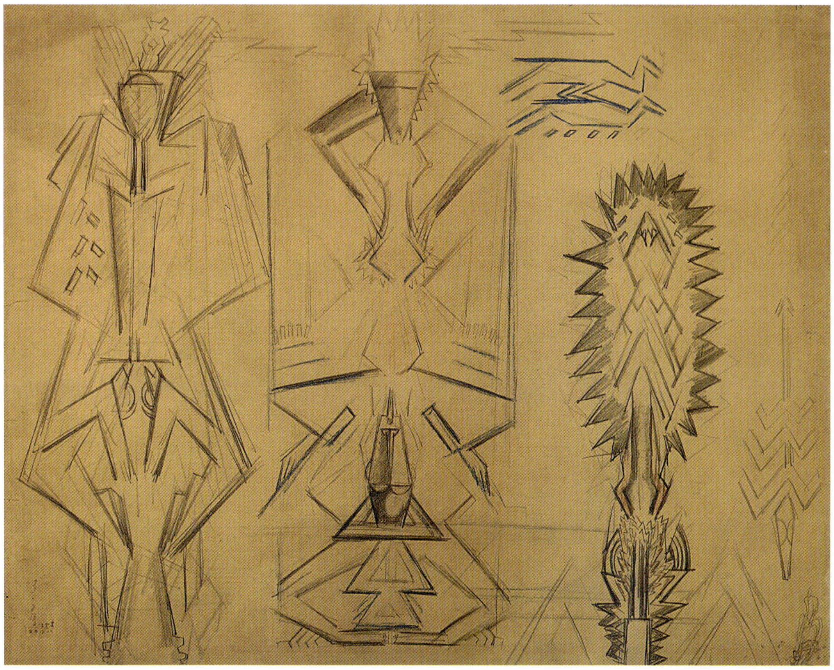

Fig.12
Jacob Epstein
Studies for 'Rock Drill' 'Venus' and 'Doves' c.1913
(no.2)

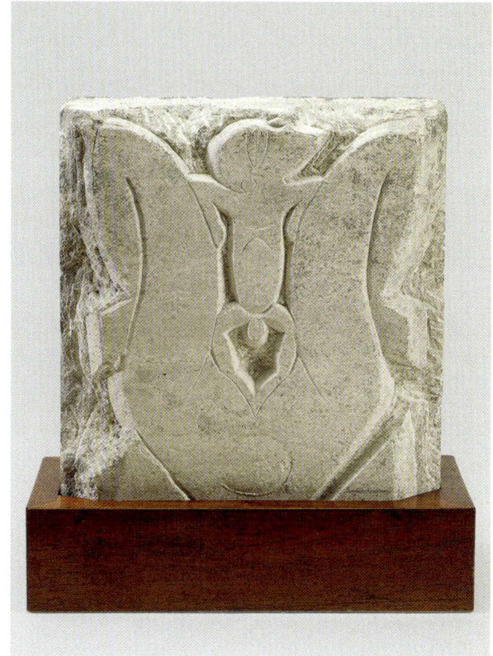

Fig.13
Jacob Epstein
Birth 1913–14
(no.36)

items in the Cubist Room were very far from Cubist. Frederick Etchells's *Entry into Jerusalem* c.1912 had stylised decorative figures in decidedly Bloomsbury flavour and dated from a period before he began using abstraction. The change is evident from two Analytical Cubist heads, that may be the drawings illustrated in *Blast*, no.1, pages ix and x.[25] These early seeds in Etchells's growth towards geometric abstraction later flowered in his Doré exhibits.

In the overall catalogue introduction, James Bolivar Manson, former secretary of the Camden Town Group, wrote positively of the avant-garde gathering, continuing his belief in a unified new alliance:

> To conceive a limit to artistic development is an admission of one's own limitations. Nothing is finally right in art; the rightness is purely personal, and for the artist himself. So in the London Group ... all modern methods may find a home. Cubism meets Impressionism, Futurism and Sickertism join hands and are not ashamed, the motto of the Group being that sincerity of conviction has the right of expression ... the vital qualities in modern art should be concentrated in one definite group, instead of being scattered in the medley of modern exhibitions.[26]

This position was visibly untenable. At the exhibition opening, Mayor J.L. Otter said in his speech that the council offered the show as 'a sign of the times' and praised the revolutionary spirit in art, such as the Pre-Raphaelites. He felt 'staggered and a little puzzled' by the Cubist Room, but said that 'in spite of all that the pictures were deeply interesting. They [the public] might scoff at them – some of them perhaps – but still be deeply interested because they were the work of accomplished men.'[27] Following him, Sickert too was 'puzzled with some manifestations of modern art', but these exhibitions 'gave opportunities to anyone who had anything to say ... when men were producing things manifestly unsuitable there was a considerable strain of heroism ... Men were seeking out fresh paths for their ideas quite apart from imitations of nature.'[28] This defence of the Lewis group slyly criticised their commercial and intellectual viability. Privately Sickert was appalled by the Cubist Room: 'At Brighton the Epstein – Lewis – Etchells room made me sick & I publicly disengaged my responsibility,' he wrote to Nan Hudson. When Epstein's 'so-called drawings' and Lewis's *Creation* were shown at Fitzroy Street, he was further outraged: 'The Epsteins are pure pornography – of the most joyless soit dit – and the Lewis is pure impudence ... I don't believe in them, and, further, I think they make any consideration of serious painting impossible.'[29] The battle lines between innovation and tradition were drawn. Sickert resigned from the London Group in protest and began fighting a guerrilla war, sniping at targets from his position as a writer for the *New Age*. With astonishing hypocrisy as the painter of sordid Camden Town nudes with indistinct faces, Sickert complained in March 1914:

> We hear a great deal about non-representative art. But while the faces of the persons suggested are frequently nil, non-representation is forgotten when it comes to the sexual organs. Witness Mr Wyndham Lewis's 'Creation', exhibited at Brighton, Mr [Henri] Gaudier-Brzeska's drawing in last week's New Age, and several of Mr Epstein's later drawings ... The Pornometric gospel amounts to this. All visible nature with two exceptions is unworthy of study, and to be considered pudendum. The only things worthy of an artist's attention are what we have hitherto called the pudenda![30]

Lewis's response was calmly magisterial. Dismissing Sickert's moralising accusations, he calmly consigned Sickert and his art to the irrelevant wilderness of the past. 'For twenty or thirty years', Lewis wrote, Sickert was 'the scandal of the neighbourhood (as a painter) ... the Bohemian plague-spot on clean English life.' But now 'he has survived his sins, and has sunk into the bandit's mellow and peaceful maturity. He sits at his open door and invents little squibs and contrivances to discomfort the young brigands he hears tales of, and of whose exploits he is rather jealous.'[31] Sickert's time was over. Lewis now claimed the future for the Vorticists.

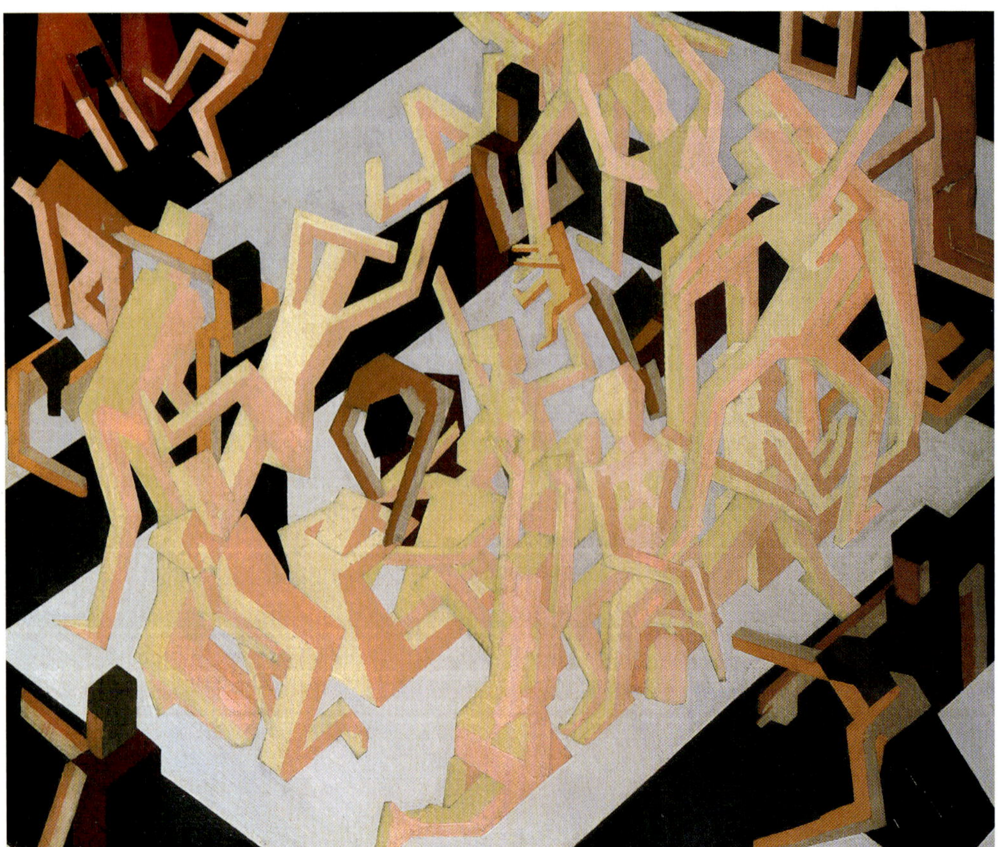

Fig.14
David Bomberg
Vision of Ezekiel 1912
Oil on canvas
114.3 x 137.2 cm
Tate. Purchased with assistance from the Morton Bequest through the Contemporary Art Society 1970

NOTES

1 Wyndham Lewis, 'The Cubist Room' in *An Exhibition of the English Post-Impressionists, Cubists, and others*, exh. cat. (Brighton: Brighton Public Art Gallery, 1913), pp.11, 12.

2 See Quentin Bell and Stephen Chaplin, 'The Ideal Home Rumpus: Wyndham Lewis and Roger Fry', *Apollo*, vol.80, no.32 (October 1964), pp.284–91.

3 Wyndham Lewis, 'The Round Robin', October 1913, quoted in *Letters*, ed. W.K. Rose (London: Methuen, 1963), p.49.

4 'The Cubists: Astounding Pictures at Brighton', *Brighton Gazette*, 17 December 1913.

5 Lewis, Brighton 1913, p.10.

6 Ibid., p.11.

7 Ibid.

8 Ibid., pp.11–12.

9 This work is untraced; see Walter Michel, *Paintings and Drawings: Wyndham Lewis* (London: Thames and Hudson 1971), p.426, U.10.

10 'The Cubists of Camden Town', *Brighton Herald*, 20 December 1913.

11 Ibid. The eroticism of the painting would surely have evoked Nijinsky's controversial performance in the Ballets Russes *Prélude à l'après midi d'un faune* premiered in Paris on 29 May 1912.

12 George R. Halkett, 'Art & Artists: The Revolutionaries of British Painting', *Observer*, 21 December 1913, p.9.

13 'Round the Galleries: The London Group', *Sunday Times*, 18 January 1914.

14 Lewis showed: *Creation* (£25), *L'Après-midi d'un Faune* (£25), *Group* (£30) and what may have been, to judge by their prices, three works on paper *Group* (£9), *Classic Group* (£6), and *Brothers* (£9).

15 Wyndham Lewis, 'Modern Art', *The New Age*, vol.14, no.22 (2 April 1914), p.703; reprinted in *Letters*, p.59.

16 See 'The Cubists of Camden Town'.

17 See Michel 1971, p.8.

18 Lewis, Brighton 1913, p.12.

19 Ibid.

20 Lewis, 'Modern Art'.

21 Alongside *Primeval Decoration* (£50), Bomberg showed various studies: *Wind and Water* (£12), *Study in Oil Paint* (£26), *Chalk Study* (8 gns), *Drawing for 'Primeval Decoration'* (£30) and *Summer Night* (£15).

22 David Bomberg manuscript autobiography; see Richard Cork, *Vorticism and Abstract Art in the First Machine Age*, vol.1 (London: Gordon Fraser 1976), p.136.

23 Nevinson's prices were listed as *Dawn at Southwark* (£25), *Gare St Lazare* (£25), and *Camden Town* (£20); his three works on paper, *Waiting for the Robert E. Lee*, *Limehouse* and *Gare St Lazare* were 7 guineas each.

24 The prices would suggest that *The Sand Pit* (£25) was Wadsworth's only oil. He priced *The Pells, Lewes* and *Sussex Farm* at 5 gns and 10 gns respectively, and also showed *Fortifications* (5 gns), *Still Life* (10 gns), *Issy les Molineux* (12 gns), and *The Iron Bridge* (15 gns).

25 Etchells's *Entry into Jerusalem* c.1912 was only priced at £10, while the Analytical Cubist heads were £4 each.

26 James Bolivar Manson, 'Introduction', Brighton 1913, p.8.

27 'The Cubists: Astounding Pictures at Brighton'.

28 'Impressionist Opens the Brighton Exhibition: His Views of the New School', *Sussex Daily Advertiser*, 17 December 1913.

29 Walter Sickert to Nan Hudson, [February] 1914; Tate Gallery Archive.

30 Walter Sickert, 'On Swiftness', *The New Age*, vol.14, no.21 (26 March 1914), pp.655–6; Anna Gruetzner Robins (ed.), *Walter Sickert: The Complete Writings on Art* (Oxford: Oxford University Press 2000), p.347.

31 Lewis, 'Modern Art'.

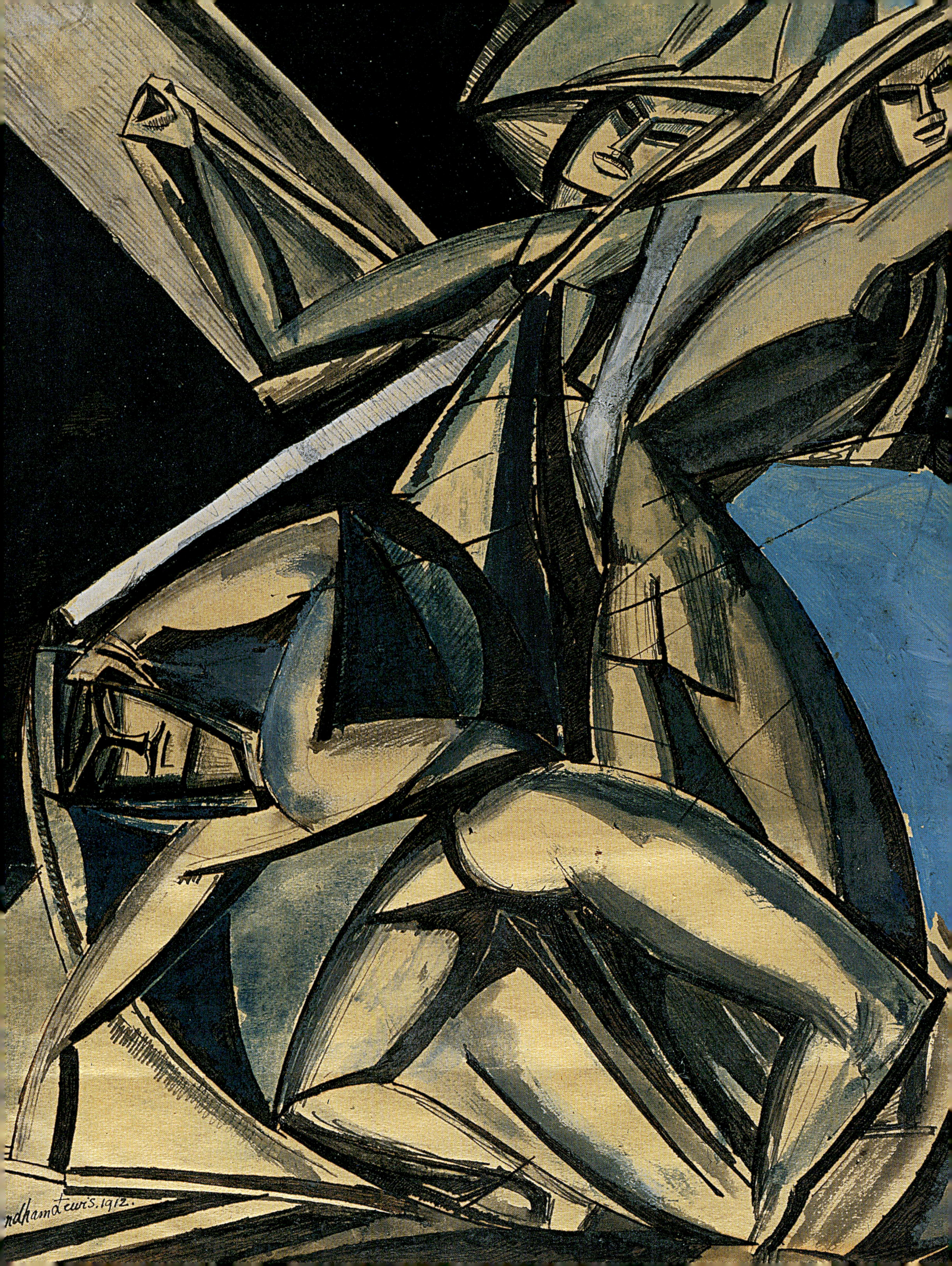
ndham Lewis, 1912.

WYNDHAM LEWIS'S VORTICISM: A STRANGE SYNTHESIS

Paul Edwards

Surveying the scene in Europe in 1929 and looking forward to a 'world-art' unrestricted by political nationalism and cultural isolationism, Wyndham Lewis gave the broadest definition of Vorticism:

> What has fact on its side is still this strange synthesis of cultures and times (which we named Vorticism in England) and which is the first projection of a world-art, and also I think the clearest trail promising us delivery from the mechanical impasse.[1]

The synthesis was 'strange' presumably because its particular form and elements were to some extent fortuitous. To account for Lewis's version of this synthesis (which took its final Vorticist form in the geometrical abstractions he produced from 1913 to 1915), a number of histories are needed. One would relate London's art-politics from around 1910, including Lewis's separation from the Camden Town Group (of which he was a semi-detached member); his uneasy relationship with Bloomsbury, culminating in his walk-out from Roger Fry's Omega Workshops in 1913 along with painters who would join him in the rival Rebel Art Centre; then Lewis's qualified welcome of F.T. Marinetti and Futurism, followed by a repudiation of certain aspects of Futurist ideas and practice in the name of a specifically English movement, for which Ezra Pound invented the title, Vorticism. Lewis became the chief spokesman and theorist of this new movement through editing the avant-garde magazine *Blast* (1914–15) and writing its manifestos. Alongside this history is an aesthetic one, driven by Lewis's ambition to produce a distinctive and advanced form of painting, as from 1910 onward he tried, first, the formulae of Cubism, as in *Girl Asleep* 1911; then a disciplined version of Henri Matisse's linear technique, as in *Courtship* 1912; followed in 1912 by a taut Cubo-Futurist style dominated by the colour blue. After a further transitional stage in which he abandoned the use of tonal gradients of colour to indicate volume, he restricted his formal means to geometrically delineated, intersecting forms filled with unmodulated colour, black or white, or grimy passages of pencil and chalk. A third history would trace the development of Lewis's ideas, which were inspired by his education in antipositivism, particularly the ideas of Henri Bergson, Friedrich Nietzsche, and Georges Sorel,

Detail from Wyndham Lewis *The Dancers* 1912 (fig.18)

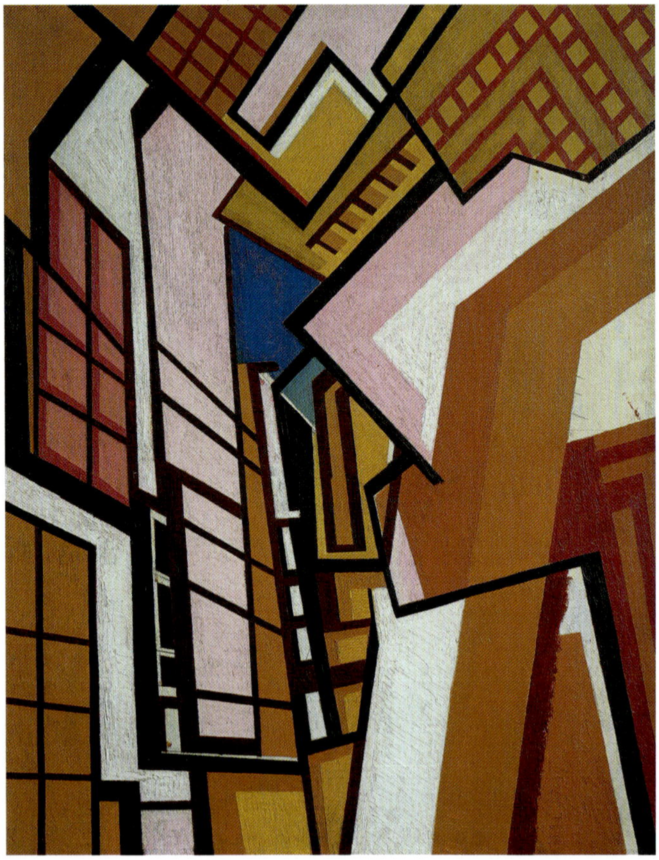

Fig.15
Wyndham Lewis
Workshop c.1914–15
(no.19)
[D; P]

which dominated the thought of young advanced painters in Paris before the First World War. This history would also trace his interest in oriental art and its aesthetic; his knowledge of Siberian Shamanism; his reactions to Futurist ideas, to Vasily Kandinsky, to the formalist aesthetics of Roger Fry and Clive Bell; and finally his reception of Wilhelm Worringer's thinking as transmitted through the lectures and conversation of T.E. Hulme. These were the ingredients in Lewis's Vorticist synthesis.

The histories are intertwined, and each predominates at different moments in Lewis's development towards Vorticism. This essay is concerned mainly with the way his painting engages with Bergson's philosophy and provides only a partial account of Vorticism's development and rationale. Anyone who stands in front of Lewis's *Workshop* c.1914–15 (fig.15) or *Timon of Athens* 1913 (fig.16) will respond to them as dynamic but rather impenetrable works that withhold their ultimate secrets. The pink, brown, and mustard colours of *Workshop* and its (in places) curiously smeared paint, along with the intricate yet indecipherable mechanomorphic forms of *Timon of Athens*, to adapt T.S. Eliot's phrase, communicate before they are understood. Indeed, no amount of visual and historical analysis can subdue them completely to the understanding. The forms employed by a painter never map perfectly onto a philosophical system, and those used by experimental painters before the First World War have no inevitable or intrinsic relationship with the systems of thought that were used to explain them. In the case of one of the most influential philosophies of the period, it was, as the title of Mark Antliff's account of painting in Paris suggests, a case of 'inventing' Bergson.[2] Lewis's deployment of various stylistic innovations (in which, with the exception of geometrical abstraction, he was a follower rather than an initiator) shows him questioning the philosophies for which he understood other artists were inventing them to express. He was not simply absorbing styles. As Lisa Tickner has said, 'Lewis can't be adequately mapped in terms of a medley of continental "isms". His intelligent interrogation of *what they were good for* served a quite idiosyncratic pictorial project.'[3] Idiosyncratic in some respects it may have been, but in 1913–14 it suddenly resulted in a 'synthesis' around which the London avant-garde could, with reservations, rally. Its concerns with Bergson's metaphysics (and physics) were scarcely peripheral.

Thomas Kush, in 1981, was the first to make the somewhat surprising case for Bergson's importance to Lewis's early painting.[4] Bergson is, after all, 'blasted' on page 21 of *Blast*, no.1 (1914), and in *Time and Western Man* (1927) Lewis denounced him as the fountainhead of all the 'time-philosophies' that he sought to counter and defeat. Yet, we have Lewis's own word for the early influence of the philosopher upon him: 'Bergson was an excellent lecturer, dry and impersonal. I began by embracing his evolutionary system.'[5] This system was part of Bergson's attempt to show that the nineteenth-century 'nightmare of determinism', in which the possibilities of life were circumscribed by the mechanical laws of cause and effect, was at least partly an illusion. Nature (or what underlies it) is not really circumscribed but creative and free. A continuous upsurge of cosmic energy – a form of spirit – aspires to realise itself in forms that preserve as much freedom as possible. The various grades of matter and biological forms (matter itself, plants, insects, higher animals, and finally human beings) correspond to the degrees and manners in which these spiritual explosions have achieved this goal. Natural forms represent the reach of cosmic energy when it meets the resistance of inertia as matter. This liberatory philosophy holds out the hope of humanity transcending its condition and 'natural' limitations. Bergson seemed to show that the inertia may be overcome, and his philosophy was received across Europe as an optimistic call for spiritual transformation.

But there is a less optimistic way of interpreting Bergson's system that stresses material inertia: 'Prostration is our natural position. A worm-like movement from a spot of sunlight to a spot of shade, and back, is the type of movement that is natural to men.'[6] Look at Lewis's *Sunset among the Michelangelos* c.1912 (fig.17) or *Two Mechanics* c.1912. The Cubist influence is immediately apparent, but they are not what we think of as Cubist because at no level are they concerned with a problem of knowledge. Unlike a figure in a Cubist portrait by Pablo Picasso, in which we infer a relationship between the unlikely forms on the canvas and a normal human being as sitter (however disrupted the inference is by the signs that prompt it), Lewis's figures are what they seem: lumpish, devitalised, and barely risen above a vegetable or vermiform existence. Their resemblance to human beings is metaphorical, and the condition of material collapse that these works explore has for Lewis both tragic and comic possibilities, though his figures tend to be more pitiable than tragic.

During the same period Lewis was also interested in the outbursts of energy that underlie Bergson's theory of creation; his famous lost painting *Kermesse* 1912, designed as a decoration for the Cave of the Golden Calf, was originally shown in July 1912 under the title *Creation* at the Allied Artists' Association exhibition at the Royal Albert Hall.

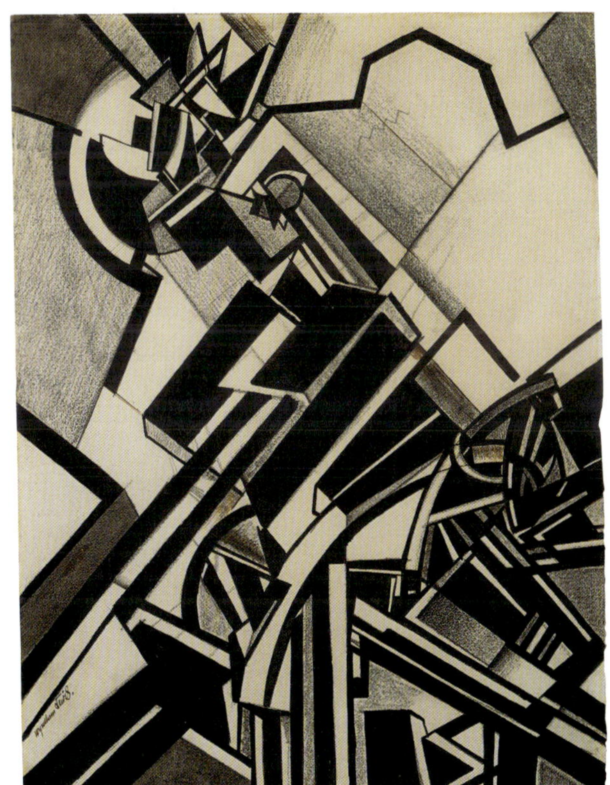

Fig.16
Wyndham Lewis
Timon of Athens 1913
(no.32)
[B1; P]

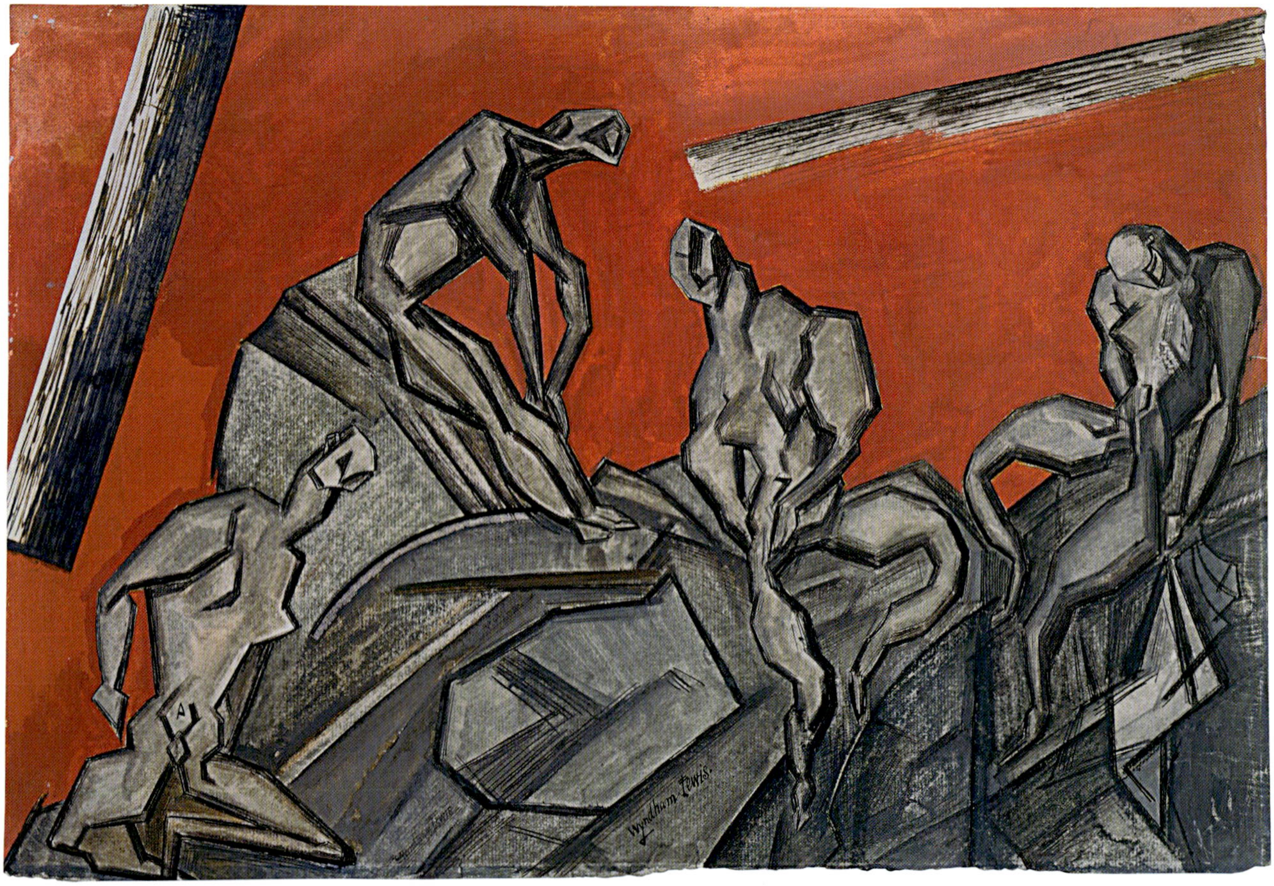

Fig.17
Wyndham Lewis
Sunset among the Michelangelos c.1912
Ink and gouache on paper
32.3 x 47.8 cm
Victoria and Albert Museum, London

Another *Creation* (along with a watercolour of the same name) was included in Fry's *Second Post-Impressionist Exhibition: British, French and Russian Artists* (1912–13).[7] *Kermesse* and its surviving related drawings depict dancing figures – a common motif of European paintings at the time: most famously Matisse's *The Dance* 1909. Unlike his vegetable figures, Lewis's dancers (especially in *The Dancers*, also known as *The Dancers: Study for Kermesse* 1912, fig.18) transform their surroundings and flood them with violent energy. But they too seem to be stopped short by some form of limit. The painting thus contains opposites, as the energy of creation is ultimately arrested by its material vehicle.

This enforced limitation was, in an oblique way, also the theme of Lewis's series of drawings for *Timon of Athens*, intended for an illustrated edition (1913) of William Shakespeare's play *The Life of Timon of Athens*. The importance of the series is signalled by the fact that two later works that exemplify his mature Vorticist style of geometric abstraction, are also related to the play: *Timon of Athens* itself and *Composition: Later Drawing of Timon Series* 1913 (fig.19). The earliest drawings, adaptations of the Cubo-Futurist style seen in the study for *Kermesse*, point most clearly to this continuity. In *The Thébaïde* 1912, violent energy issues from Timon's screaming mouth, animating the scene into spikes, sharp wedges, and incisive curves. Timon is a tragic figure who has conceived the world and humanity as generous and kind and acted accordingly. His violent misanthropy is his reaction to the discovery, on the contrary, that his fellows are mean, selfish, and brutal; his frustrated cry is also an analogue of the violent energy of Lewis's dancers, but with less chance than they of escaping the material limitations of ordinary life.

These works, all dominated by Lewis's favourite (in 1912) range of blues and browns, reveal a more secure grasp of what might be called the 'epistemological' side of Cubism,

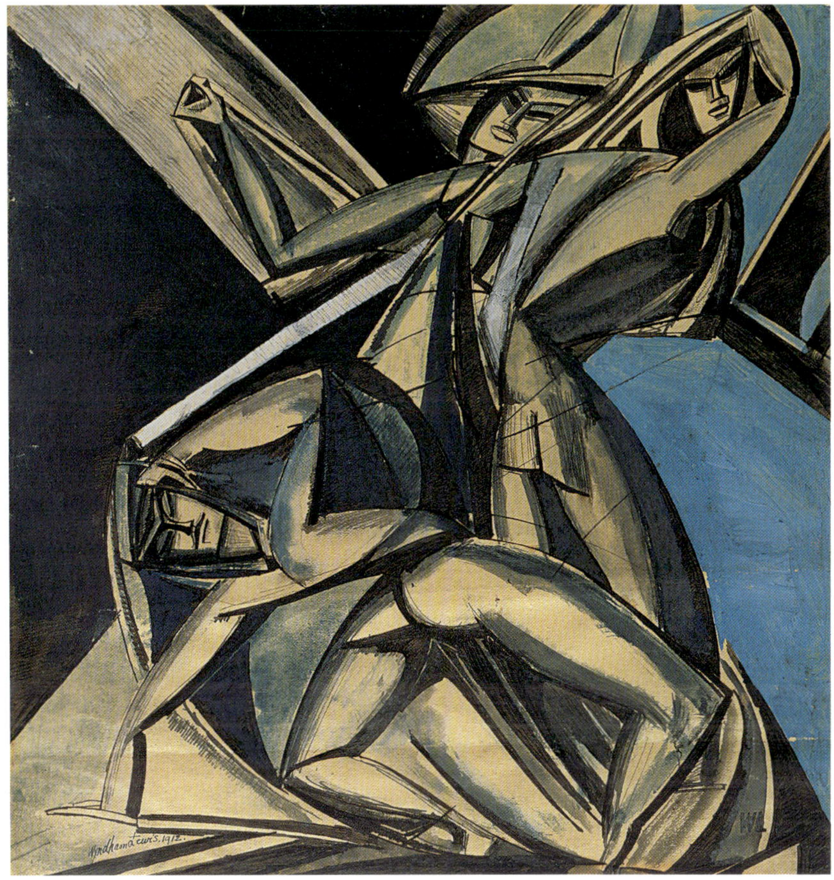

Fig.18
Wyndham Lewis
The Dancers 1912
Ink and watercolour on paper
30.1 x 29.2 cm
[P]

as the construction of the two female figures in the left foreground of *The Thébaïde* demonstrates. Nevertheless, Lewis still seems primarily to make an ontological point: the ultimate inseparability of the figures from the matrix of lines, passages, and planes that compose them is an analogue for the unavoidable limitation of energy within the forms of matter, and Lewis's Cubism is again employed for its metaphorical and expressive capacity, rather than for any reflection on modes of perception or representation of the world. Before Lewis could invent the mode of abstraction known as Vorticism, he needed to reconceive the nature of pictorial space – or the plane on which the artist makes marks – and the kinds of signification those marks could serve. The transition occurs in an intermediate stage of the Timon project in which he radically reduced his pictorial resources, probably to facilitate economical printing in line-block rather than full-colour on coated paper. The subtitle pages for the Acts show Lewis using the picture plane as a designer uses it, laying out his forms, arranging them on the flat, and not thinking of pictorial space as a virtual representation of three dimensions. At the same time, a drawing like *Timon* 1912 (no.58) relates the reduced range of visual elements to the machine forms of the modern environment: the figure of Timon is simply a particular configuration brought about when these components mesh in a certain way. This is a Futurist vision – almost a postmodern vision – but also a tragic one, as is appropriate for the play.

As I have suggested, Lewis's work of 1912 in a sense illustrates Bergson's ideas about energy, matter, and creation. Curiously, though Bergson is 'blasted' in *Blast*, no.1, Lewis becomes in 1913 a more intrinsically Bergsonian artist, though of a peculiarly perverse and rebellious kind. Bergson's system contains an epistemology that plays a crucial role in enabling his evolutionary system to claim to overcome the old nightmare of determinism. His philosophy is at one level a theory of false consciousness, arguing that the tendency to perceive the world in Kantian or Newtonian ways as a set of discrete things is false or misleading. Instead, through a form of intuition, achieved through an intensification of attention that fuses all time and space into an act of pure perception and bypasses the commonsense world that physics studies, we can be liberated into the realm of creative freedom and indeterminacy of the *élan vital*, the spirit-force. In this act we become one with *la durée*, or duration, a version of creative time that Bergson distinguishes from mechanical clock time. This intuitive seizing of reality is the element of Bergsonism usually associated with modernism.[8]

Intuition therefore leaves normal perception behind it as too limited a perspective on the world and our own capacities. However, another form of 'knowledge' equally goes beyond the commonsense world but proceeds in the opposite direction. This is pure intellectuality, whose epistemological paradigm is geometry, which is the foundation of humanity's ability to understand and work on its surroundings, calculate, and exercise mechanical control over them. But this form of knowledge is intimately connected to the limitations of our material world – to the extent of 'causing' them. Even though we do not go so far as to actually perceive the world as abstract geometry, we deduce geometry by extending through logic the tendency of human perception to construct the world according to the three-dimensional manifold. Ordinary life is lived somewhere between these poles of rigid geometry and emancipated intuition, which are equivalent to matter and spirit, those themes of the agon in Lewis's work of 1912. Lewis becomes a Vorticist, one could say, when he not only depicts this conflict but also conceives of the picture space and pictorial elements themselves as instances of it. Different relationships with reality and ways of knowing (as well as being) now seem to govern the work's emergence.

From Bergson's descriptions, one can derive a phenomenology of space that can be thought of as a spectrum, with the commonsense world at its centre. At one end is the pure, homogeneous, unqualitied space of classical geometry, which our intellect deduces as the conceptual armature of matter. Other animals, especially insects, are near the other end of the spectrum, and for them 'space is not so homogeneous ... and ... determinations of space, or directions, do not assume ... a purely geometrical form'.[9] Animals live in a different reality, because they have an immediate perception of the 'very ground of our experience' and may, for example, sense different directions as different colours:

> we have to do with two different kinds of reality, the one heterogeneous, that of sensible qualities [that is, the 'space' of insects and intuition] the other homogeneous, namely space. This latter, clearly conceived by the human intellect, enables us to use clean-cut distinctions, to count, to abstract, and perhaps also to speak.[10]

Our world is a product of this misleading intellectual consciousness, and Bergson conceives of the task of philosophy as to overcome the merely relative truths of physics and reverse our dependence on intellectual faculties; in truth the whole world of matter, with its regularities and determinate form, results from a failure of the *élan vital* to mount the slope that has matter at its bottom and emancipated spirit at its top. In this rather gnostic philosophy, the entire material world becomes a kind of cosmic mistake, and philosophy must help the cosmos surpass it. Bergson asks rhetorically whether the task of metaphysics is not:

> to bring back matter to its origins [in spirit, or *élan vital*], and to build up progressively a cosmology which would be, so to speak, a reversed psychology? All that seems *positive* to the physicist and to the geometrician would become, from this new point of view, an interruption or inversion of the true positivity, which would have to be defined in psychological terms.[11]

Of course much of modernism signed up to this project, the paradigm case being Kandinsky, whose paintings draw us back up the slope that has materiality at its bottom. His abstraction takes us to that boundary where material objects and their significations dissolve and the spiritual shines through as pure heterogeneous quality.

Lewis's abstractions do the opposite – though this is by no means all that they do. In them the capacity to abstract intellectually (which 'seems *positive* to the physicist and geometrician' but to Bergson damagingly limited) determines the basic mode of the artist's activity. His practice is thus an idiosyncratic but logical corollary of a true Futurism that embraces modernity, for modernity has been produced precisely through the power of intellectual apprehension to 'externalise' the world and transform it with mechanical invention and production. A comprehensive reflection of the modern world must engage with this fact. Lewis embraced it rather than disparaging it, as he believed Bergson did, but his was, as he later said, a 'stoic embrace'.[12]

For Bergson, the object world has no ontological validity independent of the functions we discover in it through our search for intellectual purchase on it: 'The bodies we perceive are, so to speak, cut out of the stuff of nature by our *perception*, and the scissors follow, in some way, the marking of lines along which *action* might be taken.' And again:

> The distinct outlines we see in an object, and which give it its individuality, are only the design of a certain kind

of *influence* that we may exert on a certain point of space: it is the plan of our eventual actions that is sent back to our eyes, as though by a mirror, when we see the surfaces and edges of things.[13]

In this light, the world of commonsense objects is to some extent an arbitrary one since, farther along the spectrum away from spatiality and materiality, it interfuses and iridesces with heterogeneous qualities, while in the other direction, it becomes more conceptual, reduced to the geometrical and other simple physical components of the physical laws that work at that particular point. They never apply completely, because reality is not, ultimately, geometrical,[14] but they work well enough for us to control and supplement nature with machines.

Such Vorticist designs as *Abstract Composition III* 1914–15 create a kind of space that clearly demonstrates this reciprocal relationship between a geometrical epistemology and ontology. From simple geometric elements and their intersections, areas of solidity and differentiated space emerge, and the field in front of us becomes an array of pathways for the mind to follow. But it can never trace one without meeting resistance from another that it must also assess as a direction that leads to a divergent understanding of the forces and energies in play before it. The contradictions of these possible pathways seem to exceed our ability to subdue them into a clear, coherent whole. The drawing thus provides a visual paradigm of the phenomenology of technologized man or woman in the modern city, though it does not represent them mimetically. Lewis describes this new kind of humanity in 'The New Egos' in *Blast*, no.1:

> But the modern town-dweller of our civilization sees everywhere fraternal moulds for his spirit, and interstices of a human world.
>
> He also sees multitude, and infinite variety of means of life, a world and elements he controls.
>
> Impersonality becomes a disease with him.
>
> ... the frontiers interpenetrate, individual demarcations are confused and interests dispersed.[15]

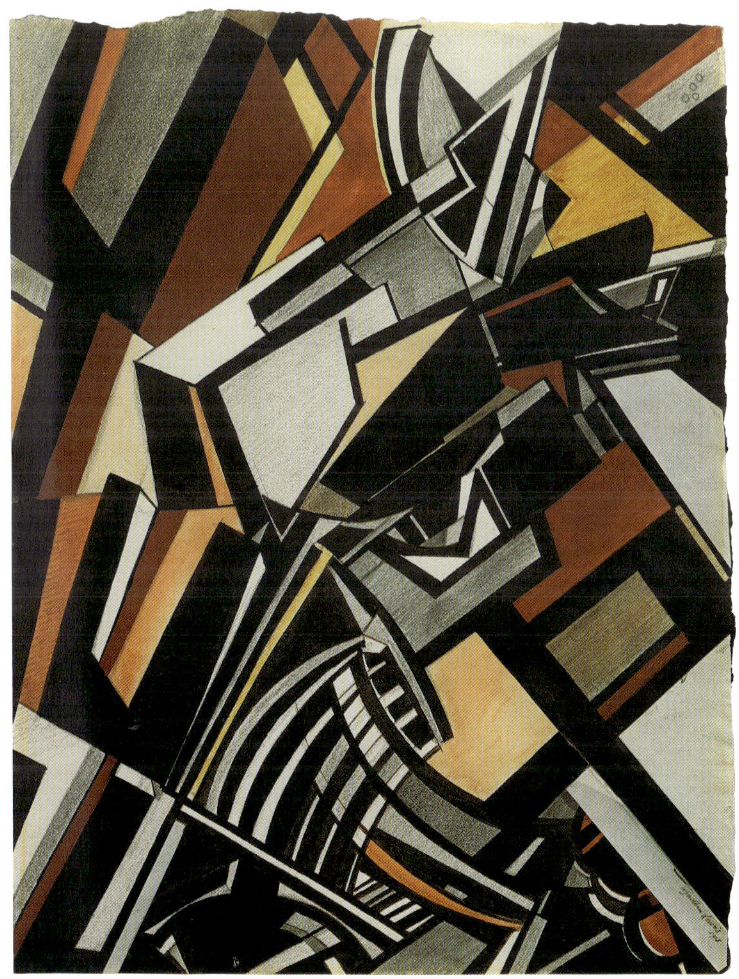

Fig.19
Wyndham Lewis
Composition 1913
(no.64)
[P]

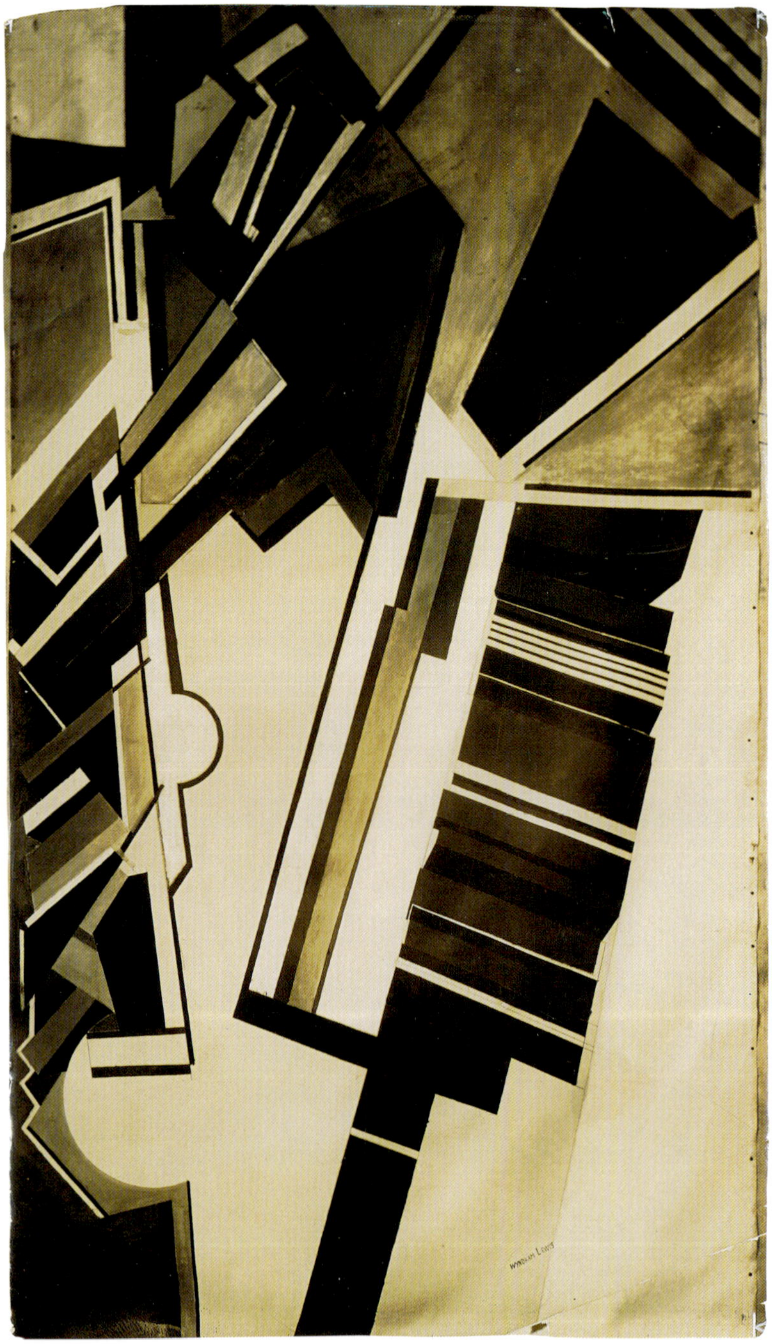

Fig.20
Wyndham Lewis
Plan of War 1913–14
(Lost)
[B1; P]

This interpenetration and confusion of demarcations are visible in *Abstract Composition III*, one of Lewis's most abstract works. As a plan like Bergson's geometry, it can never simply be reconciled with any materialization that would fully agree with commonsense perception. In the second issue of *Blast*, Lewis complained that most Cubists were 'mostly converted Impressionists, and inclined naturally to cube over their first effort, merely, instead of making any fresh start.'[16] Lewis, instead, rethinks the visual field in accordance with the characteristics of a certain way of interacting with the world: the analytic method that has produced modernity. He creates a virtual space animated by forces and occupied by different grades of material that would be reality for us if we saw and lived our world in the way that our industrial and intellectual techniques imply. Another work, *Design for Red Duet* 1915 (fig.29 on p.62), does represent the human figure as it would exist on this part of the phenomenological spectrum. Lewis is not 'cubing' onto a preconceived human figure but designing a plan of it from a limited range of conceptual and visual elements suited to the needs and functions of man within a technologized, urban environment. The culmination or epitome of the picture as a plan is the lost *Plan of War* 1913–14 (fig.20). The painting does not tell us how Lewis feels about the idea of war, except that, even if not the 'world's only hygiene' in Marinetti's words, it is an essential ingredient in – perhaps the culmination of – modernity. Though a plan in Bergson's sense, as the title suggests, it does not cut through reality without opposition, just as a military commander's scheme is necessarily modified by resistance.[17] It does not, unlike one of Kandinsky's apocalypses, aspire to break through to a realm of pure spirit.

Lewis carried over this reconception of the picture space to his *Timon* project. *Composition: Later Drawing of Timon Series* (no.64) depicts a dancing couple (the male more abstracted, robotic, and threatening than the female in *apache* dance posture beneath him).[18] As in the earlier Timon works, dynamism is again impeded, blocked by the sheer recalcitrance of the matter it organises. Not all of Lewis's Vorticism partakes of this mood, however. *Planners* 1912–13 (fig.21), originally titled *A Happy Day*, displays relaxed and airy geometries and colours. *Portrait of an Englishwoman* 1913 on the other hand is humorous, adapting intellectual geometry to a witty caricature of the 'prunes and prisms' English bourgeoisie. Ironically this work, reproduced in Russia in Aleksandr Belenson's journal *Strelets* (*The Archer*) in 1915, may well have inspired a quite different use of similar pictorial elements in the work of Kazimir Malevich and in Suprematism.[19] This exemplifies my earlier point that a visual style does not map directly onto a philosophy unless we bring the philosophy to it as a supplement. Geometry, interpreted from another set of assumptions (Theosophical ones, for example), may seem like a symbol of our spiritual transcendence of matter, rather than of the techniques of marshalling and controlling but also locking us into it.

Bergson's dualism is a competitive relationship, epistemologically between intuition and spatializing intellect, or, ontologically between a spiritual life-force and a recalcitrant matter, and such relationships are inherent in Lewis's Vorticism, starting with the playful co-presence of 'Blasts' and 'Blesses' in the magazine: England and France are both blasted, but equally, both are blessed. Lewis's repudiation of a consistent and indivisible personality is also related, along with his interest in 'duets', as in *Red Duet* 1914 (fig.30 on p.64). In similar fashion, *The Crowd* 1914–15 (no.7) simultaneously celebrates the mystic violence of the anarchist and critiques its limitations within the monolithic structures of the modern industrial city.

The truth is that Lewis does not want his paintings to belong exclusively to the world of matter. Their uncompromising geometry and earthy textures evoke matter and the geometricizing intellect, but their dynamism and vibrant colours conjure spirit and transcendent intuition. Not that their two aspects are (or should be) as distinct as this analysis suggests, for the point of Lewis's Vorticism is that it is a 'synthesis' however 'strange'. On the spiritual side, Lewis enlisted a variety of non-rational compulsions to determine his formal decisions, an aspect of his practice he emphasised many years later in explaining Vorticist abstractions:

> The way those things were done – are done, by whoever uses this method of expression – is that a mental-emotive* impulse is let loose upon a lot of blocks and lines of various dimensions and encouraged to push them around and to arrange them as it will. It is of course not an accidental, isolated, mood: but it is recurrent groups of emotions and coagulations of thinking, as it were, that is involved.
>
> *By this is meant subjective intellection, like magic or religion.[20]

Lewis's types of compulsion are mentioned in *Blast*, where, in 'Fêng Shui and Contemporary Form', he compares the artist to the clairvoyant or Chinese geomancer, who is in touch with forces deeper than reason. These powers appear as a compulsion (that Lewis elsewhere called an 'inferior religion'), determining, beyond calculation or reason, the form of the painting:

> In a painting certain forms MUST be SO; in the same meticulous, profound manner that your pen or a book must lie on the table at a certain angle, your clothes at

night be arranged in a set personal symmetry, certain birds be avoided, a set of railings tapped with your hand as you pass, without missing one.[21]

But it is important to realise that Lewis wished his work to belong neither entirely to the realm of matter nor to spirit. He felt that Kandinsky's aspirations to purge matter and reveal an entirely spiritual order were not appropriate to the kind of beings that humans inescapably are (at least until they become ghosts).[22] Conversely, he thought that Picasso's small constructions (of absinthe glass and spoon, for example) remained too locked into the purely material dimension, untransformed by the spiritual energy that makes a work of art live.[23]

Early in the climactic peroration that comprises the last few pages of chapter three in *Creative Evolution*, Bergson begins to give a totalizing perspective on the cosmic competition he has outlined:

> Life as a whole, from the initial impulsion that thrust it into the world, will appear as a wave that rises, and which is opposed by the descending movement of matter. On the greater part of its surface, at different heights, the current is converted by matter into a vortex. At one point alone it passes freely, dragging with it the obstacle which will weigh on its progress but will not stop it. At this point is humanity; it is our privileged situation.[24]

Asked to explain the meaning of Vorticism, Lewis said, 'You think at once of a whirlpool. At the heart of the whirlpool is a great silent place where all the energy is concentrated, and there at the point of concentration is the Vorticist.'[25] Only in light of Bergson's statement does this idea take on much meaning. In Lewis's modification of the French thinker, though, he typically reserves the position of stillness and freedom not for humanity as a whole, but for the avant-garde Vorticist.

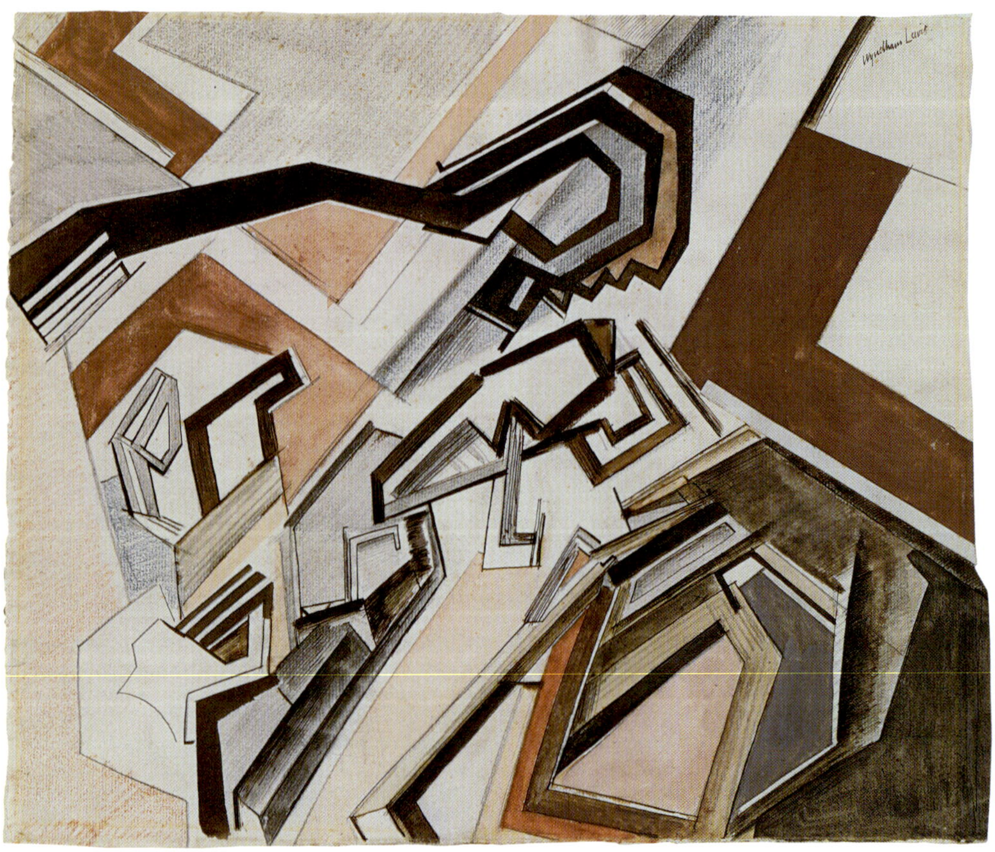

Fig.21
Wyndham Lewis
Planners: Happy Day 1912–13
(no.63)
[P]

NOTES

1 Wyndham Lewis, 'A World Art and Tradition' (1929), in *Wyndham Lewis on Art: Collected Writings* 1913–1956, ed. Walter Michel and C.J. Fox (London: Thames and Hudson, 1969), p.259.

2 Mark Antliff, *Inventing Bergson: Cultural Politics and the Parisian Avant-Garde* (Princeton: Princeton University Press, 1993).

3 Lisa Tickner, 'A Lost Lewis: The Mother and Child of 1912', *Wyndham Lewis Annual*, vol.2 (1995), p.8.

4 Thomas Kush, *Wyndham Lewis's Pictorial Integer* (Ann Arbor, Mich.: UMI Research Press, 1981).

5 Wyndham Lewis to Theodore Weiss, 19 April 1949, *The Letters of Wyndham Lewis*, ed. William K. Rose (London: Methuen, 1963), p.489. Lewis followed Henri Bergson's lectures while an art student in Paris before the First World War.

6 Wyndham Lewis, *The Art of Being Ruled* (1926; repr., ed. Reed Way Dasenbrock, Santa Rosa, Calif.: Black Sparrow Press, 1989), p.248.

7 The work was illustrated in the *Daily Mirror*, 3 October 1912. See Paul Edwards, 'Wyndham Lewis at the Second Post-Impressionist Exhibition: New (Old) Reproductions of Three Lost Works', *Wyndham Lewis Annual*, vols.9–10 (2002–3), pp.73–9.

8 See Henri Bergson, *Time and Free Will: An Essay on the Immediate Data of Consciousness*, trans. F.L. Pogson (London: George Allen and Unwin, 1912), pp.99–101, for an account of 'pure duration' like the one that modernist painter Lily Briscoe experiences in Virginia Woolf's *To the Lighthouse* (1927).

9 Ibid., p.96.

10 Ibid., p.97.

11 Henri Bergson, *Creative Evolution*, trans. Arthur Mitchell (London: Macmillan, 1911), pp.219–20. Note that Bergson suggests that the character of the cosmos can change as a result of the way we think about it; in other words that epistemology is so closely geared to ontology that it can ratchet it back under its own power.

12 Wyndham Lewis, 'The Skeleton in the Cupboard Speaks' (1939), in *Wyndham Lewis on Art*, p.341.

13 Bergson 1911, p.12.

14 'Science is contingent, relative to the variables it has chosen, relative to the order in which it has successively put the problems'. It succeeds because 'mathematics represents the side to which matter inclines.' Ibid., pp.231–2.

15 Wyndham Lewis, 'The New Egos', *Blast*, no.1 (July 1914), p.141.

16 Wyndham Lewis, 'A Review of Contemporary Art', *Blast*, no.2 (July 1915), p.39.

17 Noel Yeates, in an unpublished essay, draws attention to the origin of the title in the English translation of Carl von Clausewitz's *Vom Krieg* (*On War*, 1832).

18 Alan Munton, in conversation with the author, was the first to identify this motif.

19 Anthony d'Offay discovered the connection in the 1960s.

20 Wyndham Lewis to Charles Handley-Read, 2 September 1949, *Letters*, p.504.

21 Wyndham Lewis, 'Fêng Shui and Contemporary Form,' *Blast*, no.1, p.138.

22 Lewis notes, 'you may regard [the supernatural] as redundant and nothing to do with life. The art of painting, further, is ... the art most attached to life.' Lewis, 'A Review of Contemporary Art', p.44.

23 In 'Relativism and Picasso's Latest Work', Lewis complains that they are not 'MACHINES OF LIFE, a sort of LIVING plastic geometry'. *Blast*, no.1, p.140.

24 Bergson 1911, p.284. Compare 'A Review of Contemporary Art': 'The moment the Plastic is impoverished for the Idea, we get out of direct contact with these intuitive waves of power, that only play on the rich surface where life is crowded and abundant. We must constantly strive to ENRICH abstraction till it is almost plain life.' p.40.

25 Wyndham Lewis, quoted in Douglas Goldring, *South Lodge: Reminiscences of Violet Hunt, Ford Madox Ford and the English Review Circle* (London: Constable, 1943), p.65.

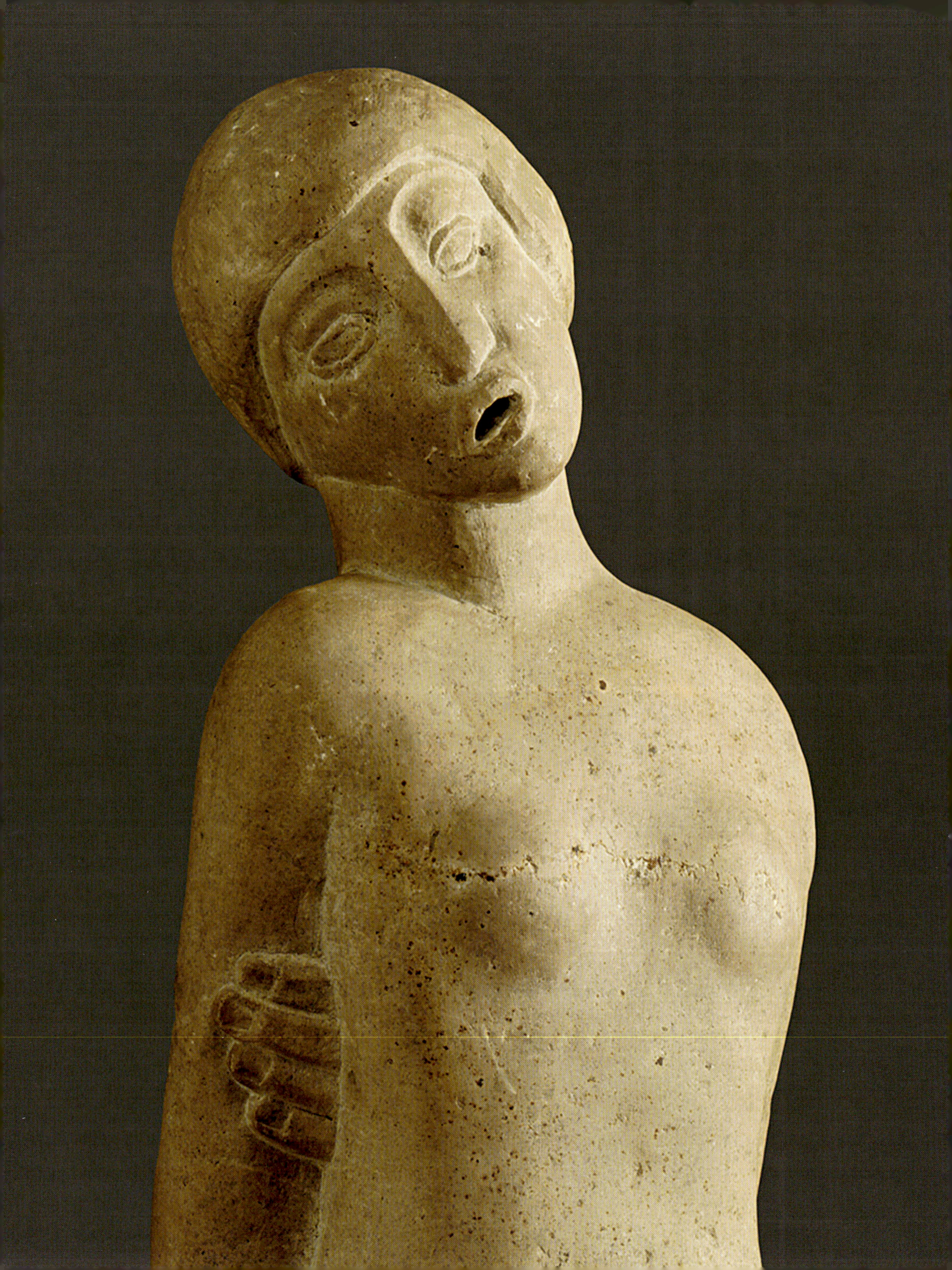

SCULPTURAL NOMINALISM/ ANARCHIST VORTEX: HENRI GAUDIER-BRZESKA, DORA MARSDEN, AND EZRA POUND

Mark Antliff

Following their initial encounter in July 1913, the sculptor Henri Gaudier-Brzeska (fig.22) and the poet and impresario Ezra Pound (fig.1 on p.16) developed a strong friendship, which lasted until the former's untimely death in June 1915; yet the political dimension of that alliance remains to be understood. This lacuna is especially striking given the profound impact of Dora Marsden, the editor of *The New Freewoman* (June–December 1913) and *The Egoist* (January 1914–December 1919), on Pound's political views from the summer of 1913 onwards;[1] Gaudier-Brzeska's earlier allegiance to anarchism;[2] and *The Egoist*'s status as the literary vehicle chosen by Gaudier-Brzeska and Pound to promote their emerging theory of Vorticist sculpture.

Marsden championed an anarcho-individualist interpretation of the egoist philosophy of Max Stirner, author of *Der Einzige und sein Eigentum* (1844), translated into English as *The Ego and his Own* in 1907.[3] Historians have pointed to Stirner and Marsden's espousal of nominalism – the belief that universals, classes, and abstractions distort rather than reveal reality – as inspiring Pound's anarcho-individualist and egoist championing of an art of particulars, first in his imagist poetry, then in his Vorticist aesthetic, with its basis in the dynamic qualities of the ideogram.[4] Anarchist nominalism also inspired Marsden and Pound to reject representational forms of government as well as status quo concepts of religion, the state, the citizen, and other universals. Marsden followed Stirner in declaring such generalizing terms illusory myths, designed to dupe the individual into subordinating his or her interests to those of the plutocratic state or the capitalist elite.[5] To counteract such coercive forms of collectivism, Stirner and Marsden called for a 'union of egoists' wherein individuals voluntarily formed a group to egoistically achieve maximum corporeal and creative satisfaction.[6] Thus egoism not only bolstered Pound's prior call for a poetics of the image as a more direct conduit to sensate experience, it led him to promote the anarchist ideology of direct action, in principled opposition to party politics.[7] Such tenets first emerged in Pound's writings for *The New Freewoman* in the autumn of 1913, but his most explicit statement appeared in his essay 'The New Sculpture', published in a February 1914 edition of *The Egoist*.[8] In that article Pound announced that 'primitivists' such as Jacob Epstein and Gaudier-Brzeska had rejected the 'folly' of democratic institutions to affirm their individual freedom

Detail from Henri Gaudier-Brzeska *Singer* 1913 (fig.27)

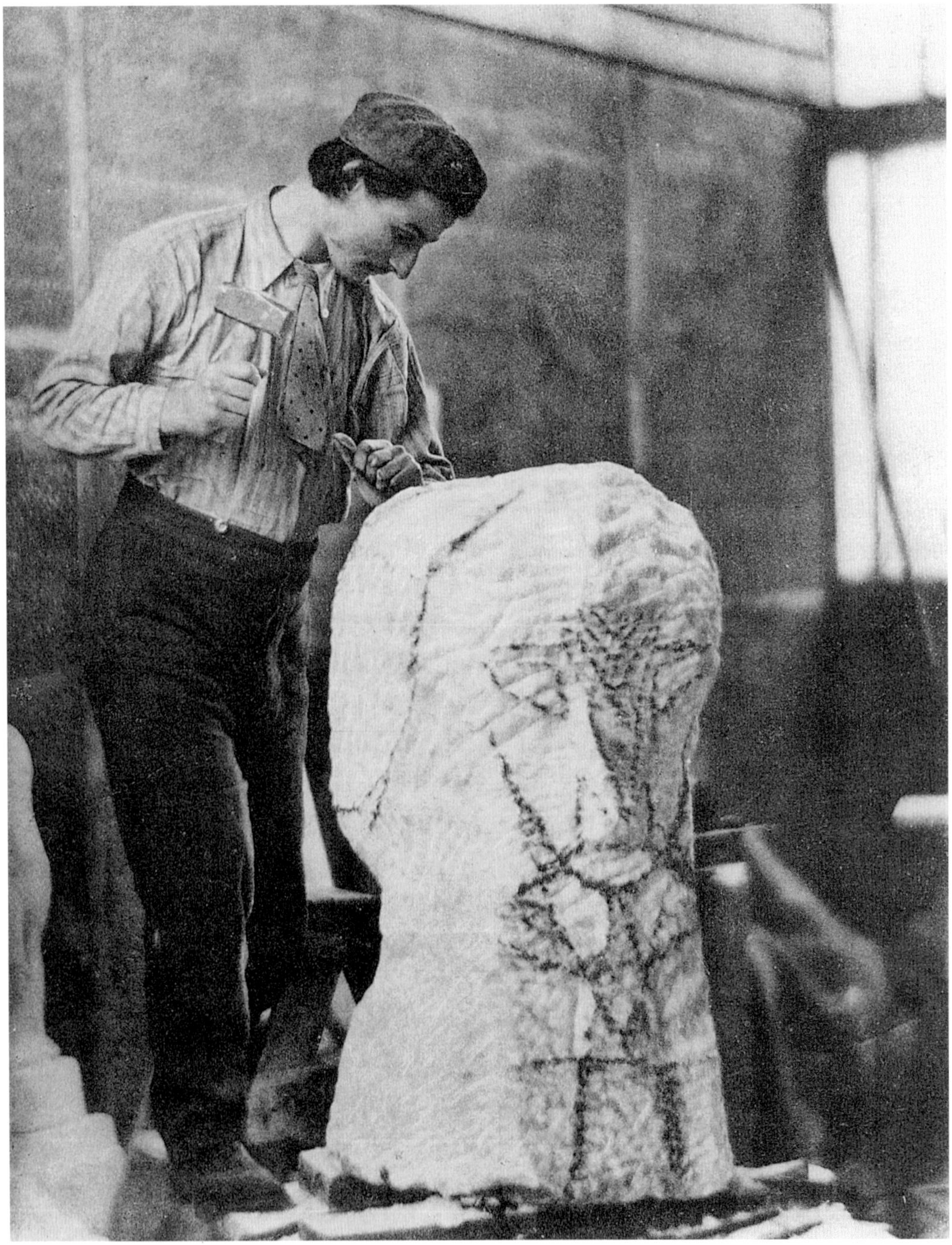

Fig.22
Henri Gaudier-Brzeska carving
Hieratic Head of Ezra Pound 1914
Photograph by Walter Bennington

from societal constraints.[9] Writing in *The Egoist* shortly after the appearance of the Vorticist journal *Blast* (1914–15) in June 1914, Pound affirmed his status as an atrabilious 'syndicalist' who was hostile to all 'political institutions'.[10]

While Marsden's impact is well documented, Gaudier-Brzeska's role in reinforcing Pound's new-found allegiance to anarchism has yet to be examined. Gaudier-Brzeska first declared himself an anarchist in October 1910, and following his move to London in January 1911, he renewed his contact with anarchist circles.[11] Pound in his 1916 memoir of Gaudier-Brzeska recalled that his early conversations with the sculptor in 1913 consisted of 'long, gay, electrified arguments over [Pound's] skepticism as to the impracticability of anarchy'.[12] Given Gaudier-Brzeska's anarchist affiliations, one can assume that he aided Pound's political evolution during the autumn of 1913. Such interactions pertain especially to Gaudier-Brzeska's professed commitment to direct carving in January 1913,[13] which arguably took on ideological import following his exposure to Pound's and Marsden's anarcho-individualism during that summer.

Philosophical Anarchism

Among the shared enthusiasms connecting Gaudier-Brzeska to *The Egoist* was a politicized interpretation of the French philosopher Henri Bergson's work. Gaudier-Brzeska and Marsden's endorsement of Bergson's critique of the 'fixed idea' in his seminal book *Evolution créatrice* (*Creative Evolution*, 1907) is particularly relevant.[14] In the December 1913 issue of *The New Freewoman*, Marsden asserted that Stirner's egoist philosophy 'anticipated Bergson', and to reinforce that claim, she reproduced an extract from *Creative Evolution* titled 'The Philosophy of Ideas', which proved central to her nominalist critique of fixed ideas.[15] In the essay, Bergson disparaged language for its inability to grasp 'duration', Bergson's term for temporal change. Language, in Bergson's view, is a pragmatic tool of the intellect, which transforms the radically individuated, qualitative, and heterogeneous nature of duration into homogenizing categories and static concepts. As a result of the practical function of our intellect, these generalizing terms come to be substituted for the permeable, inner flow of our felt emotions and the qualitative complexity of our sensory experience. Such prejudices, stated Bergson, are at the root of what philosophers mean by ideas. To prove his point Bergson traced the word 'idea' back to its Greek origin, 'eidos', a term that corresponded to 'three essential categories of language', which constitute 'the stable view taken of the instability of things'. From Plato onwards, fixed ideas were considered more real than the sensory, durational flux they displaced. This intellectual ossification had a verbal equivalent 'in our habits of language' for fixed ideas 'are all that [language] is capable of expressing'.[16]

Concurrent with Gaudier-Brzeska and Pound's arguments over the merits of anarchism, Marsden adapted Bergson's critique of language and of the intellect to her anarcho-individualist agenda. In a July 1913 essay, she claimed that the intellect examines all things in a comparative manner, rather than empathetically lingering on their particularity. It converts our ever-changing sensate experience into fixed concepts such as 'Truth, Humanity, Justice', classificatory 'Essences' extracted from a 'subjugated Soul'.[17] In a February 1914 edition of *The Egoist*, Marsden wrote a nominalist diatribe against standardized notions of 'Order' and 'Culture', promoted by the state through its laws and institutions. Having dismissed governmental concepts of 'statutory law' as 'delusions', Marsden then marshalled Bergson's distinction between intellectual and vital order in *Creative Evolution*[18] to support her anarchist critique.[19] Gaudier-Brzeska surely would have read this issue since it included Pound's first art criticism specifically devoted to Gaudier-Brzeska's sculpture, and a full-page reproduction of his art (fig.26). Marsden held that standardized concepts of 'Culture' likewise oppress individuals by causing them to doubt their own senses. Moneyed elites and government institutions promulgate such fixed ideas, which succeed in making people doubt 'the few things which their own individual power to perceive makes them aware of through the channels of their senses'. 'The clutter of cultural concepts ... – mere words', wrote Marsden, 'are choking the frail tentacles of perception.'[20] In an earlier article on art, Marsden followed Bergson in arguing that poetry rather than prose is the ideal means of capturing 'the soul motion', for poetry constitutes a concise use of language in the forms of sensory 'images', created in an elevated state of 'self-consciousness'.[21] By autumn 1913, Marsden and Pound regarded the poet's recourse to the sensual immediacy of the image and rejection of discursive abstractions as the linguistic corollary to anarchist direct-action strategies.[22] I would argue that Gaudier-Brzeska and Pound developed a sculptural correlate to Marsden's anarchist nominalism following the launch of *The Egoist* in January 1914.

Sculptural Nominalism and the Embodied Ego

In February and March 1914, Pound and Gaudier-Brzeska published a series of articles in *The Egoist* that amount to a nominalist interpretation of abstract art. Pound launched this campaign in 'The New Sculpture', pitting humanist aesthetics, which he associated with classical Greek art, its legacy in realism, and support of the political status quo, against an alternative vision of the artist as an anarchist rebel in revolt against democracy and humanism. Proponents of humanism believed that the classical Greek idealization of the body set an eternal standard that all art should aspire to; furthermore, this humanism was deployed

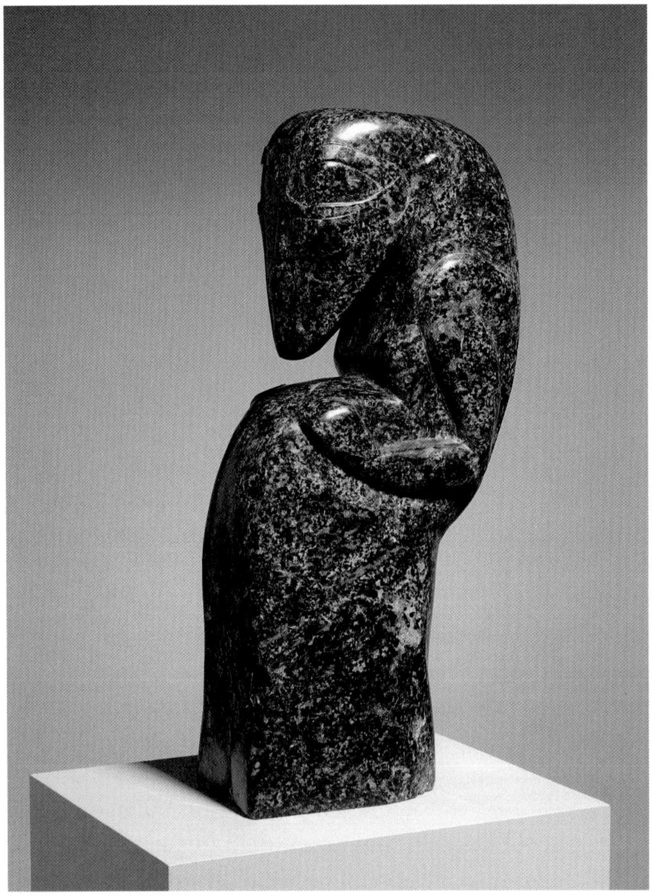

Fig.23
Jacob Epstein
Female Figure 1913
(no.34)

by the educated elite as a means of converting the public to its ideals. The humanists' attempt to 'lead and persuade humanity' also resulted in the birth of realist aesthetics, which, in literature, sought to win over the public through analyzing societal 'degeneration'. Pound by contrast declared his hostility to classical idealism, the 'analytical' novel, and the state-sanctioned cultural establishment.[23] One is reminded of Marsden's antirationalist diatribe against fixed ideas and unchanging concepts. For Pound, the aesthetic equivalent to eidos is the eternal classical ideal and an analytic rather than emotive approach to art. Thus the new sculpture eschews classical idealism and the analytic methods of the realist, finding its raison d'être in the unmediated expression of 'desire' and emotive 'forces'.[24] A focus on forces, especially the emotional drive intrinsic to the creative process, is the subject of the new sculpture. The ideological counterpart to such nominalist intransigence is open warfare against the political and cultural status quo. Unlike the humanist, the 'egoist' sculptor recognizes that 'the war between him and the world is a war without truce'. Further, 'he has no intention of trying to rule by general franchise... The artist has been at peace with his oppressors long enough. He has dabbled in democracy and he is now done with that folly'. Rejecting classical idealism and realist analysis, the 'new wild sculpture' taps the irrational wellsprings of the so-called primitive art of the non-European 'savage' who 'must live by craft and violence'. Thus the classical 'fashion plates' sculpted by Praxiteles are rejected in favour of 'Djinns, tribal gods, fetishes, etc'.[25]

Intransigence, combined with primitivism, underlines Epstein and Gaudier-Brzeska's sculpture in Pound's review, in a March 1914 issue of *The Egoist*, of the first exhibition of the London Group, held at the Goupil Gallery that month.[26] In keeping with Stirner's egoism, Pound relished the corporeal fecundity of Epstein's primitivized sculpture of a pregnant female in *Female Figure* in 'flenite' 1913 (fig.23), describing it as inspired by Egyptian art and 'the tragedy and enigma of the germinal universe'. Gaudier-Brzeska's *Boy with Coney* 1914 in turn 'is Chou, or suggests slightly the bronze animals of that period'. The sculpture of these two artists recalls 'the gods of the Epicureans'. Indeed, 'it is as if some realm of "Ideas", of Platonic patterns, were dominated by Hathor.' Here Pound asserted that the Egyptian cow-goddess of fertility, in tandem with an Epicurean delight in sensual pleasure, has overridden the ethereal realm of pure, disembodied 'Ideas'. Pound merged a Bergsonian and Stirner-inspired contempt for Platonic absolutes with a primitivist celebration of pagan gods, as manifest in Gaudier-Brzeska's and Epstein's 'new wild sculpture'.[27]

In this same issue Pound and Gaudier-Brzeska joined forces in a two-pronged rebuttal of *The Egoist* contributor and poet Richard Aldington, who, under the pseudonym 'Auceps', had ridiculed Pound's rejection of classical norms.[28] Pound's opening salvo took aim at the antinominalist status given to Greek art in Auceps's imagination. Pound declared himself and his artist allies 'liberated' from Auceps's devotion to 'THE BEAUTIFUL' for 'we have ceased to regard work as good or bad in accordance with whether it approaches or recedes from the "Antique", the "Classical" models'.[29] Pound's capitalization of the 'BEAUTIFUL', the 'Antique', and the 'Classical' recalls Marsden's equally mocking capitalization of fixed 'Essences'.[30] Thus Auceps refused 'to see the force of other conventions, by resolutely entrenching himself in prejudice'. An emotive response to such 'force' constitutes Pound's means of aesthetic 'appreciation', which he pointedly distinguishes from Auceps's idealist 'art criticism'.[31]

Pound's letter is followed by 'Mr. Gaudier-Brzeska on "The New Sculpture"'.[32] Just as Pound valued sculpture that subordinates Plato to Hathor, Gaudier-Brzeska exalted primitivism over the classical ideal as defined by cultural arbiters like 'the impertinent Auceps'. Gaudier-Brzeska accused him of brandishing 'false and arrogant scholastics', a reference to the classical method of dialectical reasoning to reconcile contradictions through analysis. Plato and the Scholastics had been subjected to a scathing critique by Stirner and Bergson; moreover, Gaudier-Brzeska echoed Pound in accusing Auceps of upholding the classical as an aesthetic norm. Auceps judged the new sculpture 'with, as a standard, the superficial qualities of the Greeks'. 'It would be better if he had the courage to say, "I am a dry intellect and I can *understand* but *to feel* is impossible."'[33] 'The modern sculptor', by contrast, 'works with instinct as his inspiring force' and since expression of that 'intense feeling' takes the form of 'abstraction' his sculpture bears no relation to 'classic Greek', but is instead 'continuing the tradition of the barbaric peoples of the earth'. Gaudier-Brzeska associated such barbarity with male sexuality. Having condemned the 'sterile' Auceps for embracing the 'light voluptuous modeling' typical of Hellenic sculpture,[34] Gaudier-Brzeska, in a June 1914 article, brashly described his own sculpture as 'virile' by virtue of his direct carving.[35] Art historians have frequently analyzed the male Vorticists' preoccupation with themes of virility,[36] but we also need to examine the anarchist import of Gaudier-Brzeska's self-fashioning as a virile rebel. Gaudier-Brzeska actively cultivated the persona of an anarchist *apache*, a derisive term

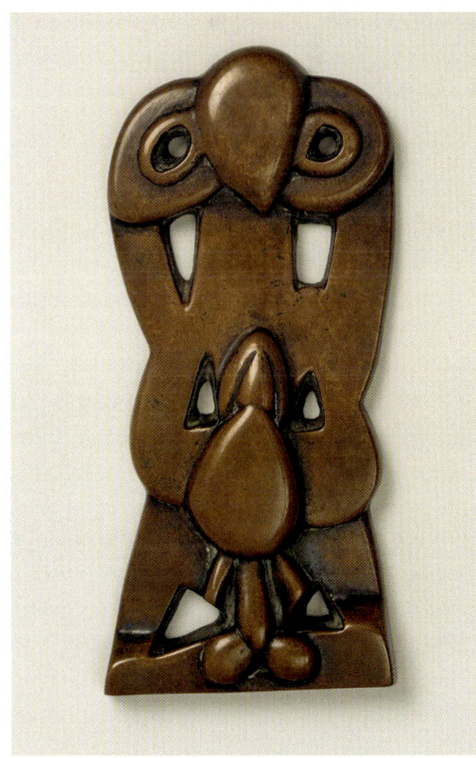

Fig.24
Henri Gaudier-Brzeska
Doorknocker 1914
Brass
17.8 x 8.5 x 1 cm

applied in the French and foreign press to describe male youths from the criminal underclass who frequented seedy cafés and dance halls and openly engaged in sexual relations out of wedlock.[37] Gaudier-Brzeska's Vorticist sculptures, such as his *Knuckleduster* 1914 or his sculpted *Doorknocker* 1914 (fig.24), depicting a copulating couple, are manifestations of this persona, which intertwined unbridled sexuality with pugilist aggression.[38]

Male virility had anarchist import for Gaudier-Brzeska and took on additional significance following his exposure to Stirner's philosophy in 1913–14. A central tenet of Stirner's theory is his celebration of the ego as wholly carnal, the polar opposite of Georg Wilhelm Friedrich Hegel's absorption of the human ego into some ethereal realm of the Absolute Spirit. Thus the first part of *The Ego and his Own* examines various fabrications of the ego, including notions of God, justice, and human essence, which are then condemned as illusory conceptions of a nonexistent, transcendental reality.[39] Stirner calls on humanity to denounce these universals and recognize the individual ego as the embodied repository of our creative abilities. Only when the individual 'has fallen in love with his corporeal self, and takes a pleasure in himself as a living flesh and blood person' will the ego achieve self-realization. The egoist is, first and foremost, 'a mortal creator'; moreover, Stirner wanted individuals to destroy the false 'corporeality' granted to abstract ideas like God and the state to achieve an affirmative realization that 'I alone am corporeal'.[40] To behave egotistically requires one to act in response to one's corporeal interests and desires: Stirner's nominalism therefore constitutes a frontal assault against any notion that mind and body, spirit and the flesh, somehow occupied two separate realms.[41] Readers of *The New Freewoman* and *The Egoist* were very familiar with this argument, for Marsden frequently asserted that the 'desiring' ego found its raison d'être in gender-neutral 'sexual passion' and the anarchist doctrine of free love.

With such thoughts in mind, we can look again at Gaudier-Brzeska's *Hieratic Head of Ezra Pound* 1914 (no.1), a collaborative piece commissioned by Pound in early 1914 and completed in late March. Starting with a four-foot block of Pentelicon marble, Gaudier-Brzeska carved a primitivist image that startlingly combines a bust of Pound's head with a bulbous erect penis. When seen from the front, the viewer confronts Pound's totemic visage, but when viewed from the back, the bust resolves into a brazen display of male sexual desire (fig.25).[42] From an egoist perspective, the work exemplifies Stirner's rebellious claims that Spirit cannot exist without the flesh and that the egoist seeks self-affirmation through the sensual enjoyment of his or her corporeal being. Whereas traditional portrait busts emphasize the life of the mind and inner character by exaggerating the size of the cranium, forehead, and hair, Gaudier-Brzeska highlights the link between mental and sexual fertility,[43] dispelling any illusion that the human imagination exists as a free-floating entity, detached in its contemplation of Platonic absolutes. Further, the revelatory effect of encountering two radically different images as the viewer moves around the statue not only embodies *The Egoist*'s endorsement of imagism, but also evokes Bergson's conjecture, in *Introduction à la métaphysique* (*An Introduction to Metaphysics*, 1903), that the confluence of 'different images' could 'direct consciousness to the precise point where there is a certain intuition to seize on'.[44] The choice of Pentelic marble also resonates ideologically; as Jon Wood has pointed out, this material is Greek, quarried near Athens, and the same marble used for the Parthenon's architecture and sculpture, also on display at the British Museum.[45] Its use in creating a brash ode to Pound's virility was an egoist means of further mocking Auceps's 'rationalist' veneration of classical Greek sculpture. Thus *Hieratic Head of Ezra Pound* fulfils Gaudier-Brzeska and Pound's desire to create a sculptural equivalent to Stirner's nominalist declaration that 'I alone am corporeal'.

Direct Carving

For Gaudier-Brzeska and Pound, this anarchist paradigm also confirms the modernist embrace of direct carving, which to their minds ensures that the sculpted work is a product of the artist's unmediated, emotive response to the particular quality of the chosen medium. Direct carving, like direct action in politics or imagism in literature, stands for an anarchist rebellion against forms of representation considered anathema to the nominalist. To fully appreciate this aspect of the Vorticists' ideological praxis, we need briefly to consider the sculptural techniques Gaudier-Brzeska and Pound revolted against from a nominalist perspective: sculpting in wax to produce casts and the related use of mechanical tools to translate clay or plaster models into marble.

During the nineteenth century, sculptors commonly reproduced stone sculpture from a clay, plaster, or wax model using mechanical aids and studio assistants. Having produced a three-dimensional design, sculptors then employed a pointing machine to fabricate an exact stone replica or enlargement of their clay or plaster model by taking a series of measured points on it and then transferring these points to a copy. Thus a technical device for measurement facilitated the creation of multiples in various sizes, with smaller versions designed for the domestic market. In addition academic sculptors preferred the relative softness of marble due to the smoothness and detailed finish it made possible – the sculptural counterpart to the so-called licked surface of academic painting. As a result, these sculptures

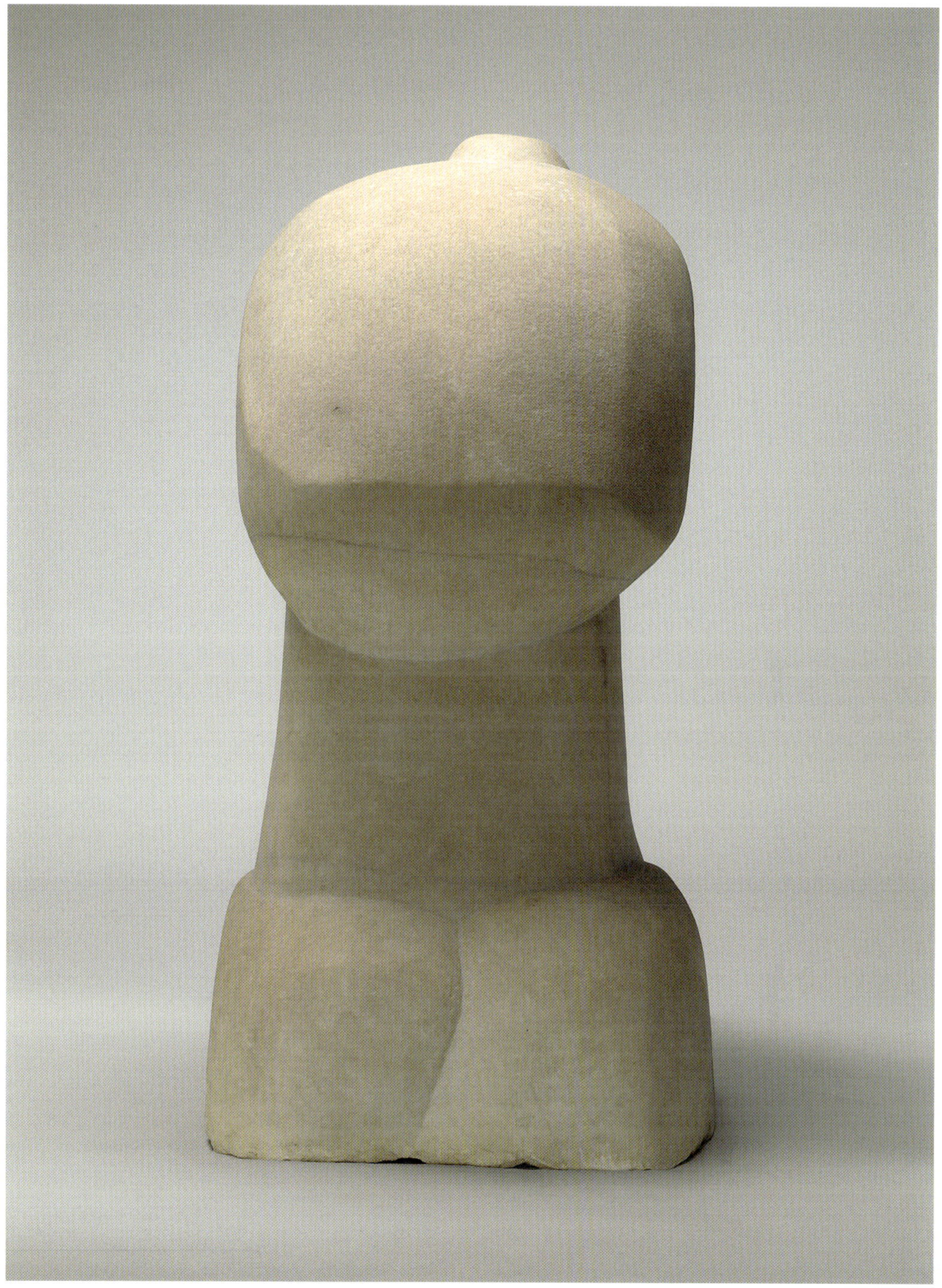

Fig.25
Henri Gaudier-Brzeska
Hieratic Head of Ezra Pound 1914
(back view of no.1)

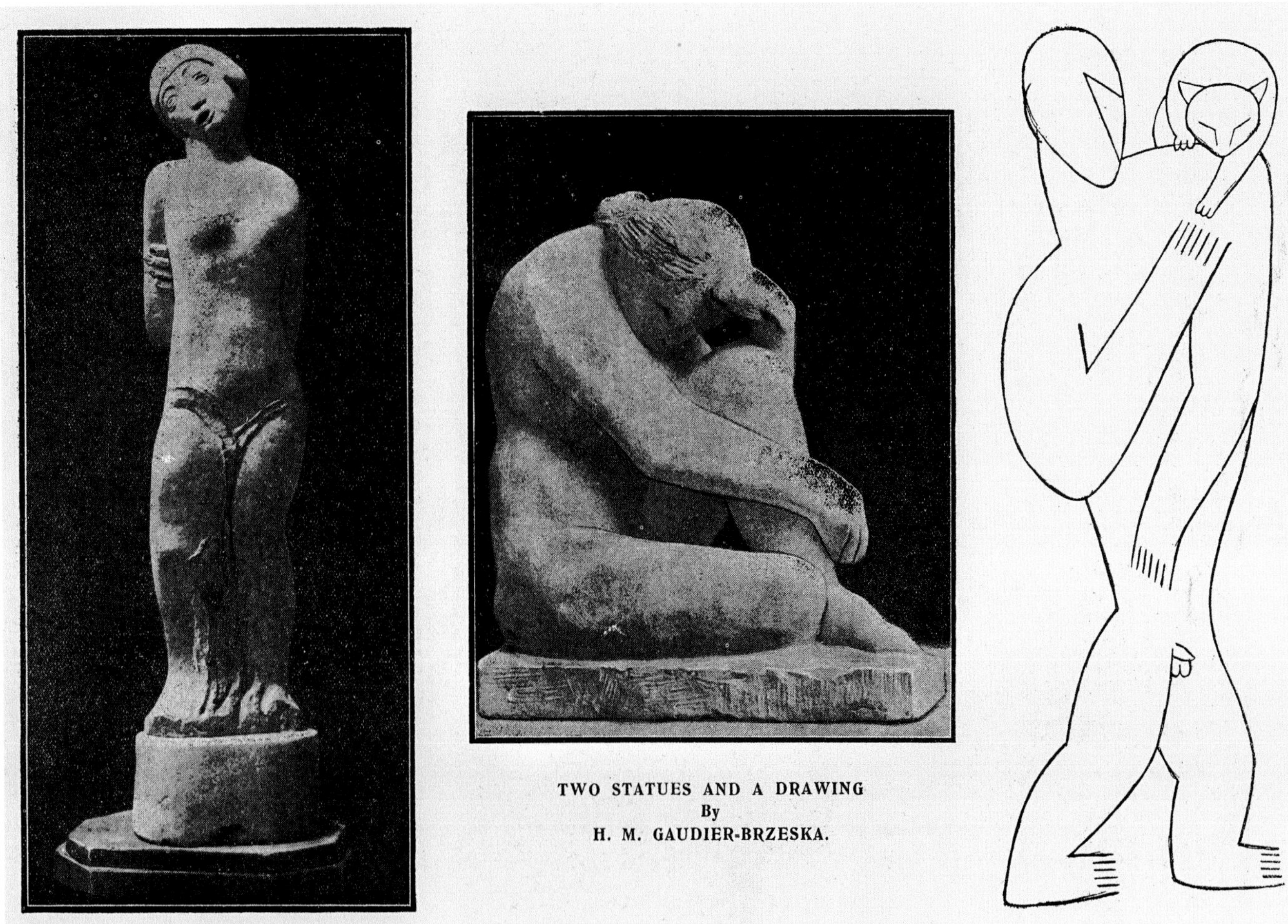

Fig.26
'Two Statues and a Drawing by H.M. Gaudier-Brzeska', *The Egoist*, vol.1, no.14 (16 February 1914), p.80

often have a standardized appearance as if they had been machine-tooled. Another technique for producing multiples was casting, wherein reusable plaster moulds taken from a wax model could be employed to mass-produce replicas. In both instances, studio assistants rather than the principal sculptor executed the end product – whether a smooth white marble surface or a bronze cast. Even modernists such as Auguste Rodin employed accomplished sculptors who executed the majority of the work, with Rodin himself only occasionally taking up the chisel to add the final touches to his works in marble.[46]

From a nominalist perspective such techniques are anathema. Adherence to anarcho-individualism calls for a direct, expressive relationship between artist and medium. Casting techniques to produce multiple copies violates the egoist veneration of the unique, while pointing assures that the sculptor's subjective and physical response to the material is subordinate to the stultifying effects imposed by a scientific measuring tool. Pound and Gaudier-Brzeska's interventions in *The Egoist* repeatedly attacked casting and copying techniques as well as the academic penchant for plaster casts, smooth white marble, and classical subject matter, while celebrating direct carving as a corollary to the anarchist nominalism propagated by the journal. In 'The New Sculpture', Pound opened his anarchist defence of Gaudier-Brzeska and Epstein by declaring their work

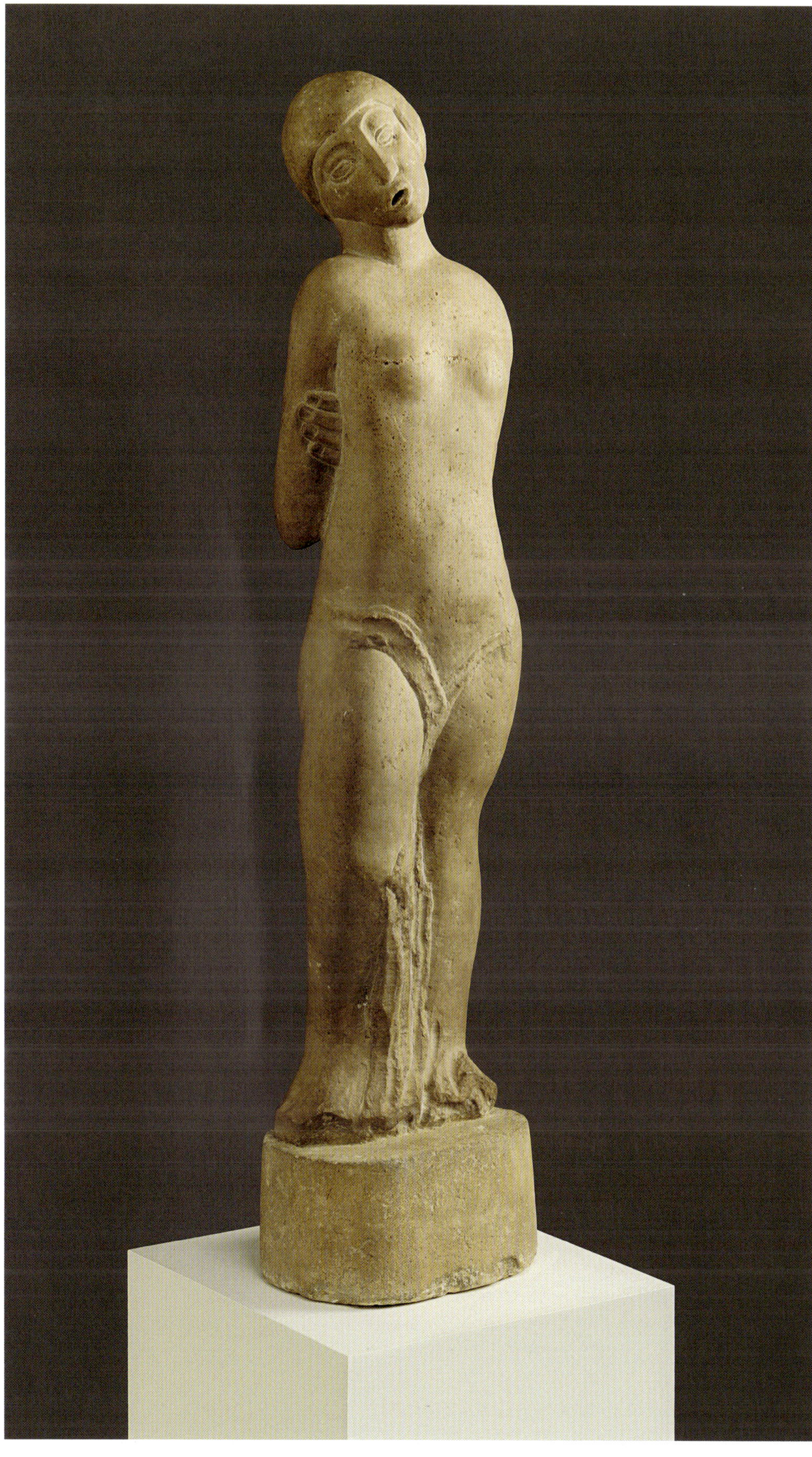

Fig.27
Henri Gaudier-Brzeska
Singer 1913
Derby stone
85.1 x 21.6 x 15.9 cm
[D]

'a d—n sight more interesting than Rodin at his plaster-castiest' and dismissed Greek sculpture for reminding 'all rightly constituted futurists' of 'plaster of Paris'.[47] The same issue introduced *The Egoist* readers to Gaudier-Brzeska's sculpture with a full-page reproduction of two examples of his direct carving, his funerary sculpture *Grief* 1913 carved in bath stone, and his *Singer* 1913, sculpted from a hard Derby stone (fig.26). The photograph highlights his tools' markings: the *Singer*'s stone surface is dotted with marks from a pointed chisel (fig.27), while Gaudier-Brzeska's vigorous use of a claw chisel is clearly visible on the base of *Grief*. Pound in his memoir of Gaudier-Brzeska venerated his friend as a protean genius who 'cut direct', rejected casting, and 'never cut in one sort of stone a work more fitting another sort'.[48] In the 15 June 1914 issue of *The Egoist*, Gaudier-Brzeska reiterated this nominalist paradigm, proclaiming his admiration for 'the work of master craftsmen, for whom every inch of surface is won at the point of a chisel'.[49] Practitioners of direct carving, we are told, will not engage in 'arbitrary translations of designs in any material' for 'they are fully aware of the different qualities and possibilities of woods, stones, and metals'. Gaudier-Brzeska then referred to the individual qualities realisable through direct carving, citing his red-veined alabaster *Boy with Coney*, his *Green Stone Charm* 1914 (no.26), and his brass *Doorknocker* (fig.24) as able to elicit radically different emotional responses.[50] Gaudier-Brzeska's allegiance to direct carving and the virility needed to carve into hard substances was further underscored in the 1915 *First Vorticist Exhibition* at London's Doré Galleries where he exhibited eight sculptures, all carved from stone.[51]

Gaudier-Brzeska's demand that sculptors respond to the material's unique qualities was such that it emerged as the central tenet of his manifesto 'Vortex. Gaudier-Brzeska', published in the June 1914 issue of *Blast*.[52] He asserted that the 'direct energy', 'feeling for form', and 'intensity' native to the sculpture of non-Western 'primitives' was wholly absent in the sculpture of the Greeks. Whereas Pound and Gaudier-Brzeska had previously condemned classical sculpture as a normative ideal, they now attacked representational content *as such* and celebrated what Pound referred to as 'the primary media' in his contiguous manifesto 'Vortex. Pound'.[53] While Pound dismissed all art based on 'likeness or mimicry', Gaudier-Brzeska's declaration argued that the Greek artist's singular focus on human resemblance guaranteed that 'HIS SCULPTURE WAS DERIVATIVE his feeling for form secondary'.[54] By rejecting Greek art, Gaudier-Brzeska claimed that the Vorticists had not only resuscitated the primitives' 'feeling for form' and 'direct energy', they had also harnessed the imperious egoism Marsden and Pound declared central to anarcho-individualism and modernist aesthetics. 'We have been influenced by what we liked most, each according to his individuality ... to express our abstract thoughts of conscious superiority. Will and consciousness are our VORTEX'.[55]

The Final Vortex

Sculptural nominalism thus constituted the visual-art counterpart to Marsden's egoism, but by the time of Gaudier-Brzeska's *Blast* manifesto and the outbreak of the First World War in August 1914, Marsden's anarchist project was in disarray.[56] While Marsden condemned nationalist warmongering and Pound remained a noncombatant, Gaudier-Brzeska sided with those anarchists who interpreted the defence of France as synonymous with a defence of the revolutionary tradition, leading him to enlist in the French army in September 1914.[57] Concurrently he tempered his allegiance to Marsden's egoism, as evidenced by his wartime manifesto 'Vortex. Gaudier-Brzeska', written in November 1914 and published in the July 1915 edition of *Blast*.[58] Whereas his article in *Blast*, no.1, proclaimed art an expression of 'individuality', that 'will and consciousness are our VORTEX', the new one identified the vortex with life itself, 'THE MOVING AGENT THAT PERMITS THE SMALL INDIVIDUAL TO ASSERT HIMSELF'. Life is now described as a perpetual force, and war 'A GREAT REMEDY' that 'SERVES AS A PURGE TO OVER-NUMEROUS HUMANITY'. Although Gaudier-Brzeska still claimed to derive his emotions 'SOLELY FROM THE ARRANGEMENT OF SURFACES', the emotion itself was the product of 'the intensity of Life', an abstract life force, indifferent to human suffering.[59] Rather than acting as a free agent, Gaudier-Brzeska was now captive to a 'moving agent', for under the war's impact, Gaudier-Brzeska's imperious ego had become subsumed within the vortex of what Wyndham Lewis cogently described as 'a multitude of other Blasts'.[60]

NOTES

1 See Bruce Clarke, *Dora Marsden and Early Modernism: Gender, Individualism, Science* (Ann Arbor: University of Michigan Press, 1996); Rebecca Beasley, *Ezra Pound and the Visual Culture of Modernism* (Cambridge: Cambridge University Press, 2007); Robert von Hallberg, 'Libertarian Imagism', *Modernism/Modernity*, vol.2, no.2 (April 1995), pp.63–79; David Kadlec, *Mosaic Modernism: Anarchism, Pragmatism, Culture* (Baltimore: John Hopkins University Press, 2000), pp.54–89; Paul Peppis, *Literature, Politics, and the English Avant-Garde: Nation and Empire, 1901–1918* (Cambridge: Cambridge University Press, 2000), pp.83–140; Vincent Sherry, *Ezra Pound, Wyndham Lewis and Radical Modernism* (Oxford: Oxford University Press, 1993), pp.43–69.

2 See Mark Antliff, '"Their Country": Henri Gaudier's Anarchist Anti-Militarism, 1910–1914', in Sebastiano Barassi (ed.), *'WE the Moderns': Gaudier-Brzeska and the Birth of Modern Sculpture*, exh. cat. (Cambridge: Kettle's Yard Gallery, 2007), pp.75–87; and Mark Antliff, 'Henri Gaudier-Brzeska's *Guerre sociale*: Art, Anarchism and Anti-Militarism in Paris and London, 1910–1915', *Modernism/Modernity*, vol.17, no.1 (January 2010), pp.135–69.

3 John P. Clark, *Max Stirner's Egoism* (London: Freedom Press, 1976).

4 Allan Antliff, *Anarchist Modernism: Art, Politics, and the First American Avant-Garde* (Chicago: University of Chicago Press, 2001), pp.73–80; Beasley 2007, pp.49–58, 78–111, 128–30; and Kadlec 2000, pp.54–80.

5 Clark 1976, pp.37–58.

6 Max Stirner, *The Ego and his Own*, (trans. Steven Byington, 1907; repr., London: Rebel Press, 1993), pp.37, 306–9. See also Clark 1976, pp.71–86.

7 Von Hallberg 1995; Kadlec 2000, pp.54–89; and Beasley 2007, pp.78–111.

8 Antliff 2001, pp.73–80; and Beasley 2007, pp.98–9.

9 Ezra Pound, 'The New Sculpture', *The Egoist*, vol.1, no.4 (16 February 1914), pp.67–8.

10 Bastien von Helmholtz [Ezra Pound, pseud.], 'Suffragettes', *The Egoist*, vol.1, no.13 (1 July 1914), pp.254–6.

11 On Henri Gaudier-Brzeska's anarchist roots, see H.S. Ede, *Savage Messiah: A Biography of the Sculptor Henri Gaudier-Brzeska* (1931; repr., London: Gordon Fraser, 1971), pp.21, 30–31; Antliff, '"Their Country"'; and Antliff 2010, pp.135–69.

12 Ezra Pound, *Gaudier-Brzeska: A Memoir* (New York: New Directions, 1970), p.46.

13 Ede 1971, p.135; Evelyn Silber, *Gaudier-Brzeska: Life and Art* (New York: Thames and Hudson, 1996), pp.93–101; and Sebastiano Barassi, 'A Pioneer of Avant-Garde Sculpture', in Barassi 2007, pp.5–59.

14 Ede 1971, pp.98–100, 101–2; and Clarke 1996, pp.99, 194–5.

15 Henri Bergson, 'The Philosophy of Ideas', *The New Freewoman*, vol.1, no.13 (15 December 1913), pp.246–8.

16 Ibid.

17 Dora Marsden, 'Intellect and Culture', *The New Freewoman*, vol.1, no.2 (1 July 1913), pp.21–3.

18 Henri Bergson, *Creative Evolution*, trans. Arthur Mitchell (New York: Henry Holt, 1931), pp.223–36.

19 Dora Marsden, 'Mainly Anent the Decalogue', *The Egoist*, vol.1, no.4 (16 February 1914), pp.61–5.

20 Ibid., p.65; and Dora Marsden, 'The Art of the Future', *The New Freewoman*, vol.1, no.10 (1 November 1913), pp.181–3.

21 Marsden, 'The Art of the Future', p.183; and Henri Bergson, *The Creative Mind*, trans. Mabelle L. Andison (New York: Philosophical Library, 1946), pp.193–6.

22 Von Hallberg 1995, pp.66–8; and Kadlec 2000, pp.57–67, 74–8.

23 Ezra Pound, 'The New Sculpture', pp.67–8.

24 Ibid.

25 Ibid.

26 Ezra Pound, 'Exhibition at the Goupil Gallery', *The Egoist* , vol.1, no.6 (16 March 1914), p.109.

27 Ibid.

28 Ezra Pound, 'The Caressability of the Greeks', *The Egoist*, vol.1, no.6 (16 March 1914), p.117; and Henri Gaudier-Brzeska, 'Mr. Gaudier-Brzeska on the New Sculpture', ibid., pp.117–18. On the debate between Richard Aldington, Pound, and Gaudier-Brzeska, see Lisa Tickner, 'Now and Then: The *Hieratic Head of Ezra Pound*', *Oxford Art Journal*, vol.16, no.2 (1993), pp.55–60; and Jon Wood, 'Heads and Tales: Gaudier-Brzeska's *Hieratic Head of Ezra Pound* and the Making of an Avant-garde Homage', in David J. Getsy (ed.), *Sculpture and the Pursuit of a Modern Ideal in Britain, c.1880–1930*, (Aldershot: Ashgate Publishing, 2004), pp.191–217.

29 Pound, 'The Caressability of the Greeks', p.117.

30 Marsden, 'Intellect and Culture', pp.21–3; and Dora Marsden, 'Liberty, Law, and Democracy', *The Egoist*, vol.1, no.1 (1 January 1914), pp.1–3.

31 Pound, 'The Caressability of the Greeks', p.117.

32 'Mr. Gaudier-Brzeska on the New Sculpture', pp.117–18.

33 Ibid., p.117.

34 Ibid., p.118.

35 Henri Gaudier-Brzeska, 'Allied Artists Association Ltd.', *The Egoist*, vol.1, no.15 (15 June 1914), pp.227–9.

36 Tickner 1993, pp.56–7; and Wood 2004, 'Heads and Tales', pp.197–8.

37 Antliff 2010, pp.143–8.

38 See Silber 1996, p.272; Antliff 2010; and Jon Wood, 'Ornaments, Talismans, and Toys: The Hand-Held Sculptures of Henri Gaudier-Brzeska', in Jonathan Black (ed.), *Blasting the Future!: Vorticism in Britain 1910–1920* (London: Philip Wilson, 2004), pp.41–8.

39 Clark 1976, pp.10–35.

40 Stirner 1993, pp.13–14, 366.

41 Ibid., pp.132, 291.

42 Silber 1996, pp.131–2; Tickner 1993, pp.56–7; and Wood 2004, 'Heads and Tales', pp.197–8.

43 Wood 2004, 'Heads and Tales', p.196.

44 Bergson 1946, p.195.

45 Wood 2004, 'Heads and Tales', p.198.

46 Nicolas Penny, *The Materials of Sculpture* (New Haven: Yale University Press, 1993).

47 Pound, 'New Sculpture', pp.67–8.

48 Pound 1970, p.19.

49 Gaudier-Brzeska, 'Allied Artists Association Ltd.', pp.227–9.

50 Ibid., p.227.

51 In the Vorticist exhibition catalogue, Gaudier-Brzeska's sculptures are listed as follows: '(a) *Boy with Coney* (alabaster). (Lent by Ezra Pound), (b) *Marble Group* (Lent by Ezra Pound), (c) *Dancer*, (d) *Caritas*, (e) *Singer*'. The list then includes the following under the subtitle *Small Objects*: '(a) *Paper-weight* (lent by G. Hyde-Lewis), (b) *Fawn* (lent by Ezra Pound), (c) *Charm*'. See *First Vorticist Exhibition*, exh. cat. (London: Doré Galleries, 1915). Of these eight sculptures, Evelyn Silber has identified the following six in her catalogue raisonné: *Boy with Coney* (no.76); *Caritas* (no.75); *Singer* (*Chanteuse Triste*) (no.51); *Paperweight* (Ornament, relief) (no.87); *Fawn* (Small Fawn in Brown Stone) (no.84); *Charm* (*Green Stone Charm*) (no.85). See Silber 1996. Roger Cole and Jeremy Lewison argue that the dancer referenced in the Doré catalogue refers to Gaudier-Brzeska's *Red Stone Dancer* c.1913, as opposed to his Rodinesque, plaster *Dancer* modelled in autumn or winter 1913 (Silber 1996, no.58). The latter work contradicted Gaudier-Brzeska and Pound's endorsement of direct carving in 1914; thus it is improbable that this work would have been chosen for the first Vorticist exhibition in 1915. On *Red Stone Dancer*, see Roger Cole, *Burning to Speak: The Life and Art of Henri Gaudier-Brzeska* (Oxford: Phaidon, 1978), p.95; and Jeremy Lewison (ed.), *Henri Gaudier-Brzeska, Sculptor 1891–1915*, exh. cat. (Cambridge: Kettle's Yard Gallery, 1983), pp.47–8; on the plaster *Dancer* of late 1913, see Silber 1996, p.264.

52 'Vortex. Gaudier-Brzeska', *Blast*, no.1, June 1914, facsimile ed. (Santa Rosa, Calif.: Black Sparrow Press, 1989), pp.155–8.

53 'Vortex. Pound', *Blast*, no.1, pp.153–4.

54 'Vortex. Gaudier-Brzeska', p.156.

55 Ibid., p.158.

56 Mark Morrisson, 'Marketing British Modernism: *The Egoist* and Counter-Public Spheres', *Twentieth Century Literature*, vol.43, no.4 (Winter 1997), pp.439–69.

57 Antliff 2010, pp.157–60.

58 Henri Gaudier-Brzeska, 'Vortex. Gaudier-Brzeska. (Written from the Trenches)', *Blast*, no.2, July 1915, facsimile ed. (Santa Rosa, Calif.: Black Sparrow Press, 2000), pp.33–4.

59 Ibid.

60 The phrase comes from the opening line of Lewis's editorial in *Blast*, no.2. See Wyndham Lewis, 'Editorial', *Blast*, no.2, pp.5–6; for *Blast*, no.2, see Peppis 2000, pp.96–132.

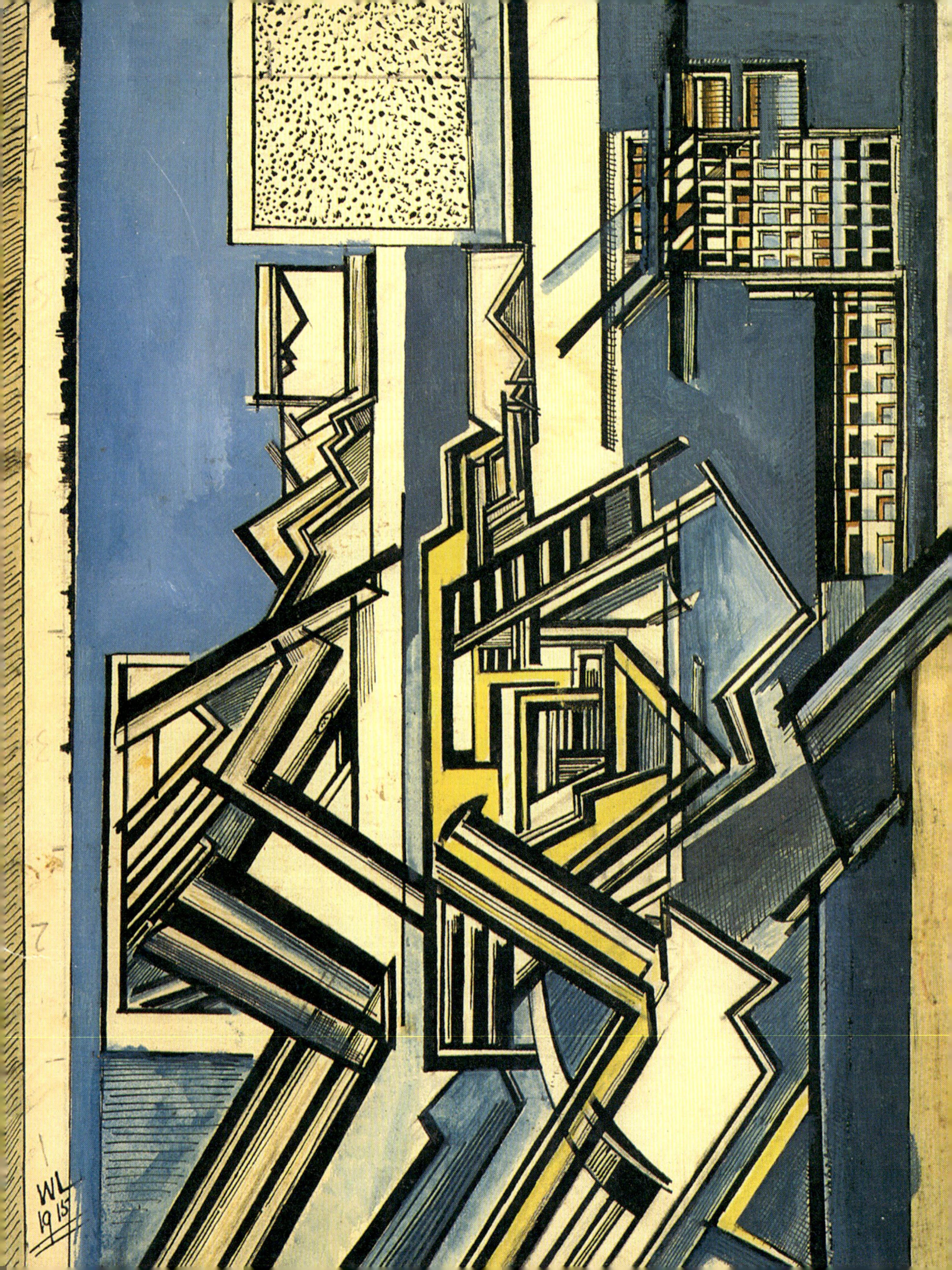

'REFORMING WITH A PICK-AXE': THE FIRST VORTICIST EXHIBITION AT THE DORE GALLERIES IN 1915

Anna Gruetzner Robins

At the *First Vorticist Exhibition*, which opened at the Doré Galleries, 35 New Bond Street on 10 June 1915,[1] seven of the eleven artists who had signed the Vorticist manifesto in the first issue of *Blast* (1914)[2] – Jessica Dismorr, Frederick Etchells, Henri Gaudier-Brzeska, Wyndham Lewis, William Roberts, Helen Saunders, and Edward Wadsworth – exhibited twenty-two paintings, eight sculptures, sixteen drawings, and three woodcuts in 'part of the principal room' of the gallery.[3] Six other artists – Bernard Adeney, Lawrence Atkinson, David Bomberg, Duncan Grant, Jacob Kramer, and C.R.W. Nevinson – were 'Invited to Show' with the Vorticists,[4] and their contribution of fifteen paintings and five drawings brought the total up to sixty-seven works (fig.28).

The exhibition was the culmination of a series of modern art exhibitions in London beginning with Roger Fry's *Manet and the Post-Impressionists* (1910–11), which together brought hundreds of modernist European works of art including Post-Impressionism, Fauvism, Cubism, and Futurism, to London.[5] The xenophobic blasting of European modernism that runs through Lewis's writing needs to be seen in the context of these exhibitions. These mini-retrospectives of major European movements highlighting artists such as Paul Cézanne, Paul Gauguin, Henri Matisse, Pablo Picasso, and Vincent van Gogh served as a blueprint for Lewis's grand plan of a distinct avant-garde British group.

The Doré show was one of the most public demonstrations of the Vorticists' identity.[6] Whether they stood as a group is another matter. Vorticist supporter Ezra Pound wrote in 1915 that the exhibition should have consisted of '40 things by Lewis and 30 by all of the other contributors' because 'most ... have simply built on one or another corner of his work, and done things "which he happened to do"'.[7] Lewis put all his energy into the show. He persuaded fellow Vorticists to contribute work, invited non-members, and hung the exhibition giving Wadsworth the prime place with a wall in the gallery while taking a screen for his own work.[8] Lewis designed the exhibition catalogue, which has a vivid orange cover, distinctive typeface, and single geometric motif and contains one of his signed drawings, after *Design for Red Duet* 1915 (fig.29). He also penned the two-page 'Note for Catalogue', featuring a potted exhibition history of the Vorticist artists. Whereas *Blast*, no.1, had been a 'sort of picture-gallery', the Doré

Detail from Wyndham Lewis *Design for Red Duet* 1915 (fig.29)

exhibition was the first time that 'a gallery [had] been used for the special exhibition of nothing but the works of this tendency by English artists'.[9] He pointed out that the Allied Artists' Association, an open London exhibition started in 1908 and based on the non-juried Salon des Indépendants, and the London Group, formed in 1914, had been two important venues for the Vorticists. He could have included the *Post-Impressionist and Futurist Exhibition* at the Doré Galleries in October 1913, organized by Frank Rutter, who drew attention to the importance of Cubism and Futurism for Lewis, Nevinson, and Wadsworth. He might also have mentioned *An Exhibition of the Work of English Post-Impressionists, Cubists and others*, held at Brighton Public Art Galleries between December 1913 and January 1914. The catalogue's introductory essays by James Bolivar Manson and Lewis explained English Post-Impressionism and English Cubism respectively.[10] The work of Lewis, Etchells, and Wadsworth along with Adeney, Bomberg, and Nevinson and the future Vorticists Jacob Epstein, Jessie Etchells, Fanny Eveleigh, and Cuthbert Hamilton were gathered together in what Lewis called the 'Cubist Room'. Six months later, in the pages of *Blast*, no.1, Lewis played down their former identity as English Cubists, wanting to rid his artists of the European labels that were being tacked onto various kinds of British avant-garde art, including Post-Impressionism, a term coined by Fry in 1910, and Futurism, which was suspect because of its Italian origins.[11] Even in his essay on the 'Cubist Room', Lewis had declared such 'terms and tags' unsatisfactory for describing the 'revolutionary painting' and sculpture of his British artists.[12]

The outbreak of the First World War in August 1914 brought an enormous destruction and loss of life. In the face of this reality many journals and newspapers prioritized war reporting and did not review the *First Vorticist Exhibition*. Prestigious journals such as the *Saturday Review* reduced its art coverage to the 1915 summer exhibition of the Royal Academy of Arts. Others referred to the Vorticist show in a summary notice,[13] or treated it as a joke. The populist *Daily Mirror*, for instance, claimed that 'any child ... can be a first rate Vorticist if it is given some lightly coloured paints, bottle of blacking and mamma's new white tablecloth'. The paper reproduced Wadsworth's *Blackpool* 1915 and *Combat* 1915 and Frederick Etchells's *Pigeon Juggler* 1915 with the caption 'Blackpool residents would never recognise their own town if they visited the Vorticist exhibition at the Dore Galleries. It is evident that in "the combat" somebody has been badly knocked about.'[14] Moreover, Lewis had made enemies of several important critics. That these included Fry and Walter Sickert may explain why neither reviewed the exhibition. Fabian, poet, and *Times* art critic Arthur Clutton-Brock joined the list of adversaries, after the latter had compared the works by Lewis, Roberts, and Wadsworth seen at the London Group in March to 'Prussian[s] in their spirit', who 'execute a kind of goose-step', before suggesting 'perhaps if the Junkers could be induced to take to art, instead of disturbing the peace of Europe, they would paint so and enjoy it'.[15] This was hardly the sort of comment that Lewis could ignore. He took Clutton-Brock to task in *Blast*, no.2, where he misquoted him and pointed out that because Vorticist paintings 'are rather strange at first sight, they are regarded as ferocious and unfriendly. They are neither ... We are not cannibals.'[16]

Plans for the Doré show had been well advanced by April, but wartime and deadline pressure meant that several works by Gaudier-Brzeska, Lewis, and Wadsworth first seen at the London Group in March were exhibited again in the exhibition in June.[17] This may be another reason why the press overlooked it.[18] Clutton-Brock was not the

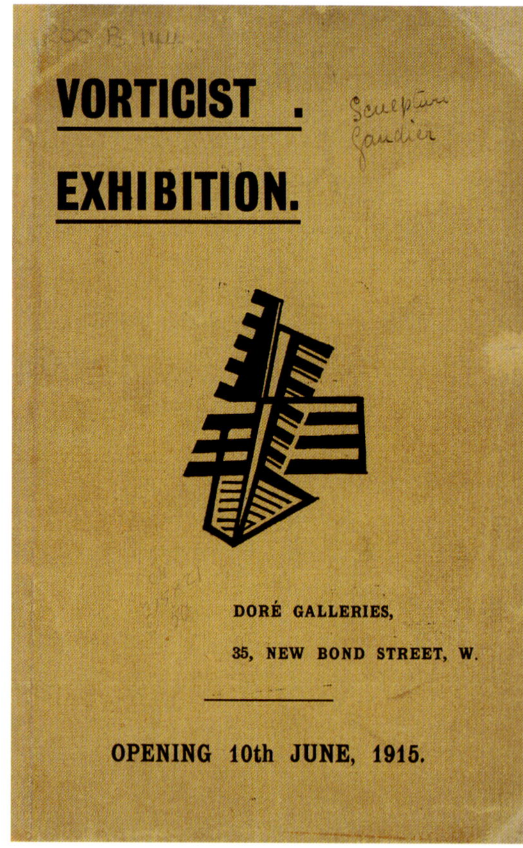

Fig.28
Catalogue of the *Vorticist Exhibition* 1915
Doré Galleries, London
Above: cover, designed by Wyndham Lewis
Right: List of exhibited works

THE VORTICIST GROUP.

MEMBERS.

DISMORR.

ETCHELLS.

GAUDIER-BRZESKA.

ROBERTS.

SANDERS.

WADSWORTH.

WYNDHAM-LEWIS.

The first Exhibition of the Vorticist Group, opening 10th June, 1915.

PICTURES.

1. DISMORR.
   (a) Shapes.
   (b) Interior.
   (c) Movement.
   (d) Design.

2. ETCHELLS.
   (a) The Pigeon-Juggler.
   (b) Painting.

PICTURES (continued).

3. ROBERTS.
   (a) Overbacks.
   (b) Twostep.
   (c) Jeu.
   (d) Theatre.

4. SANDERS.
   (a) Atlantic City.
   (b) English Scene.
   (c) Swiss Scene.
   (d) Cliffs.

5. WADSWORTH.
   (a) Combat.
   (b) Blackpool.
   (c) Interior.
   (d) Dry Dock.

6. WYNDHAM-LEWIS.
   (a) Two Shafts.
   Man and Woman.
   (b) Red Duet.
   (c) Democratic Composition.
   (d) Workshop.

SCULPTURE.

GAUDIER-BRZESKA.
(a) Boy with coney (alabaster). (Lent by Ezra Pound).
(b) Marble Group. (Lent by Ezra Pound).
(c) Dancer.
(d) Caritas.
(e) Singer.

SMALL OBJECTS.

(a) Paper-weight. (Lent by G. Hyde-Lees).
(b) Faun. (Lent by Ezra Pound).
(c) Charm.

DRAWINGS.

1. ETCHELLS.
   (a) Hyde Park.
   (b) Drawing.

2. ROBERTS.
   (a) Drawing.
   (b) Religion.

3. SANDERS.
   (a) Island of Laputa.
   (b) Black and Khaki.

4. WADSWORTH.
   (a) Centrifuge.
   (b) Enclosure.
   (c) Tentative Drawing.
   (d) Rigid Drawing.

   WOODCUTS.

   (a) Rotterdam.
   (b) Harbour of Flushing.
   (c) Newcastle.

5. WYNDHAM-LEWIS.
   (a) Design for "Red Duet."
   (b) Harsh Design.
   (c) A Ceremonious Scene.
   (d) Bathers.
   (e) Design for Painting.
   (f) Design for "Conversation in Jack."

LIST OF WORKS BY THOSE INVITED TO SHOW.

1. ADENEY — Landscape.

2. ATKINSON
   (a) Painting.
   (b) Painting.
   (c) Painting.

3. BOMBERG.
   (a) Decorative Experiment.
   (b) Decorative Experiment.
   (c) Small Painting.
   } Paintings.

   (a) Design in white.
   (b) Design in colour.
   (c) Design in colour.
   } Drawings.

4. DUNCAN GRANT
   (a) One
   (b) Two
   } Paintings.
   (c) Three Still Life.

5. KRAMER.
   (a) Man and Woman.
   (b) Pebbles.
   } Paintings.

   (a) Dance of Death.
   (b) The Heart.
   } Drawings.

6. NEVINSON (Futurist)
   (a) War Crowd.
   (b) The wound.
   (c) Caught. A night attack on Dunkirk.

Leveridge & Co., Harlesden, N.W.

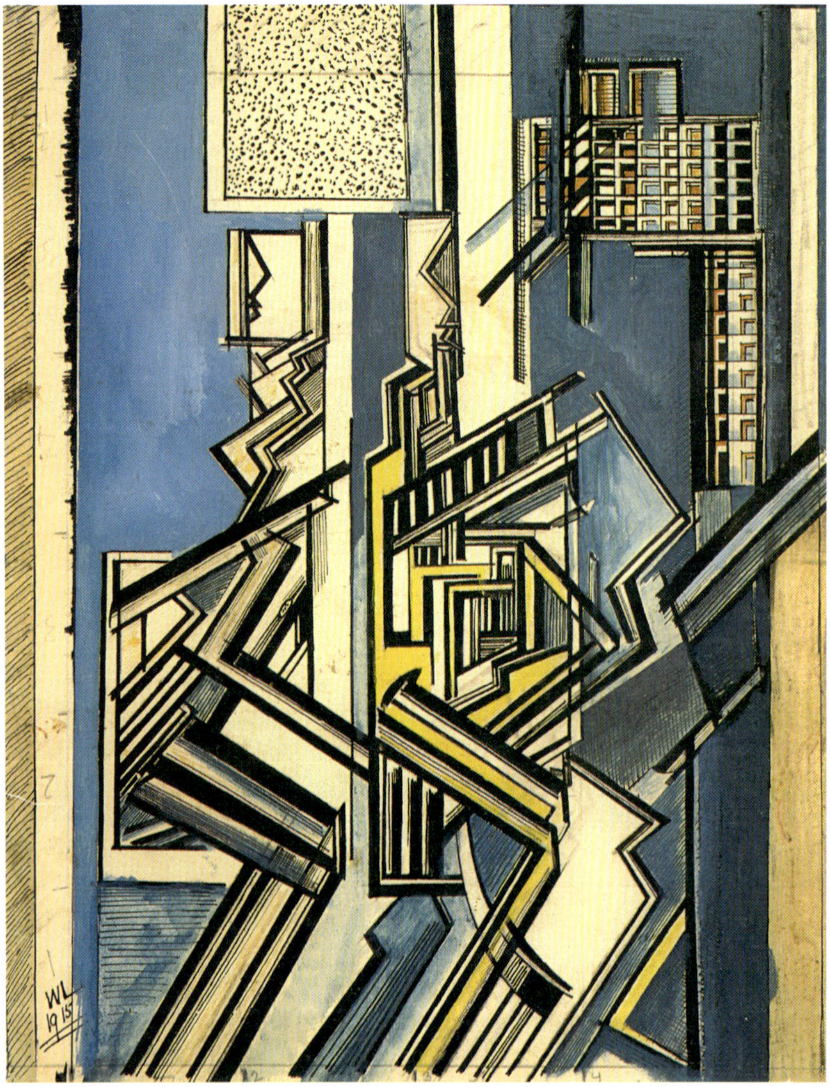

Fig.29
Wyndham Lewis
Design for Red Duet 1915
Pencil, pen, ink, watercolour, and gouache on paper
31.8 x 24.8 cm
Private collection
[D; B2; P]

only critic who thought that the advanced abstraction of Vorticist art and Lewis's bombastic, heckling tone in the catalogue preface were inappropriate during a time of war. 'Thirteen in all, all in the Vortex; and so very little chance that they will ever get out again, for the Vortex is one of those furious primordial things that can only be defined in negatives', wrote J.[ohn] M.[iddleton] M.[urray] in the *Westminster Gazette*. Turning his attention to Nevinson and Gaudier-Brzeska, he chastised them for banishing 'the representative element from [their] art'.[19] P.G. Konody, who had been hostile to the Vorticists efforts in the past, ignored the exhibition until Gaudier-Brzeska was killed in action. His death 'should disarm the anger which might otherwise be aroused', Konody advised, because 'the "Vorticists" continue their antics in times as serious and critical as the present.'[20] Gaudier-Brzeska had 'remained a "Vorticist"' by producing Vorticist sketches in the trenches, which convinced Konody of the artist's seriousness and thus that of the other painter-members. 'When six artists like Dismore [sic], Etchells, Roberts, Sanders [sic], Wadsworth and Wyndham-Lewis show such absolute oneness of purpose and similarity of method ... one cannot believe in collective insanity'. Nonetheless, he continued, 'it is permissible to hesitate to accept these pictures and drawings as legitimate works of art'.[21] The Vorticist experiment with abstraction was meaningless, he believed, because the works failed to convey emotion though at times they achieved 'pleasant combinations of colours and shapes'.[22] Few critics recognized the difference between Cubist, Futurist, and Vorticist pictures. Lewis and Wadsworth had much in common with these other modernists, the *Athenaeum* suggested, because they 'fill their canvases with systems of interacting movement, the co-ordinations and antagonisms of which are admirably stressed'.[23]

Not everyone was unsympathetic. Rutter, the only art critic to appear on Lewis's list of the 'Blessed' in *Blast*, no.1, was also curator of Leeds Art Gallery and an exhibition organizer with a long-standing interest in avant-garde movements.[24] His *Revolution in Art: An Introduction to the Study of Cézanne, Gauguin, van Gogh, and Other Modern Painters* (1910) had been dedicated to 'the rebels of either sex all round the world over who in any way are fighting for freedom of any kind'.[25] Writing in the *Sunday Times* in June 1915 he applauded the Vorticists' radical spirit. 'The critics who told us that the war would kill all the newer and more revolutionary art movements are doomed to disappointment', he wrote, 'because they will find the extremists very much alive.'[26] The Vorticists represented 'the extreme left' of the London art world. Moreover, there was no contest between Lewis and the other exhibitors, because he 'is so clearly and admittedly the ablest of the vorticists' (no wonder Lewis blessed Rutter in *Blast*). No apology was needed, he explained, 'for dwelling principally on his work, and to understand it we should remember that it is always significant and not meaninglessly decorative'. Anticipating public hostility to Lewis's abstract arrangements based on the war, Rutter explained that Lewis 'is entitled to construct a pattern on a theme suggested by the disposition of military forces' as the Pre-Raphaelite artist Edward Burne-Jones had when using Arthurian legend.[27]

Rutter also discussed Wadsworth, comparing him to Vasily Kandinsky. Rutter, however, had little sympathy for Kandinsky's theory of abstraction and suggested that Wadsworth's 'brilliant colour and patterning would not suffer if, like Mr. Etchells and Mr. Bomberg, he leant a little more heavily on natural form for the under structure of his designs.'[28] Rutter placed Epstein, who did not exhibit (but had shown at the London Group), together with Lewis in his estimation. He did not mention Gaudier-Brzeska, but a month later he paid tribute to him as 'one of the most brilliant and promising' sculptors in London whose 'noble if deliberately archaic sense of form is manifest in his stone statuette ... the moving and extraordinarily haunting *Singer*' 1913 (fig.27 on p.55).[29] According to Rutter, most works in the Vorticist exhibition were 'puzzling and obscure to the general public' except for Gaudier-Brzeska's sculpture because of its associations with 'the beauty of Gothic figures and the nobility of archaic Greek and Assyrian sculpture.'[30]

The catchy titles of Etchells's *Pigeon Juggler*, Roberts's *Two-Step* 1915, Saunders's *Atlantic City* 1915, Wadsworth's *Blackpool*, and Lewis's *Red Duet* 1914 (fig.30) along with their abstract aims confounded many British critics who had little experience with abstract art and lacked the terminology to discuss it. 'Vorticism leaves both pictorial expression and decoration in the pothook and hanger stage, and ... reduces paint to the flat statement of the house painter', commented the *Evening Standard and St James Gazette* critic, who was probably Charles Marriott.[31] 'A good diagram is better than a bad picture; designing in pot-hooks and hangers is a good introduction to designing in natural forms, and, when all is said, paint is paint.' Vorticism was a cataclysmic force necessary when 'art needs reforming with a pick-axe.'[32] This is not edifying criticism, but neither is it hostile. This original art needed a new critical language, which Marriott, subsequently author of *Modern Movements in Painting* (1920), was still struggling to formulate.

Was Lewis's ambition to form a distinct Vorticist group successful? In retrospect, Etchells denied that there was a close affiliation between the Vorticists and claimed that he was 'always a slightly unwilling adherent of this movement which seemed mostly to "boost" Wyndham Lewis'. He explained, 'most of us were anxious to help him, but we all passed on to other aspects very shortly. I think the movement was therefore short lived and rather abortive'.[33] Furthermore, artist Horace Brodzsky claimed in 1917 that Gaudier-Brzeska 'was not a Vorticist, and had nothing in common with them' and that 'his works should not be included in ... any future exhibitions of the Vorticists.'[34]

Six non-Vorticists were included in the exhibition so that 'specimens of the work of every notable painter working at all in one or other of the new directions' were seen. This is puzzling. Yet, Lewis may have had underhand reasons for his selection.[35] He wanted Bomberg, who presented three paintings and three drawings and whose early critical success would have made him a valuable member of the Vorticist group.[36] Bomberg, however, remained a resolute Cubist and many years later was distressed to be included as a minor Vorticist in the 1956 exhibition *Wyndham Lewis and Vorticism* at the Tate Gallery.[37] Possibly Lewis saw the others' work as a foil for the Vorticists' revolutionary experiments, and, moreover, he had a few scores to settle. He had had a spectacular falling out with Nevinson in June 1914 when the latter had, without permission, added Lewis's name together with those of Atkinson, Bomberg, Epstein, Frederick Etchells, Hamilton, Roberts, and Wadsworth to 'Vital English Art: Futurist Manifesto,' which he published with F.T. Marinetti in various London papers.[38] Nevinson also used Lewis's Rebel Art Centre as their address.[39] The antagonism between Nevinson and his former associates

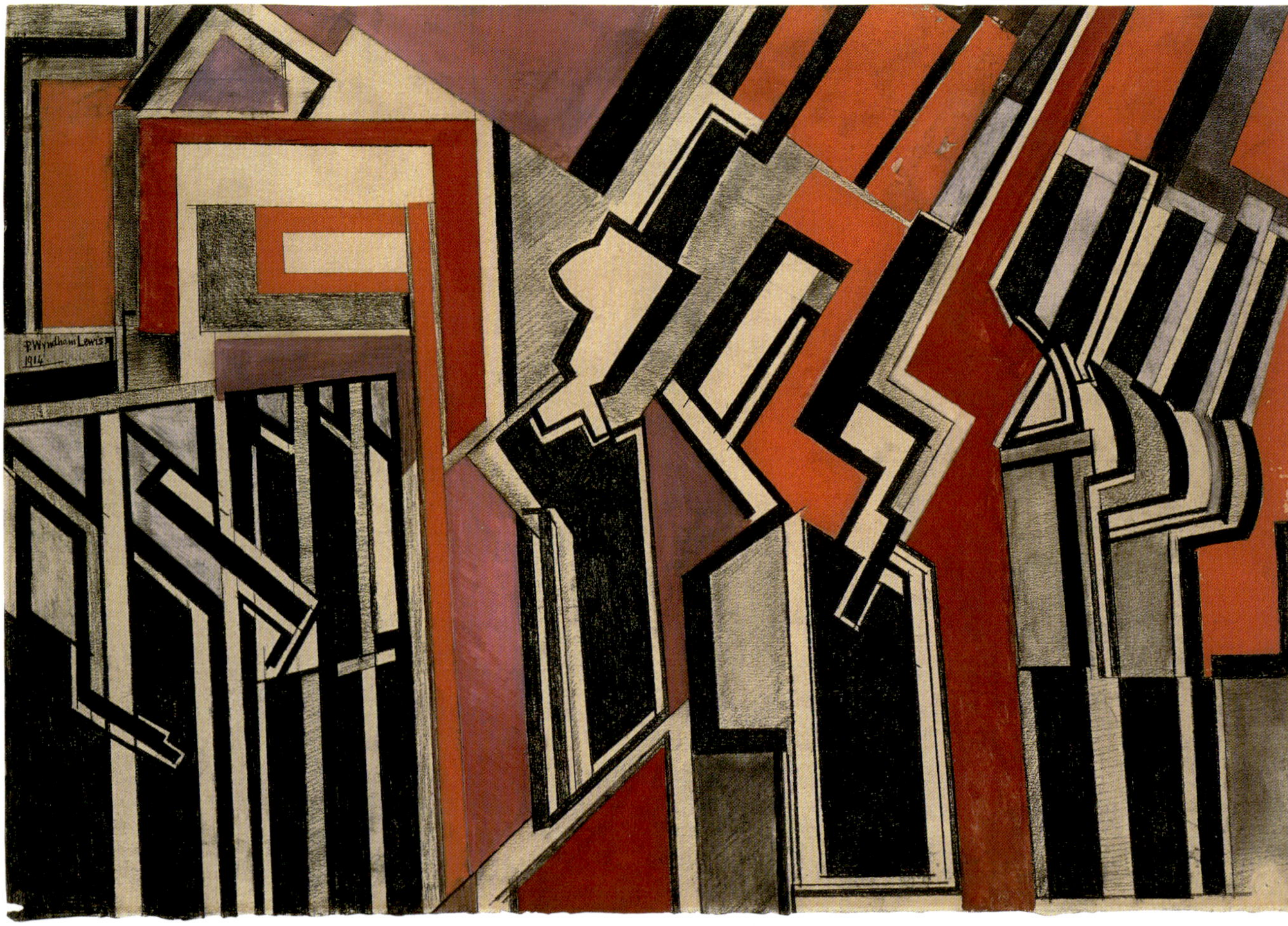

Fig.30
Wyndham Lewis
Red Duet 1914
Chalk and gouache on paper
38.5 x 56 cm
Ivor Braka Ltd, London
[D]

culminated in a clash later that month when Lewis and his gang of anti-Futurists attacked Marinetti and Nevinson during a Futurist event at the Doré Galleries.[40] At the same venue a year later, Lewis may have hoped that Nevinson's Futurist works, with their recognisable imagery and fractured forms, would seem less 'advanced' to British critics than the Vorticists' more abstract works. As Konody pointed out, 'in this strange company Mr. Nevinson's Futurist paintings look absolutely normal and almost academic'![41] The presence of Duncan Grant, who had close ties with Fry, a man with whom Lewis had had an even more public row in 1913, is even more surprising. Lewis may have used his inclusion as an opportunity of giving his grudge against Fry another public airing.[42] Grant's works have not been identified, but Konody's description of his abstract paintings as 'bits of firewood glued on to a dirty canvas, with here and there a few vertical stripes of colour'[43] bring to mind the most recent collages by Picasso, whom Grant admired. Lewis, however, dismissed such collages in his catalogue introduction, suggesting that they placed Picasso 'in the same category as a dressmaker'.[44]

The *First Vorticist Exhibition* gave abstract art by British artists a public platform for the first time. While the critical reaction to the show was less than satisfactory, Lewis achieved his aim of creating a distinct identity for the Vorticists in the London art world.

NOTES

My title comes from C.[harles] M.[arriott], 'Vorticism', *Evening Standard and St James Gazette*, 28 June 1915, p.7. I am grateful to Dorothy Hill for her help with research for this essay.

1 'The catalogue does not give the exact closing date; however, *Blast*, no.2, published in July 1915, announced that the exhibition would 'end about the second week in July'.

2 For a discussion of the dissenters, see Richard Cork, *Vorticism and Abstract Art in the First Machine Age*, vol.1 (London: Gordon Fraser, 1976), p.275.

3 'The Vorticists: A New Group of Artists', *Glasgow Herald*, 11 June 1915, p.9.

4 The group's membership as presented in the exhibition catalogue was not cast in iron. Although Lawrence Atkinson had signed the Vorticist manifesto, he was not listed with the Vorticists in the exhibition catalogue. The signatories of the Vorticist manifesto also included artist Cuthbert Hamilton, poets Richard Aldington and Ezra Pound, and photographer Malcolm Arbuthnot. *Blast*, no.1 (July 1914), p.43.

5 For a discussion of these exhibitions, see Anna Gruetzner Robins, *Modern Art in Britain, 1910–1914*, exh. cat. (London: Merrell Holberton in association with Barbican Art Gallery, 1997).

6 Rebecca Beasley, *Ezra Pound and the Visual Culture of Modernism* (Cambridge: Cambridge University Press, 2007), p.137.

7 Harriet Zinnes (ed.), *Ezra Pound and the Visual Arts* (New York: New Directions, 1980), p.234.

8 This information about Wyndham Lewis's role in the exhibition appears in a letter from Ezra Pound to John Quinn, dated 23 August 1915, published in part in Zinnes 1980, pp.234–5. I am grateful to Vivien Greene for this reference.

9 Wyndham Lewis, 'Note for Catalogue', *Vorticist Exhibition* (London: Doré Galleries, 1915), in *Wyndham Lewis on Art: Collected Writings, 1913–1956*, ed. Walter Michel and C. J. Fox (New York: Funk and Wagnalls, 1969), pp.96–8.

10 For an analysis of the Brighton exhibition, see Robert Upstone's essay, pp.27–33 above.

11 Percy Wyndham Lewis, 'The Cubist Room', *Catalogue of an Exhibition of the Work of English Post-Impressionists, Cubists and others* (Brighton: Public Art Galleries, 1913) in *Wyndham Lewis on Art*, p.56.

12 Ibid.

13 For example, *Colour* informed its readers: 'The first exhibition of works by a number of painters and a sculptor who have hitherto been known as cubists or futurists or both, opened at the Doré Galleries on June 10. Some of the paintings have been seen before, also most of [Henri] Gaudier-Brzeska's sculpture has been repeatedly shown. The writer of "Notes [sic] for catalogue" tells us at great length what Vorticism means, but it is noticed that he has invited Nevinson (Futurist) and Adeney who sends a naturalist landscape, to contribute to the show.' 'Vorticist Exhibition', *Colour*, vol.1, no.2 (July 1915), p.198.

14 'Vorticists' Picture Puzzles', *Daily Mirror*, 11 June 1915, p.2.

15 [Arthur Clutton-Brock], 'Junkerism in Art: The London Group at the Goupil Gallery', *Times*, 10 March 1915, p.8.

16 W[yndham] L[ewis], 'The London Group (March 1915)', *Blast*, no.2 (July 1915), p.78, in *Wyndham Lewis on Art*, p. 89.

17 In a letter to Harriet Monroe, dated 10 April 1915, Pound wrote: 'Anyhow there's a vorticist show at the Doré Gallery in June – war or no war.' Zinnes 1980, p.290.

18 Gaudier-Brzeska's *Singer* 1913, Lewis's *Workshop* c.1914–15, and Wadsworth's *Blackpool* 1915, *Rotterdam* 1914, and *Harbour of Flushing* 1914 were shown in both exhibitions.

19 J.[ohn] M.[iddleton] M.[urray], 'Vorticists and Others', *Westminster Gazette*, 18 June 1915.

20 P.G. Konody, 'The Vorticists at the Dore Galleries', *Observer*, 4 July 1915, p.9.

21 Ibid.

22 For a further discussion of the hostile reaction to the show, see Cork 1976, vol.1, pp.275–6.

23 'Vorticist Exhibition at the Doré Galleries', *Athenaeum*, 19 June 1915, p.556.

24 See *Blast*, no.1, p.28.

25 In his book *Revolution in Art: An Introduction to the Study of Cézanne, Gauguin, van Gogh, and Other Modern Painters* (London: Art News Press, 1910), Frank Rutter compares Paul Cézanne and Paul Gauguin to Karl Marx and Peter Kropotkin.

26 Frank Rutter, 'The Vorticists. Their Basic Principles', *Sunday Times*, 13 June 1915.

27 Ibid.

28 Ibid.

29 Frank Rutter, ' Sketches of the Italian War Zone: A Soldier-Sculptor's Death', *Sunday Times*, 11 July 1915, p.8.

30 Ibid.

31 C.[harles] M.[arriott], 'Vorticism', p.7.

32 Ibid.

33 Letter from Frederick Etchells to William Lipke, 30 March 1965, Tate Gallery Archive.

34 H[orace] B[rodzsky], 'Gossip from New York', *Colour*, vol.6, no.2 (March 1917), pp.57–8. I am grateful to Mark Antliff and Vivien Greene for this reference.

35 Lewis, 'Note for Catalogue', in *Wyndham Lewis on Art*, p.96.

36 For Roger Fry's and Rutter's enthusiastic reception of David Bomberg, see William C. Lipke, *David Bomberg: A Critical Study of his Life and Work* (London: Evelyn, Adams & MacKay, 1967), pp.42–3.

37 For Bomberg's reluctance to join the Vorticist group, see Richard Cork, *David Bomberg* (New Haven: Yale University Press, 1987), p.105. A letter from Lillian Bomberg to William Lipke casts light on Bomberg's position. She wrote: 'One very important point is that David Bomberg was never a member of the Vorticist Group, although some of his cubist work was included in the 1915 exhibition. He was very angry indeed and I think rightly so that he was included in the Wyndham Lewis Tate Gallery exhibition ... when indeed he [had] stood entirely alone ... and apart as early as 1912.' Als, 15 November 1964, TGA. For Bomberg's Jewish identity, see Lisa Tickner, 'David Bomberg: *In the Hold*, Jews, and Cubism', *Modern Life and Modern Subjects: British Life in the Early Twentieth Century* (New Haven: Yale University Press, 2000), pp.143–83. Tickner observes that 'Bomberg was not a practising Jew, but Jewishness was an important part of his identity', p.163.

38 F.T. Marinetti and C.R.W. Nevinson, 'Vital English Art: Futurist Manifesto', *Observer*, 1 June 1914, reprinted in Michael J.K. Walsh, *Hanging a Rebel: The Life of C.R W. Nevinson* (Cambridge: Lutterworth Press, 2008), pp.84–6.

39 Nevinson's sixth clause read: 'So we call upon the English public to support, defend, and glorify the genius of the great Futurist painters or pioneers and advance forces of Vital English Art – ATKINSON, BOMBERG, EPSTEIN, ETCHELLS, HAMILTON, NEVINSON, ROBERTS, WADSWORTH, WYNDHAM LEWIS.' Walsh 2008, p.86. All the 'signatories' (except Atkinson and Epstein), together with Richard and Lawrence Aldington, Gaudier-Brzeska, and Pound wrote to disassociate themselves from Nevinson's brand of Futurism. See 'Futurism', *New Weekly*, June 1914, cited in Walsh 2008, p.87.

40 For an account of the evening, see Walsh 2008, pp.89–91.

41 *Observer*, 4 July 1915, cited in Cork 1976, vol.1, p.275. Cork erroneously dates the review 5 July 1915.

42 Cork states that Lewis invited Fry to show in the exhibition, which is further evidence that he wanted the art in this section to serve as a foil for the Vorticist works. Cork 1976, p.276.

43 *Observer*, 4 July 1915.

44 Lewis, 'Note for Catalogue,' not paginated. For the domestic aspect of Grant's and Picasso's collages, see Christopher Reed, *Bloomsbury Rooms: Modernism, Subculture, and Domesticity* (New Haven: Yale University Press for the Bard Graduate Center for Studies in the Decorative Arts, Design, and Culture, 2004), pp.119–21, 147–63.

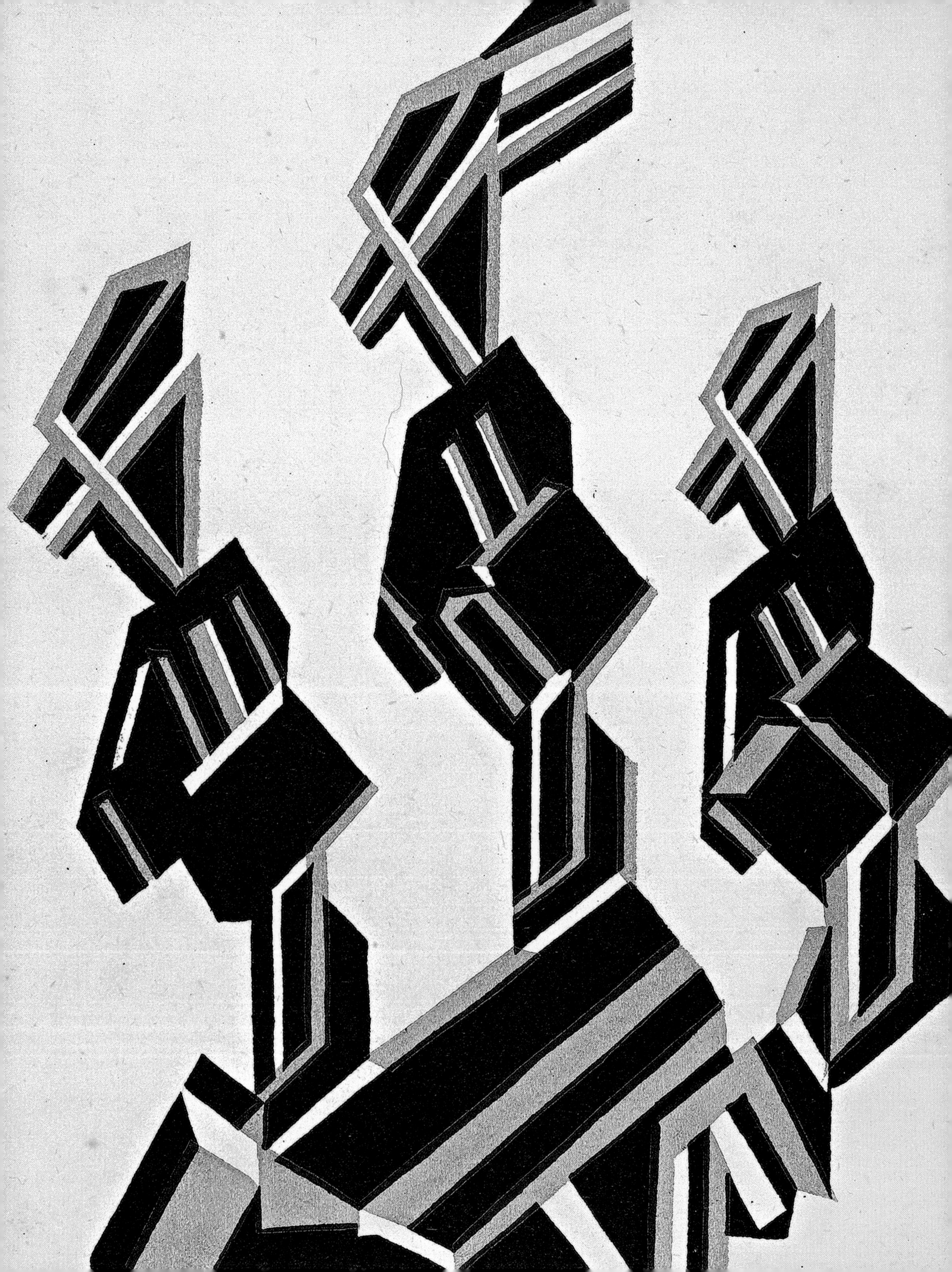

BLAST AND THE WORK OF ART IN THE AGE OF MECHANICAL REPRODUCTION

Robert Hewison

In his 1936 essay 'Das Kunstwerk im Zeitalter seiner technischen Reproduzierbarkeit' ('The Work of Art in the Age of Mechanical Reproduction'), Walter Benjamin argued that since 1900 it had become possible to reproduce any work of art mechanically, and that this had profoundly altered the way art was understood. Mechanical reproduction played a key role in shaping and communicating what became known as Vorticism, as the making of the journal *Blast* shows.[1] Benjamin's essay is principally known for his contention that the new relationship generated by the technology of reproduction led to the withering of the 'aura of the work of art'.[2] This aura was derived from the aboriginal function of the work as a ritual object, whose uniqueness is destroyed by such reproduction. But for Vorticism, mechanical reproduction was vital: graphic illustrations, which form a crucial part of its oeuvre, exist to be reproduced, and today, much Vorticist work is known only because it has survived in reproduction. The woodcuts and drawings in *Blast* (1914–15) bear out Benjamin's argument that 'to an ever greater degree the work of art reproduced becomes the work of art designed for reproducibility'.[3] What is important about Benjamin's essay, however, is the consequences of the loss of aura: 'The total function of art is reversed. Rather than being based on ritual, it begins to be based on another practice – politics'.[4] From 1909 to 1918, these were the politics of the avant-garde, as Wyndham Lewis and his associates struggled to establish a distinct identity for their art within modernism. There were, however, longer-term cultural and political implications inherent in the Vorticist project.

Mechanical reproduction via the printing press was essential to how the Vorticists communicated their ideas. The art historian Stephen Bury notes: 'Because of its very nature, traditional modes of communication and exhibition were often denied to the avant garde, it was adept at finding its own outlets, publishing its own manifestos, magazines and books, and creating new ones – the artist's book and the photo-book ... This period was the last one in which the printed format was the primary mode for communicating information.'[5] As Lewis states in the first issue, '*Blast* sets out to be an avenue for all those vivid and violent ideas that could reach the Public in no other way'.[6]

Conceived simultaneously with the Rebel Art Centre towards the end of 1913, *Blast* was funded from the same

Detail from Edward Wadsworth *Street Singers* c.1914 (fig.34)

source, a £100 advance from Lewis's artist-patron and former lover Kate Lechmere. Ironically, the Futurist disciple C.R.W. Nevinson suggested the title, but he dropped out in February 1914, discouraged by the long search for a publisher.[7] *Blast* was to be a quarterly journal, edited by Lewis, but the potential contributors had no shared idea about the critical line it would take. Its conception owes an essential debt to the Italian Futurists, in particular the propaganda of the poet F.T. Marinetti, who launched the first Futurist manifesto in 1909. In 1913 the Futurist newspaper *Lacerba* published Guillaume Apollinaire's 'L'Antitradition futuriste. Manifeste-synthèse' ('Futurist Anti-Tradition Manifesto') in Italian,[8] where the violent contrasts between 'Distruzione' and 'Costruzione' (destruction and construction) as well as 'Merda' and 'Rose' (shit and roses) anticipate the rhetoric of *Blast*'s opening pages. This anxiety of influence later turned *Blast* into a vehicle for attacking the Futurists, but as late as March 1914, Marinetti gave one of his thunderous recitals at the Doré Galleries as a fundraiser for Lewis's Rebel Art Centre, and he spoke there on 6 May.

The group shows that preceded the *First Vorticist Exhibition* in 1915, the manifestos, and two editions of *Blast* cast the movement's participants in different and confusing configurations. This 'confluence of energy' as Ezra Pound, the group's literary promoter, metaphorically described the process, crystallized as the Vortex, the visual and literary image representing a still, focal point of intellectual force.[9] Whilst the movement's magnetic, shaping influence was Lewis, as both writer and artist, the multi-authored journal, its primary means of communication, had a looser form than a manifesto: hence the contributions of fiction from Ford Madox Hueffer and Rebecca West to the first issue. They did not sign the defining manifesto in the journal, but the anti-romantic attitude of their writing justifies their presence.

Both the journal *Blast* and the term 'Vorticism' coalesced gradually. The magazine's typographically radical form borrows from the Futurist model: the 'bright puce'[10] cover of *Blast*, no.1, resembles Ardengo Soffici's cover for *I Manifesti del Futurismo* (The Futurist Manifestos) published by the *Lacerba* group in the same year.[11] A compliant printer was needed to produce *Blast*. Douglas Goldring, who had published both Lewis and Marinetti in his travel-writing magazine *The Tramp*, introduced Lewis to the small jobbing firm of Leveridge & Co. The company had the large, sans-serif type that makes such an impression in the opening

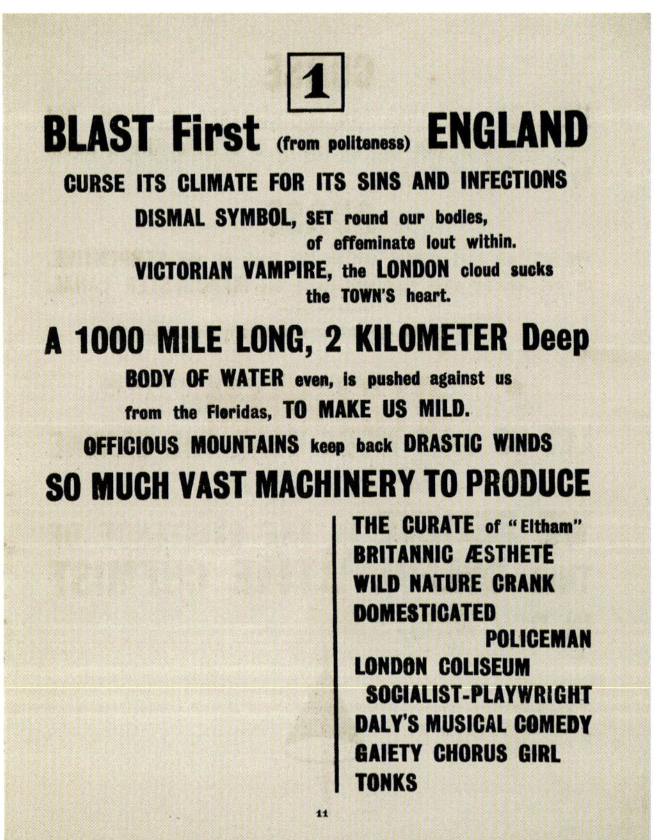
1

BLAST First (from politeness) ENGLAND

CURSE ITS CLIMATE FOR ITS SINS AND INFECTIONS

DISMAL SYMBOL, SET round our bodies,
of effeminate lout within.

VICTORIAN VAMPIRE, the LONDON cloud sucks
the TOWN'S heart.

A 1000 MILE LONG, 2 KILOMETER Deep

BODY OF WATER even, is pushed against us
from the Floridas, TO MAKE US MILD.

OFFICIOUS MOUNTAINS keep back DRASTIC WINDS

SO MUCH VAST MACHINERY TO PRODUCE

THE CURATE of "Eltham"
BRITANNIC ÆSTHETE
WILD NATURE CRANK
DOMESTICATED
POLICEMAN
LONDON COLISEUM
SOCIALIST-PLAYWRIGHT
DALY'S MUSICAL COMEDY
GAIETY CHORUS GIRL
TONKS

11

Fig.31
Blast, no.1 (July 1914), p.11

pages of *Blast*, no.1.[12] The heavy weight of the typeface signals the new brutality of a mechanical modernity (fig.31).

The assembly of the first issue shows the late adoption of the term 'Vorticism' in the journal's evolution. *Blast* was announced for publication in April 1914, subsequently revised to 20 June, and actually issued on 2 July. The inner sections, from pages 45 to 126, which contain poems by Pound, the stories by Hueffer and West, Lewis's play *Enemy of the Stars*, and Edward Wadsworth's contribution on Vasily Kandinsky, were printed first, using a serif typeface. The polemical references to the 'Great English Vortex' appear only before and after these pages and must have been printed later. It is probable that the opening 'Blast' and 'Bless' section is the manifesto that had been advertised in April, but a second manifesto that was written later and signed by eleven artists and writers follows on page 43. Lewis's 'Vortices and Notes' with contributions from Pound and Henri Gaudier-Brzeska, which appear at the end of the journal, were assembled after 27 March, when Spencer Gore, Lewis's collaborator in decorating the Cave of the Golden Calf in 1912, died, occasioning his obituary on page 150 and the reproduction of two of Gore's distinctly un-Vorticist paintings. The suffragette attacks on works of art, referred to on pages 151–2, took place from March to May and one at the Doré Galleries in June. Frida Graham, who attacked works in the National Gallery in May, is 'blessed' as 'Frieder' on page 28, as is Leveridge and the Commercial Process Co., which made *Blast*'s line block and photographic illustrations (fig.32).

The art historian Paul O'Keeffe suggests that Lewis delayed the planned April publication because of the attention being paid to the *Exhibition of the Works of the Italian Futurist Painters and Sculptors* that opened at the Doré Galleries on 24 April.[13] But it is also possible that Lewis and his Rebel Art Centre colleagues had not yet settled on the term that would in effect brand their art and values. Even in 'The Melodrama of Modernity', a late addition to *Blast*, no.1, Lewis writes: 'We may hope before long to find a new word'.[14] Pound used the phrase 'The Vortex' in a 19 December 1913 letter to describe the cultural ferment of London[15] and gave a talk on Vorticism at the Rebel Art Centre, but the term, which took on real critical significance in the writings of Lewis and Pound, did not appear in print until 13 June 1914. It came in the form

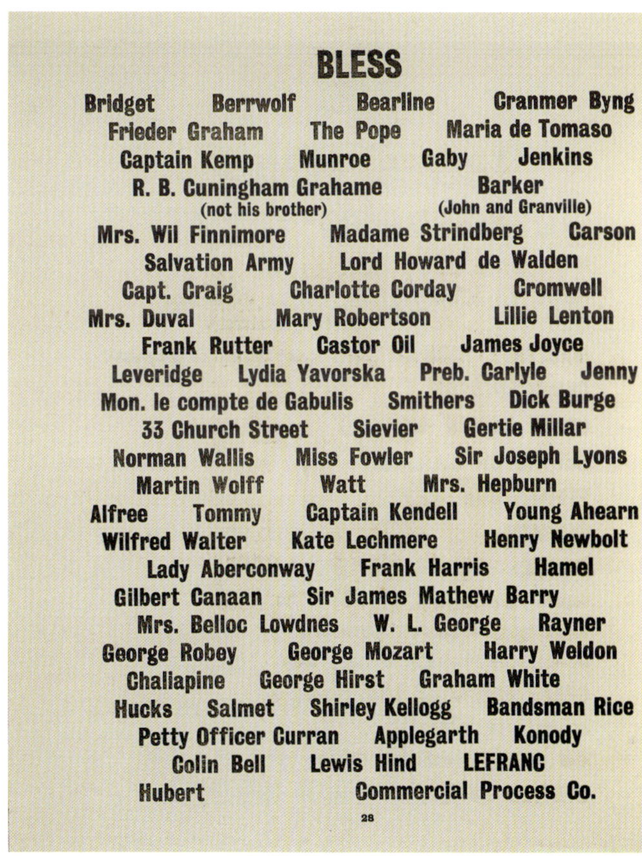

BLESS

Bridget Berrwolf Bearline Cranmer Byng
Frieder Graham The Pope Maria de Tomaso
Captain Kemp Munroe Gaby Jenkins
R. B. Cuningham Grahame (not his brother) Barker (John and Granville)
Mrs. Wil Finnimore Madame Strindberg Carson
Salvation Army Lord Howard de Walden
Capt. Craig Charlotte Corday Cromwell
Mrs. Duval Mary Robertson Lillie Lenton
Frank Rutter Castor Oil James Joyce
Leveridge Lydia Yavorska Preb. Carlyle Jenny
Mon. le compte de Gabulis Smithers Dick Burge
33 Church Street Sievier Gertie Millar
Norman Wallis Miss Fowler Sir Joseph Lyons
Martin Wolff Watt Mrs. Hepburn
Alfree Tommy Captain Kendell Young Ahearn
Wilfred Walter Kate Lechmere Henry Newbolt
Lady Aberconway Frank Harris Hamel
Gilbert Canaan Sir James Mathew Barry
Mrs. Belloc Lowdnes W. L. George Rayner
George Robey George Mozart Harry Weldon
Chaliapine George Hirst Graham White
Hucks Salmet Shirley Kellogg Bandsman Rice
Petty Officer Curran Applegarth Konody
Colin Bell Lewis Hind LEFRANC
Hubert Commercial Process Co.

28

Fig.32
Blast, no.1 (July 1914), p.28

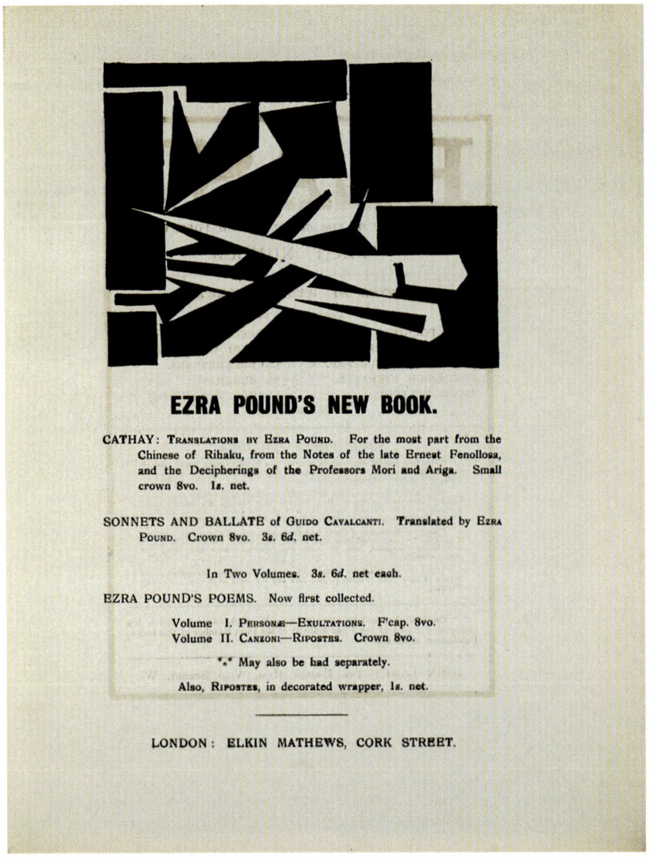

Fig.33
Blast, no.2 (July 1915), p.103, with illustration by Dorothy Shakespear

of an advertisement placed in *The Spectator*, a literary and political weekly:

> *THE MANIFESTO OF THE VORTICISTS. THE ENGLISH PARALLEL MOVEMENT TO CUBISM AND EXPRESSIONISM. IMAGISM IN POETRY. DEATH BLOW TO IMPRESSIONISM AND FUTURISM AND ALL THE REFUSE OF NAIF SCIENCE.*[16]

Lewis wrote the copy, which neatly positions Vorticism within the culture wars of the period, and John Lane of the publishing house The Bodley Head placed the advertisement. Lane had belatedly come on board as publisher of the magazine in May – without bearing any financial risk. He did feel, however, that he was at legal risk and insisted that three lines from Pound's poem 'Fratres Minores.' – 'With minds still hovering above their testicles' and 'That the twitching of three abdominal nerves / Is incapable of producing a lasting Nirvana' – be blacked out with a handstamp. This delayed publication further until 2 July.[17] By the end of July, the Rebel Art Centre was closed, following Lewis's falling out with his patroness Lechmere. She later sued him for the £97 she had lost on *Blast*.[18]

The advertisement is significant, for it declared war on Futurism. On 7 June Marinetti and his English disciple Nevinson had published 'Vital English Art: Futurist Manifesto' in the Sunday *Observer*, hailing Lawrence Atkinson, David Bomberg, Jacob Epstein, Frederick Etchells, Cuthbert Hamilton, Lewis, William Roberts, and Wadsworth as Futurists using the Rebel Art Centre's address. Jealous of Marinetti's skilful self-publicity and not one to have his leadership challenged, on 12 June Lewis took his Rebel Art Centre troops, describing themselves as Vorticists, into action to break up a Marinetti–Nevinson manifestation at the Doré Galleries. On 14 June Richard Aldington, Atkinson, Etchells, Gaudier-Brzeska, Hamilton, Lewis, Pound, Roberts, and Wadsworth disassociated themselves from Marinetti in a letter to the *Observer*, which Bomberg signed as an independent.

The sequence of events and the late arrival of the Vortex as a conceptual term in *Blast* might suggest that Vorticism was merely a counterstrike against what Lewis later called Marinetti's 'Futurist *Putsch*'.[19] Yet as this exhibition and catalogue show, by the time *Blast*, no.1, was published, Vorticism stood for a coherent set of stylistic and critical principles, expressed through the medium of mechanical reproduction.

As is well known, on 4 August 1914, the bloodless battles of the artists were overwhelmed by the all too bloody outbreak of the First World War. *Blast*, no.2, did not appear until 20 July 1915, and at Wadsworth's suggestion, it was a 'war number'.[20] Two more issues were promised but never appeared. *Blast* was again printed by Leveridge & Co., which also produced the catalogue of the *First Vorticist Exhibition* that opened at the Doré Galleries on 10 June (fig.28 on p.60). Thinner, with 108 pages, it has a suitably warlike brown and black cover by Lewis (no.37). There were three new contributors: Jessica Dismorr with poetry and prose; T.S. Eliot who had met Lewis through Pound in September 1914, with two poems, in his first appearance in English print; and a poem by Helen Saunders. (It has been suggested that the misspelling of Saunders as 'Sanders' throughout was a pseudonym,[21] but *Blast* is full of misprints.) In addition to Dorothy Shakespear, Dismorr and Saunders also contributed convincingly Vorticist images. Gaudier-Brzeska is represented by brief notes sent from the trenches before his death on 5 June 1915, and a photograph of his sculpture *Hieratic Head of Ezra Pound* 1914 (no.1).

Visually *Blast*, no.2, is more consistent than its predecessor, partly for technical reasons. Except for the photograph of Gaudier-Brzeska's work and the abstract Vorticist graphic decorations, all illustrations are line blocks, fifteen of which are full page and all but one printed on one side of the sheet only. They demonstrate a cohesive Vorticist aesthetic aside from Jacob Kramer's expressionist *Types of the Russian Army* 1915. The confident contrasts of the black-and-white blocks in *Blast* convey that distinctive aesthetic much more clearly than the somewhat murky reproductions and make the most coherent argument for Vorticism as an independent modernist movement. From Wadsworth's *Newcastle* c.1913 (no.30), which opens the first issue, to Shakespear's abstract design promoting Pound's new publications, which closes the second[22] (fig.33), this visual vigour anticipates modernist graphic art and advertising post-1918. Wadsworth's *Rotterdam* 1914 (no.38), which may have been influenced by the German woodcutters with whom he showed during the Twenty-One Gallery's *Modern German Art* exhibition in March 1914, has an openness and dynamism that also appears in Roberts's *Combat* c.1915 and Dismorr's *The Engine* c.1915. Their radical modernism and the machine aesthetic that governs it are fully supported by the literary content of the only two issues of *Blast*.

Lewis's quarrel with Marinetti and Futurism has obscured the important fact that Vorticism was that rare event, a genuinely British avant-garde movement. This assault on the soft, decaying, 'feminine' culture of late-Victorian and Edwardian England, summed up in Lewis's deliberately loose term 'Impressionism' had to be blasted away by a cultural revolution. The Vorticists' 'masculine' machine aesthetic that would achieve this destruction was not Futurism's 'accelerated impressionism'[23] but a purifying hardness. The idea can be traced back to the philosopher T.E. Hulme's 1909 'A Lecture on Modern Poetry', which asserts that poetry should aspire to the condition of sculpture rather than music. Hulme's ideas encouraged Pound towards imagism, the reforming poetic movement that he abandoned in 1913 for the revolutionary zeal of Vorticism. Intellectual and sexual rivalry with Lewis led to Hulme's absence from *Blast*, but the arguments and vocabulary of his lecture 'Modern Art and Its Philosophy' in January 1914 – 'austere, mechanical, clear cut, and bare'[24] – anticipates Vorticist values. Hulme, the critical champion of Epstein, advocated the 'new geometrical art' and its change in sensibility.[25]

Wadsworth worked closely with Lewis on *Blast*, no.1. He was well placed for the Kandinsky commission, for he had studied both German and engineering drawing in Munich in 1906, where he also learned to make woodcuts and discovered his vocation as an artist. Within the pages of *Blast*, Wadsworth's translation and commentary on Kandinsky's *Über das Geistige in der Kunst. Insbesondere in der Malerei* (*On the Spiritual in Art: And Painting in Particular*, 1912) draws a fine line between Vorticism and Kandinsky's total abstraction. Wadsworth's article, appropriately interrupted by two figure-based drawings by Epstein, argues that 'the artist can employ any forms (natural, abstracted or abstract) to express himself, if his feelings demand it'.[26] In his own practice, he moved from the semi-figurative woodcut *Street Singers* c.1914 (fig.34) to the coloured abstraction of *Interior* 1917 (no.72) and back again. His commitment to the machine aesthetic is evident in *Newcastle* and in the more sophisticated *War-Engine* 1915 in *Blast*, no.2. However, the apogee of Wadsworth's Vorticist art was reached only at the beginning of 1918 when he returned from service in the Mediterranean to supervise the application of the recently devised system of 'dazzle' camouflage to ships.[27] These vivid designs, intended to confuse enemy submarines about the ship's direction, inspired a sequence of woodcuts that creatively combine war and Vorticist abstraction.[28]

Lewis feared that war would kill modernism, hence his insistence in *Blast*, no.2, that modern art was beyond war. As Gaudier-Brzeska had written from the trenches, even when looking at a German-held hill: 'I shall derive my emotions solely from the *arrangement of surfaces*'.[29] As an artist, writer, and theoretician, Lewis took the machine aesthetic of Etchells and Wadsworth; the muscular figurative geometry of Epstein and Roberts; the urban literary satires of Dismorr, Eliot, and Pound, and tried to forge them into 'an abstract and universal art'.[30] As author of half the contents of the second issue, he used conventional art criticism to promote this future international style while continuing his disputes with Cubism, Expressionism, and Futurism. But his most radical written contributions are purely literary: his reflections on the outbreak of war in his story 'The Crowd Master' in *Blast*, no.2, bear a correspondence with his painting *The Crowd* 1914–15 (no.7). In the nightmare play *Enemy of the Stars* in *Blast*, no.1, a darker side of Vorticism is visible.

The unperformable *Enemy of the Stars* is more psychodrama than theatrical piece. Its words are hammered together by sheer linguistic will power, as though reaching for a verbal form of Vorticist abstraction. The violent conflict between Arghol and Hanp, which ends in Arghol's murder and Hanp's suicide, enacts Lewis's Nietzschean vision of the negative relationship of the artist to society, of the master to the herd, with Arghol as the pure individual, Hanp as sensual humanity. The literary critic Hugh Kenner explains this dialectical relationship as 'the two principles of action – he calls them Self and Not-self – whose quarrel in Lewis's mind guarantees the energy of his books and pictures'.[31] Lewis states: 'There is Yourself: and there is the Exterior World, that fat mass you browse on.'[32] Trapped in an identity forced on him by external contingencies, a Not-self against the Self, the artist is set against the world. Art is opposed to life, and Vorticism will purge British culture.

Thus the artist must be above the crowd, as in Lewis's painting, but this position leads to a fatally false faith in the strong man: 'Every real individuality and excellence would welcome conditions where there would inevitably be a hierarchy of power and vitality. The Best would then be Free.'[33] Ideas such as these in the 1930s led to Lewis's flirtation with Adolf Hitler, Eliot's with Oswald Mosley, and Pound's commitment to Benito Mussolini. Nor can one ignore the anti-Semitism that tainted all three.

In the epilogue to his 1936 essay, Benjamin reminds us that the age of mechanical reproduction was also the age of mass society, which Communism and Fascism were competing to control: 'The logical result of Fascism is the introduction of aesthetics into political life'. The only possible outcome, he argues, is violence: 'All efforts to render politics aesthetic culminate in one thing, war. War and war only can set a goal for mass movements on the largest scale while respecting the traditional property system.'[34]

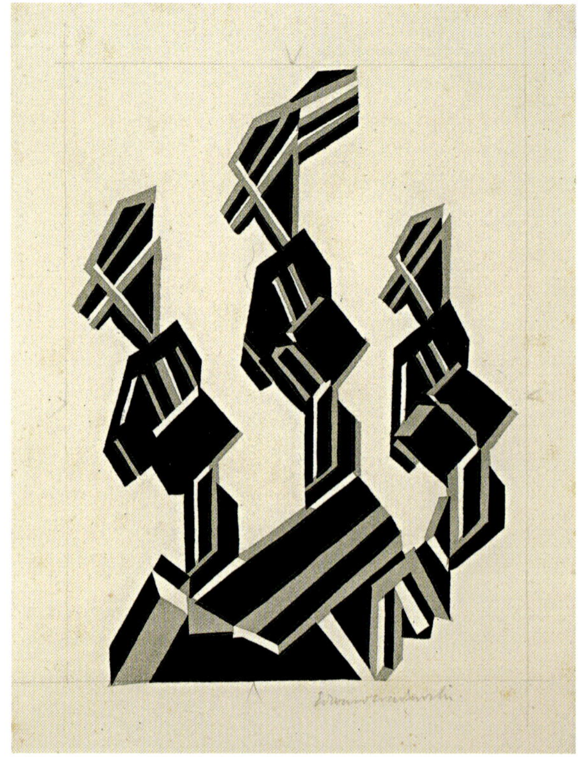

Fig.34
Edward Wadsworth
Street Singers c.1914
Woodcut on paper
sheet: 17.8 x 14 cm

The deaths of Gaudier-Brzeska and Hulme; the military experiences of Bomberg, Lewis, Nevinson, Roberts, Wadsworth, and their friends; 'The Death of Vorticism' that Pound tried to deny in 1919,[35] were enough to disillusion the *Blast* contributors about the poetics of war. But the aesthetics of Vorticism may merit Benjamin's criticism. Because war destroyed the movement and prevented its artists from getting the recognition they deserved, it may be that Lewis and Pound were pushed towards the views they later embraced. Had war not come, the Vorticists might have achieved a modernist revolution. Yet, despite what happened later, the maximum intellectual and imaginative energy of the Vortex remains 'white and abstract with its red-hot swiftness'.[36] Even in reproduction, *Blast* has not lost its aura.

NOTES

1 Walter Benjamin, 'The Work of Art in the Age of Mechanical Reproduction' (1936), in *Illuminations*, ed. Hannah Arendt, trans. Harry Zohn (1970; repr., London: Pimlico, 1990), p.211.

2 Ibid., p.215.

3 Ibid., p.218.

4 Ibid.

5 Stephen Bury (ed.), *Breaking the Rules: The Printed Face of the Avant Garde 1900–1937* (London: British Library, 2007), p.8.

6 *Blast*, no.1 (July 1914), facsimile ed. (Santa Rosa, Calif.: Black Sparrow Press, 1997), p.7.

7 William C. Wees, *Vorticism and the English Avant-Garde* (Toronto: University of Toronto Press, 1972), p.159.

8 "L'Antitradizione Futurista," *Lacerba*, 29 January 1919, pp.202–3. See Richard Cork, *Vorticism and Abstract Art in the First Machine Age*, vol.1 (London: Gordon Fraser, 1976), p.249.

9 Ezra Pound, 'Affirmations II – Vorticism', *The New Age*,vol.16, no.11 (14 January 1915), p.227.

10 Wyndham Lewis, *Blasting and Bombardiering* (1937; repr., London: Calder and Boyars, 1967), p.37.

11 Reproduced in Claudia Salaris, *Bibliografia del Futurismo 1909–1944* (Rome: Biblioteca del Vascello, 1998), p.74.

12 Michael Leveridge, 'The Printing of Blast', *Wyndham Lewis Annual* vol.7 (2000), pp.20–31.

13 Paul O'Keeffe, 'The Troubled Birth of Blast: December 1913–June 1914', in Andrew Wilson (ed.), *Vorticism*, special issue, *ICSAC Cahier* (Brussels), no.8/9, (December 1988), p.46.

14 Lewis, 'Vortices and Notes', *Blast*, no.1, p.143.

15 *The Letters of Ezra Pound, 1907–1941*, ed. D.D. Paige (London: Faber and Faber, 1951), p.65.

16 *Spectator*, 13 June 1914, p.1015.

17 Wees 1972, p.162.

18 Paul O'Keeffe, *Some Sort of Genius: A Life of Wyndham Lewis* (London: Jonathan Cape, 2000), p.171.

19 Lewis 1967, p.33.

20 Edward Wadsworth to Wyndham Lewis, 19 August 1914, quoted in Barbara Wadsworth, *Edward Wadsworth: A Painter's Life* (London: Michael Russell, 1989), p.54.

21 Wees 1972, p.176.

22 *Blast*, no.2, p.103.

23 Ezra Pound, 'Vorticism', *Fortnightly Review*, vol.96, no.573 (September 1914), p.461. See, for example, Giacomo Balla's *Dynamism of a Dog on a Leash* 1912, Albright-Knox Art Gallery, Buffalo, New York.

24 T.E. Hulme, *Speculations: Essays in Humanism and the Philosophy of Art*, ed. Herbert Read (London: K. Paul, Trench, Trubner &Co.; New York: Harcourt, Brace&Co., 1936), p.96.

25 Ibid., p.104.

26 '"Inner Necessity": Review of Kandinsky's Book by Edward Wadsworth', *Blast*, no.1, p.122.

27 'Dazzle Camouflage Supervised by Edward Wadsworth', in Cork 1976, vol. 2 (Berkeley: University of California Press, 1976), p.521.

28 For example, *Drydocked for Scaling and Painting* 1918, Imperial War Museum, London.

29 *Blast*, no.2, facsimile ed. (Santa Rosa, Calif.: Black Sparrow Press, 2000), p.34.

30 Wyndham Lewis, 'The Art of the Great Race', *Blast*, no.2, p.72.

31 Hugh Kenner, *Wyndham Lewis* (London: Methuen, 1954), p.9.

32 Wyndham Lewis, 'Vortex "Be Thyself"', *Blast*, no.2, p.91.

33 Lewis, 'The Art of the Great Race', p.72.

34 Benjamin, 'The Work of Art in the Age of Mechanical Reproduction', p.234.

35 Ezra Pound, 'The Death of Vorticism', *Little Review* vol.5, no.10–11 (February–March 1919), pp.45–8.

36 Lewis, 'Vortices and Notes', p.149.

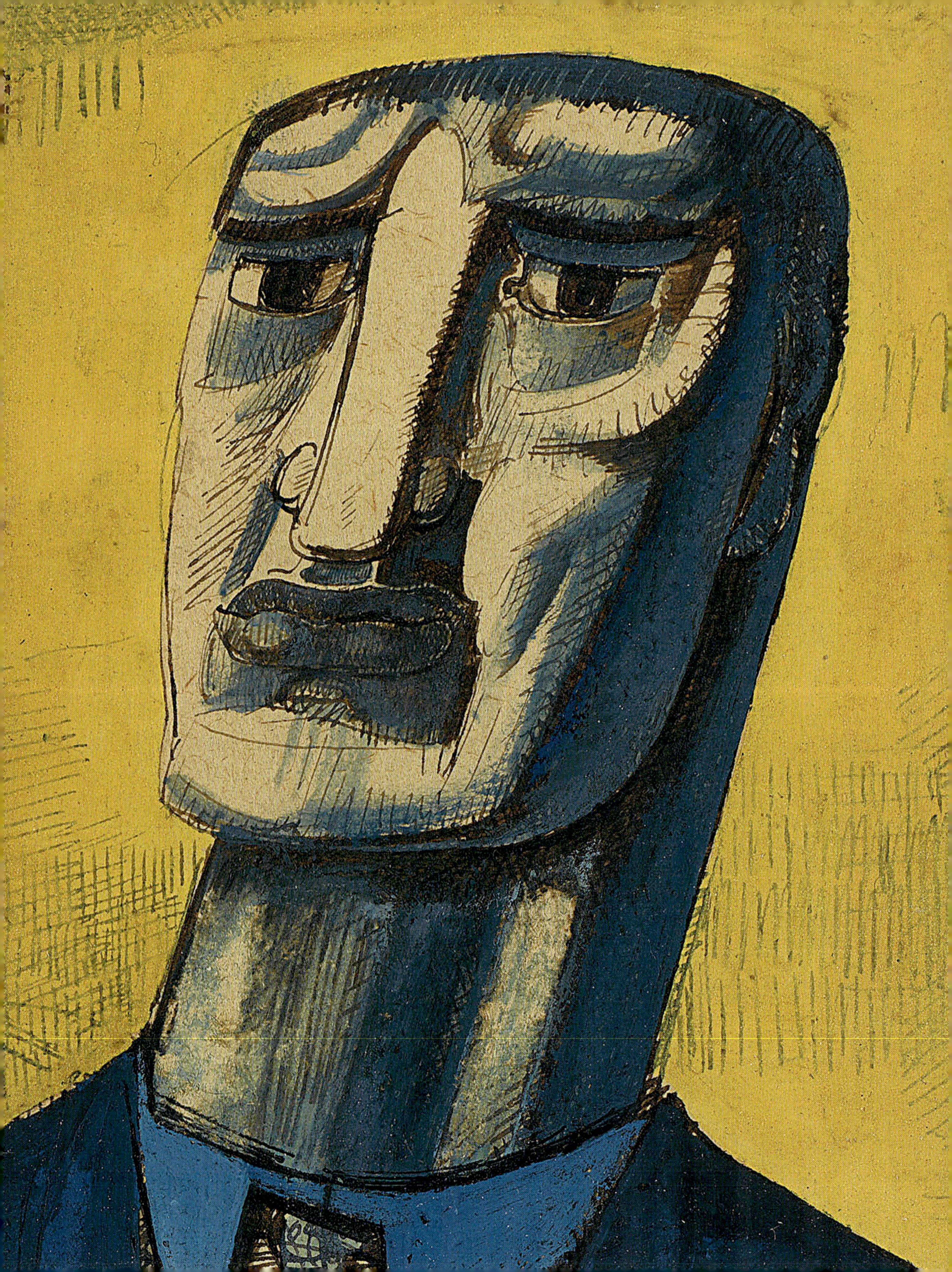

EZRA POUND AND JOHN QUINN
THE 1917 PENGUIN CLUB EXHIBITION

Vivien Greene

'It goes a step further than Cubism and Futurism, and is sponsored by [Henri Gaudier-]Brzeska, [Jacob] Epstein, and others. Its official mouthpiece is a cerise magazine called Blast', the *New York Times* announced about Vorticism, the new, polemical London-based avant-garde.[1] Published in 1914, the year of Vorticism's birth, this article's appearance in a major American newspaper was a harbinger of the Vorticist ties between England and the United States or, more precisely, between London and New York. This connection depended on the exchange between two men – both American and neither an artist – the expatriate poet Ezra Pound and the collector John Quinn. Their allegiance to these artists led to the Vorticist exhibition at the Penguin Club in New York in 1917, shaping an important chapter of the movement's history.[2]

Pound was a tremendous conduit for the flow of cultural innovations to the United States. He remained abroad for much of his career after moving in 1908 to London, where he discovered a freedom unavailable to him in American literary circles.[3] In a letter published in *The Dial* in 1915, aptly titled 'A Blast from London', he blamed the United States' cultural stodginess for the diaspora of creative Americans to Europe.[4] Soon after his arrival in London, Pound infiltrated the avant-garde literary circles of figures such as Ford Madox Hueffer, the Shakespears, T.E. Hulme, and F.S. Flint and befriended the established Irish poet whom he admired, William Butler Yeats.

Pound and Wyndham Lewis developed a camaraderie born from their similar positions as interlopers on the English scene and conflicts with the Bloomsbury group led by Roger Fry.[5] They shared a love of disruptive and direct artistic expression, whether the stripped-down clarity and mordant verse of Pound's imagist poems or the caustic savagery and reductive form of Lewis's images. Through this fertile friendship, Pound became one of Lewis's early champions and had a similar relationship with Gaudier-Brzeska. The foreign editor for *Poetry* (1912–) from 1913 to 1917 and London editor for *The Little Review* (1914–29) from 1917 to 1924, Pound also published his work in the United States and secured patronage and publishers for young poets and writers, and patronage for artists, notably the Vorticists.

On American soil, Quinn was pivotal for Vorticism's early fortunes, buying works, supporting the impecunious

Detail from Wyndham Lewis *Architect with Green Tie* 1909 (fig.35)

artists, and underwriting the Penguin Club exhibition. A son of Irish immigrants, Quinn became a successful New York lawyer.[6] Wishing to be 'a man of [his] own day and time', he sponsored and collected contemporary art and literature. As well as a major collection of Parisian avant-garde painting and sculpture (Picasso, Braque, Gleizes, Duchamp, Duchamp-Villon, Brancusi), he collected Lewis's paintings, Gaudier-Brzeska and Epstein's sculptures, and supported Pound and T.S. Eliot's poems.[7] He initially entered this Anglo- and Irish-American world through the painters John Butler Yeats and Augustus John. Then Pound, a tireless advocate of the Anglo-American avant-garde, became a primary link.

Quinn's longstanding investment in English art and literature inexorably led him to Vorticism, a movement encompassing both. The first artist whose work he bought, albeit associated peripherally with the movement, was Epstein, whom he had met in London in 1912 through John. In 1915, he began corresponding with Pound, affirming his commitment to modern artists, penned in response to the poet's condemnation of American collectors in *The New Age*.[8] Pound helped ignite Quinn's interest in Gaudier-Brzeska with an article he had published on the young artist.[9] Upon Gaudier-Brzeska's death during the First World War, in June 1915, Quinn instructed Pound to buy for him everything he could.[10]

Pound's espousal of Lewis compelled Quinn to begin collecting the upstart painter. Because Lewis's production was all overseas, Quinn relied on Pound's recommendations. In April 1915 Pound sent Quinn Lewis's *Timon* portfolio 1913 (nos.48–9)[11] for him 'to get used to', along with his article on the artist.[12] He concluded, 'Anyhow your collection is not complete until you have a few of his best things'.[13] Soon after the Doré exhibition closed, Quinn bought three Lewis drawings: *Kermess* [sic] 1912 (no.60),[14] *Timon* (later one) 1913 (no.64),[15] and *Design for Red Duet* 1915 (fig.29 on p.62).[16] He also purchased a Helen Saunders drawing, *Island of Laputa* 1915 (no.17) trusting Pound's assertion that:

> The things I personally would buy if I had the cash are. Sanders [sic] 'Island of Laputa'. (tendency to placidity in upper right ¼ of picture counteracted by great energy in her waves convention. This is Miss S. with Lewis, so to speak, 'sitting on her head') Still it is her picture.[17]

Quinn responded positively, asking Pound to acquire Saunder's work and *Kermesse* and writing: 'If there are any other things in the Dore exhibition that you think are significant and the price reasonable, I should be glad to have you get them for me'.[18]

Pound encouraged Quinn to assemble a collection of Vorticist painting and drawing revolving around Lewis:

> you ought to have the big 'Kermess', [sic] i.e. the big painting not this ink study ... In a collection like yours, seeing that you can afford the big things, I should think you would want the monumental single works, and that you would do well to guard against loading up with too much small stuff.'[19]

Even before Quinn had seen his first round of purchases, he asked his friend to identify other Lewis works. He eventually bought five drawings and the *Kermesse* painting, for which he paid in advance in January 1916, as the artist was being sent to war and sorely in need of funds.[20] Aside from *Kermesse*, this acquisition constituted more of a hold on five drawings of Quinn's choice to be selected once the artworks for the exhibition arrived in New York.[21] The only other artist Quinn bought before the 1917 show, always premised on Pound's opinion, was Frederick Etchells. The purchase of *Drawing of Head* c.1913 was based on a reproduction Pound had posted to him.[22]

Pound and Quinn began discussing the New York Vorticist exhibition in 1915. They wished at first to mount a memorial exhibition for Gaudier-Brzeska, but given the problems with his heir, Sophie Brzeska, they planned a larger presentation and Quinn agreed to underwrite a Vorticist exhibition to be held at the Montross Gallery on Fifth Avenue.[23] Quinn regarded this as an opportunity to see more works in person, especially those by Lewis.[24] The project evolved further when it became evident that Gaudier-Brzeska's sculptures would not be available for a protracted period and Pound campaigned for an exhibition hinging on Lewis but including the other active Vorticists:

> I swing onto this proposition, rather than hammering on [a] 'vorticism show', because of the indefinite and agrivating [sic] and uncertain nature of the delay about the Brzeska stuff.
>
> And so far as I am concerned 'VORTICISM', and the reason why I have embroiled myself with a tribe of former friends etc. etc. etc. ad infinitum has been solely Brzeska and Lewis.
>
> [Edward] Wadsworth does occasional good things, Etchells, does desulatory good things, Miss Sanders [sic] has done one, but I cant [sic] say that they feed <u>me</u> (i.e. my mind). And I can most certainly say that without Lewis there would be no vorticist school, no vorticist painting, (and even, in infinitiely [sic] less degree, no gay and irritant Blast).[25]

He then somewhat optimistically suggests that 'a Lewis show might raise up in New York an equal number of vorticists quite as good as the rest of the crowd here'.[26]

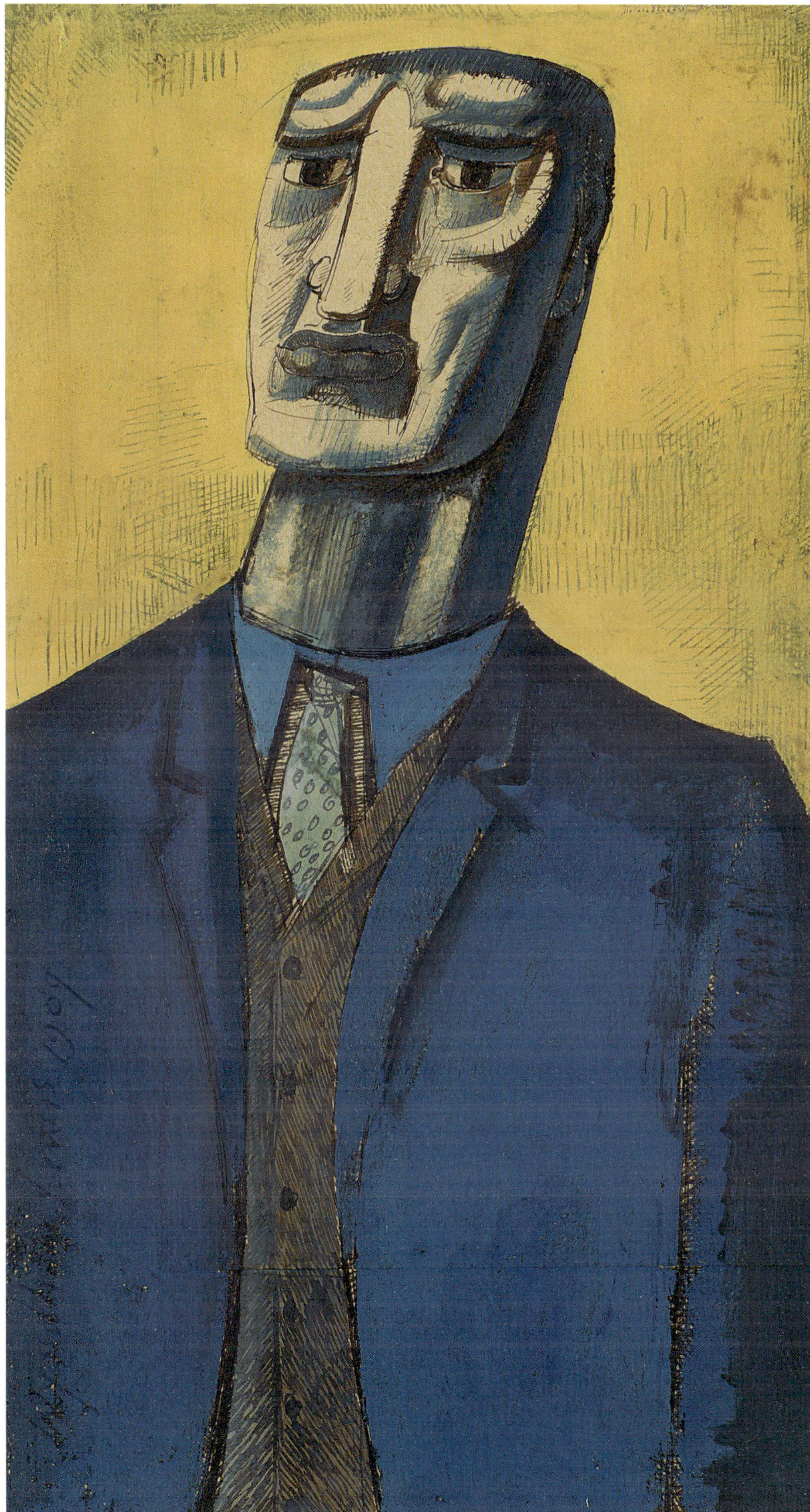

Fig.35
Wyndham Lewis
Architect with Green Tie 1909
Gouache, pen, and ink on
cut and pasted papers
23.5 x 13.3 cm
[P]

Facing major logistical problems,[27] the show did not come to pass until the beginning of 1917. In addition to the wait for the Gaudier-Brzeskas, Lewis required a leave from the Front to prepare some works for shipment.[28] After all the works were sent to the United States, the Montross Gallery withdrew from the project. Finally, this undertaking was, of course, planned against the backdrop of the war in Europe (the United States had yet to enter): communications were delayed or censored, torpedoes threatened shipments, and artists such as Lewis and William Roberts were at the Front, while Jessica Dismorr was nursing the wounded in France.

Pound's efforts – not only as Lewis's advocate, but also as unofficial curator and agent for all the Vorticists – were prodigious. He chose many of the works to be exhibited in New York and itemized his choices in a letter to Quinn shortly after the London show closed.[29] He later reiterated, 'The 40 or so drawings I sent over were selected mostly by me from stuff on [Lewis's] floor. I think they show his variety fairly well'.[30] Lewis was represented by three paintings, forty-three works on paper, and a portfolio of eleven sketches, spanning his still short career, from the primitivism of his more representational *Architect with Green Tie* 1909 (fig.35)[31] to his latest experiments with abstracted figures, evoking architectural rather than human forms, in *Design for Red Duet* (fig.29 on p.62). The other Vorticists shown, with fewer works, were Dismorr, Etchells, Roberts, Saunders, and Wadsworth.

Pound corresponded with Quinn almost daily in early 1916, sending cables, receiving payments, transferring them to the artists, obtaining signed receipts, and mailing them back to Quinn. Pound also organized the art shipment: he coordinated picking up works, oversaw their crating, arranged their insurance, and directed the shipment with the transport company.[32] These tasks were all the more onerous for an amateur during wartime. Ships often could not sail, customs and export documents were complex, and art shipments hardly a priority.[33]

Pound's exertions were well rewarded: the works were delivered safely to Quinn's home in June 1916. There Quinn could cull the best. He responded most positively to Lewis, writing to Pound: 'some of the Lewis things impressed me tremendously with their abounding vitality and power'.[34] Quinn's affinity for Lewis pleased Pound: 'I am glad you dont [sic] think me a fool about the dynamics of Lewis' stuff'.[35] By 19 August 1916, Quinn had selected twenty-four Lewis drawings and watercolours to purchase. The titles are listed in Quinn's ledger:[36] *Portrait of an Englishwoman* 1913, *The Flute Player* 1915, *On the Shore* (date unknown), *Soldiers* 1915, *El Ojo* (date unknown), *Faunesque* 1912, *Hell for Iron* 1914, *In The Forest* 1912, *Mountain of Loves* [sic] 1912, *Ascension* 1916, *A Happy Day* 1912–13 (no.63),[37] *Argol* [sic] 1914 (no.62), *The Starry Sky* 1912 (no.59),[38] *Timon* 1912 or 1915,[39] *Primitive Deshabille* (date unknown), *Mamie* 1911, *Kermess* [sic] *(drawing)* 1912,[40] *18th-Century Amazons* 1912, *Silvan Trilogy*

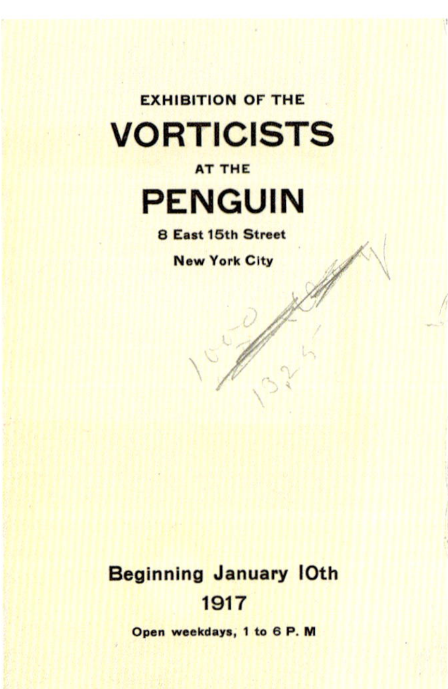

EXHIBITION OF THE

VORTICISTS

AT THE

PENGUIN

8 East 15th Street

New York City

Beginning January 10th

1917

Open weekdays, 1 to 6 P. M

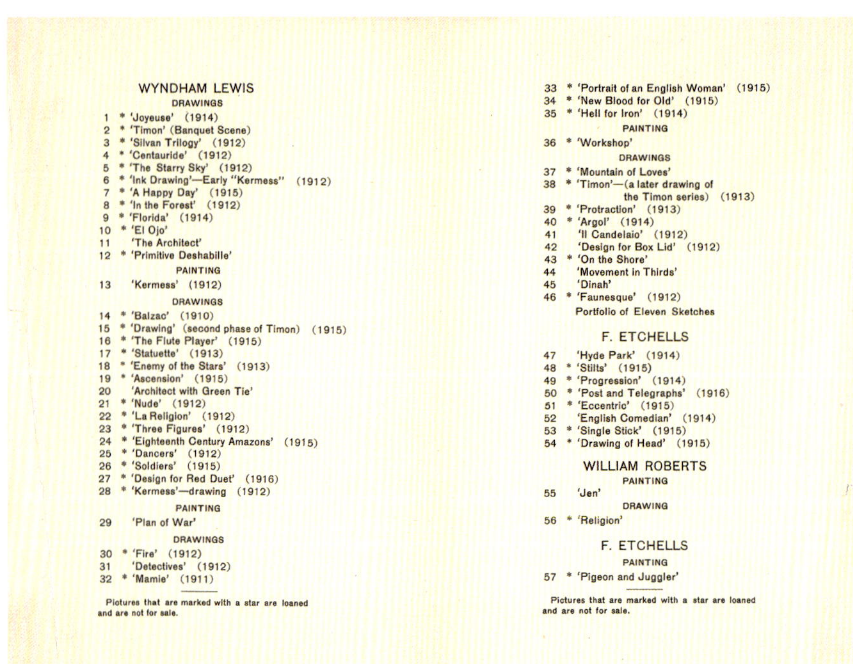

WYNDHAM LEWIS

DRAWINGS

1 * 'Joyeuse' (1914)
2 * 'Timon' (Banquet Scene)
3 * 'Silvan Trilogy' (1912)
4 * 'Centauride' (1912)
5 * 'The Starry Sky' (1912)
6 * 'Ink Drawing'—Early "Kermess" (1912)
7 * 'A Happy Day' (1915)
8 * 'In the Forest' (1912)
9 * 'Florida' (1914)
10 * 'El Ojo'
11 'The Architect'
12 * 'Primitive Deshabille'

PAINTING

13 'Kermess' (1912)

DRAWINGS

14 * 'Balzac' (1910)
15 * 'Drawing' (second phase of Timon) (1915)
16 * 'The Flute Player' (1915)
17 * 'Statuette' (1913)
18 * 'Enemy of the Stars' (1913)
19 * 'Ascension' (1915)
20 'Architect with Green Tie'
21 * 'Nude' (1912)
22 * 'La Religion' (1912)
23 * 'Three Figures' (1912)
24 * 'Eighteenth Century Amazons' (1915)
25 * 'Dancers' (1912)
26 * 'Soldiers' (1915)
27 * 'Design for Red Duet' (1916)
28 * 'Kermess'—drawing (1912)

PAINTING

29 'Plan of War'

DRAWINGS

30 * 'Fire' (1912)
31 'Detectives' (1912)
32 * 'Mamie' (1911)

Pictures that are marked with a star are loaned and are not for sale.

33 * 'Portrait of an English Woman' (1915)
34 * 'New Blood for Old' (1915)
35 * 'Hell for Iron' (1914)

PAINTING

36 * 'Workshop'

DRAWINGS

37 * 'Mountain of Loves'
38 * 'Timon'—(a later drawing of the Timon series) (1913)
39 * 'Protraction' (1913)
40 * 'Argol' (1914)
41 'Il Candelaio' (1912)
42 'Design for Box Lid' (1912)
43 * 'On the Shore'
44 'Movement in Thirds'
45 'Dinah'
46 * 'Faunesque' (1912)
Portfolio of Eleven Sketches

F. ETCHELLS

47 'Hyde Park' (1914)
48 * 'Stilts' (1915)
49 * 'Progression' (1914)
50 * 'Post and Telegraphs' (1916)
51 * 'Eccentric' (1915)
52 'English Comedian' (1914)
53 * 'Single Stick' (1915)
54 * 'Drawing of Head' (1915)

WILLIAM ROBERTS

PAINTING

55 'Jen'

DRAWING

56 * 'Religion'

F. ETCHELLS

PAINTING

57 * 'Pigeon and Juggler'

Pictures that are marked with a star are loaned and are not for sale.

[sic] 1912, *Florida* 1912, *Joyeuse* 1912, *New Blood for Old* 1915, *Centauride* 1912,[41] and *Dancers* 1912 (fig.18 on p.39).[42] A week later he made offers on *Workshop* c.1914–15 (no.19),[43] [*The*] *Enemy of* [*the*] *Stars* 1913, *Balzac* 1910, *Nude* 1912, *Three Figures* 1912, *Statuette* 1913, *Protraction* 1913 (no.61), *Fire* 1912,[44] and *La Religion* 1912.[45]

Quinn also gravitated towards Wadsworth's prints, earmarking a full suite of the woodcuts: *View of* [*a*] *Town* 1914 or 1916 (possibly no.75),[46] *Mytholmroyd* 1914 (fig.37), *Landscape* 1914 (no.74), *Interior* 1917 (no.72), *Slack Bottom* c.1914 , *Yorkshire Village* 1914 (no.71), *Rotterdam* 1914 (no.38), *Harbor of Flushing* 1914, *New Castle* c.1913 (no.30), *Fustian Town* 1914–15, *Railway Embankment* 1914 (no.77), and *Head* (not identified).[47] Later he decided on Wadsworth's *Drawing* 1915.[48] He also bought two drawings by Roberts, *Dancer* 1913–14[49] and *Religion* 1913–14,[50] and Etchells's [*The*] *Pigeon and Juggler* c.1915,[51] *Progression* 1914–15 (no.41),[52] and *Eccentric* 1915.[53] Then he took *Posts and Telegraphs* 1916 and, subsequently, offered to buy *Stilts* 1914–15 (no.67) and *Single Stick* 1915.[54]

Quinn was disinclined to accept the other artists, and asserted:

> I am not attracted much by the drawings of Desmoor [sic] or by the Desmoor paintings, or by the drawings of Saunders, nor by any of the paintings of Wadsworth, nor by the drawings of Wadsworth.[55]

Nonetheless, he bought some of these works out of an apparent sense of responsibility:

> Perhaps I am violating my own feeling and also your feeling that I should have only 'representative things', in buying the two Etchell [sic] things I ordered last week and the one this week, and in taking the drawing of Wadsworth or the drawings of Roberts. But, poor devils, they sent the things over here and no one else is likely to buy them. If I were thinking only of myself I wouldn't take any of the others and concentrate on the Lewis drawings.[56]

In fact, Quinn wrote that he had also acquired Dismorr's *Movements* (date unknown), and Saunders's *Canon* c.1915 (no.70), *Dance* c.1915 (no.69), and *Balance* c.1915 (no.68).[57] All the works marked with a star in the Penguin Club catalogue (fig.36) as being on loan represent the art Quinn bought.

Paralleling Pound's travails, Quinn's own trouble and expense to realize this exhibition were extraordinary. Following the Montross Gallery's withdrawal, he sought another location. The artist Walt Kuhn, Quinn's close friend, provided a space at the Penguin Club. This short-lived establishment, located at 8 East 15th Street, was

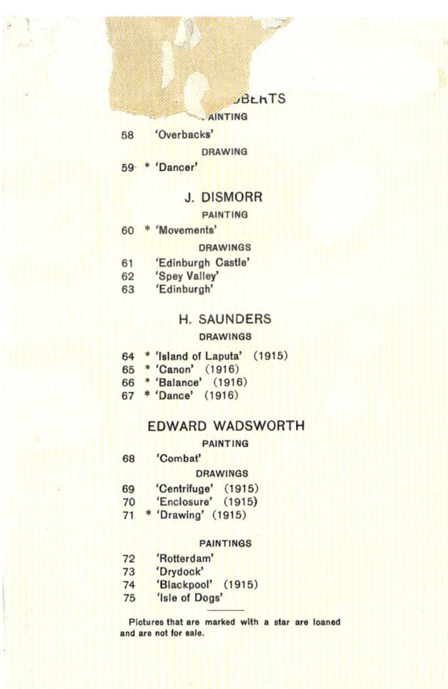

BERTS
AINTING
58 'Overbacks'
DRAWING
59 * 'Dancer'

J. DISMORR
PAINTING
60 * 'Movements'
DRAWINGS
61 'Edinburgh Castle'
62 'Spey Valley'
63 'Edinburgh'

H. SAUNDERS
DRAWINGS
64 * 'Island of Laputa' (1915)
65 * 'Canon' (1916)
66 * 'Balance' (1916)
67 * 'Dance' (1916)

EDWARD WADSWORTH
PAINTING
68 'Combat'
DRAWINGS
69 'Centrifuge' (1915)
70 'Enclosure' (1915)
71 * 'Drawing' (1915)

PAINTINGS
72 'Rotterdam'
73 'Drydock'
74 'Blackpool' (1915)
75 'Isle of Dogs'

Pictures that are marked with a star are loaned and are not for sale.

Fig.36
Exhibition of the Vorticists at the Penguin 1917
Front cover and list of works from the exhibition catalogue, Penguin Club, New York

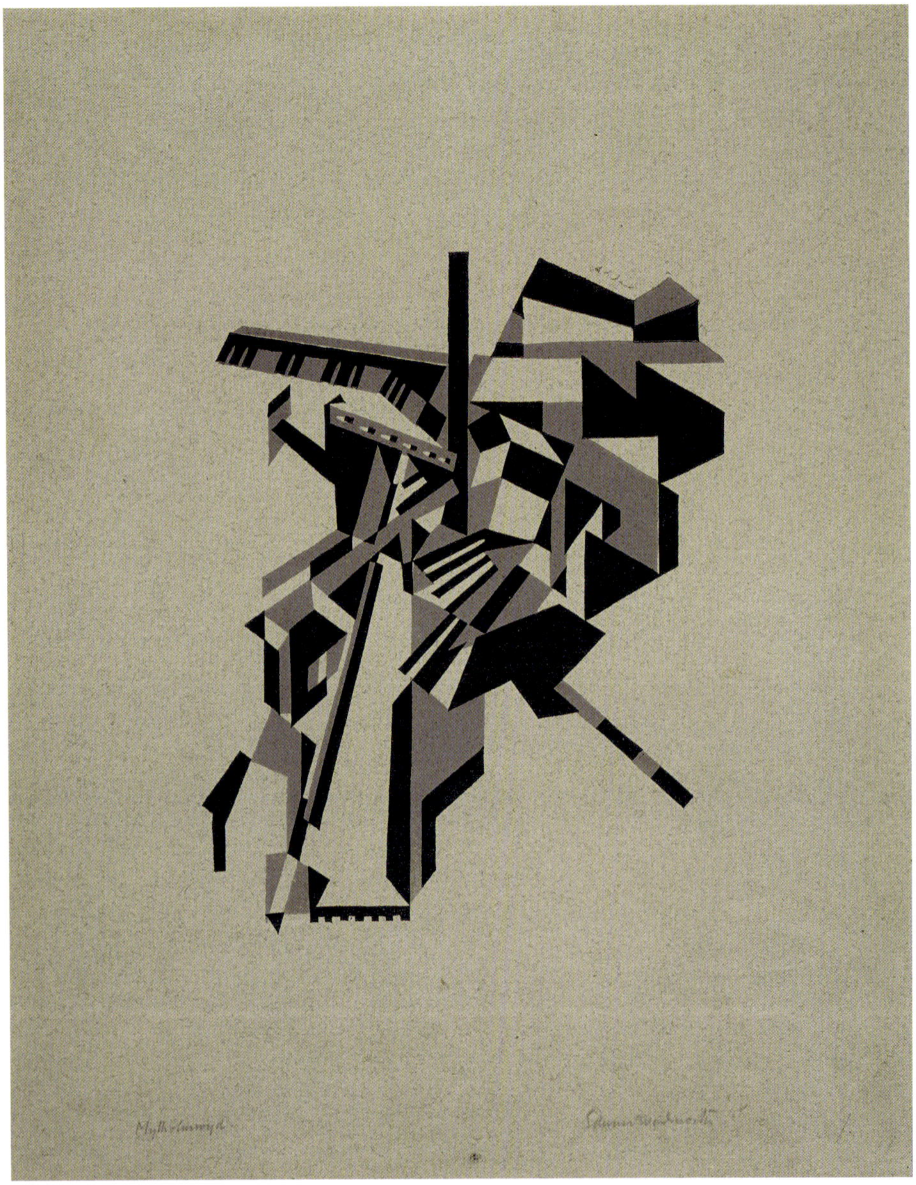

Fig.37
Edward Wadsworth
Mytholmroyd 1914
Woodcut on paper
sheet: 38 x 30.4 cm
image: 21.6 x 17.8 cm
[S]

an artist-run association Kuhn had formed with friends. Though he did not particularly like the work, Kuhn hosted the show as a favour to Quinn, who had helped fund the Penguin Club. Ultimately, Quinn assumed all the exhibition costs and almost single-handedly mounted the presentation.[58] Immediately after it opened in January 1917, he related to Pound:

> They have got a verygood [sic] room, and the Vorticist pictures (not the Brzeska drawings) have been put in, and they look very well ... Everything is hung, the drawings as well as the paintings, and they look very fine indeed. I read the proofs for the catalogue. The things appear on the catalogue just as they are numbered and hung on the walls, and that accounts for the fact that drawings are mixed in with paintings and that Roberts' things are separated by a painting of Etchells' ... Kuhn wanted to open the show in November, but I hadn't a moment's time, not even to sort out the things and to arrange them and to have the catalogue written. As it was I did it only a few nights ago, going over the things with your invoice and writing the names, at my apartment till late into the night, on the back of each picture.[59]

On view from 10 January to 1 February 1917, the Penguin Club exhibition did not fare well. It elicited no buyers and won neither public approbation nor press recognition. Although notices were mailed, barely a newspaper remarked upon the show. A brief notice in *The World* made dismissive, if ill-informed, remarks:

> Tendencies that had meteoric vogue some years ago and were supposed to have run their course for pictorial purposes are revived in an exhibition of the Vorticists ... The walls are brilliant with hangings in which intricacy of design and color harmonies and contrasts are effectively shown. Such work was long ago recognized by the public as ingenious. It failed to win enduring favor because it belongs to mechanical or ornamental design rather than to art ... Their arrival in the field would seem to be belated.[60]

Vorticism no longer represented the 'new' among the high modernist movements of the early 1910s seen in New York at the Armory Show in 1913 (which Quinn had also supported). Its shock value had faded by 1917. The 'motion and vitality' of Vorticist imagery, which alternately celebrated technology, fetishized the machine, fragmented bodies and forms, and reconceptualized space was now familiar.

However, Quinn had predicted that this would happen, prior to the exhibition. In a letter to Lewis, he attributed the phenomenon, in part, to American critics feeling negatively towards Pound and Kuhn.[61] Pound had also foreseen: 'I don't think anyone will be very much dissappointed [sic] in not selling to the public. You are the recognized American public, and the show was sent for your inspection, I think, rather than for anything else'.[62] This was true. Quinn's commitment to Vorticism grew. Following the exhibition's closing, determined to own a representative collection of Vorticist art, he made yet another selection of works. Still employing Pound as his go-between with all but Lewis, to whom he wrote directly, the staunch patron proposed to buy: Wadsworth's *Rotterdam* c.1914–15,[63] and *Combat* 1915, Roberts's *Jen* 1915[64] and *Overbacks* (date unknown), and Etchells's *Hyde Park* 1914–15[65] and [*The*] *English Comedian* 1914–15 (no.65).[66] He told Lewis that he would take the other two paintings, *Kermesse* and *Plan of War* 1913 (fig.20 on p.42),[67] as well as the balance of the drawings – *The Architect* (date unknown), *Architect with Green Tie*, *Detectives* 1912, *Il Candelaio* 1912,[68] *Design for Box Lid* 1912, *Movement in Thirds* 1912, and *Dinah* (date unknown) – and the portfolio of eleven sketches of *Fishermen and Port Hangers-on* (date unknown).[69] Whilst not necessarily his first choice – 'Some of Lewis' things I like very much better than others'[70] – after consulting with Pound and deliberating whether to send the unsold Lewis works back for a selection, he decided to keep what was in New York. He bargained with all the artists on prices.[71] These relatively unknown painters, struggling with the additional wartime strictures, all accepted Quinn's offers.

Quinn did not acquire everything. He sent the avant-garde bookstore, Sunwise Turn, the remaining unsold works: Wadsworth's paintings *Blackpool* c.1914–15, *Dry Dock* 1915, and *Isle of Dogs* (date unknown), his drawings, *Centrifuge* 1915 and *Enclosure* 1915, and twenty-seven woodcuts, together with Dismorr's drawings, *Edinburgh* (date unknown), *Edinburgh Castle* 1914–15 (no.66), and *Spey Valley* (date unknown).[72] They attracted no buyers. Finally, Quinn posted these last works back to Wadsworth, sending the Dismorr drawings to his care.[73]

While Vorticism did not gain currency in the United States, the Penguin Club exhibition is a landmark for the movement. Quinn continued to collect Lewis and Gaudier-Brzeska. In the wake of his untimely death in 1927, his works were auctioned, and some made their way into American collections. In this way, the Penguin Club show disseminated Vorticist works in the United States. More importantly, the exhibition is a document of the powerful Pound–Quinn collaboration, an alliance that provided indispensable support to the Vorticist movement during its short life.

NOTES

I am grateful to Guggenheim Museum Curatorial Interns Emma Enderby as well as Natalia Lauricella and Katherine Boccard for their tireless assistance copying the Quinn Papers at the New York Public Library (hereafter NYPL) and fact-checking respectively. I also thank Mark Antliff for identifying and locating several artworks discussed in the essay. I must acknowledge the NYPL, especially the use of the Wertheim Study room, without which my research would not have been possible.

All artwork titles cited from the Quinn correspondence or his ledgers are reproduced as they appear in the originals. When works have been securely identified, their dates and present title (if different) are noted. On occasion, dates differ from those given in the illustrated Penguin Club catalogue checklist. Some of the letters cited also are reproduced in Harriet Zinnes (ed.), *Ezra Pound and the Visual Arts* (New York: New Directions, 1980), but here I have quoted the original documents.

1 'Vorticism: The Latest Cult of Rebel Artists', *New York Times*, 9 August 1914, p.SM10.

2 For the Penguin Club exhibition, see Richard Cork, *Vorticism and Abstract Art in the First Machine Age*, vol.2 (Berkeley: University of California Press, 1976), pp.490–5. See also Rebecca Beasley, *Ezra Pound and the Visual Culture of Modernism* (Cambridge: Cambridge University Press, 2007), pp.141–4.

3 For Ezra Pound's early years in London, see James J. Wilhelm, *Ezra Pound in London and Paris, 1908–1925* (University Park: Pennsylvania State University Press, 1990) and Robert M. Crunden, *American Salons: Encounters with European Modernism, 1885–1917* (New York: Oxford University Press, 1993), pp.195–273.

4 Ezra Pound, 'A Blast from London', *The Dial*, 16 January 1915, pp.40–1.

5 For Wyndham Lewis, see Paul Edwards, *Wyndham Lewis: Painter and Writer* (New Haven: Yale University Press, 2000) and Tom Normand, *Wyndham Lewis the Artist: Holding the Mirror up to Politics* (Cambridge: Cambridge University Press, 1992).

6 For John Quinn's biography, see B.L. Reid, *The Man from New York: John Quinn and his Friends* (New York: Oxford University Press, 1968) and Judith Zilczer, *'The Noble Buyer': John Quinn, Patron of the Avant-garde*, exh. cat. (Washington, DC: Smithsonian Institution Press, 1978).

7 John Quinn to Gwen John, 5 January 1911, Quinn Papers, NYPL. All the Quinn correspondence and ledgers cited are from the Quinn Papers at the NYPL.

8 Quinn to Ezra Pound, 25 February 1915, and Ezra Pound, 'Affirmations 3: Jacob Epstein', *The New Age*, vol.16, no.12 (21 January 1915), pp.380–2.

9 Ezra Pound, 'Affirmations 5: Gaudier-Brzeska', *The New Age*, vol.16, no.14 (4 February 1915), pp.409–11.

10 Quinn to Pound, 27 July 1915, and in a cable dated 24 August 1915. A drawn-out negotiation with the unbalanced Sophie Brzeska – with Pound acting as mediator – yielded few works. See Roger Cole, *Gaudier-Brzeska: Artist and Myth* (Bristol: Sansom & Co., 1995), pp.128–44.

11 Dating for the Wyndham Lewis works throughout this essay relies on Walter Michel, *Wyndham Lewis: Paintings and Drawings* (Berkeley: University of California Press, 1971), unless otherwise noted.

12 Pound to Quinn, 18 April 1915. The article was Pound, 'Wyndham Lewis', *The Egoist*, vol.1, no.12 (15 June 1914), pp.233–4.

13 Pound to Quinn, 18 April 1915.

14 This is titled *Ink Drawing – 'Early Kermess'* in the Penguin catalogue. Michel identifies it as *Kermesse*.

15 Cork identifies this work as likely being *Composition* (now in the Tate collection, dated 1913) and dates it 1913–14. Richard Cork, *Vorticism and Abstract Art in the First Machine Age*, vol.1 (Berkeley: University of California Press, 1976), pp.126, 305n.91.

16 'I cabled a reply at once naming £30, which sum would be due Lewis for Blasts and the three drawings, (one ink, two in colours) which I had ordered for you, as per former correspondence'. Pound to Quinn, 23 December 1915. The drawing titles are listed in Quinn's ledger, p.186.

17 Pound to Quinn, 11 August 1915.

18 Quinn to Pound, 26 August 1915. The Lewis and Saunders works he purchased in 1915 were shipped in April and arrived in New York on 6 May 1916. Quinn to Pound, 10 June 1916.

19 Pound to Quinn, 7 September 1915.

20 Pound cabled Quinn on 17 December 1915. 'Lewis Enlisted Needs Money Debts = Pound'. Quinn answered, 'Please cable best price Lewis Kermess and two or three other important and representative works against immediate payment London draft'. Quinn to Pound, 15 January 1916. Pound responded, 'Kermess eighty pounds next recommend five drawings ten pounds each all one hundred twenty pounds'. Pound to Quinn, by 19 January 1916.

21 'However I am not chosing [sic] your 5. but leaving it to you in N.Y.' Pound to Quinn, 12 March 1916. Quinn did not initially keep *Kermesse* as it appeared for sale in the Penguin catalogue. This money was applied to the cost of the other works he chose. See receipt from Wyndham Lewis sent via Pound to Quinn 'Received of Ezra Pound £40 (forty pounds) as part of payment for drawings purachased [sic] by John Quinn. £140 to be paid in future on a deal for £300 worth of drawings which is to replace former agreement for purachase [sic] of Kermes [sic] and five drawings'. 2 September 1916.

22 Quinn said he would take it in his 27 July 1915 letter. The receipt signed by Frederick Etchells, confirming payment of £5 for 'Drawing of Head', is included in Pound to Quinn, 23 August 1915. The Etchells was shipped with the works for the Penguin exhibition. Cork assigns c.1913 as the date: Cork 1976, vol.1, pp.112, 305n49. Cork's identification and dating of the Penguin works has been indispensable.

23 Pound to Quinn, 13 July 1915, and Quinn to Pound, 27 July 1915.

24 Quinn to Pound, 27 July 1915.

25 Pound to Quinn, 23 August 1915.

26 Ibid.

27 See Quinn to Pound, 2 March 1916; Pound to Quinn, 18 March 1916; Quinn to Pound, 20 March 1916; and Pound to Quinn, 4 April 1916.

28 Pound to Quinn, 13 April 1916.

29 Pound to Quinn, 23 August 1915.

30 Pound to Quinn, 11 April 1917.

31 Cork identifies this title and date in Cork 1976, vol.2, pp.14, 300n57.

32 Quinn's instructions to Pound give a sense of what this entailed: 'Now as to packing the "representative Vorticist show": The whole thing can be charged to and paid for at this end ... The best packers are G.W. Sheldon & Co. ... Of course the works should be (a) insured against war and marine risk and (b) there should be a consular invoice that they are original works of art ... [Jack] Knewstub of the Chenil Gallery might take charge of the packing and shipping and consular declaration and insurance'. Quinn to Pound, 11 February 1916.

33 See his long letters to Quinn, 18 March, 25 April, 29 April, and 26 May 1916.

34 Quinn to Pound, 7 July 1916.

35 Pound to Quinn, 19 July 1916.

36 Quinn's ledger, pp.187–8.

37 Now *Planners: Happy Day* (Tate). Dating per Tate.

38 Now *Two Women* (Arts Council Collection, London).

39 Date depends on whether, more likely, it is *Timon (Banquet Scene)* now *Timon of Athens, Act I. Banquet Scene* (Courtauld Gallery, London), or *Drawing (second phase of Timon)*, which Cork identifies as possibly *Timon of Athens* 1913–14 (private collection). *Vorticism and its Allies*, exh. cat. (London: Arts Council of Great Britain, 1974), p.77. I am thankful to Paul Edwards for bringing the location of the former work to my attention.

40 Now *Design for Programme Cover: Kermesse* (British Museum, London). I am indebted to Edwards who also flagged this work's location.

41 Now *Centauress* (Cecil Higgins Art Gallery, Bedford).

42 Now *The Dancers* (Manchester City Art Galleries).

43 Dating per Tate.

44 The Penguin catalogue lists this work as 1912, and Michel undated.

45 Quinn to Pound, 25 August 1916.

46 The dates for Wadsworth's prints are all from Jeremy Greenwood, *The Graphic Work of Edward Wadsworth* (Woodbridge: Wood Lea Press, 2002). *View of a Town* could either be *Bradford, View of a Town 1914* or *View of a Town* 1916.

47 See Quinn to Pound, 5 August 1916, and Quinn's ledger, p.190. *New Castle* corresponds to *Newcastle*. *Fustian Town* corresponds to *Fustian Town: Hebden Bridge*, whereas *Railway Embankment* is *Platelayers Sheds*.

48 Quinn to Pound, 12 August 1916. Dating per Penguin catalogue.

49 Cork suggests it could be *Study for Dancers*. Cork 1976, vol.1, pp.188, 308n9.

50 Ibid., pp.189–90, 308n16.

51 This is *The Pigeon-Juggler* c.1915. Cork 1976, vol.2, pp.406, 561n7.

52 Dating per Cecil Higgins Art Gallery, Bedford.

53 Quinn to Pound, 5 August 1916, and Quinn's ledger, pp.189, 191. Dating for *Eccentric* is from the Penguin catalogue.

54 Quinn to Pound, 12 August and 25 August 1916 and Quinn's ledger, p.189. Dates for *Posts and Telegraphs* and *Single Stick* from the Penguin catalogue. Cork identifies *Stilts* as possibly *Gouache: Stilts (?)* 1914–15.Cork 1976, vol.2, pp.404–5, 561n4. Now *Composition* 1914–15 (British Council Collection).

55 Quinn to Pound, 1 July 1916.

56 Quinn to Pound, 12 August 1916.

57 Quinn to Pound, 25 August 1916. Saunders dates are per The David and Alfred Smart Museum of Art, The University of Chicago.

58 He paid over $460. See Quinn's ledger, pp.192–4.

59 Quinn to Pound, 12 January 1917.

60 Frederick W. Eddy, 'News of the Art World', *The World*, 28 January 1917, p.10M.

61 Quinn to Lewis, 15 March 1917.

62 Pound to Quinn, 19 July 1916.

63 Dating for Wadsworth's paintings and drawings relies on Jonathan Black, *Edward Wadsworth: Form, Feeling, and Calculation. The Complete Paintings and Drawings* (London: Philip Wilson, 2005), unless otherwise noted.

64 Cork identifies *Jen* as *Jeu* 1915. Cork 1976, vol.2, pp.493, 381, 560n20.

65 Ibid., pp.326–7, 561n9.

66 See Quinn to Pound, 15 March 1917, for *Rotterdam*, *Jen*, and *Overbacks*. He adds offers on *Hyde Park*, *English Comedian*, and *Combat* in a 29 April 1917 letter to Pound. *The English Comedian* date is per the Victoria and Albert Museum, London.

67 Edwards, *Wyndham Lewis*, p.128.

68 Date is from the Penguin catalogue.

69 Quinn to Lewis, 15 March 1917. Portfolio title is from Quinn's ledger, p.195. Michel titles it *Sketches of Fishermen and Bargees*. Per note 39, above, either *Timon (Banquet Scene)* or, more probably, *Drawing (second phase of Timon)* remains unaccounted for in the ledgers. As Quinn did not send it back, one can speculate that perhaps a clerical error confused the latter work with *Timon* (a later drawing from the *Timon* series).

70 Quinn to Pound, 29 April 1917.

71 Ibid. See prices and counter-offers in Quinn's ledger, pp.195–6.

72 Quinn to Edward Wadsworth, 7 June 1917. Cork identifies *Edinburgh Castle* as possibly *Landscape: Edinburgh Castle* c.1914–15. Cork 1976, vol.2, pp.418, 561n38. Now *Edinburgh Castle*1914–15, Victoria and Albert Museum, London.

73 Quinn to Wadsworth, 14 May 1919.

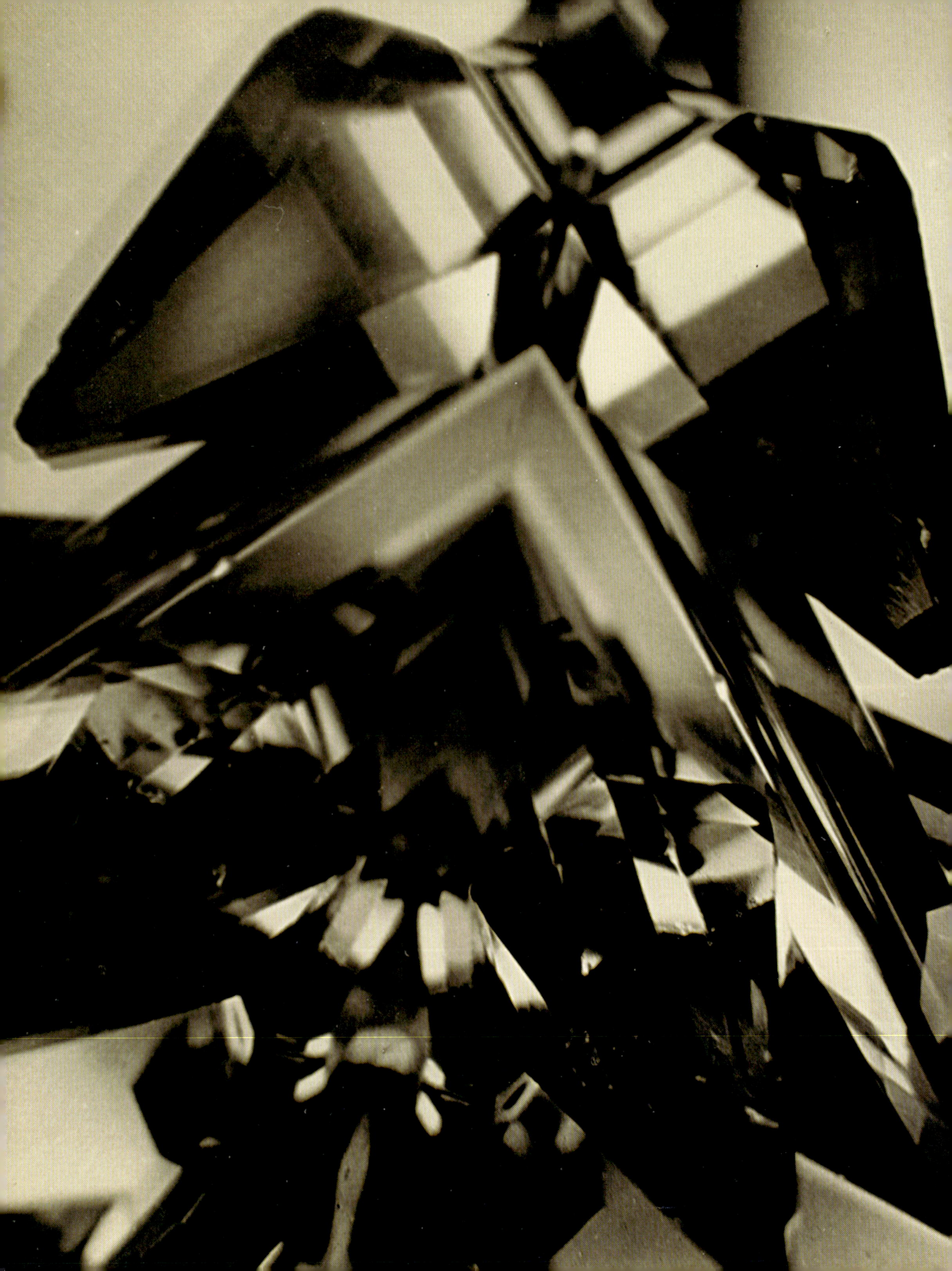

ALVIN LANGDON COBURN AND THE VORTOGRAPHS

Tom Normand

The 'vortographs' (what is there after all in a name)
Alvin Langdon Coburn 1917[1]

In late November 1960 Alvin Langdon Coburn was in correspondence with the eminent photographic historian Helmut Gernsheim. On 17 November Gernsheim wrote: 'I am just putting the finishing touches to a book on Aesthetic Trends in Photography, to be published next autumn by Faber and Faber. You figure in it several times: as a member of the Photo-Secession, with your portraits of Men of Mark, and as the first person to make an abstract photograph.'[2] Gernsheim's list of achievements certainly acknowledges Coburn's importance to the history of photography, noting his role as an esteemed Pictorialist, a portraitist of distinction, and an innovator of extraordinary talent. But, the subsequent correspondence highlights Coburn's desire, late in life, to be fully recognised as the progenitor of photographic abstraction. He wrote:

> I expect you have seen the recent edition of 'CONTEMPORARY PHOTOGRAPHER' entitled 'The Sense of Abstraction' in which one of my Vortographs is acknowledged to be the earliest example of Abstraction in Photography![3]

In a later, undated letter, Gernsheim replied: 'I have not seen the recent issue of 'The Contemporary Photographer' to which you refer, but I had already independently arrived at the conclusion that your Vortographs were the first abstract photographs.'[4] He then asked a number of questions about the naming, making, and mode of reproducing the Vortographs to which Coburn replied:

> 1. Ezra Pound invented the title of Vorticists for a group of poets and painters of which he was one of the chief exponants [sic]. Vortographs are Vorticist-Photographs!
> 2. They were made by placing the lense [sic] of a camera within a triangular tube lined with mirrors.
> 3. With abstract pictures, if they are a good pattern, it does not see [sic] to me to greatly matter if they are reversed, or which way is the top![5]

This last, astonishing confession was in response to Gernsheim having noted that the Vortograph reproduced in Beaumont Newhall's book *On Photography: A Source Book of Photo History in Facsimile* (1956) had been printed

Detail from Alvin Langdon Coburn *Vortograph* 1917 (fig.42)

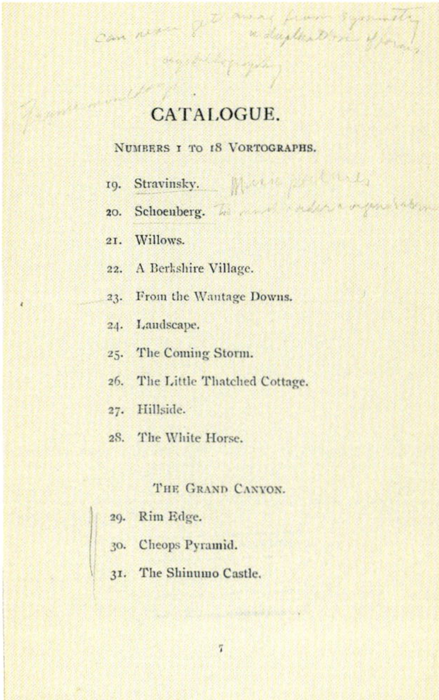

CATALOGUE.

NUMBERS 1 TO 18 VORTOGRAPHS.

19. Stravinsky.
20. Schoenberg.
21. Willows.
22. A Berkshire Village.
23. From the Wantage Downs.
24. Landscape.
25. The Coming Storm.
26. The Little Thatched Cottage.
27. Hillside.
28. The White Horse.

THE GRAND CANYON.

29. Rim Edge.
30. Cheops Pyramid.
31. The Shinumo Castle.

7

fig.38
The Camera Club exhibition checklist of Vortographs and paintings by Alvin Langdon Coburn, 1917

in reverse, but Gernsheim was to correct this error in his *Creative Photography: Aesthetic Trends, 1839–1960* (1962), in which he noted that 'at the end of World War 1 under the influence of his friend the Cubist painter Max Weber, Alvin Langdon Coburn felt a similar need to experiment.'[6] Indeed, as early as the end of 1916, Coburn had adapted the technology of photography by attaching a 'triangular tube lined with mirrors' to his camera lens, and with this not-so-simple act, he revolutionised the camera's method of production and created what he was pleased to call the 'first abstract photographs'.

Interestingly, this particular narrative of the Vortographs contains three principal protagonists: Coburn and Pound, two American émigrés working in London during 1917; as well as Weber, an American born in Russian-occupied Poland who had spent the years from 1905 to 1909 working in Paris and who became a figurehead in the New York avant-garde in the period around the First World War. Their core involvement is notable because the theme of the émigré is central to Vorticism, which, though a London-based movement, included individuals either alien to British society or on the margins of the cultural establishment. In part this cultural difference provided the platform for this radical and incendiary movement and offered an opening for the challenge that was the Vortograph.

Coburn had immigrated to Britain from the United States in 1912. Thirty years old, he was already a singular voice in photography and had been a prodigy in this field, his work having been exhibited in his native Boston before his sixteenth birthday. He had travelled to London with photographer F. Holland Day in 1899, where he met with Frederick Evans and later showed work at the Royal Photographic Society. In 1902 he opened his first studio in New York and eventually became a member of Alfred Stieglitz's Photo-Secession movement. Simultaneously, he joined the Linked Ring Brotherhood, a London-based Secessionist group that propagated fine-art photography. His reputation was such that he encountered the intelligentsia of his age and celebrated its members in a series of outstanding portraits, eventually published as *Men of Mark* in 1913. His portfolio by this period included some Pictorialist masterpieces, a number of exceptional views of the Grand Canyon and Yosemite National Park, and an extraordinarily modernist project interrogating the abstract urban space of New York, most celebrated in *The Octopus* 1912 (fig.39). With these cityscapes Coburn came closest to the sentiment of Vorticist painting. *The Octopus* and Coburn's epic *House of A Thousand Windows* 1912 were both exhibited at the Goupil Gallery in London during the October 1913 show *Camera Pictures by Alvin Langdon Coburn*. Shortly thereafter Wyndham Lewis produced his archetypal Vorticist works *New York* 1914, *Workshop* c.1914–15 (no.19), and *The Crowd* 1914–15 (no.7), all of which demonstrate a debt to Coburn's vision.[7] In this respect at least, Coburn might be described as a progenitor of Vorticism.

An insistent Anglophile, Coburn moved permanently to Britain, residing first in London. As part of the expatriate community he met Pound, whose portrait he first took in October 1913 (fig.1 on p.16). By that time, Pound had lived in London for five years, and his restless creativity had marked him as one of the most ambitious modern poets and a cultural entrepreneur. In late 1913 Pound joined Lewis in founding what would become the Vorticist movement, and their combined energies shaped it until its demise in 1919. Pound introduced Coburn to Vorticist rhetoric, and this initiation was sealed when Coburn made portraits of Jacob Epstein, Lewis, and Edward Wadsworth in the following years (figs.2–4 on pp.16–17). Pound, moreover, identified the camera's potential to advance the movement's machine aesthetic, especially during the period when Vorticism was dissipating under the contingencies of the war. In September 1916 Pound wrote to his father, 'Coburn and I have invented Vortography. The idea is one no longer need photograph what is in front of the camera, but can use one's element of design.'[8] This claim to partial authorship of the invention and controlling interest in the 'idea' is somewhat of a conceit, but there is little doubt that between September 1916 and early

January 1917, Pound was midwife to the birth of a purely abstract photographic form.

Coburn, however, was the parent, and his intuition and ambition occasioned these extraordinary works. The raw history of this development has been part of Coburn's testament. In his edited autobiography,[9] Coburn notes:

> It was in 1914 that Wyndham Lewis founded the avant-garde movement named by the American painter and writer Ezra Pound 'Vorticist'. I did not see why my own movement should lag behind modern art trends, so I aspired to make abstract pictures with the camera. For this purpose I devised the Vortoscope late in 1916. The instrument was composed of three mirrors fastened together in the form of a triangle. The mirrors acted as a prism splitting the image formed by the lens into segments. The objects I photographed were usually bits of wood and crystal.[10]

In fact Coburn had presaged this radical experimentation in a statement from 1916. Writing in *Photograms of the Year 1916*, he presented a declaration of intent:

> being interested particularly in photography, it has occurred to me, why should not the camera throw off the shackles of conventional representation and attempt something fresh and untried? Why should not its subtle rapidity be utilised to study movement? Why not repeated successive exposures of an object in motion in the same plate? Why should not perspective be studied from angles hitherto neglected or unobserved. Think of the joy of doing something which it would be impossible to classify, or to tell which was the top and which the bottom![11]

In the conservative world of fine-art photography, this was sedition, but Coburn proceeded to realise his aspiration in winter 1916.

Coburn produced more than forty Vortographs during his period of interest in this project. In part they conform to the Pictorialist aesthetic, for Coburn championed the Pinkham and Smith 'Semi-Achromatic' lens. It was most probably to this that he added his mirror device. Because of his soft-focus lenses, his Vortographs are angular and geometric like Vorticist painting but diffuse and 'feathered' in their form and

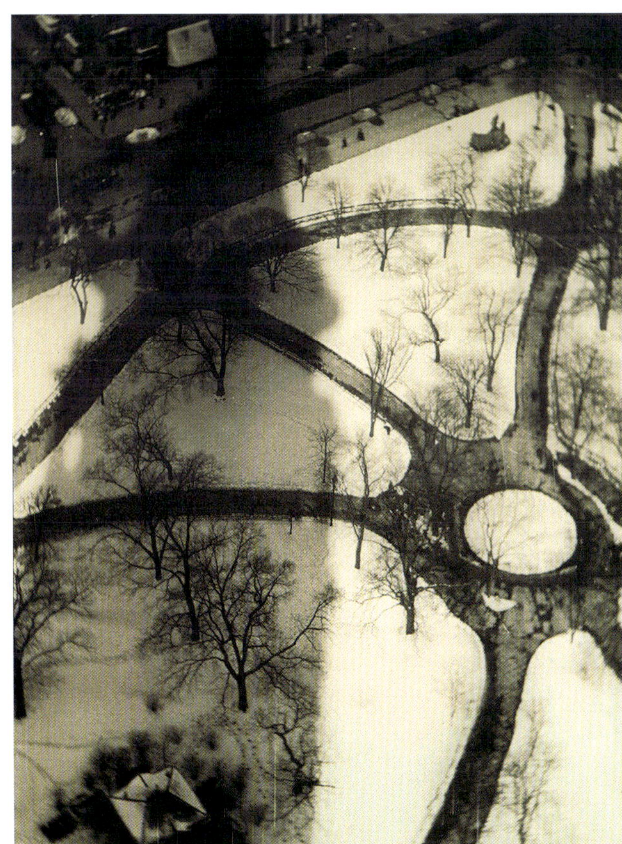

Fig.39
Alvin Langdon Coburn
The Octopus, New York 1912
Platinum print
41.8 x 31.8 cm
Metropolitan Museum of Art, New York. Ford Motor Company Collection, Gift of Ford Motor Company and John C. Waddell, 1987

shape.[12] Unlike Pictorialist photographs, they eschew narrative and sentiment and instead conjure a world of abstract design. *Vortograph* 1917 (no.83) for example, is a kaleidoscopic whirl of intense highlights and dark fissures leavened by triangular passages and strata in tones of grey. The 'bits of wood and crystal' were set on a glass tabletop in order to create maximum light refraction intensifying the feeling of explosive energy and movement. These characteristics correlate to other Vorticist experiments, which may be equally viewed within the context of Futurist art and photography.[13]

In January 1917 the Camera Club in London invited Coburn to show his work,[14] and he accepted with the proviso that there would be no conditions as to what he might exhibit. He displayed eighteen Vortographs and thirteen paintings, including *Stravinsky* c.1915 and *Schoenberg* c.1915, along with English landscapes, and three paintings of scenes from the Grand Canyon.

The catalogue cover was decorated with an abstract design by Coburn (figs.40, 41) that mirrored some of the characteristics of his Vortographs. His insistence on including his paintings caused a significant rift with Pound. In the catalogue's introductory essay, Pound began with a hostile dismissal of Coburn's graphic work:

> This note concerns only the Vortographs and not the paintings in this exhibition. Mr Coburn's paintings were done before the invention of the vortescope [sic]. He has attached no label to them, but they are, roughly speaking, post-impressionist. It should be quite clear that the paintings were not done in agreement with the work of the 'Vorticists', and that there is no connection between Mr. Coburn, as painter, and the group known as the Vorticist group.[15]

'Roughly speaking' indeed, but Pound clearly saw a recidivism in Coburn's paintings that mitigated against the Vortographs' presumed radical intent. Nevertheless, Pound's own analysis of the images tended to be couched in formalist terms, which would not have been out of place in the context of Post-Impressionist aesthetics: 'The vortescope [sic] is useless to a man who cannot recognise a beautiful arrangement of forms on a surface'.[16] In fact, this decorative formalism was echoed in Coburn's reflections on his Vortographs, but he enthusiastically defended his paintings in an addendum to Pound's catalogue essay. He wrote, 'I feel rather hurt at the manner in which he brushes aside my paintings' while confessing that 'they are not, however, the most important part of the present show. This will go down to posterity as the first example of Vortography'.[17]

The historic importance of the world's first abstract photographs was greeted with something less than rapture. Antony Guest reviewed the exhibition for *Photo-Era* and commented on the 'perplexity among the general body of visitors to this show. Indeed, at the time of [his] visit, there was some who held that the work was not to be taken seriously, and that Mr. Coburn was laughing in his sleeve at a bewildered

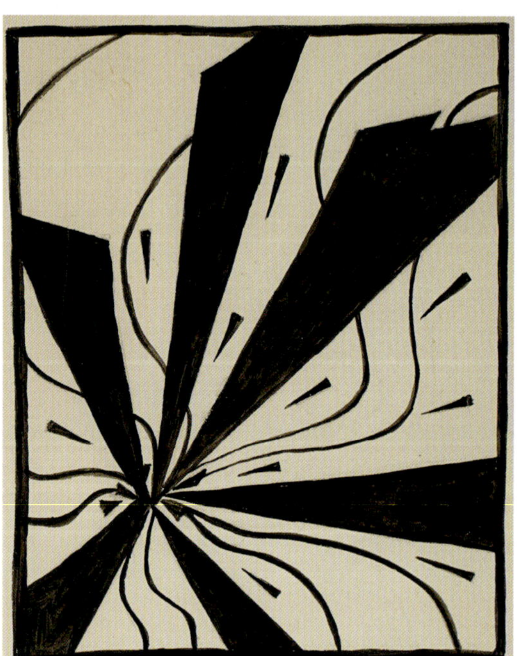

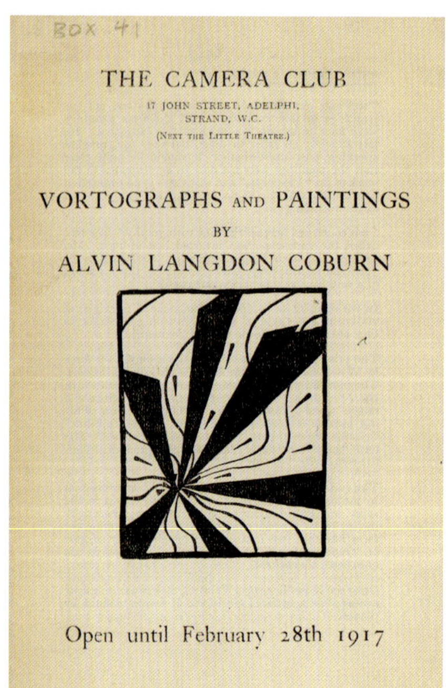

BOX 41

THE CAMERA CLUB
17 JOHN STREET, ADELPHI, STRAND, W.C.
(NEXT THE LITTLE THEATRE.)

VORTOGRAPHS AND PAINTINGS
BY
ALVIN LANGDON COBURN

Open until February 28th 1917

Fig.40
Alvin Langdon Coburn
Cover design for *Vortographs and Paintings by Alvin Langdon Coburn* exhibition catalogue, The Camera Club, London 1917
Ink on paper
16.4 x 13.2 cm
George Eastman House, Rochester, NY

Fig.41
Front cover of *Vortographs and Paintings by Alvin Langdon Coburn*, exhibition catalogue, The Camera Club, London 1917

public'.[18] Even a publication as sympathetic to Coburn as *Photograms of the Year* could not resist this comic intimation: 'A very entertaining half-hour might be spent in finding out which way up Alvin Langdon Coburn's "A Vortograph" looks best.'[19] Following the London show, the exhibition travelled to the Scottish Photographic Pictorial Circle in Glasgow, and, naturally, 'not a few photographic pictorialists' brains have been in a whirl since coming in contact with the "new art"'.[20] Even Pound seemed to cool towards Coburn during the exhibition, for his lukewarm catalogue essay testified to a creeping indifference to the Vortographs.

Coburn's eagerness for the project also quickly waned, and, while he lived another five decades, this was his last great moment as a photographer. The precise reasons for Coburn's silence remain unresolved, but he moved from an engagement with avant-garde art towards an overwhelming interest in religious mysticism. In the years following the First World War, he became increasingly committed to Freemasonry, Rosicrucianism, the Hermetic Order of the Golden Dawn, and Eastern philosophical traditions. This withdrawal from creative photography and adoption of mystical speculation were features of his character and biography that he fully recognised. When reviewing his career in the *Photographic Journal* in 1962, Coburn noted:

> Friends have asked me why I have for many years ceased to devote my energies exclusively to photography. The answer is that I think spiritual concerns are more important, and that the art of the interior life is more vital and significant to the supreme and ultimate purpose of the human soul than any other activity. [21]

Here, the 'art of the interior life' created a fundamental barrier to his development as an avant-garde modernist, proselytizing Vorticist theory.

The fact is that Coburn was temperamentally misaligned with Vorticism. Writing to Gernsheim in relation to the editing of his autobiography, he requested:

> Dear Friend Gernsheim,
>
> There is just one thing that I am still not quite happy with about the book, and that is that there is no portrait in it of Diasetz Teitaro Suzuki. Do you think it might be possible to omit the portrait of Wyndham Lewis and put Suzuki in its place?[22]

Both portraits were included, but it remains significant that Coburn asked to replace Vorticism's co-founder with the foremost advocate of Zen and Shin Buddhism. Coburn was never predisposed towards the crypto-political aesthetic of Lewis and his acolytes, nor could he connect with its aggressive masculinity. Whereas Vorticism engaged modernity by developing machine aesthetics as a counterpoint to the world of machines, Coburn looked to disengage with the social currents of the age. For this reason his Vortographs parallel and obliquely reference Vorticist art rather than express its provocative, angular, hard-edged stasis.[23]

Likewise Coburn's Vortographs move towards a soft diffusion of form and subtle tonal gradation that allies them to a Pictorialist aesthetic informed by Post-Impressionism. Their abstraction is contingent on a decorative formalism that accents notions of design. In *Photograms of the Year 1916*, he speculated on the possibility of an abstract photography, remarking: 'In last year's exhibition of the Royal Photographic Society there was a little group of prints by American workers, mostly titled "Design". They were groups of various objects photographed because of their shape and colour value, and with no thought of their sentimental associations.'[24]

His comments are not the aggressive, declamatory prose of the Vorticist journal *Blast* (1914–15), and for all that Pound claimed partial authorship of the Vortographs and presented himself as their champion and interpreter, Coburn's fullest allegiance was, in fact, with the New York-based Weber. In the same article Coburn continued:

> Weber, the Cubist painter-poet, was responsible for the idea of these designs, and Weber is one of the most sincere artists that it has ever been my good fortune to meet. In his new book, 'Essays on Art', Weber says: 'To express moods that stir the emotions from within, as does music, the plastic artist, when he conceives of energetic rhythmic interlaced forms or units, should be much more moved than even by music. It is like cementing a thought, or arresting a perfect moment of time, or like giving body to space, or solidity to air, or coloured light to darkness.'[25]

Coburn had photographed Weber in 1911 when both were initiates in the Stieglitz circle. Moreover, after moving to London, Coburn alerted Roger Fry to Weber's work and arranged for the publication of his poems.[26]

Weber's relationship to modernism paralleled Coburn's fractured vision. An innovative artist, he explored Cubism early in its history and was one of the first Americans to seek an aesthetic language that might properly express the energy of that most totemic of contemporary city spaces, New York. *Rush Hour, New York* 1915, a prime example of a dynamic, abstracted cityscape, presents an equivalent to Coburn's experiments of 1912[27] and remains the progenitor in painting of a modernist New York. Like Coburn, his sense of contemporary art was coloured by a formalism that shaded into mysticism, and he was a vocal advocate of the esoteric theory, or cult, of the Fourth Dimension. Both Coburn and Weber had, furthermore, been acolytes of Arthur Wesley Dow, the influential artist, photographer, and most especially educator. Coburn attended Dow's summer schools in Ipswich, Massachusetts, in 1902 and 1903 and was introduced to the formal aesthetics of Japanese art in that period.[28] Likewise, Weber was one of the countless American painters who learned Dow's theories while attending the Pratt Institute in Brooklyn, at age sixteen. In both cases Dow's influential aesthetic treatise *Composition: A Series of Exercises in Art Structure for the Use of Students and Teachers*, first published in 1899, reinforced their orientation towards a mystical formalism.

In Weber, Coburn saw a kindred spirit and significant artist who would take his own graphic work seriously. The correspondence between the two continued throughout 1917 and 1918 when Coburn, writing from Harlech in Wales, confessed:

> The 'Vortographs' (what is there after all in a name) will I am sure interest you. In them I feel that I have made a real contribution to the possibilities of photography, but most people do not seem to understand them at all. Not long ago I had a little show of them. It consisted of 'abstract' photographs and 'realistic' paintings, but no one saw what I was driving at in this connection either![29]

While Coburn viewed his paintings as 'realistic', the evidence points to a Post-Impressionist aesthetic governed by flat bands of vivid colour.[30] His satisfaction with this medium was evidenced elsewhere in the same letter: 'Photography still interests me but more and more I am drifting towards paint. I think it is the immediate result that I like, and the color!'[31] Here Coburn eschews photography's technical and mechanical aspects, 'drifting towards' the contemplative interaction with nature that might be realised in paint. Weber supported this development, just as he had encouraged an aesthetic based on the idea of 'design'. Given these conditions, Coburn's Vortographs were experiments in a decorative formalism one remove from the combative contest with modernity that provided Vorticism with its character and definition.

It is important to understand Coburn's Vortographs within this frame. He pushed the Pictorialist approach towards an interest in urban and modern life, subjects from the period circa 1909. Simultaneously he engaged in portraiture and subject pictures that accented a nascent spirituality and mysticism. His encounter with Pound directed him towards the Vorticist avant-garde and encouraged his desire to experiment with photographic techniques. Though evidently in contrast with the movement's core values, the result was the

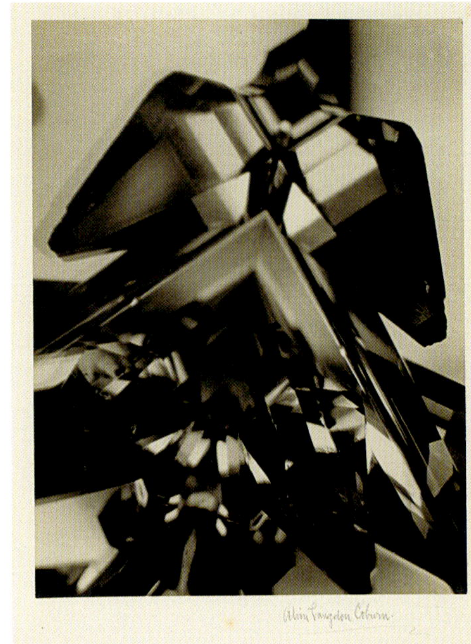

Fig.42
Alvin Langdon Coburn
Vortograph 1917
Gelatin silver print
image: 26.6 x 20.4 cm
[C]

'Vortographs' whose aesthetic root was in Post-Impressionist theory, partially supported by Coburn's friendship with Weber. This Post-Impressionism, a contemplative ideal based on the projection of 'moods and emotions', united Coburn's abstract photography to the sentiment evidenced in his Pictorialist work. All of this was directed against the industrialised, urban, mechanistic, secular, and socially expanding world that was the contemporary reality: the world embraced, explored, and contested by Vorticism. Coburn was in flight from this modernity at the very point when he created the most modern and unremittingly modernist vision in photography. His 'first abstract photographs' then were not only a triumph of his photographic imagination but also a portent of his retreat to 'the art of the interior life'.

Nonetheless, the astonishing audacity of this photographic project, the product of three minds, perhaps, all American and in their way émigrés, emerged out of the confluence of a confrontation with modernity, the ambition of an abstract modernism, and the gyre of a romantic mysticism that created the most inventive and daring of innovations in the creative arts. Coburn was surely, as Gernsheim insisted, 'the first person to make an abstract photograph' and his Vortographs mark the moment when photography first realised its potential as an avant-garde intervention.

NOTES

1 Alvin Langdon Coburn to Max Weber, 2 October 1917, Weber Papers, Archives of American Art, Smithsonian Institution, Washington, DC.

2 Helmut Gernsheim to Coburn, 17 November 1960, Harry Ransom Center, University of Texas, Austin. All correspondence between Gernsheim and Coburn cited in this essay is from this archive.

3 Coburn to Gernsheim, 20 November 1960.

4 Gernsheim to Coburn, undated.

5 Coburn to Gernsheim, 29 November 1960.

6 Helmut Gernsheim, *Creative Photography: Aesthetic Trends, 1839–1960* (New York: Dover Publications, 1991), p.161.

7 For the relationship between Coburn's photographs and Wyndham Lewis's work, see Richard Cork, *Vorticism and Abstract Art in the First Machine Age*, vol.2 (Berkeley: University of California Press, 1976), pp.495–505, and Paul Edwards, *Wyndham Lewis: Painter and Writer* (New Haven: Yale University Press, 2000), p.128.

8 Ezra Pound to Homer L. Pound, 22 September 1916, in Harriet Zinnes (ed.), *Ezra Pound and the Visual Arts* (New York: New Directions, 1980) p.293.

9 While Coburn is the acknowledged author of his autobiography, Helmut and Alison Gernsheim served as ghostwriters.

10 *Alvin Langdon Coburn, Photographer: An Autobiography*, ed. Helmut and Alison Gernsheim (London: Faber, 1966), p.102.

11 Alvin Langdon Coburn, 'The Future of Pictorial Photography', *Photograms of the Year 1916: An Annual Review of the World's Pictorial Photographic Work*, ed. F.J. Mortimer (London: Hazell, Watson & Viney, Ltd., 1916), p.23.

12 The appropriate contrast, first noted by Pound, might be with Edward Wadsworth's woodcuts. *The Letters of Ezra Pound, 1907–1941* (London: Faber and Faber, 1951), p.158. In his private collection now housed at George Eastman House, Rochester, New York, Coburn held at least five Wadsworth prints including *Rotterdam* 1914 (no.38) and *Little London City* 1914, all archetypal examples of the uncompromising hard-edged angularity of Vorticist art.

13 Anton Giulio Bragaglia, an Italian Futurist photographer, had begun exploring the idea of 'photodynamism' in 1911 and published two manifestoes of this multiexposure photography in 1912 and 1916.

14 The Camera Club offices in London were bombed during the Second World War, destroying all records of the exhibition.

15 [Ezra Pound], 'The Vortographs', in *Vortographs and Paintings by Alvin Langdon Coburn*, exh. cat. (London: The Camera Club, 1917), p.2.

16 Ibid., p.3.

17 Alvin Langdon Coburn, 'Postscript', ibid., p.6.

18 Antony Guest, 'A.L. Coburn's Vortographs', *Photo-Era*, nos.38–9 (May 1917), p.227.

19 F.J. Mortimer (ed.), *Photograms of the Year 1917–18: An Annual Review of the World's Pictorial Photographic Work* (London: Hazell, Watson & Viney, 1918), p.18.

20 See the unsigned reviews in the *Amateur Photographer* (30 April 1917) and *British Journal of Photography* (27 April 1917).

21 Alvin Langdon Coburn, 'Photographic Adventures', *Photographic Journal*, vol.102, no.5 (May 1962), p.158.

22 Coburn to Gernsheim, 2 March 1965.

23 For the disjuncture between the 'melting obfuscation of the Vortographs' and the 'solid definition' of Lewis' Vorticist paintings, see Cork 1976, vol.2, pp.501, 504.

24 Coburn, 'The Future of Pictorial Photography', p.23.

25 Ibid., pp.23–4.

26 See, especially, Frank Di Federico 'Alvin Langdon Coburn and the Genesis of Vortographs', *History of Photography*, vol.11, no.4 (October–December 1987), p.277.

27 See Susan Krane, 'Introduction', in Percy North, *Max Weber: The Cubist Decade 1910–1920*, exh. cat. (Atlanta: High Museum of Art, 1991), p.15, and Percy North, 'Max Weber: The Cubist Decade', ibid., pp.32–5.

28 See Mike Weaver, *Alvin Langdon Coburn: Symbolist Photographer* (New York: Aperture, 1986), pp.11–18.

29 Coburn to Weber, 2 October 1917. Coburn's emphasis.

30 See Coburn's watercolours in Nancy E. Green and Jessie Poesch, *Arthur Wesley Dow and the American Arts and Crafts* (New York: American Federation of Arts in association with Abrams, 2000).

31 Coburn to Weber, 2 October 1917.

PLATES

Introduction

The introductory section principally revolves around iconic works associated with Vorticism: Jacob Epstein's *Rock Drill* 1913–15, David Bomberg's *The Mud Bath* 1914, Henri Gaudier-Brzeska's *Hieratic Head of Ezra Pound* 1914, and Wyndham Lewis's *The Crowd* 1914–15. Neither Epstein nor Bomberg officially joined the group, but were credited by the Vorticists with shaping their mode of abstraction. Epstein's sculpture announces the group's embrace of machine aesthetics; Bomberg's focus on a public bath in London's East End foregrounds the Vorticist praxis of distilling representational imagery into abstract form; Gaudier-Brzeska's 'hieratic' visage registers their shared interest in primitivism; and Lewis's congested cityscape speaks to the Vorticists' engagement with contemporary politics. Whilst the Vorticists declared their movement to be resolutely English, there was exceptional diversity among those they championed: Epstein was a Jewish American émigré to England, Bomberg was also of Jewish heritage, Gaudier-Brzeska was a French expatriate, and the Canadian-born Lewis resided for many years in continental Europe before settling in London in late 1908. The poet Ezra Pound, the Vorticists' major literary spokesperson, was American. Thus the Vorticists were decidedly cosmopolitan in orientation, which accounts in part for their ambition to transform art on both sides of the Atlantic.

1
Henri Gaudier-Brzeska
Hieratic Head of Ezra Pound 1914
Marble
90.5 x 45.7 x 48.9 cm
[B2]

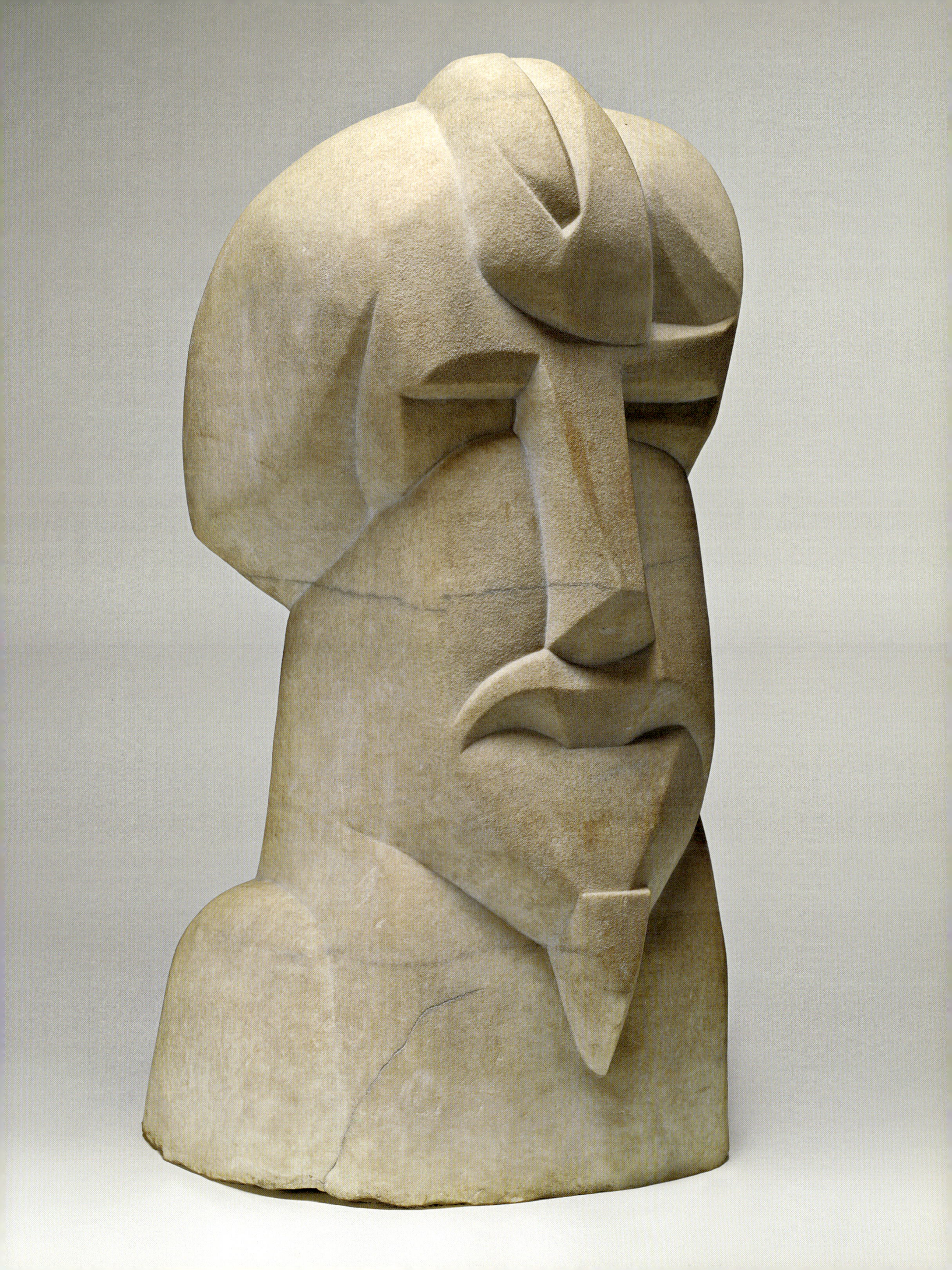

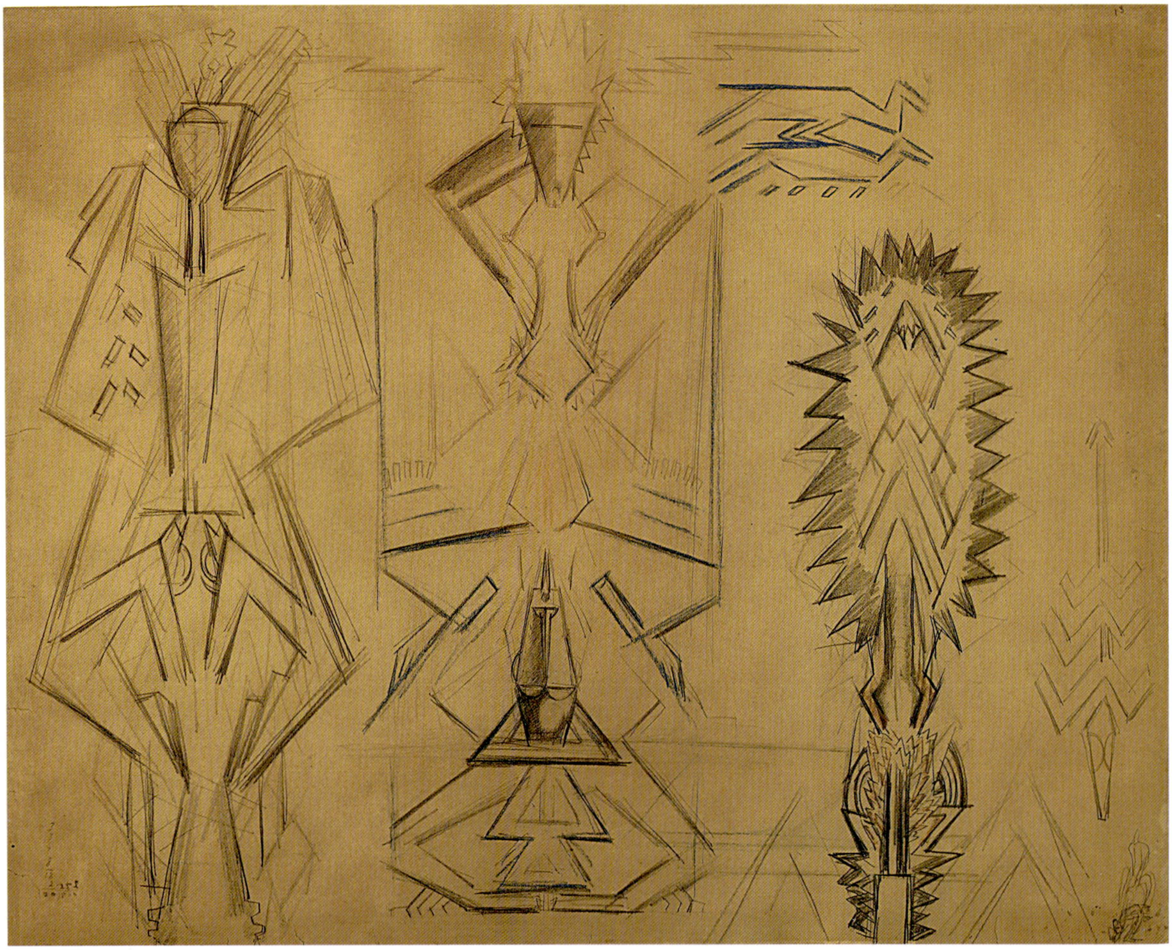

2

Jacob Epstein

Studies for 'Rock Drill'
'Venus' and 'Doves' c.1913
Crayon and pencil on paper
45.7 x 58.4 cm

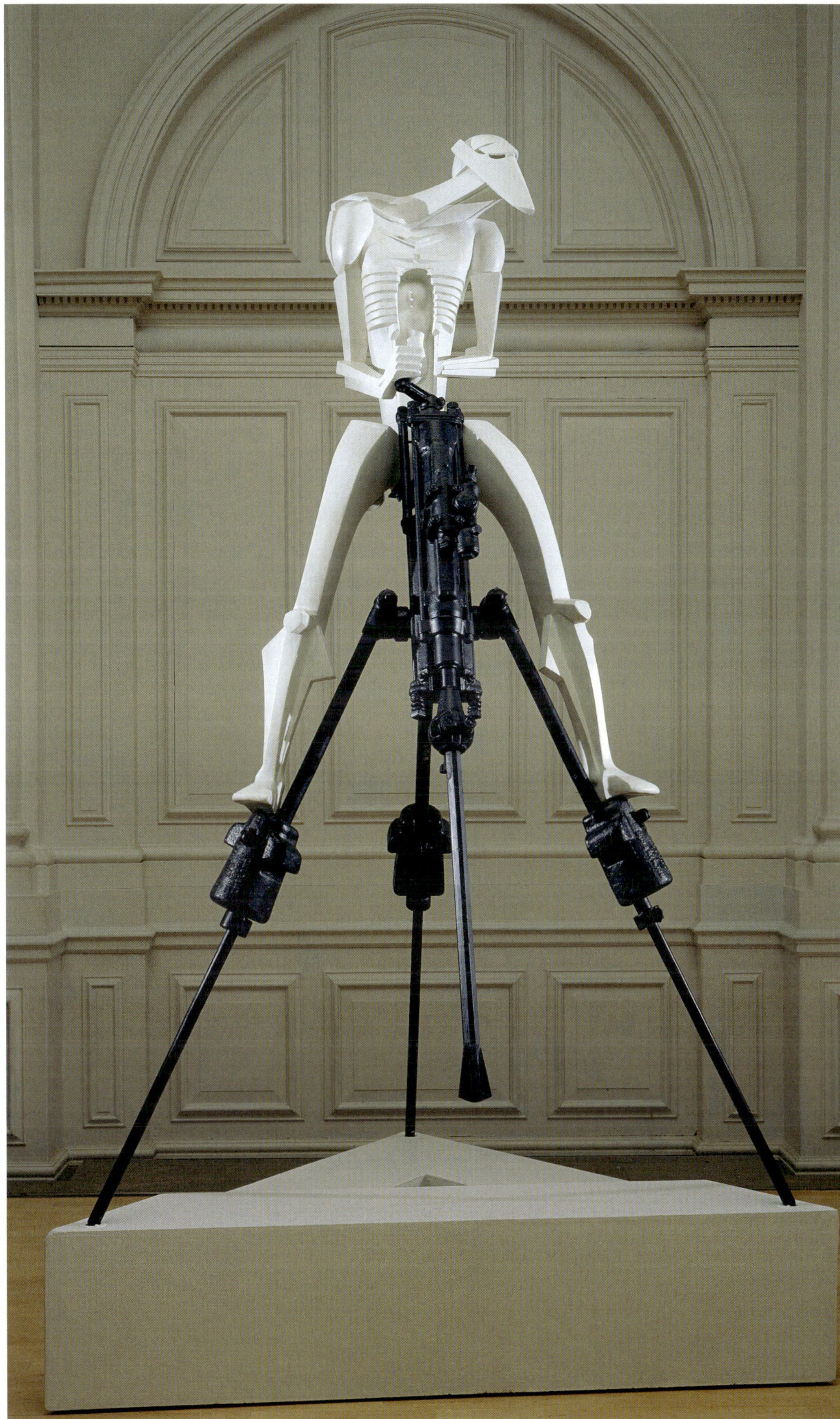

3
Jacob Epstein
Rock Drill 1913–15
[reconstruction by Ken Cook and Ann Christopher after the dismantled original, 1973–4]
Polyester resin, metal, and wood
205 x 141.5 cm

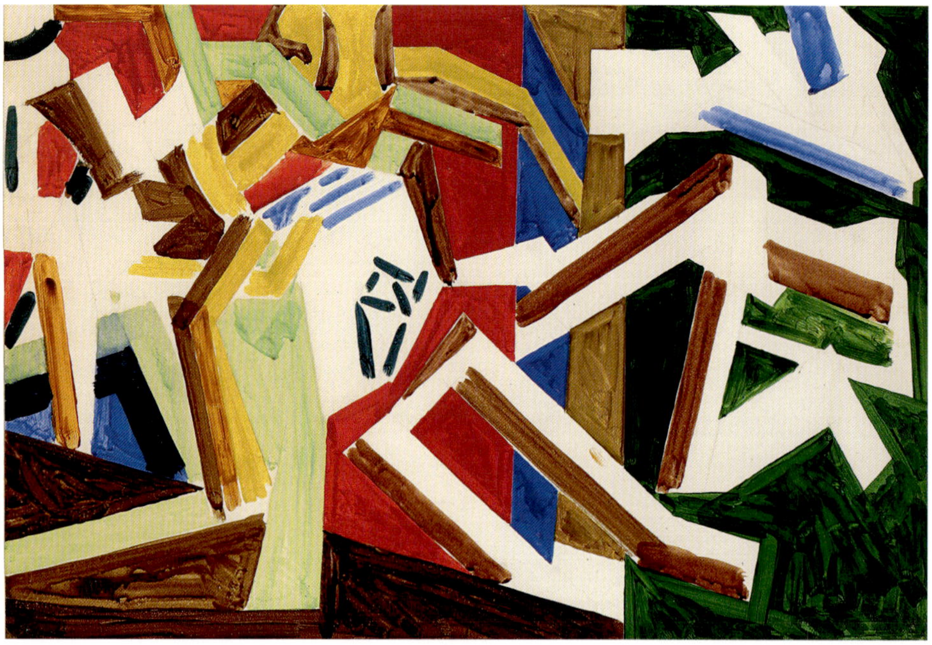

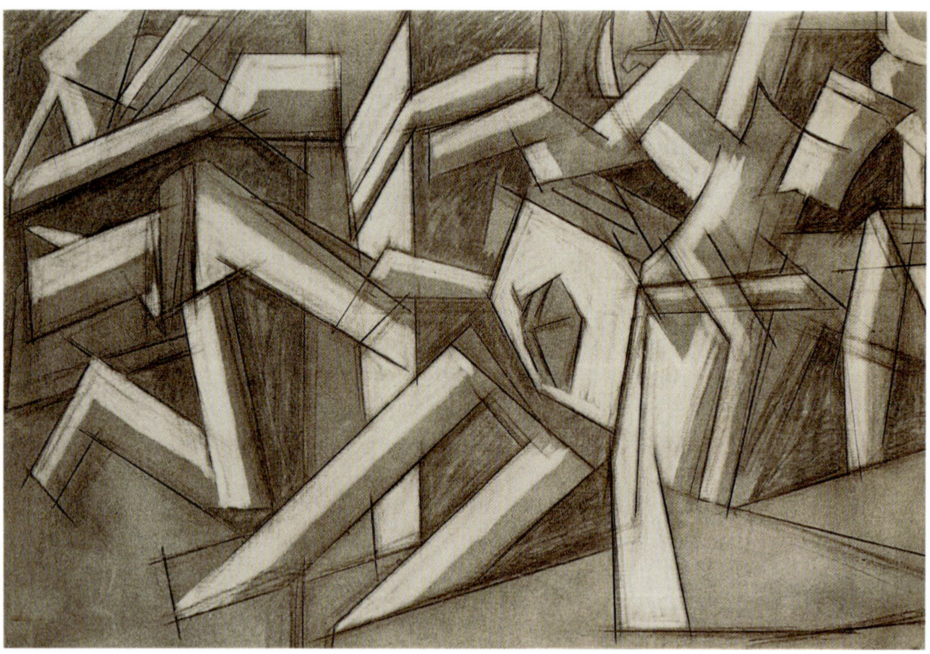

4
David Bomberg
Study for 'The Mud Bath'
(recto) c.1914
Gouache and pencil
on paper
53.4 x 70.8 cm

5
David Bomberg
Study for 'The Mud Bath'
(verso) c.1914
Gouache and pencil
on paper
53.4 x 70.8 cm

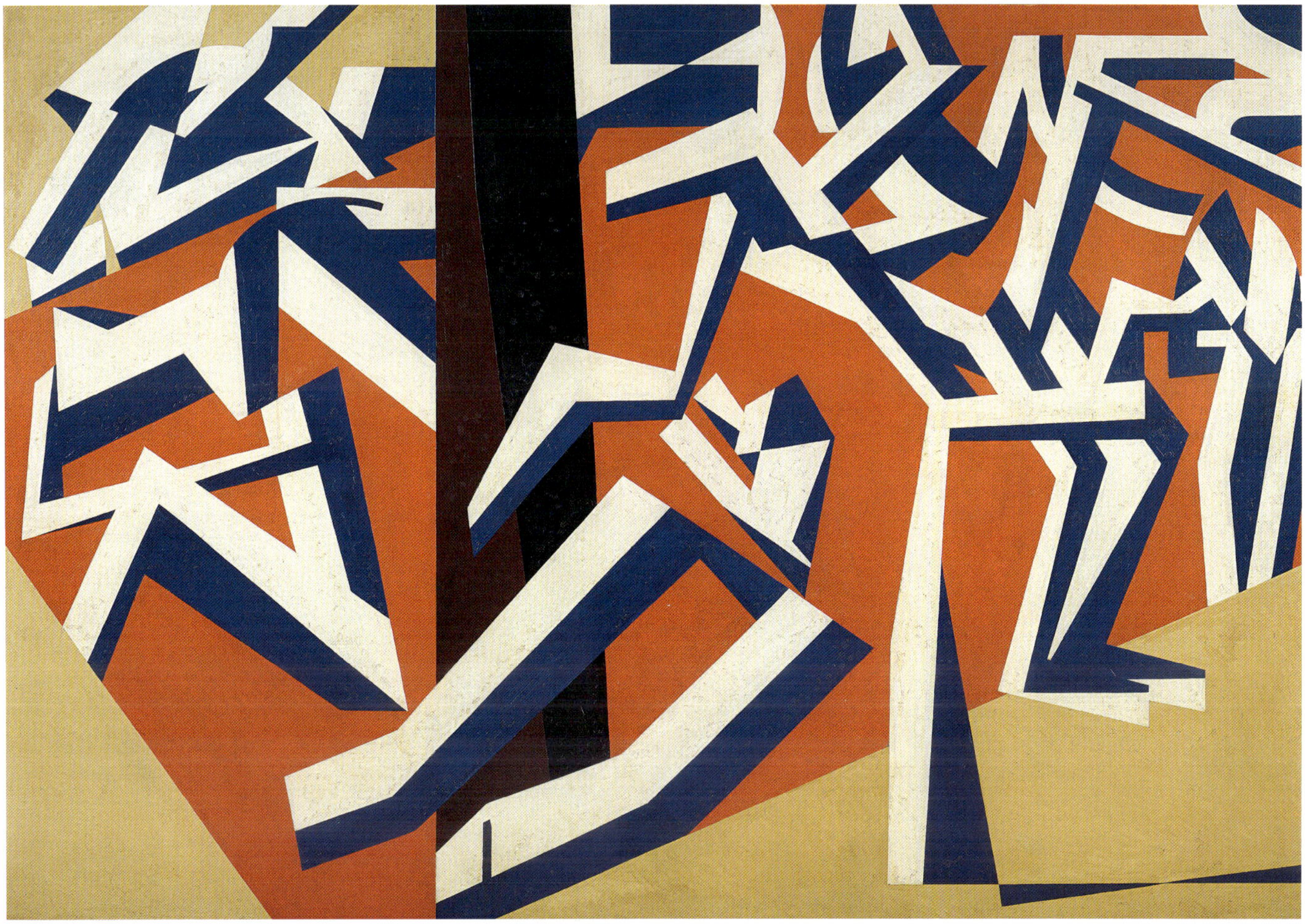

6
David Bomberg
The Mud Bath 1914
Oil on canvas
152.4 x 224.2 cm

7
Wyndham Lewis
The Crowd 1914–15
Oil and pencil on canvas
200.7 x 153.7 cm
[D]

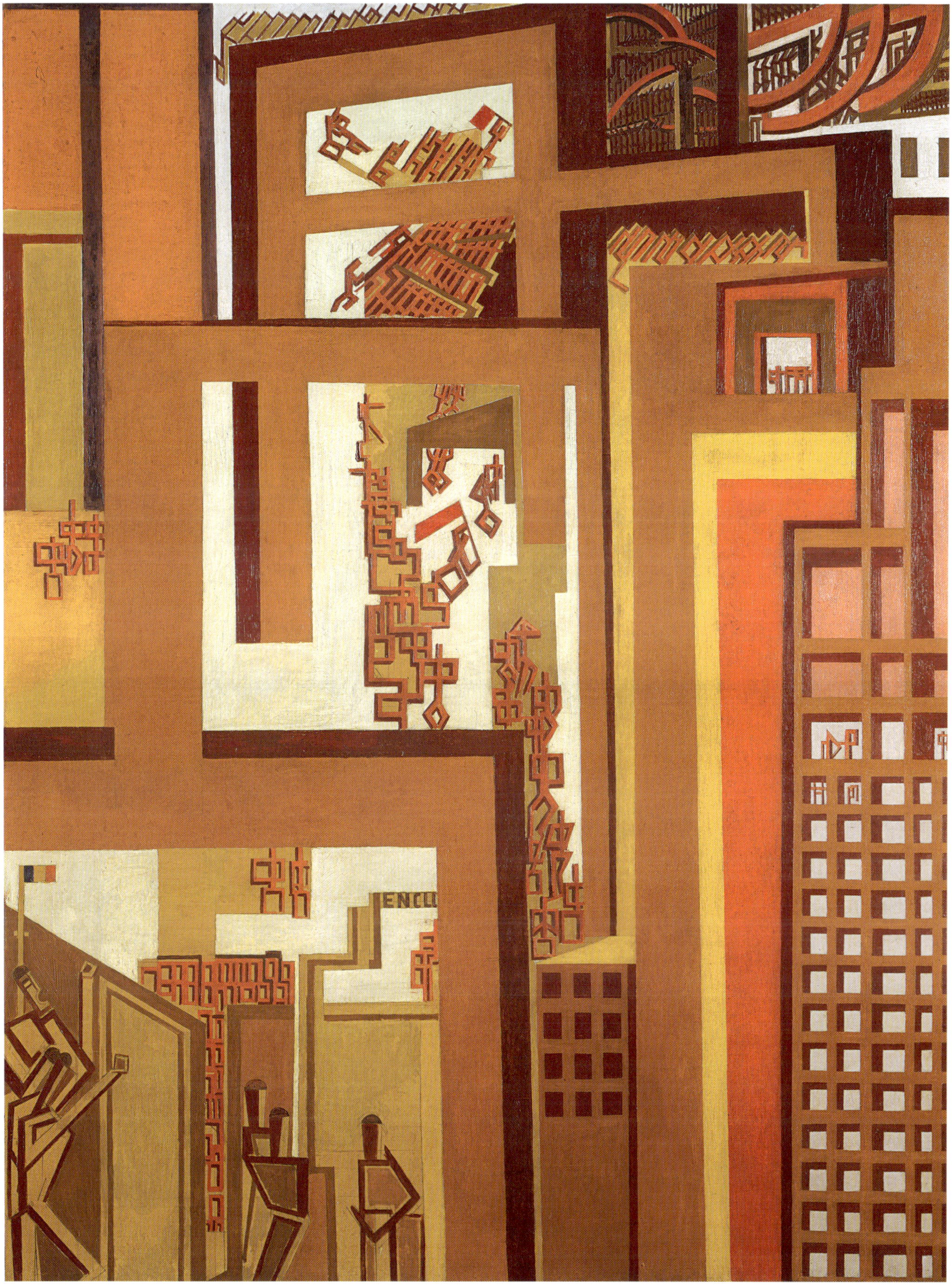
ENCL

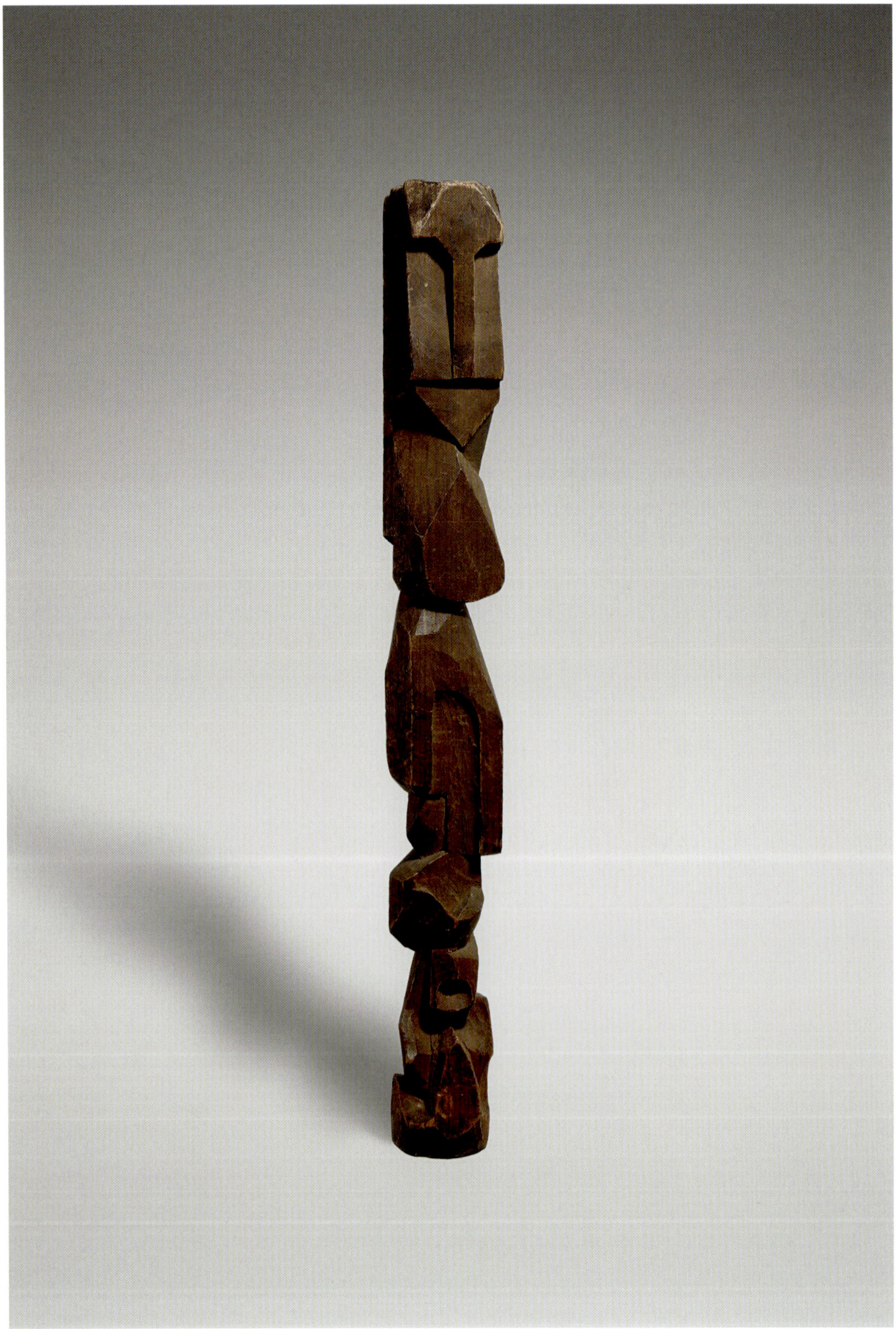

8
Henri Gaudier-Brzeska
Portrait of Ezra Pound [n.d.]
Wood
71.1 x 7.6 x 7.6 cm

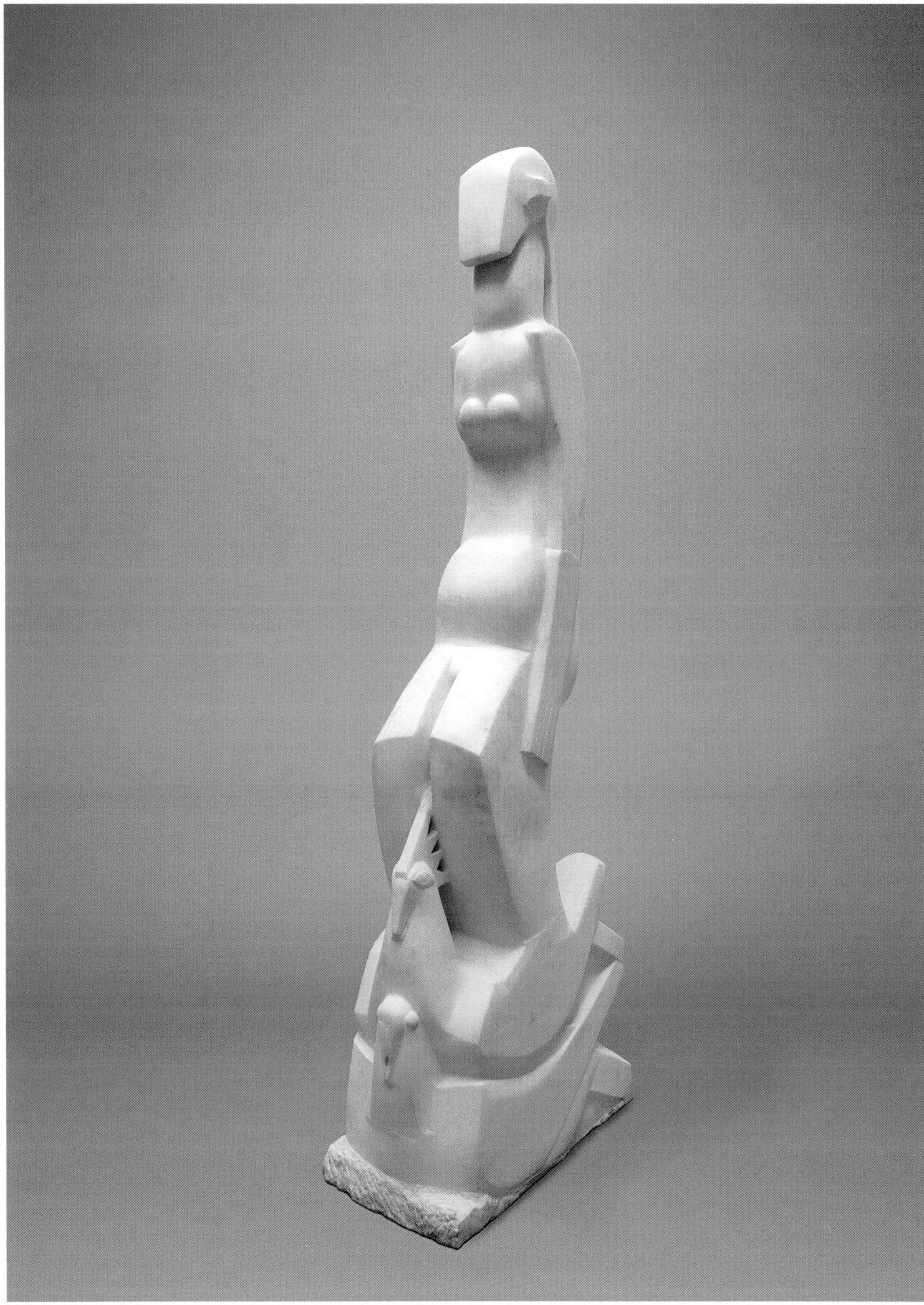

9
Jacob Epstein
Venus 1917
Marble
235.6 x 43.2 x 82.6 cm

DORE GALLERIES

The Doré Galleries' First Vorticist Exhibition

The Vorticists published their polemical manifesto in 1914, but it was not until June–July of 1915 that Wyndham Lewis presented the *First Vorticist Exhibition* at the Doré Galleries in London. Nascent Vorticists works had been included elsewhere, as with those in the Cubist Room of *An Exhibition of the Work of English Post-Impressionists, Cubists and others*, at the Brighton Public Art Galleries (December 1913 – January 1914). Vorticist artwork also had been displayed in the pages of *Blast*'s first issue in 1914. The Doré presentation, however, was the first concerted effort to gather the artists associated with the movement and show their work under the Vorticist rubric. Lewis assembled painters Jessica Dismorr, Frederick Etchells, Helen Saunders, William Roberts, and Edward Wadsworth, and sculptor Henri Gaudier-Brzeska, all of whom were labelled Vorticists in the catalogue. Additionally, he invited artists Bernard Adeney, Lawrence Atkinson, David Bomberg, Duncan Grant, Jacob Kramer, and Christopher Nevinson, but listed them separately in that publication. The absence of some Vorticist manifesto signatories and the inclusion of individuals such as Bloomsbury painter Grant hint at the notoriously shifting alliances within the group, even at this pivotal stage. But the core Vorticists transcended any personal or theoretical discord though their stylistic allegiances, witnessed by their lightning-bolt forms, lurid colours, and elemental or mechanized conceptions of the human figure. And it was through these shared radical aesthetics that the movement cohered and defined their visual identity to the British public.

10
Henry Gaudier-Brzeska
Red Stone Dancer c.1913
Red Mansfield stone
43.2 x 22.9 x 22.9 cm
[D]

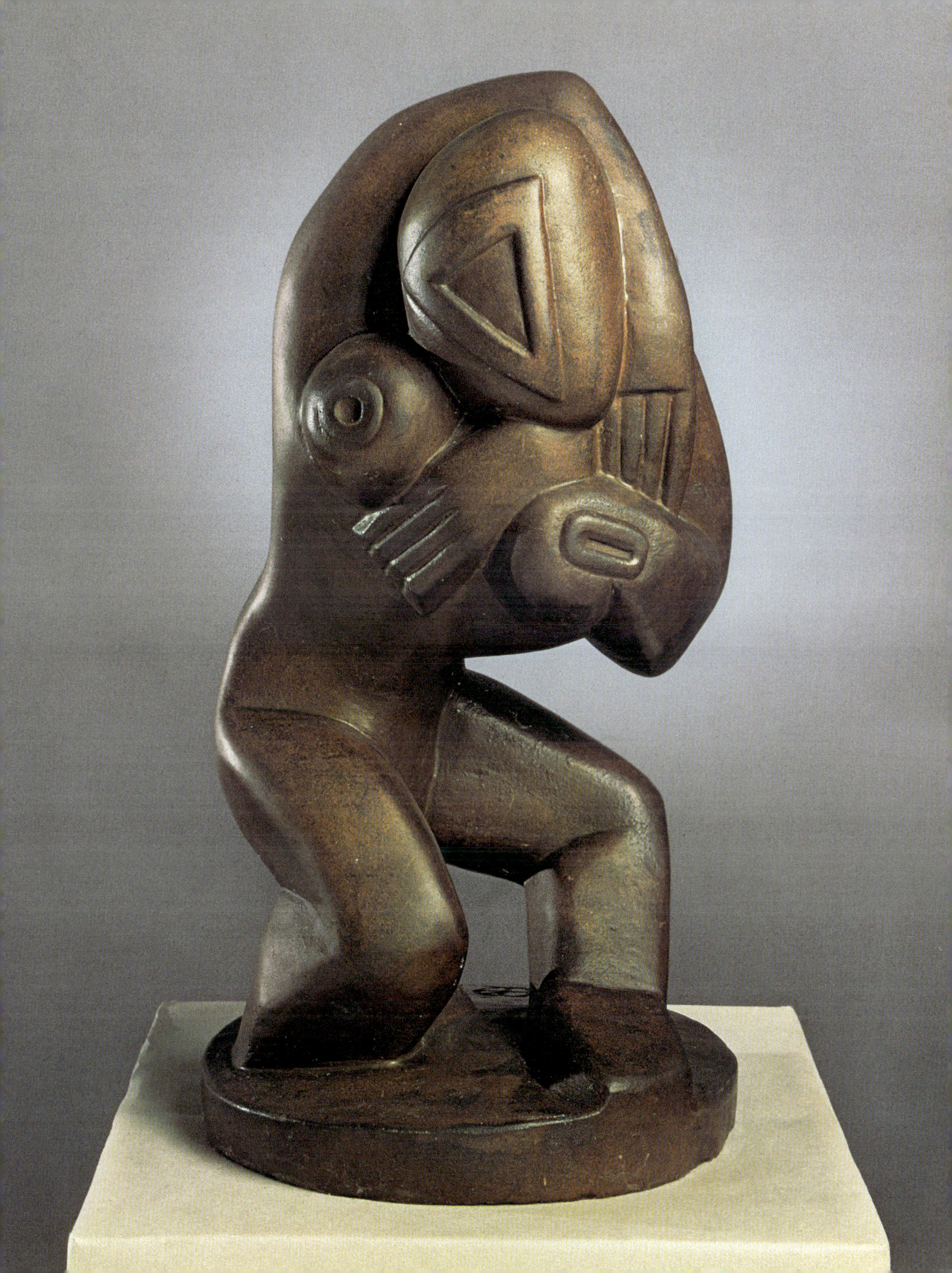

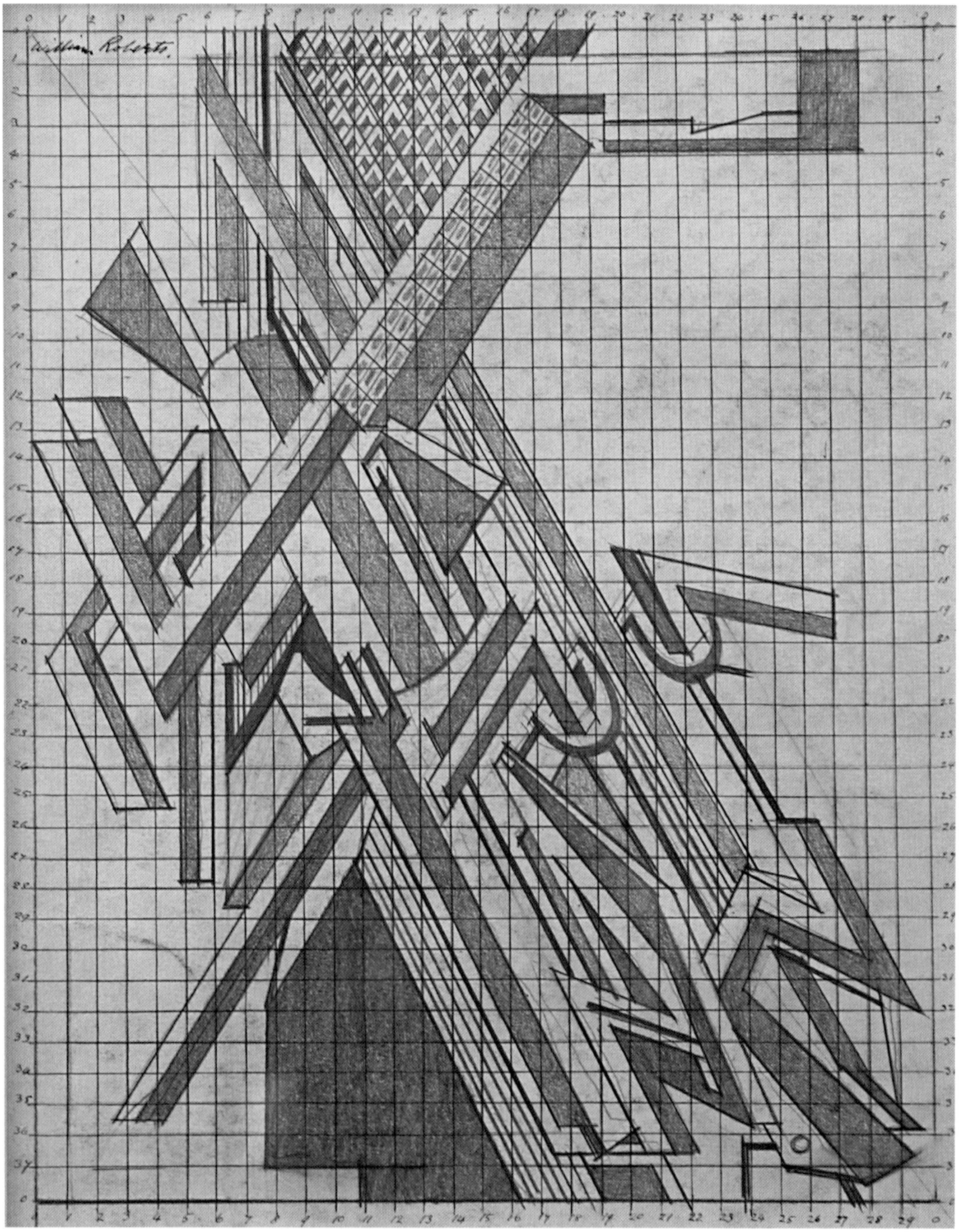

11

William Roberts

Study for 'St George and the Dragon' 1915

Pencil on paper

25.4 x 20.3 cm

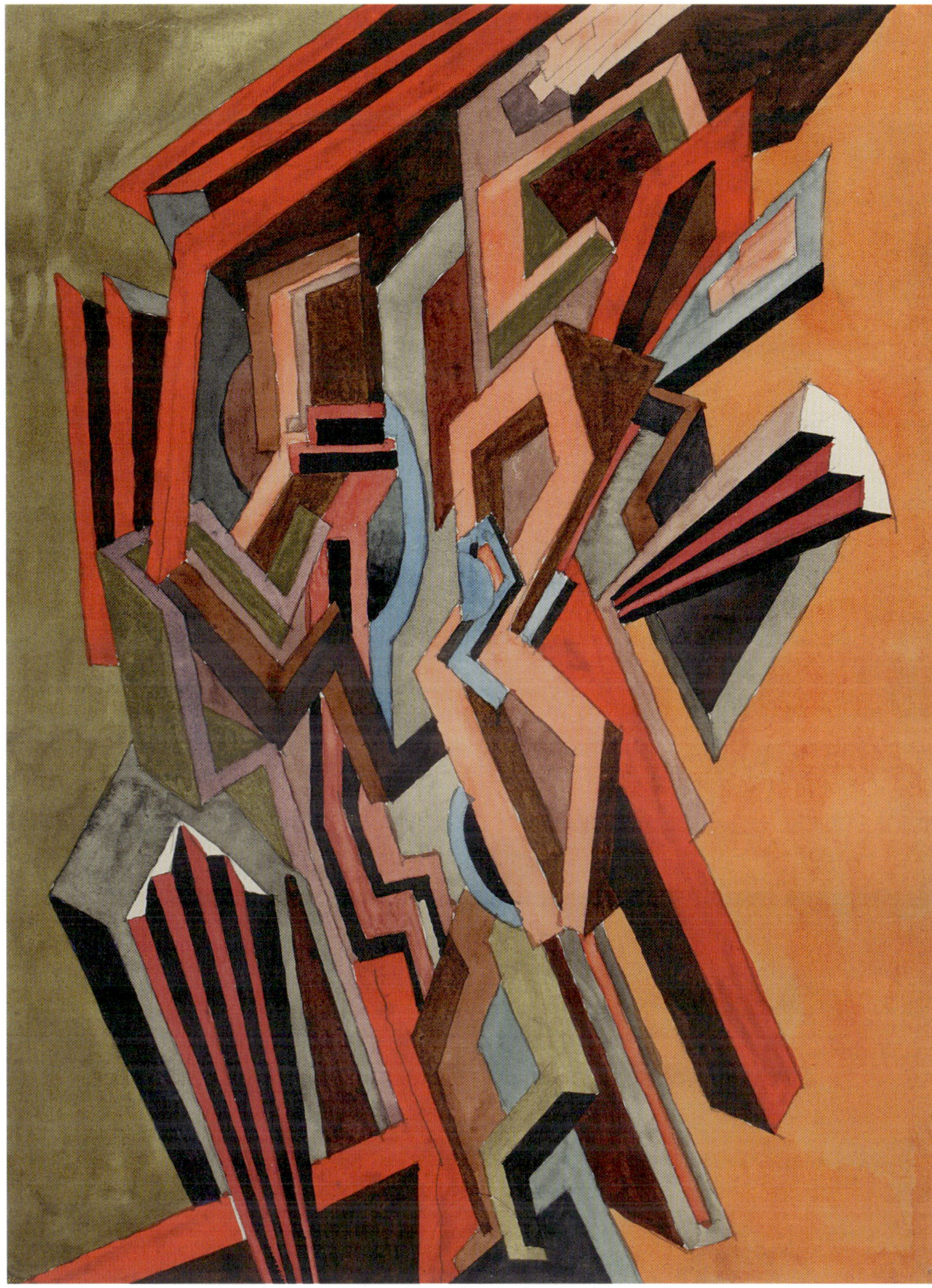

12
William Roberts
Study for the lost painting 'Two-Step' 1915
Pencil, watercolour, and gouache on paper
30 x 23 cm
[D]

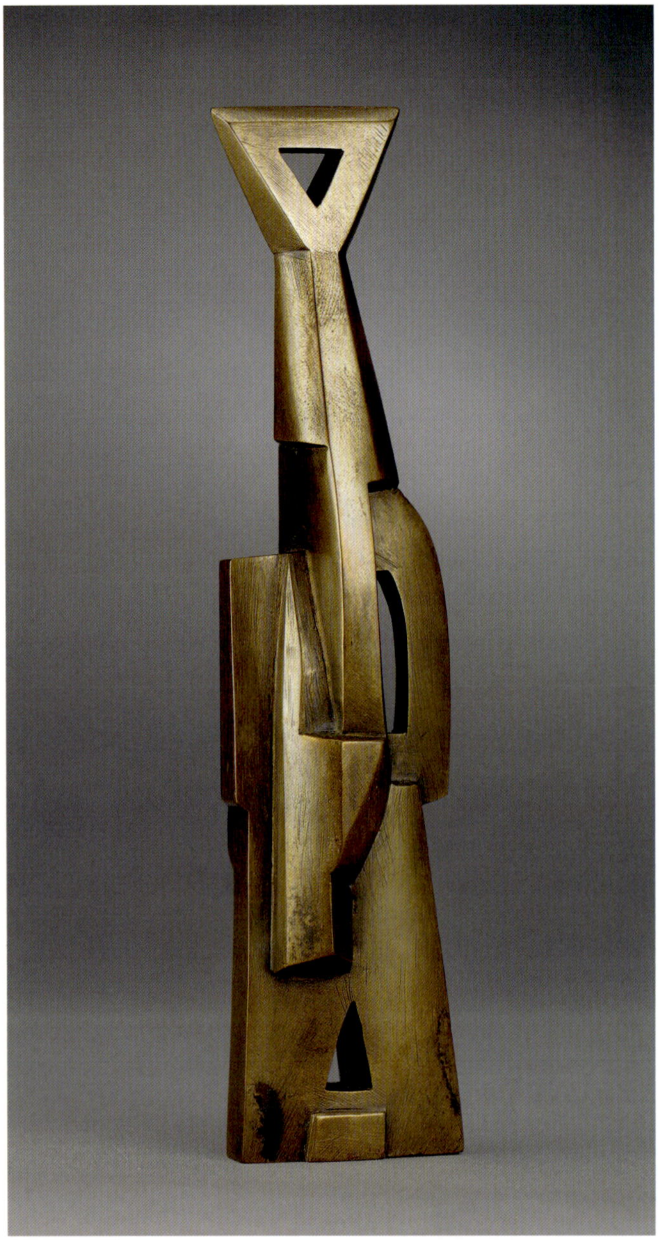

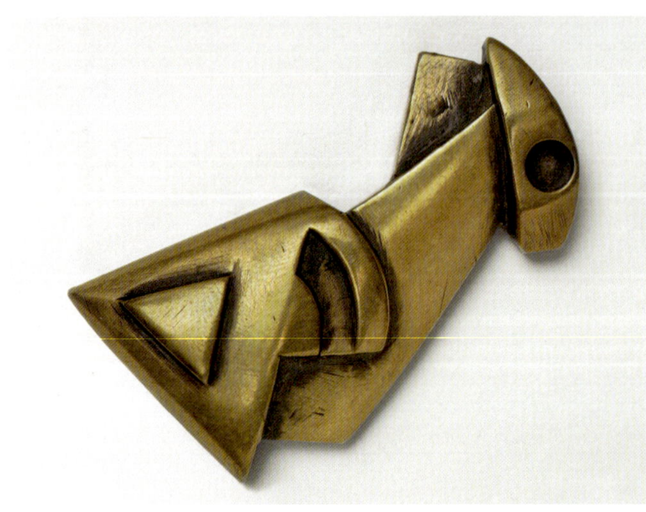

13
Henri Gaudier-Brzeska
Ornement Torpille 1914
Brass
15.9 x 3.8 x 3.2 cm

14
Henri Gaudier-Brzeska
Fish 1914
Bronze
4.8 x 3 x 0.8 cm

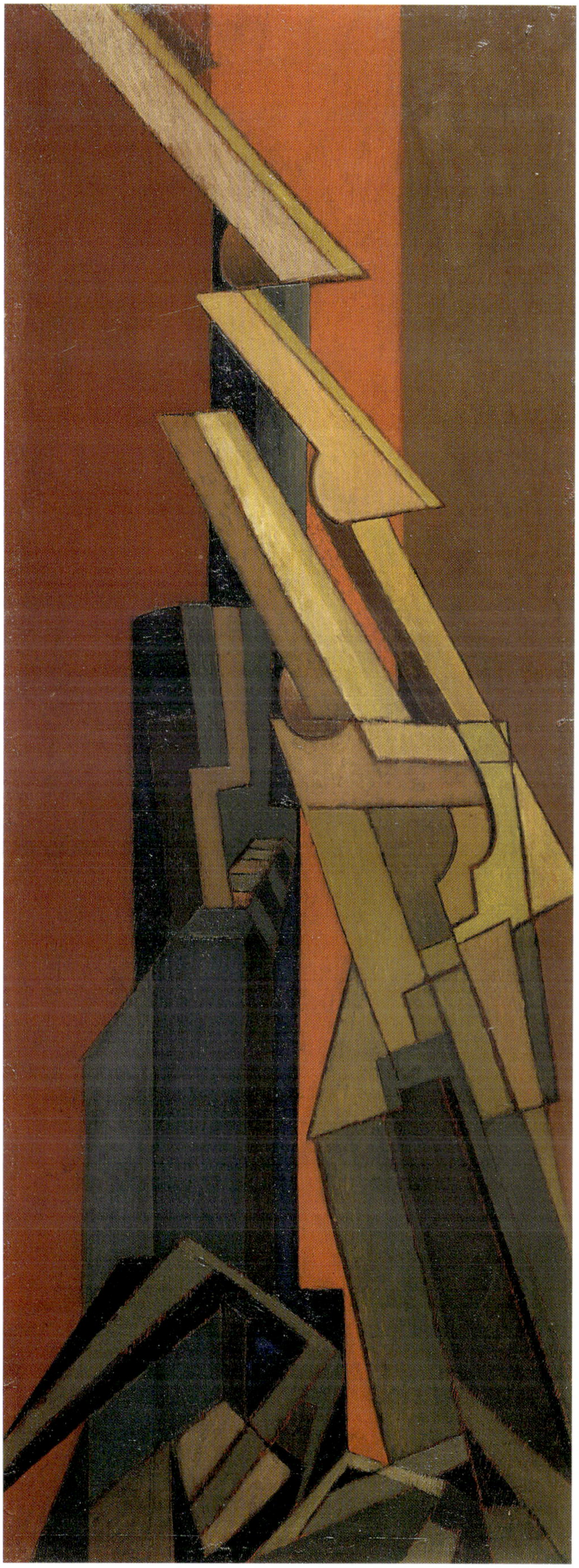

15
Lawrence Atkinson
Abstract c.1915–20
Oil on wood
129.5 x 50.8 cm

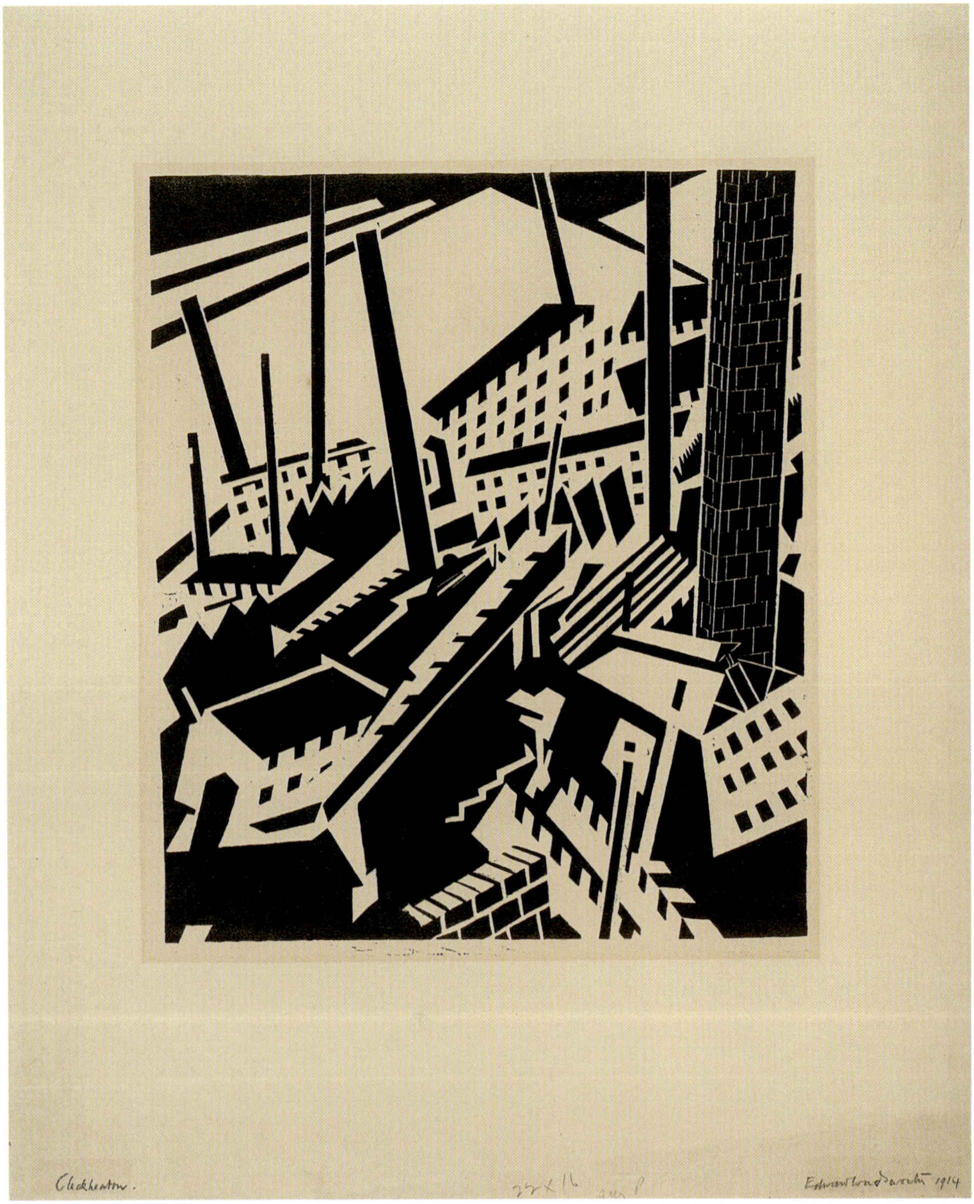

16
Edward Wadsworth
Cleckheaton 1914
Woodcut on paper
sheet: 45.1 x 36.8 cm
image: 28.6 x 24.8 cm

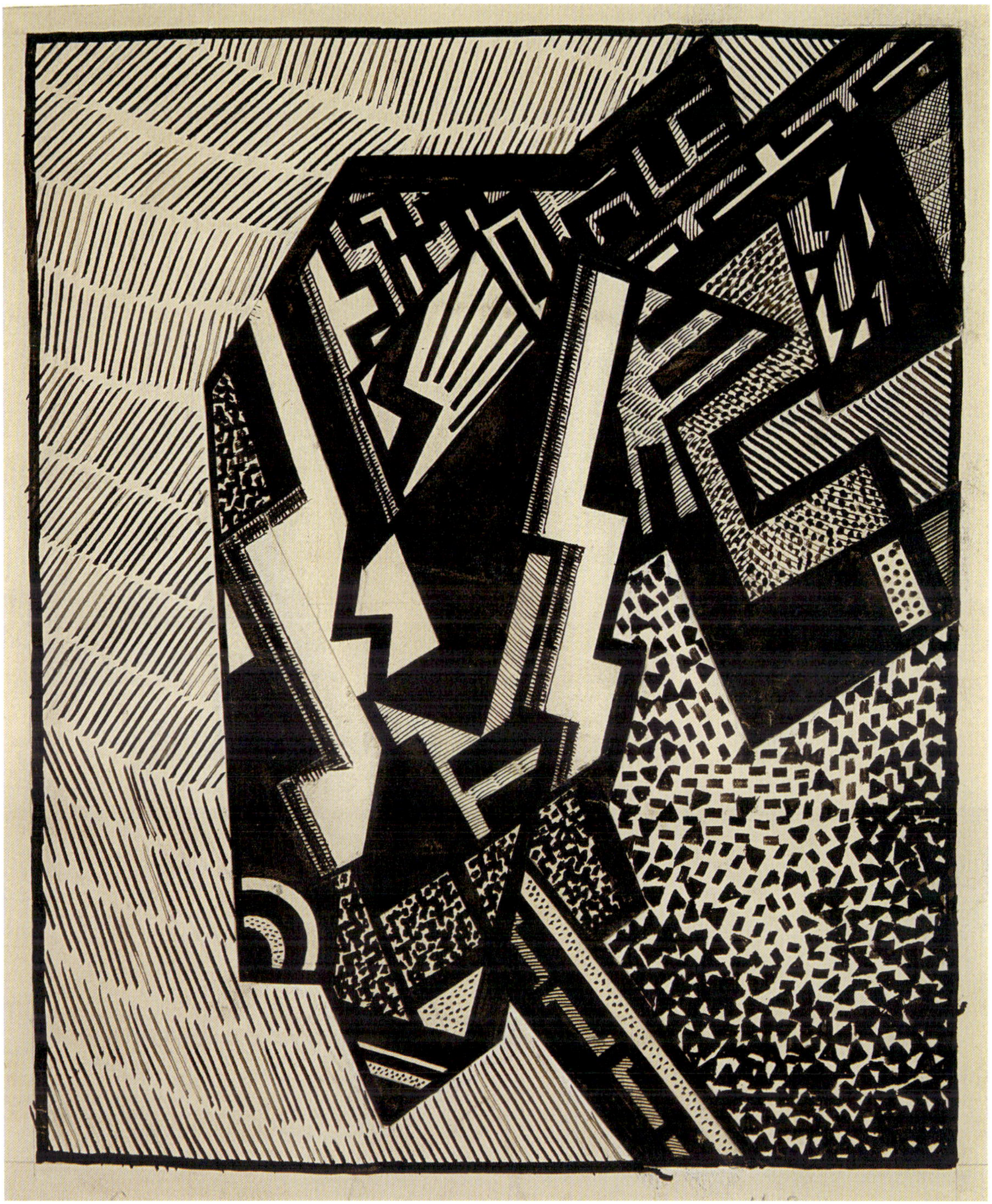

17
Helen Saunders
Island of Laputa 1915
Pen and ink, and collage
on paper
sheet: 27 x 23.2 cm
image: 25.4 x 21.6 cm
[D; B2; P]

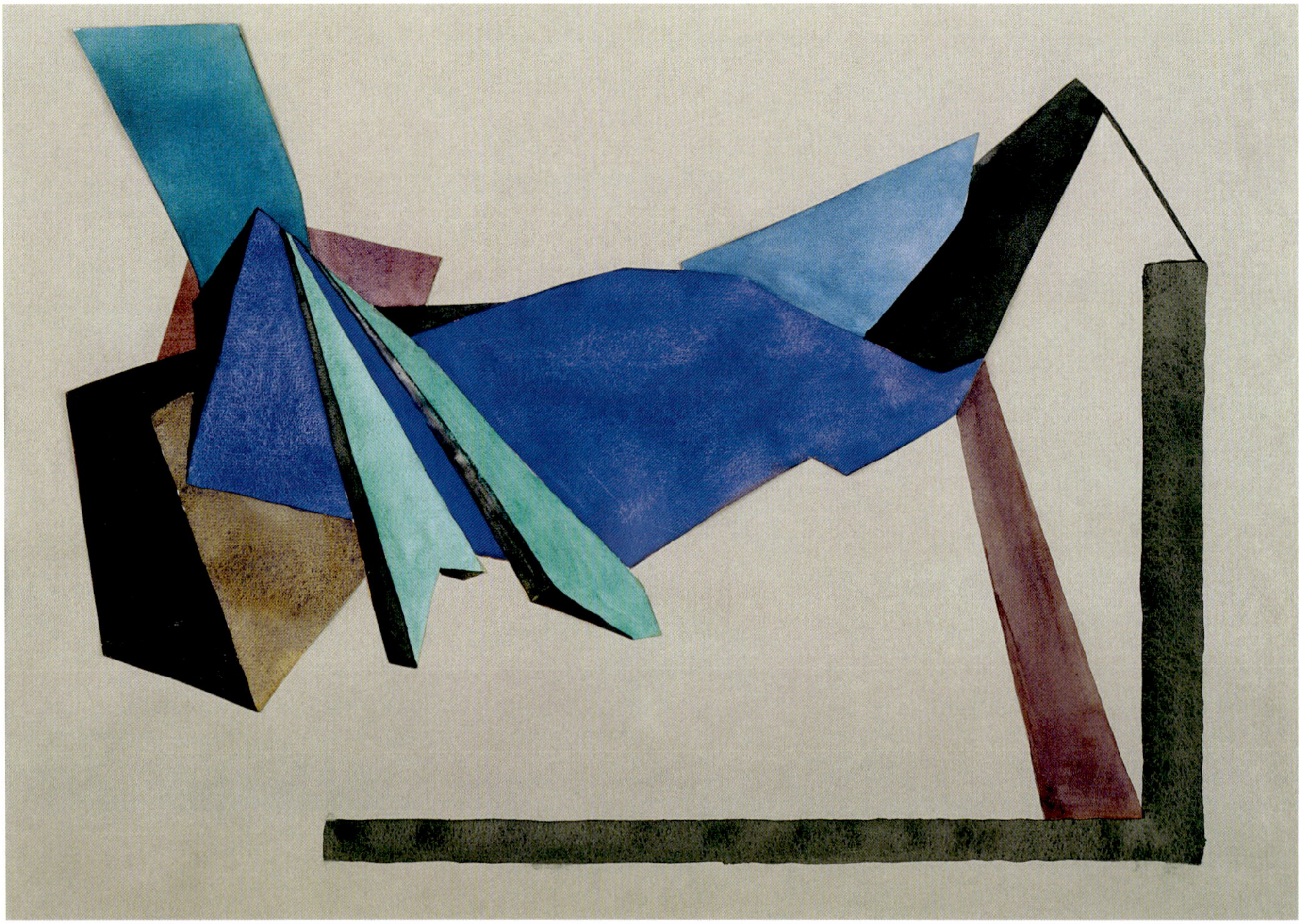

18
Dorothy Shakespear
Composition in Blue and Black
1914–15
Collage and watercolour on paper
33.7 x 46.4 cm

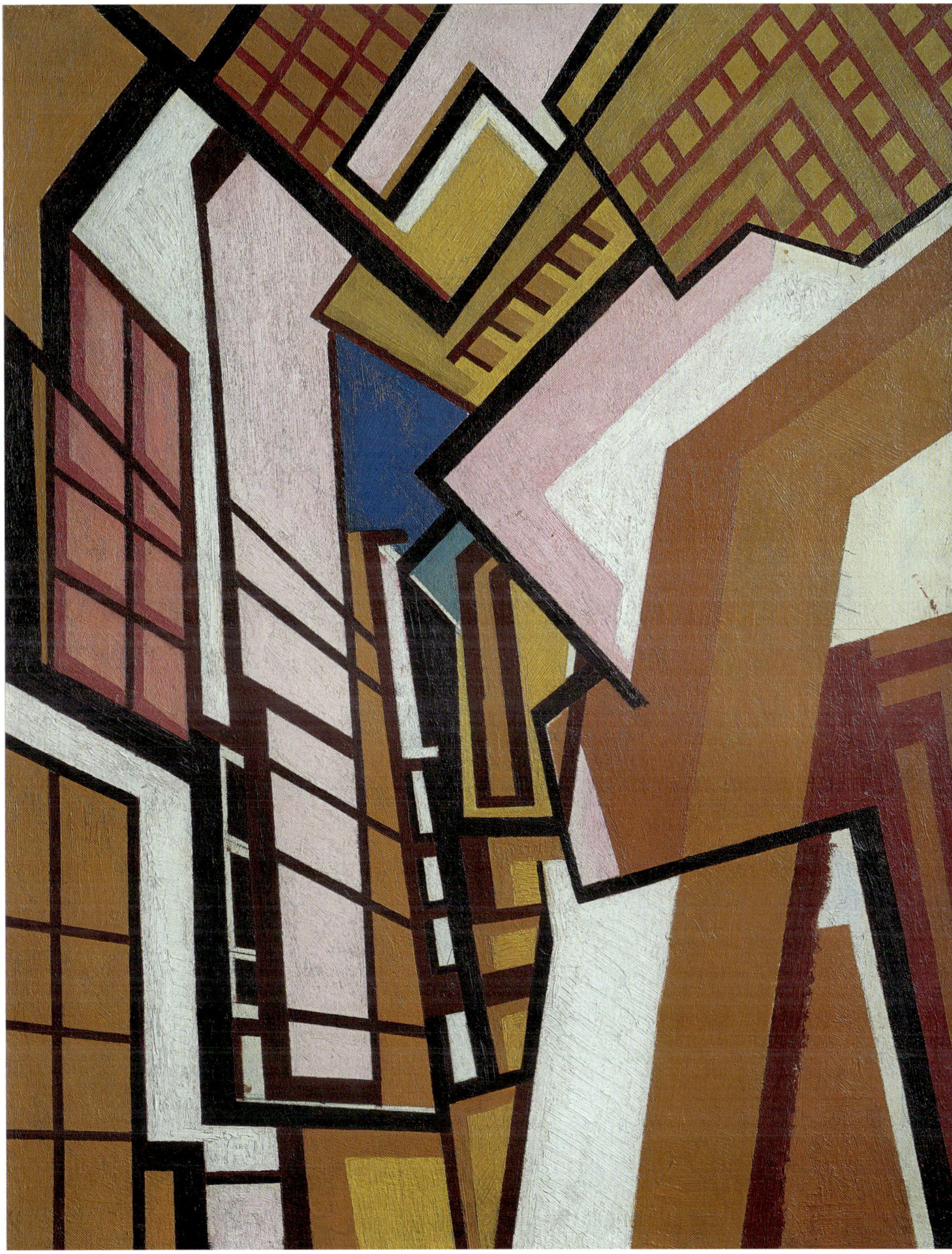

19
Wyndham Lewis
Workshop c.1914–15
Oil on canvas
76.5 x 61 cm
[D; P]

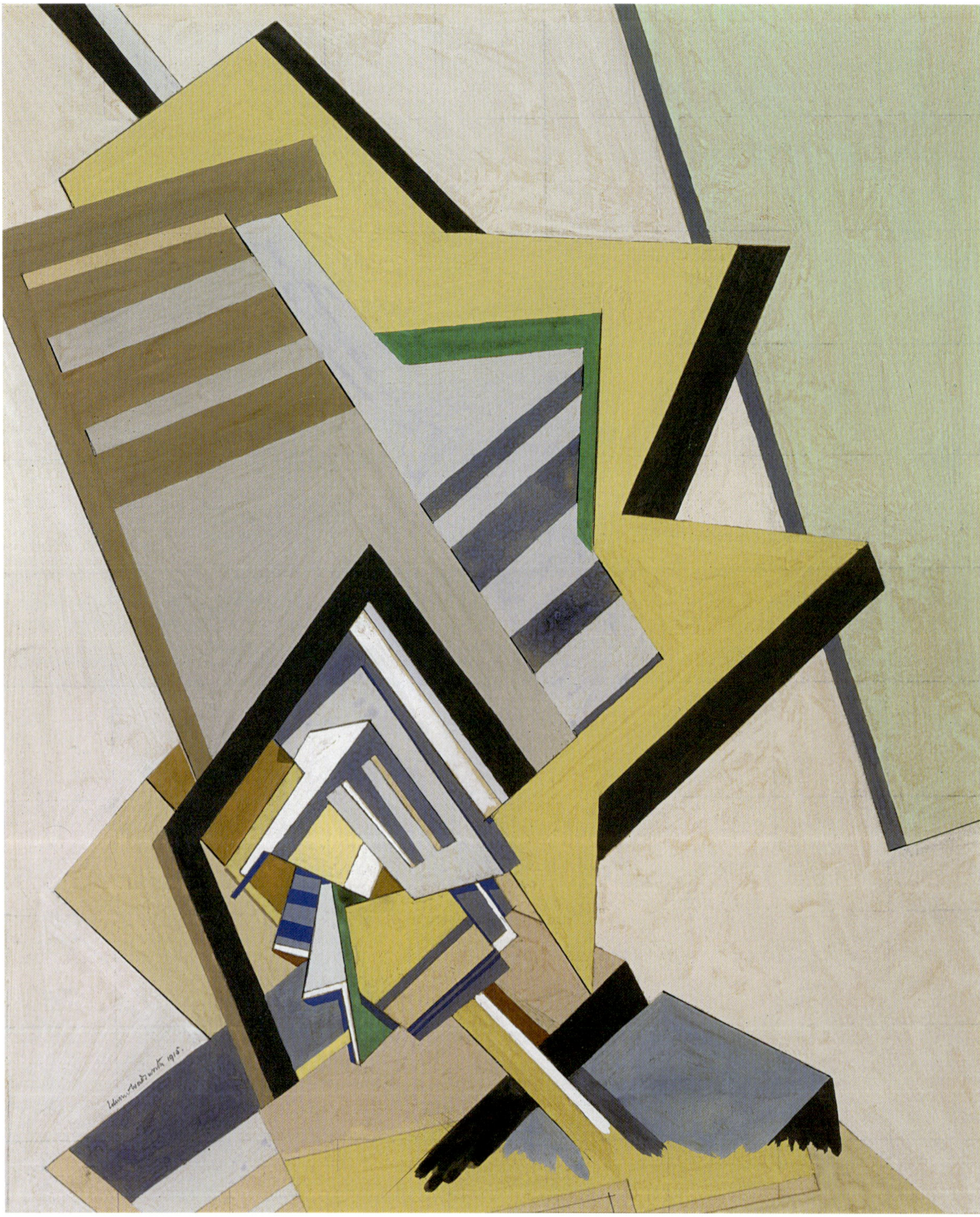

20

Edward Wadsworth

Abstract Composition 1915

Gouache, pen, and pencil on paper

41.9 x 34.3 cm

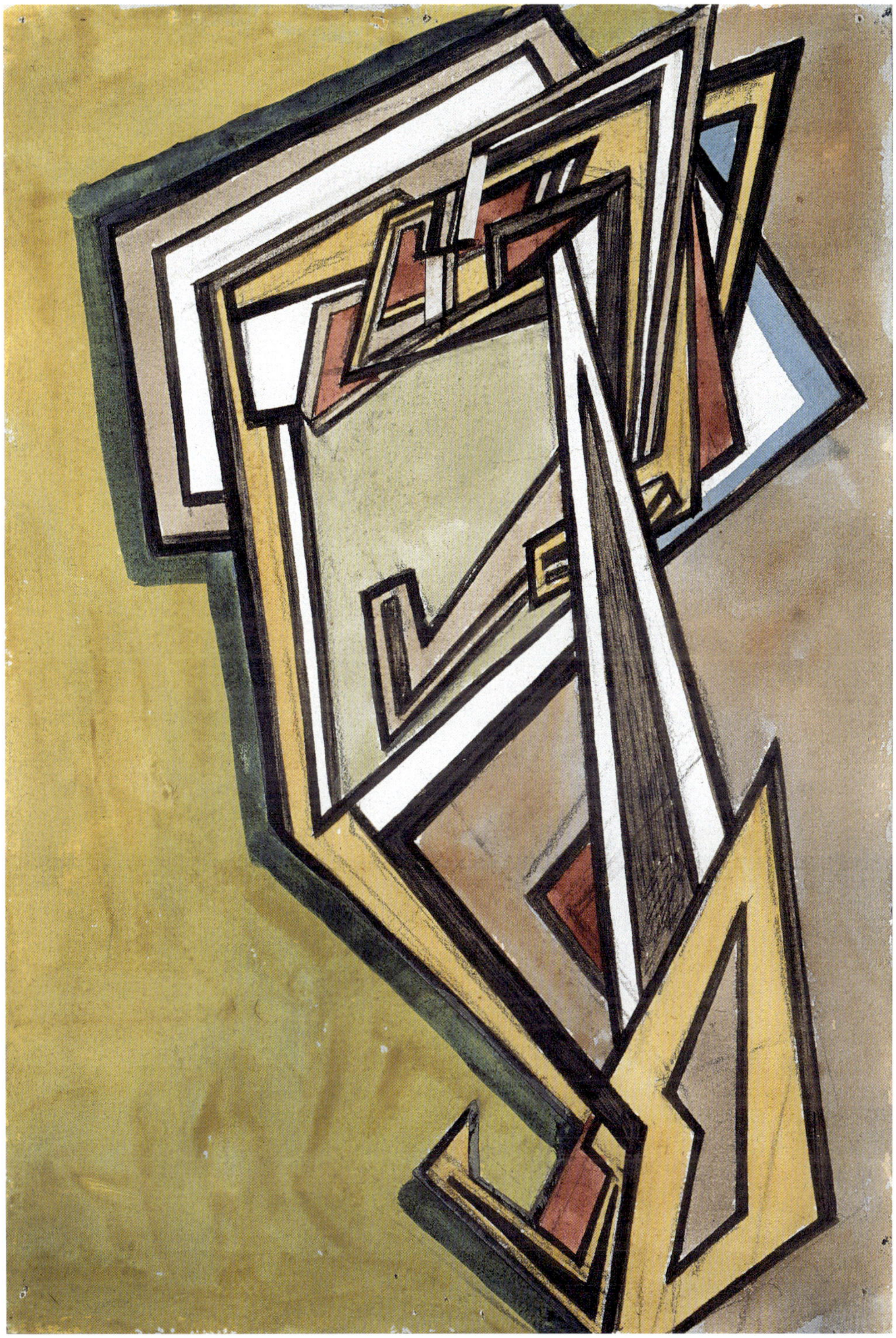

21
Helen Saunders
Study for 'Black and Khaki' (?) c.1915
Ink and watercolour on paper
25.5 x 18 cm
[D]

22
Lawrence Atkinson
Abstract Composition 1915
Ink, crayon, and watercolour on paper
33 x 21.6 cm

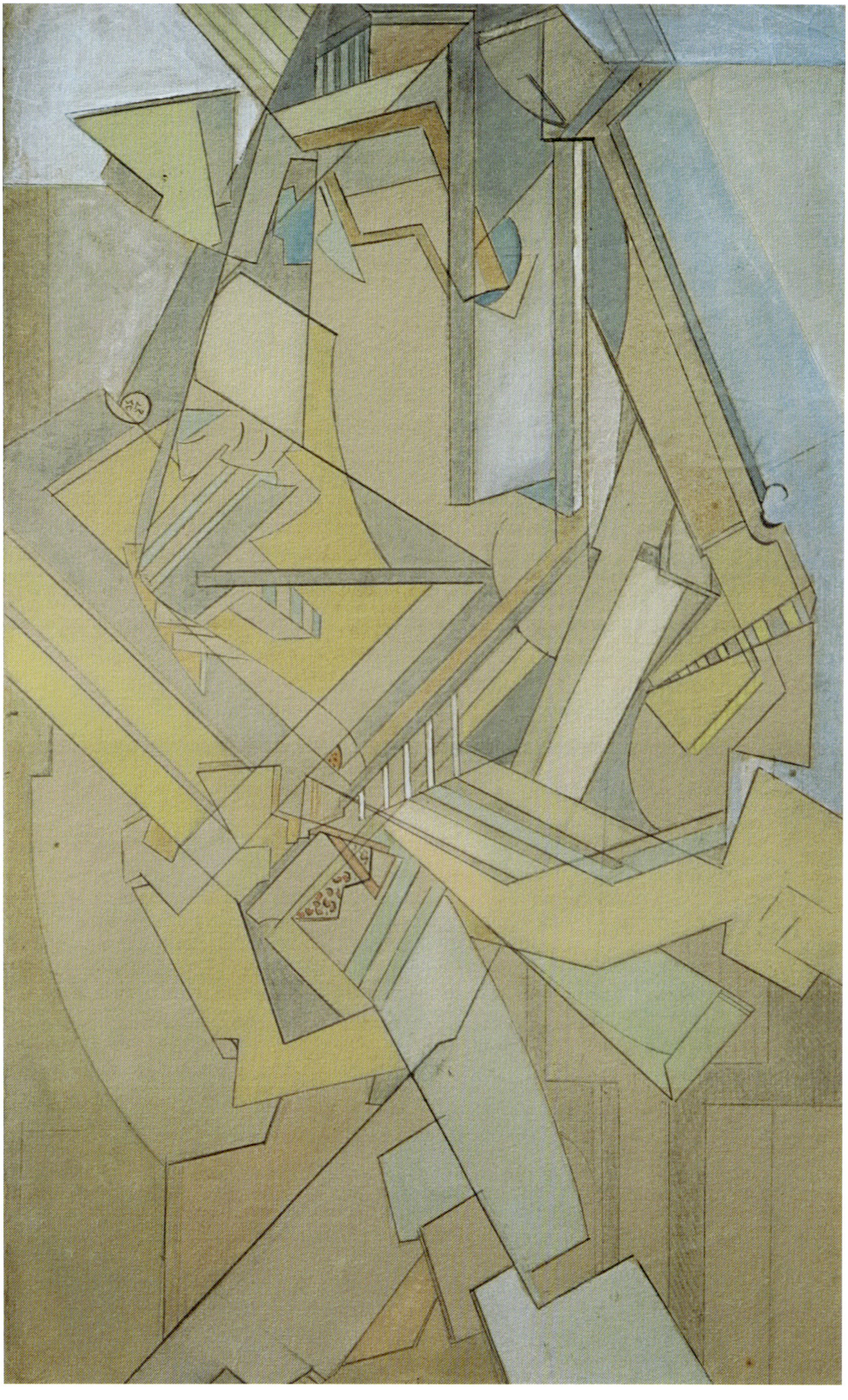

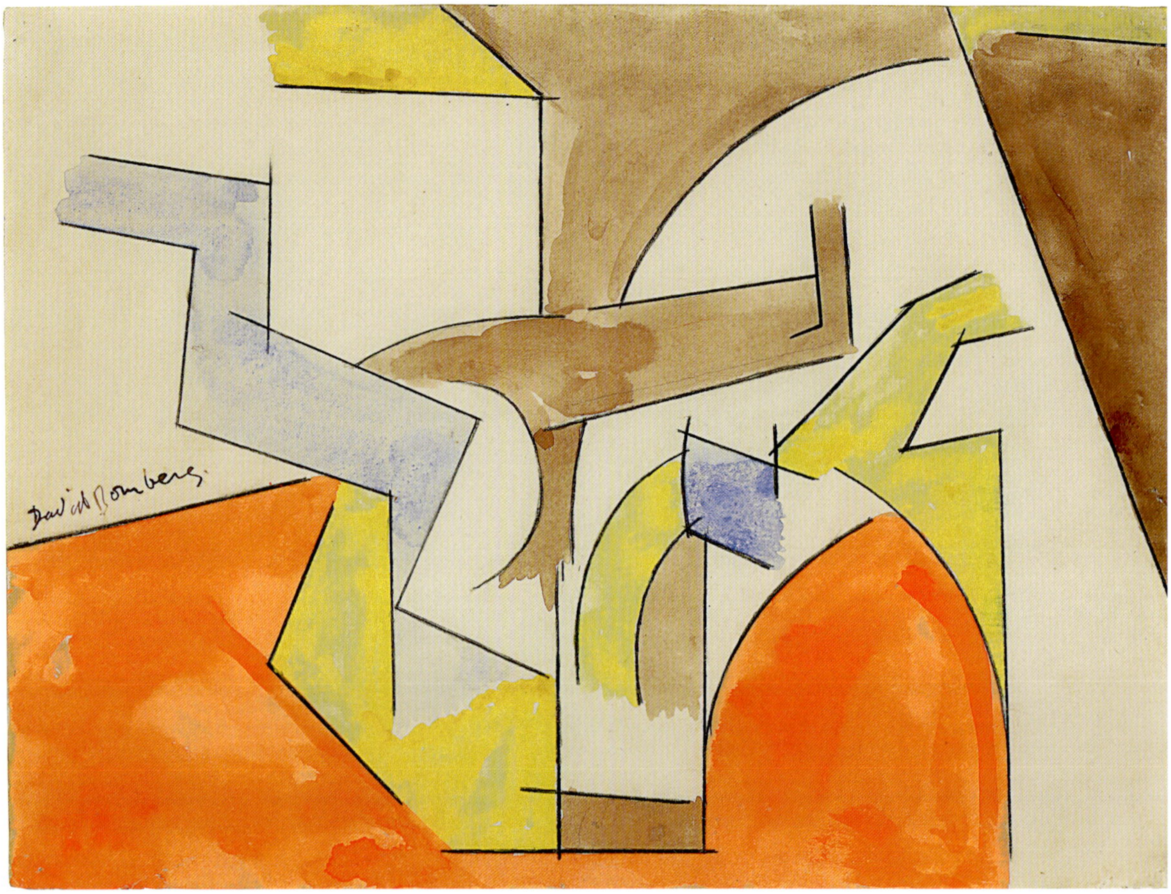

23
David Bomberg
Abstract Composition c.1914
Pencil and watercolour on paper
27.5 x 36.5 cm

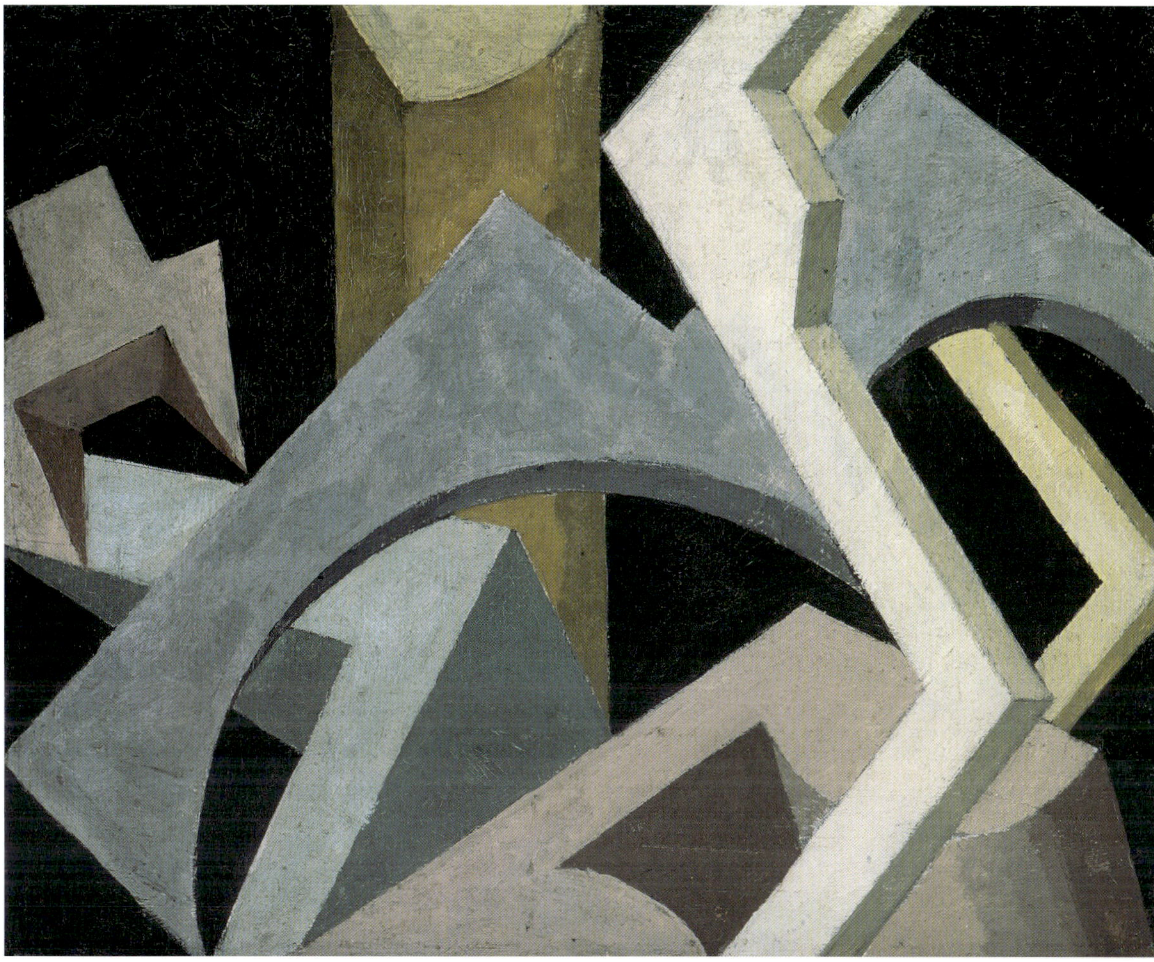

24
Jessica Dismorr
Abstract Composition c.1915
Oil on wood
41.3 x 50.8 cm

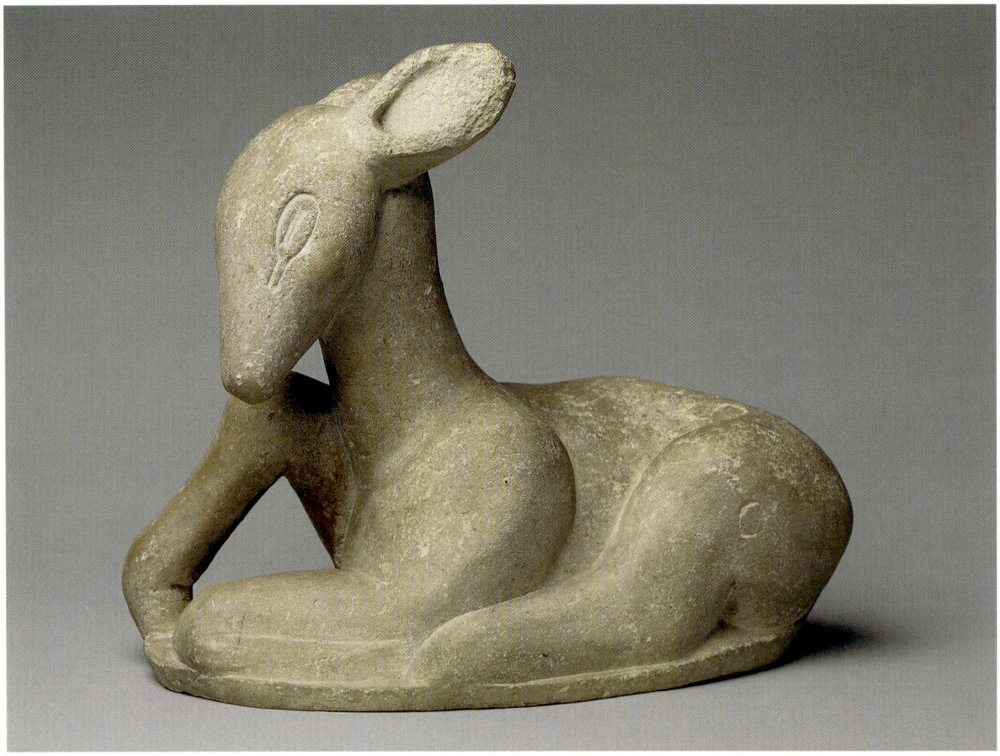

25
Henri Gaudier-Brzeska
Crouching Fawn 1913
Bath stone
30.4 x 25.3 cm
[D]

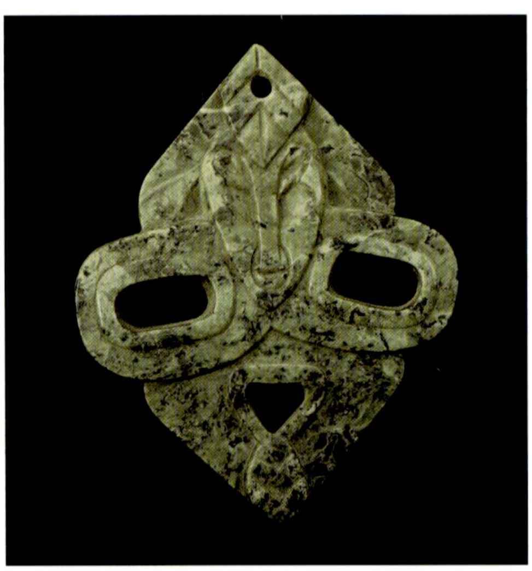

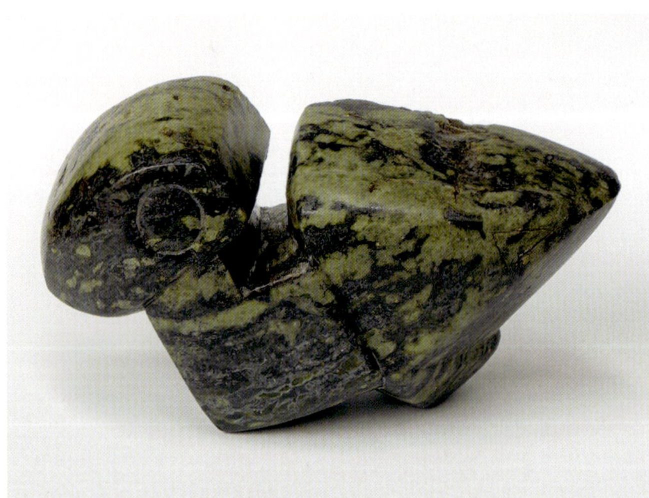

26
Henri Gaudier-Brzeska
Green Stone Charm 1914
Irish marble 10.8 x 8.9 cm
[D]

27
Henri Gaudier-Brzeska
Duck 1914
Marble
6.5 x 12 x 4 cm

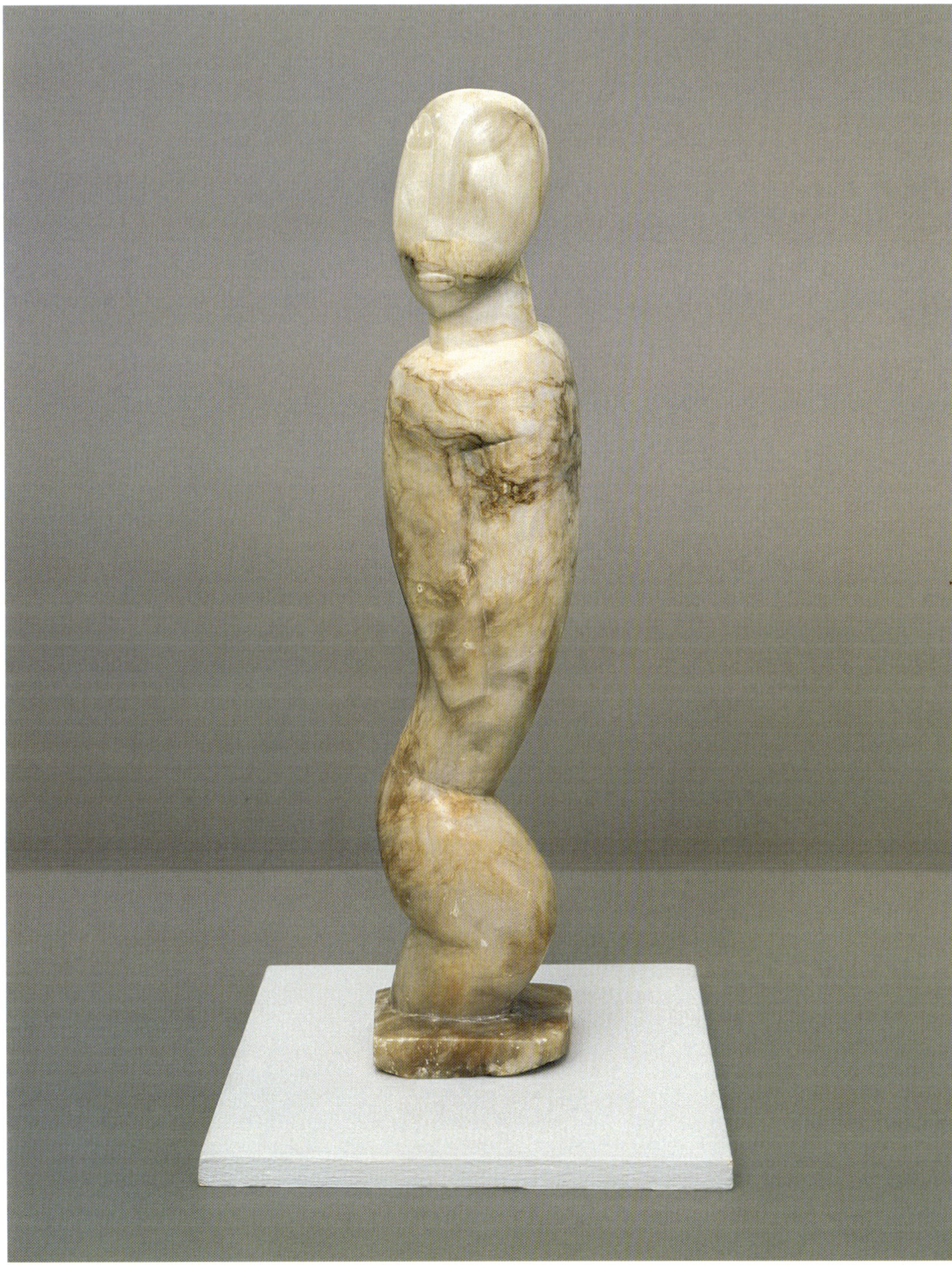

28
Henri Gaudier-Brzeska
The Imp c.1914
Alabaster
40.6 x 8.9 x 8.3 cm

BLAST

Blast and Ephemera

Blast, no.1, the 'Review of the Great English Vortex', appeared in July 1914 to signal the birth in London of an avant-garde opposed to French Cubism and Italian Futurism. Edited by Wyndham Lewis, *Blast* was designed to shock the public with its bright pink cover traversed by a diagonal title in bold black capital letters. The journal opened with a strident manifesto that alternately 'Blasted' and 'Blessed' aspects of European and American culture before declaring the movement's protagonists 'Primitive Mercenaries' who drew on England's 'mechanical inventiveness' as inspiration for their unique mode of hard-edged abstraction. Lewis later described *Blast* as 'a sort of picture gallery': appropriately, the journal interspersed poetry and prose by such luminaries as Rebecca West, T.S. Eliot and Ezra Pound, with abstract drawings and reproductions of paintings, prints, and sculptures. *Blast* also included innovative poems, manifestos, a play, and art criticism by Vorticist artists Dismorr, Gaudier-Brzeska, Lewis, Saunders, and Wadsworth. The Vorticists' embrace of print media additionally led to forays into book design and the production of myriad small ephemera, including posters and invitations to Vorticist dinners and public lectures. Whereas *Blast*, no.1 addressed such topical issues as feminism and the suffrage movement, the July 1915 issue of *Blast: War Number* struggled to assert the continued relevance of art and culture in the midst of a world war. Lewis's editorial for the second number lamented that the journal was overwhelmed 'by a multitude of other Blasts' and no further issues of *Blast* ever appeared, despite Lewis and Pound's concerted attempts to revive the review.

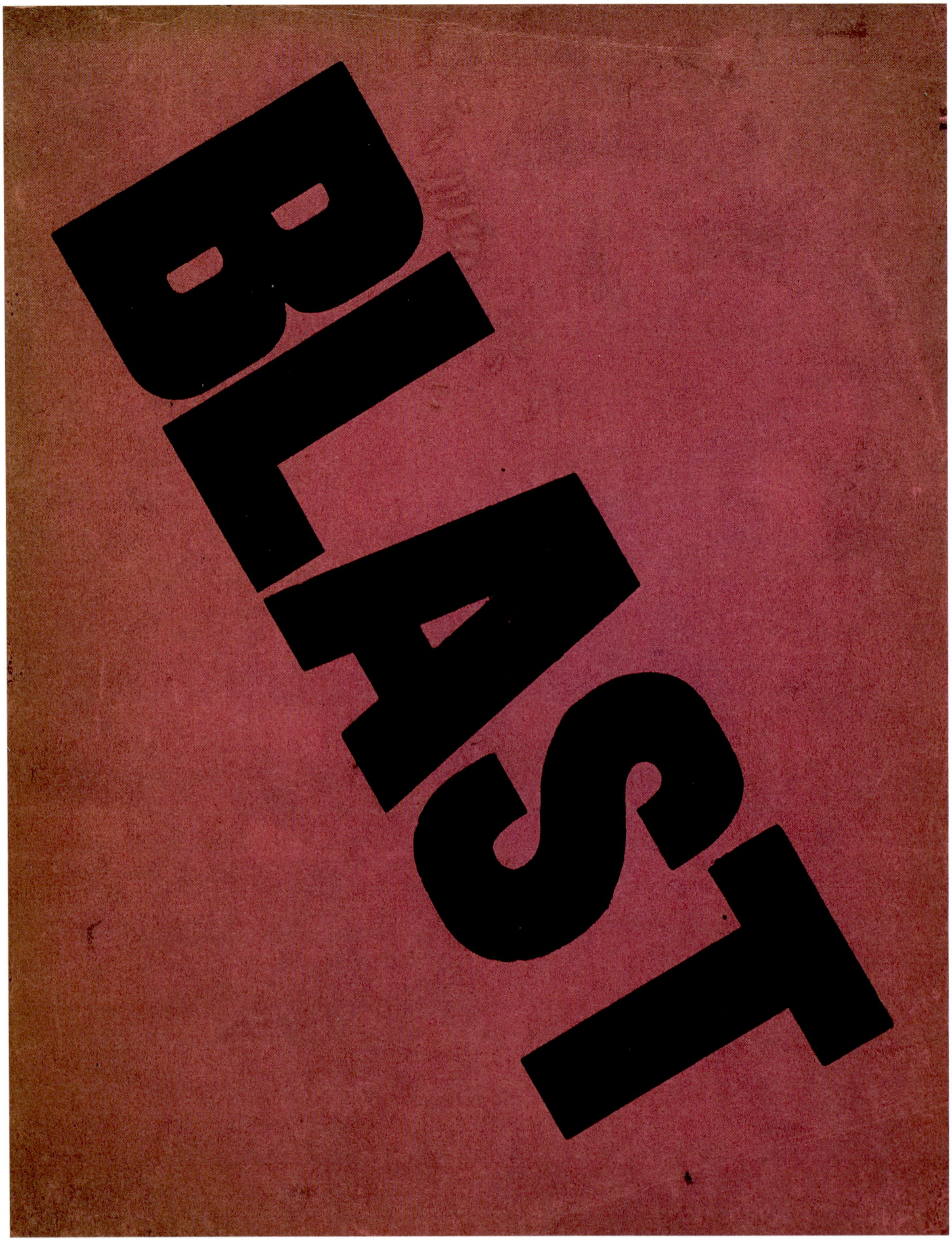

29
Blast, no.1: *Review of the Great English Vortex*, 20 June 1914
Front cover: designed by Wyndham Lewis

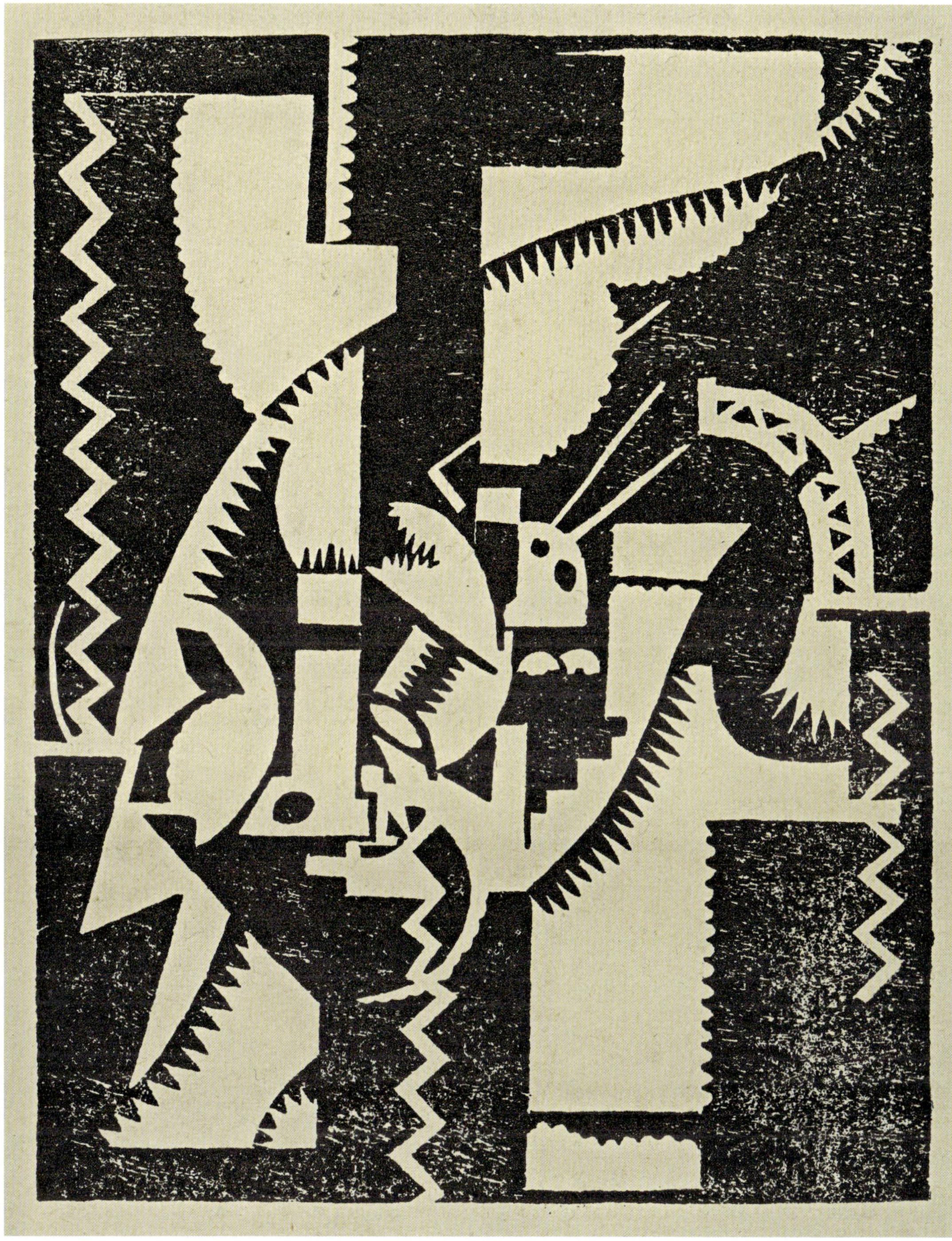

30
Edward Wadsworth
Newcastle c.1913
Woodcut on paper
sheet: 24.7 x 24.7 cm
[D; B1; S]

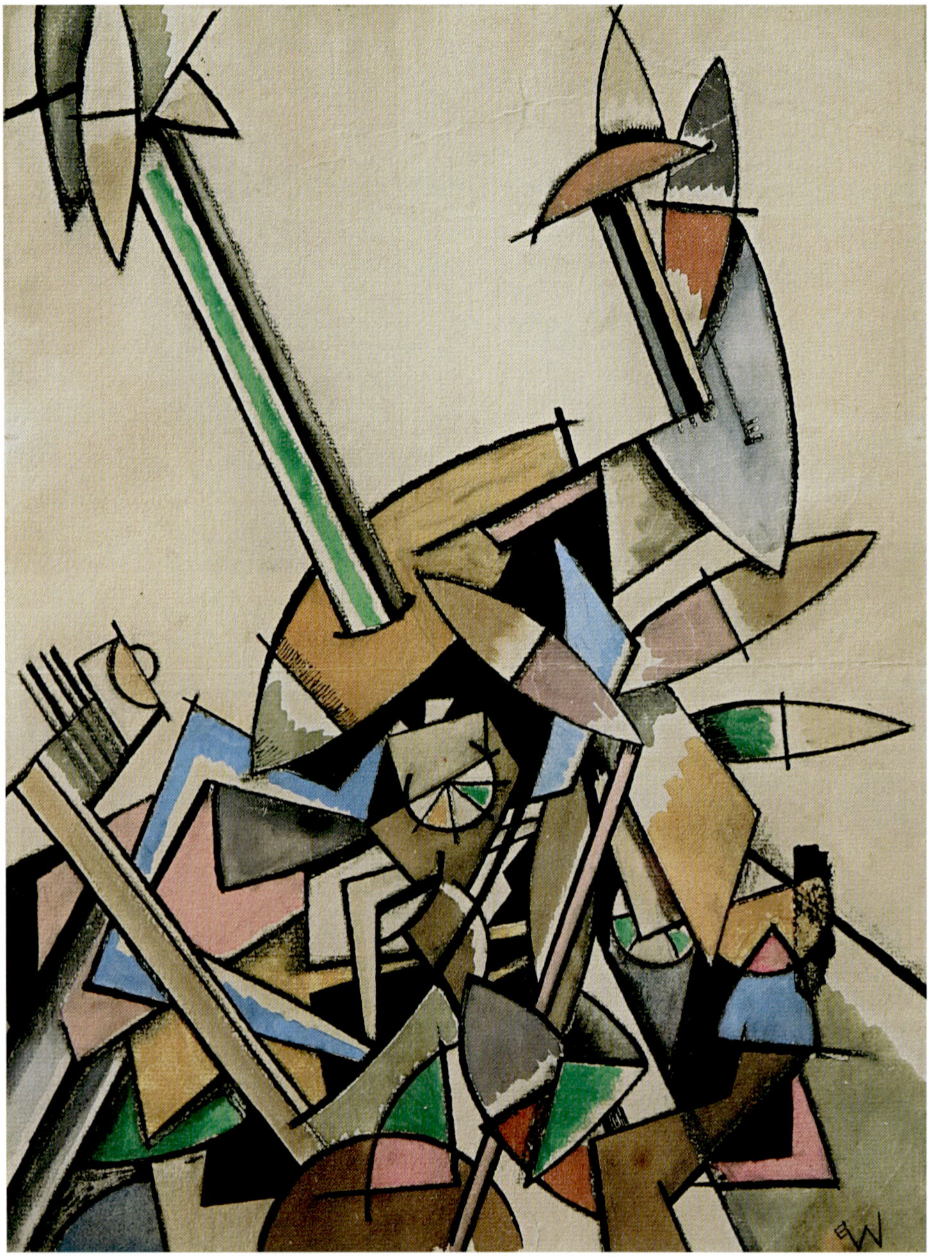

31
Edward Wadsworth
Study for 'Cape of Good Hope' 1914
Ink, crayon, watercolour, and
gouache on paper
33 x 25 cm
[B1]

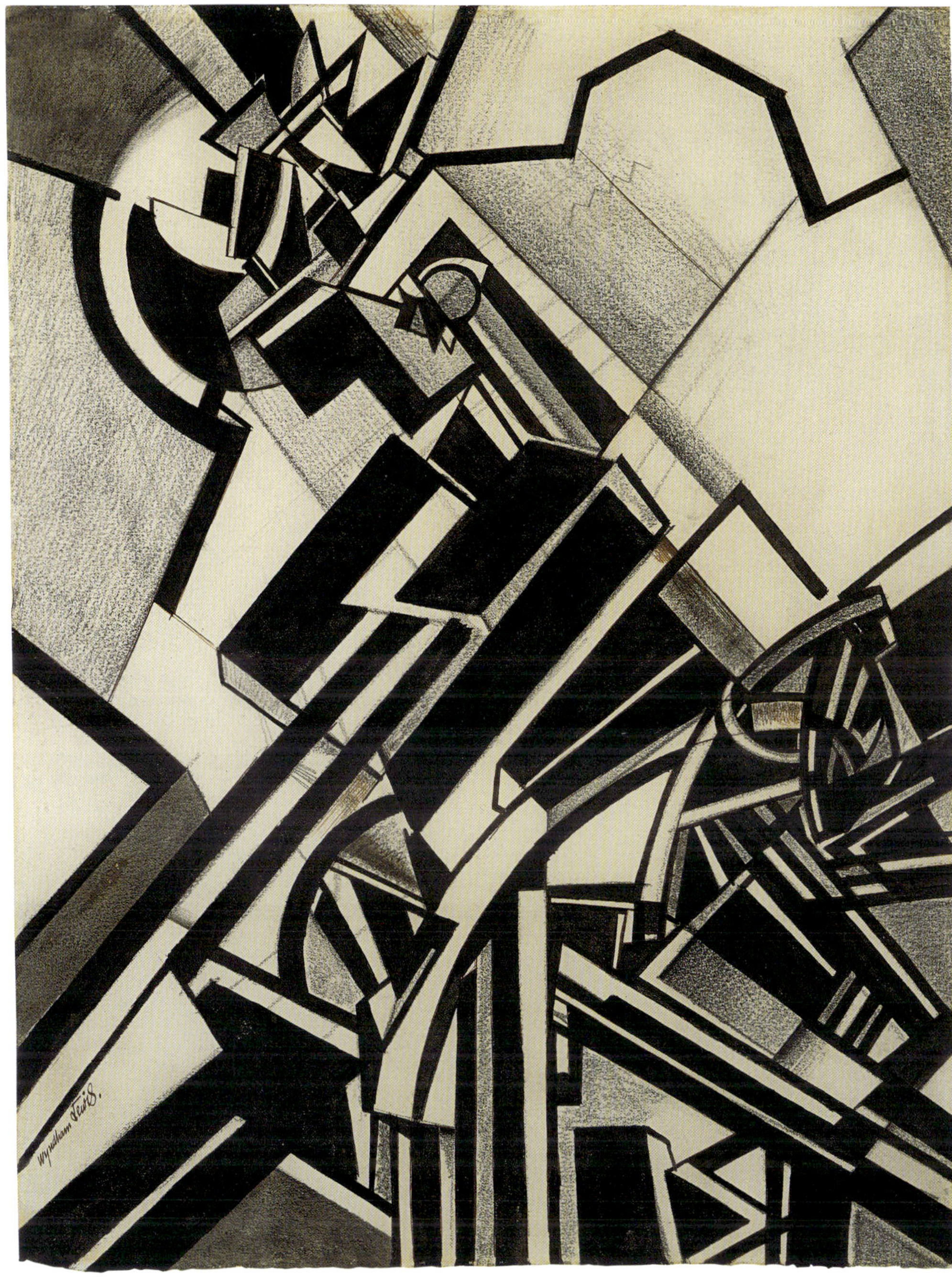

32
Wyndham Lewis
Timon of Athens 1913
Pencil, pen, and ink on paper
34.5 x 26.5 cm
[B1; P]

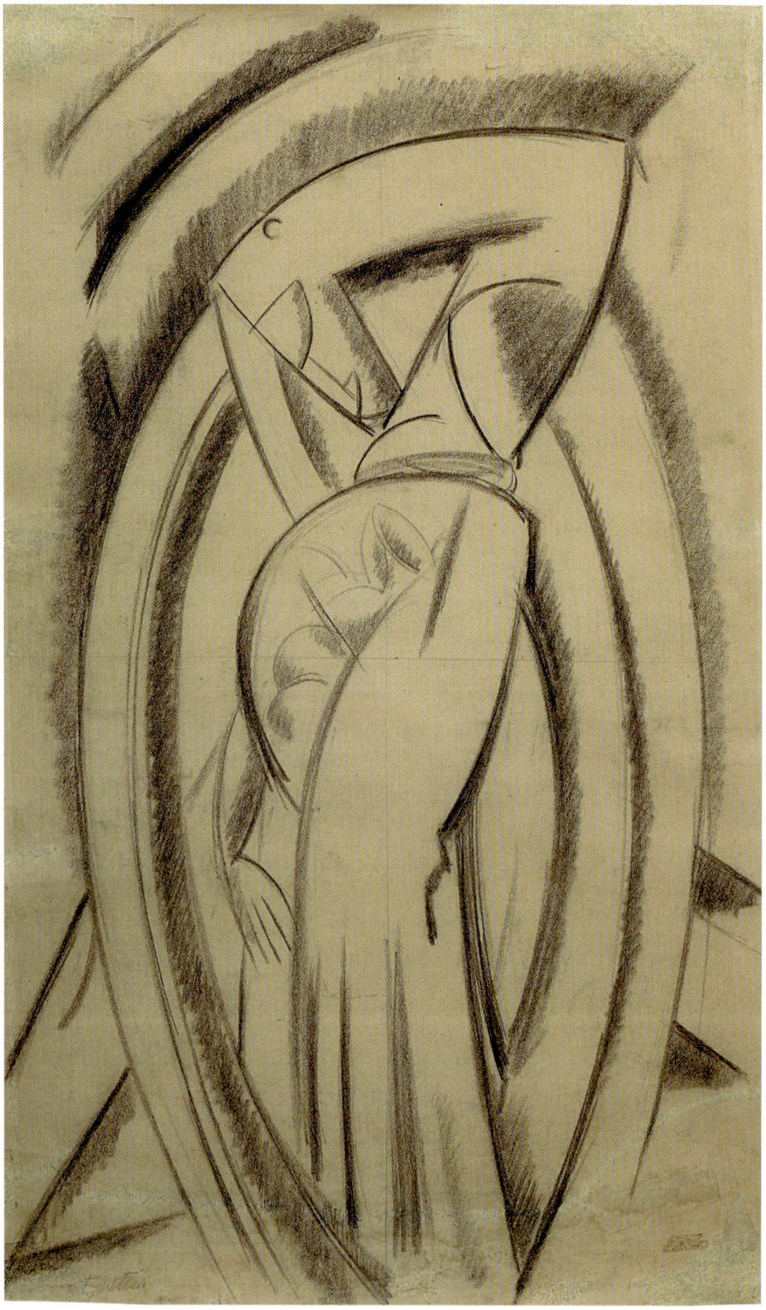

33
Jacob Epstein
Study for 'Female Figure in Flenite' c.1913
Crayon on paper
68.6 x 42.5 cm
[B1]

34
Jacob Epstein
Female Figure 1913
Serpentine [flenite]
61 x 16.2 x 28.9 cm

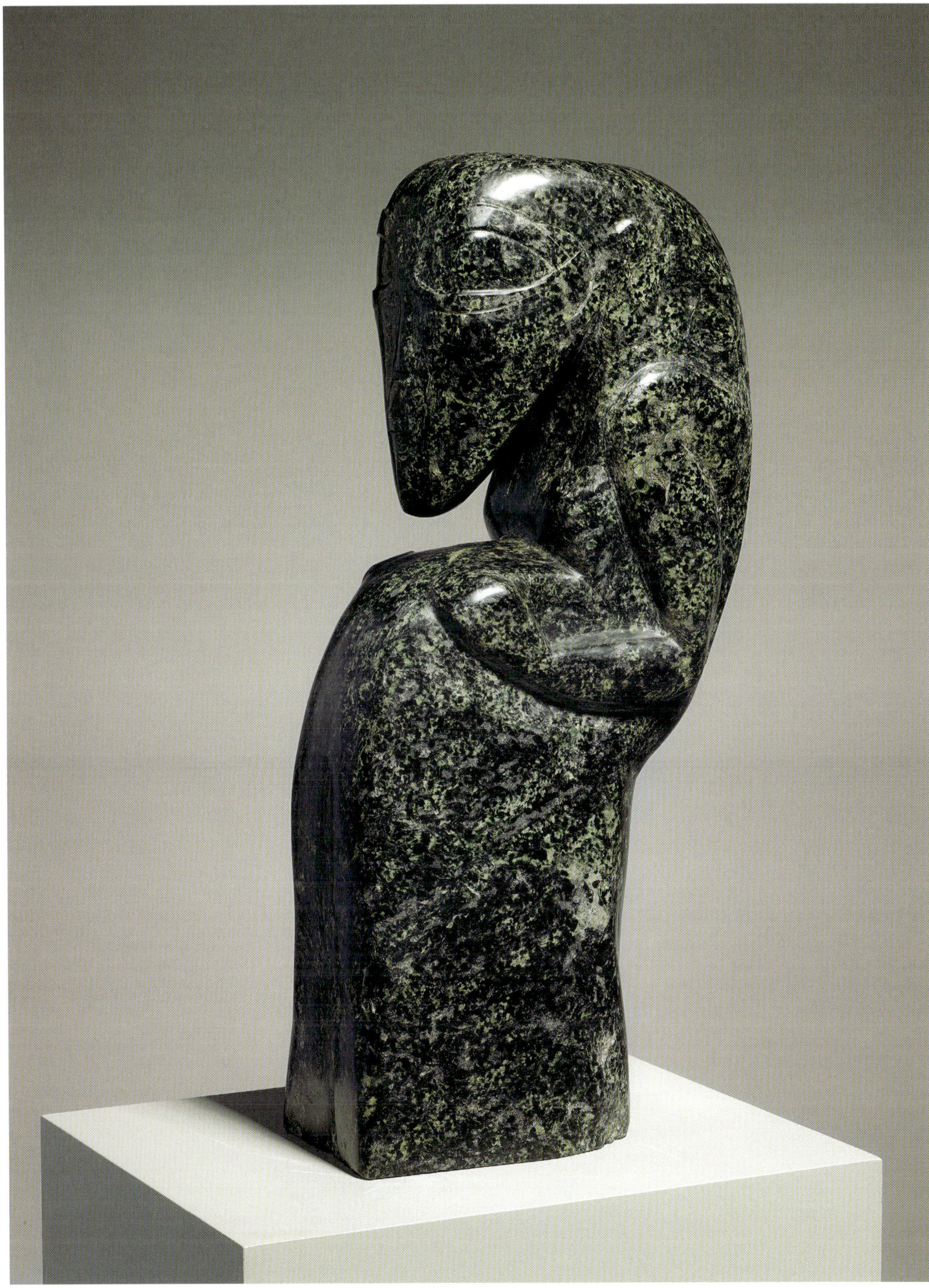

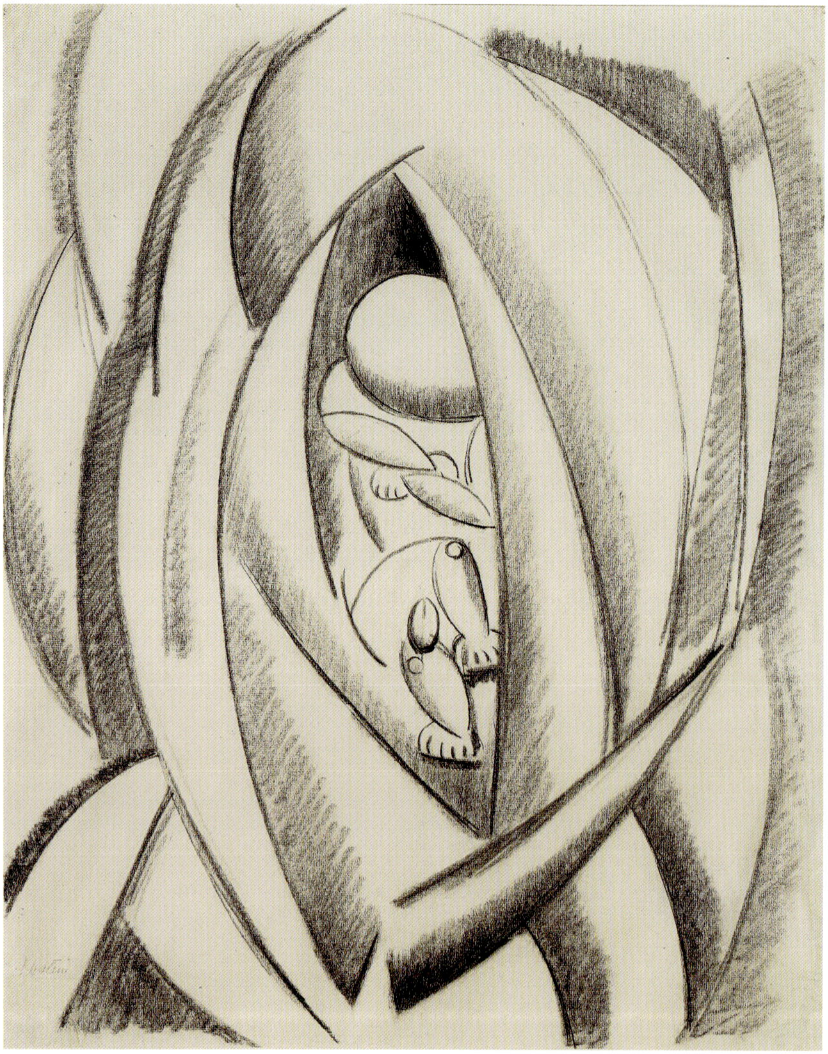

35
Jacob Epstein
Untitled (Birth) [n.d.]
Crayon on paper
63 x 52.7 cm

36
Jacob Epstein
Birth 1913–14
Stone
30.6 x 26.6 x 10.2 cm

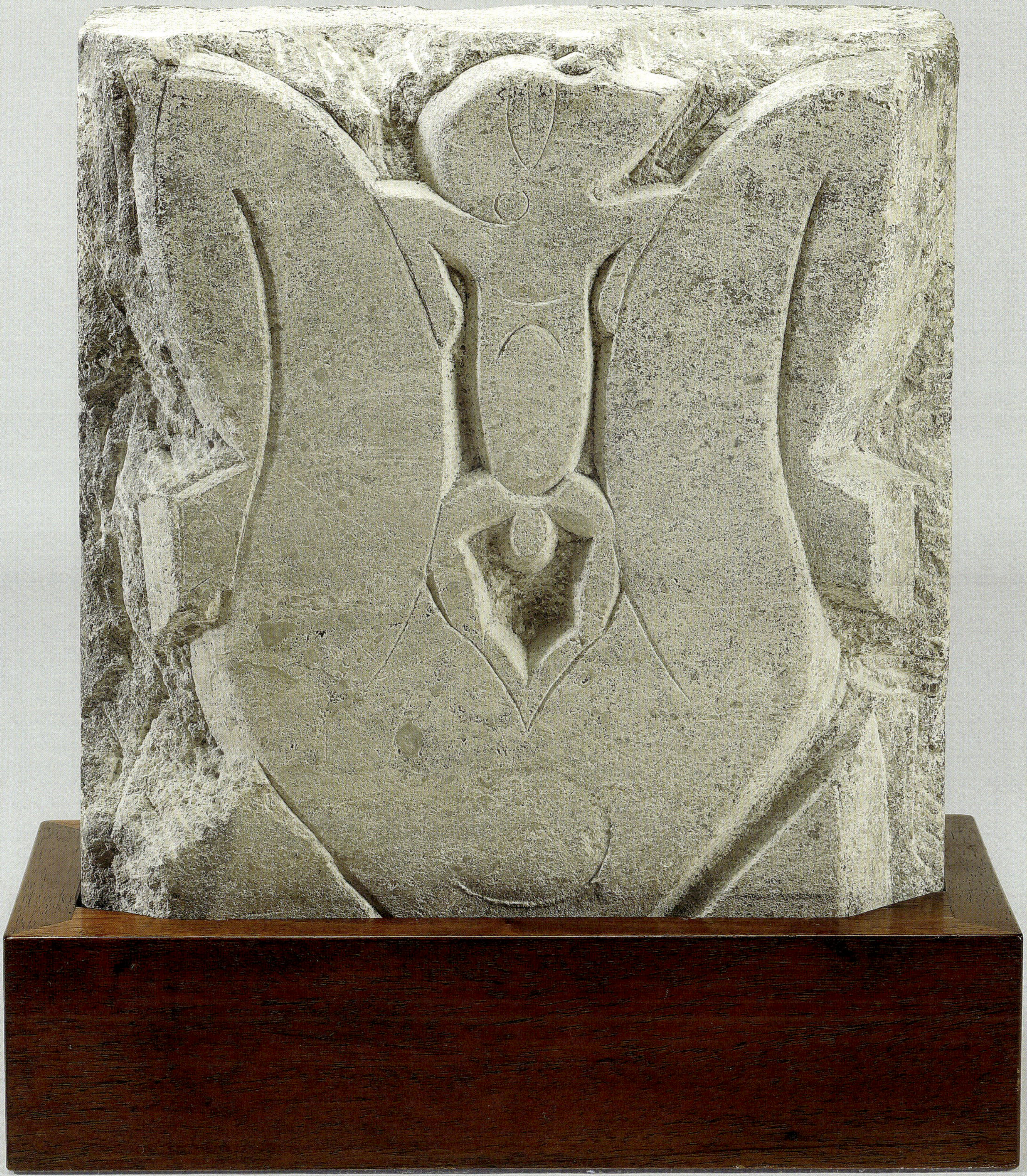

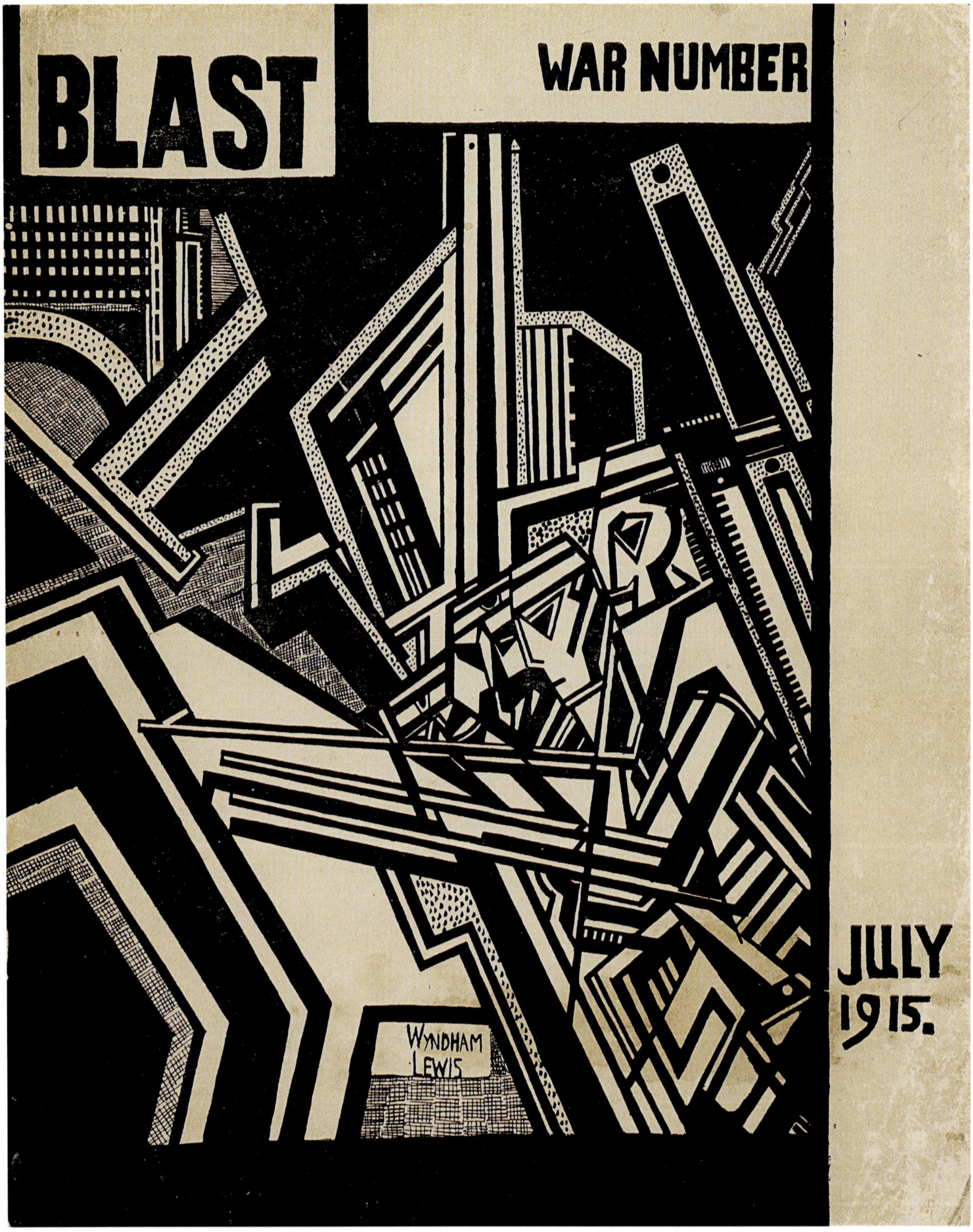

37
Blast, War Number: *Review of the Great English Vortex*, July 1915
Front cover: Wyndham Lewis,
Before Antwerp 1915

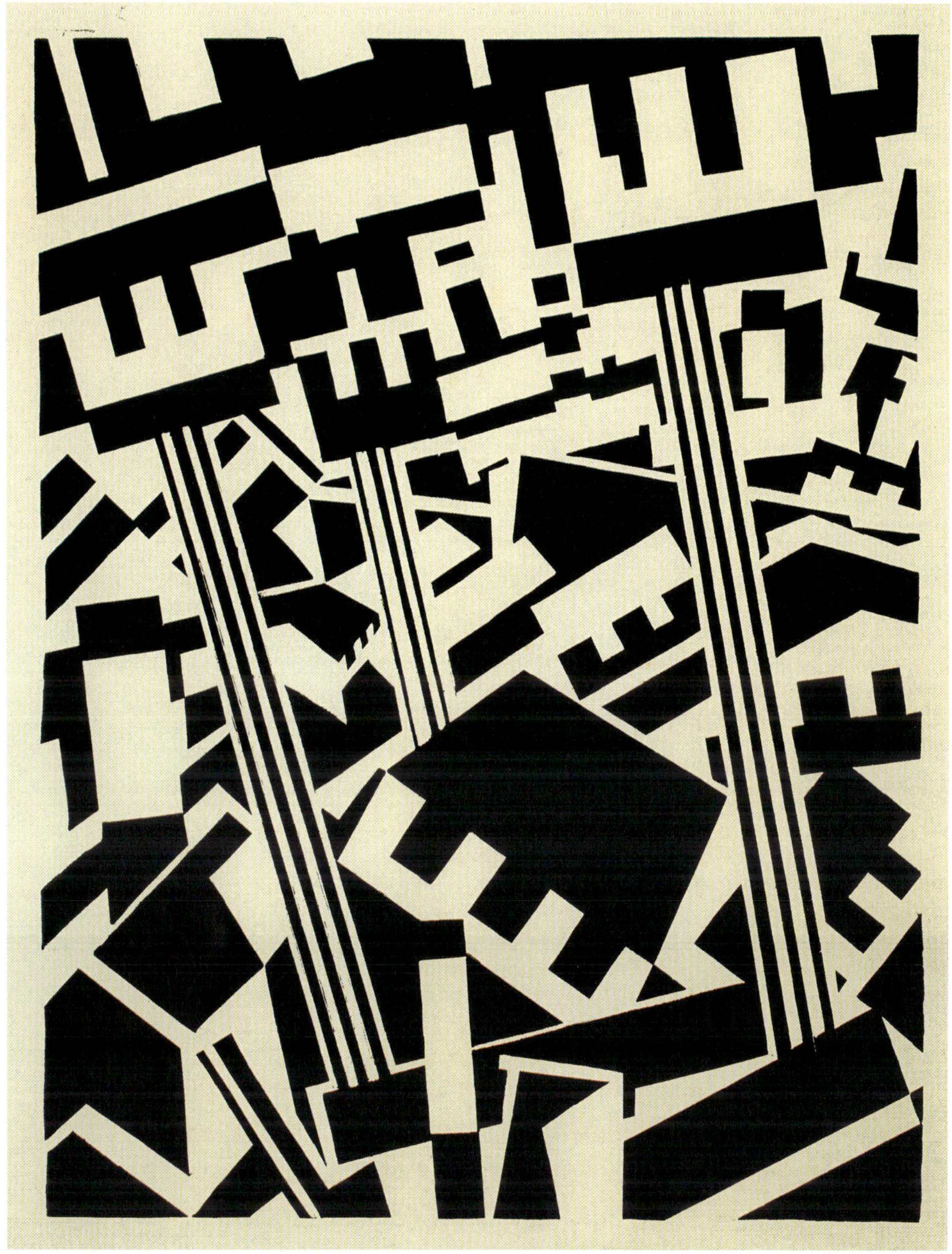

38
Edward Wadsworth
Rotterdam 1914
Woodcut on paper
sheet: 51 x 38 cm
image: 26.4 x 20.2 cm
[B2; D; S]

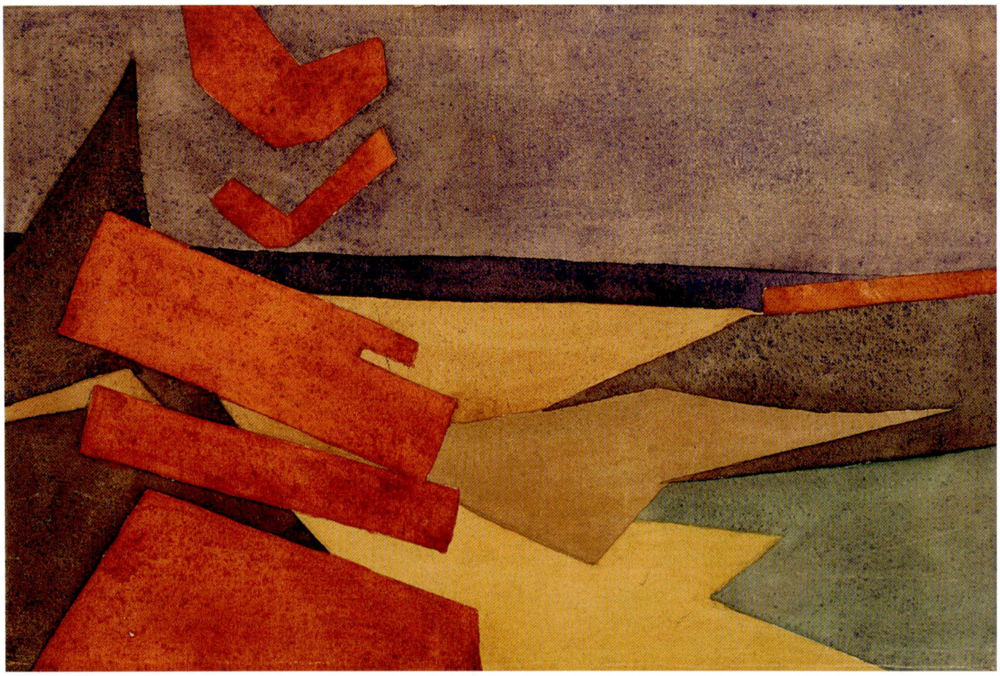

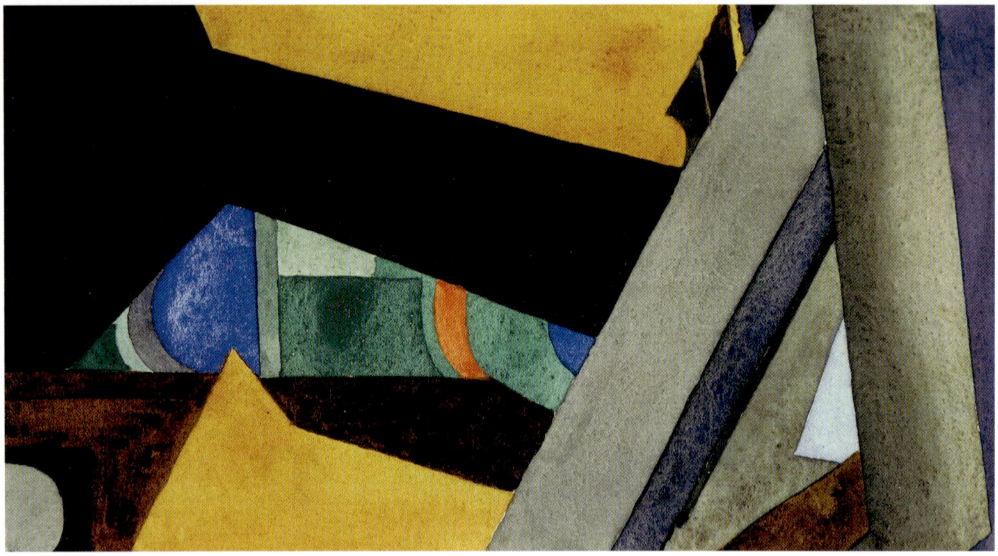

39
Dorothy Shakespear
Untitled c.1914–15
Watercolour on paper
14 x 21 cm

40
Dorothy Shakespear
Untitled (Abstract Composition) c.1914–15
Collage, watercolour, and pencil on paper
11.3 x 20.8 cm

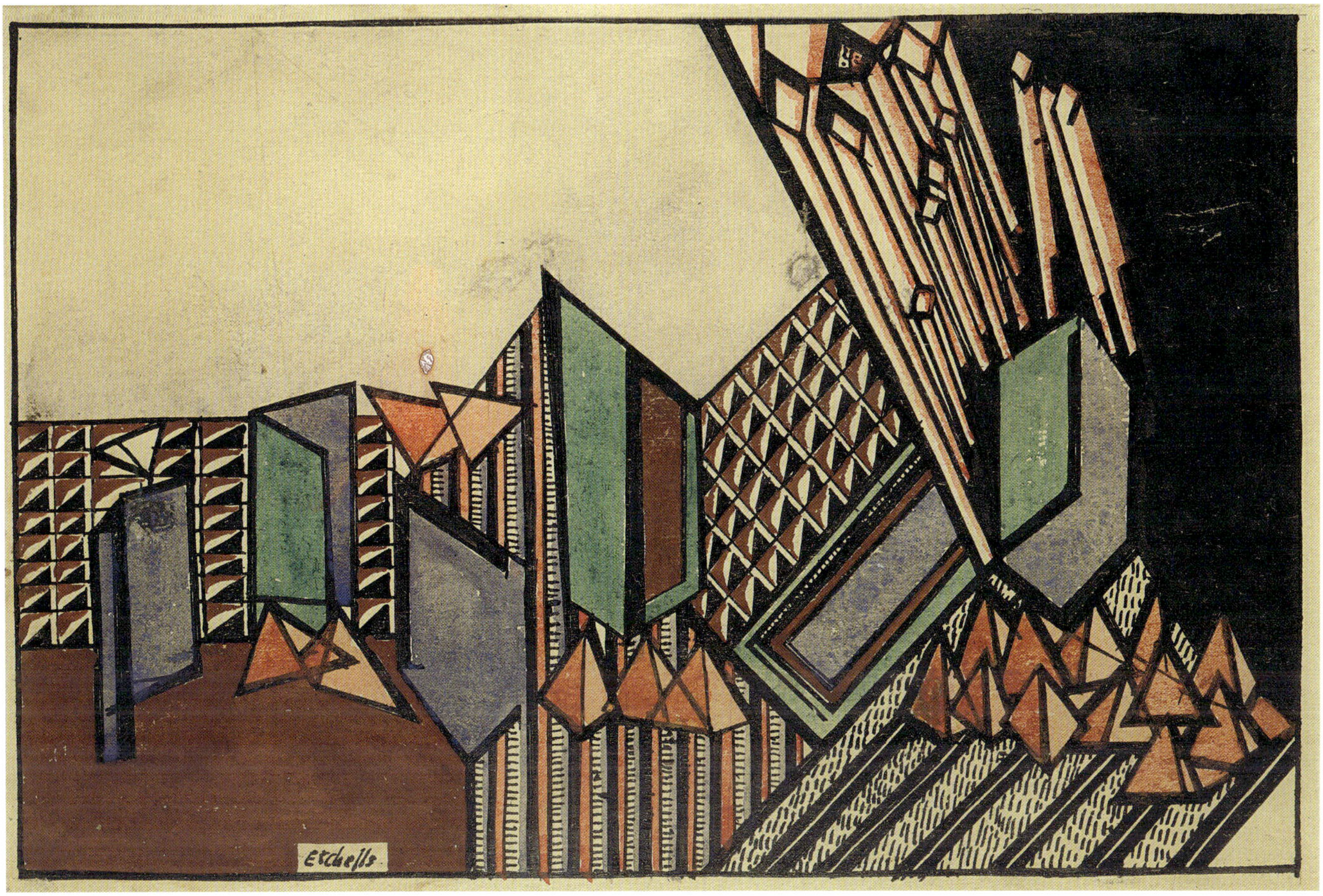

41
Frederick Etchells
Progression 1914–15
Pen and ink on paper
14.3 x 22.3 cm
[B2; P]

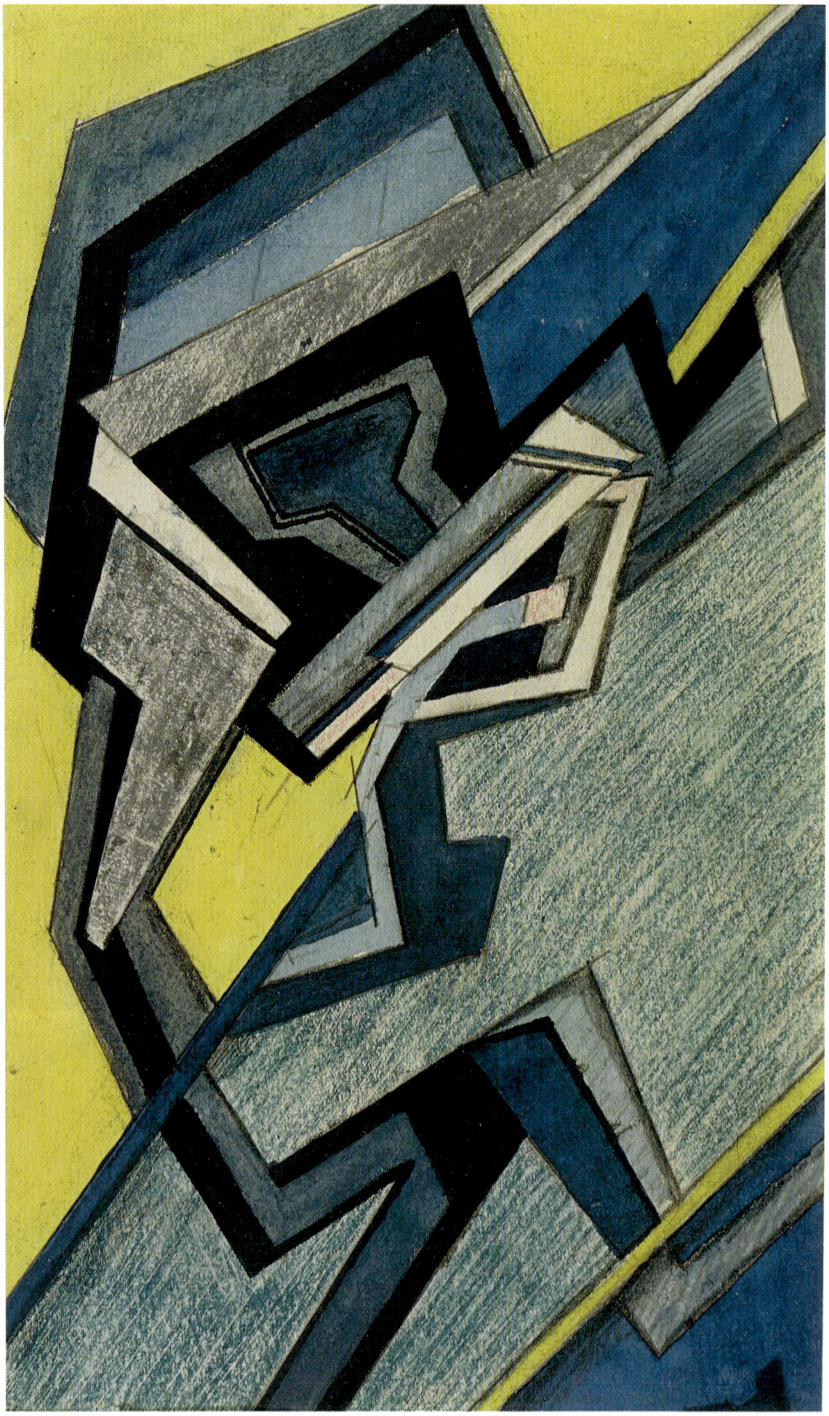

42
Helen Saunders
Abstract Composition in Blue and Yellow c.1915
Pencil, watercolour, and mixed media on paper
27.6 x 17.1 cm

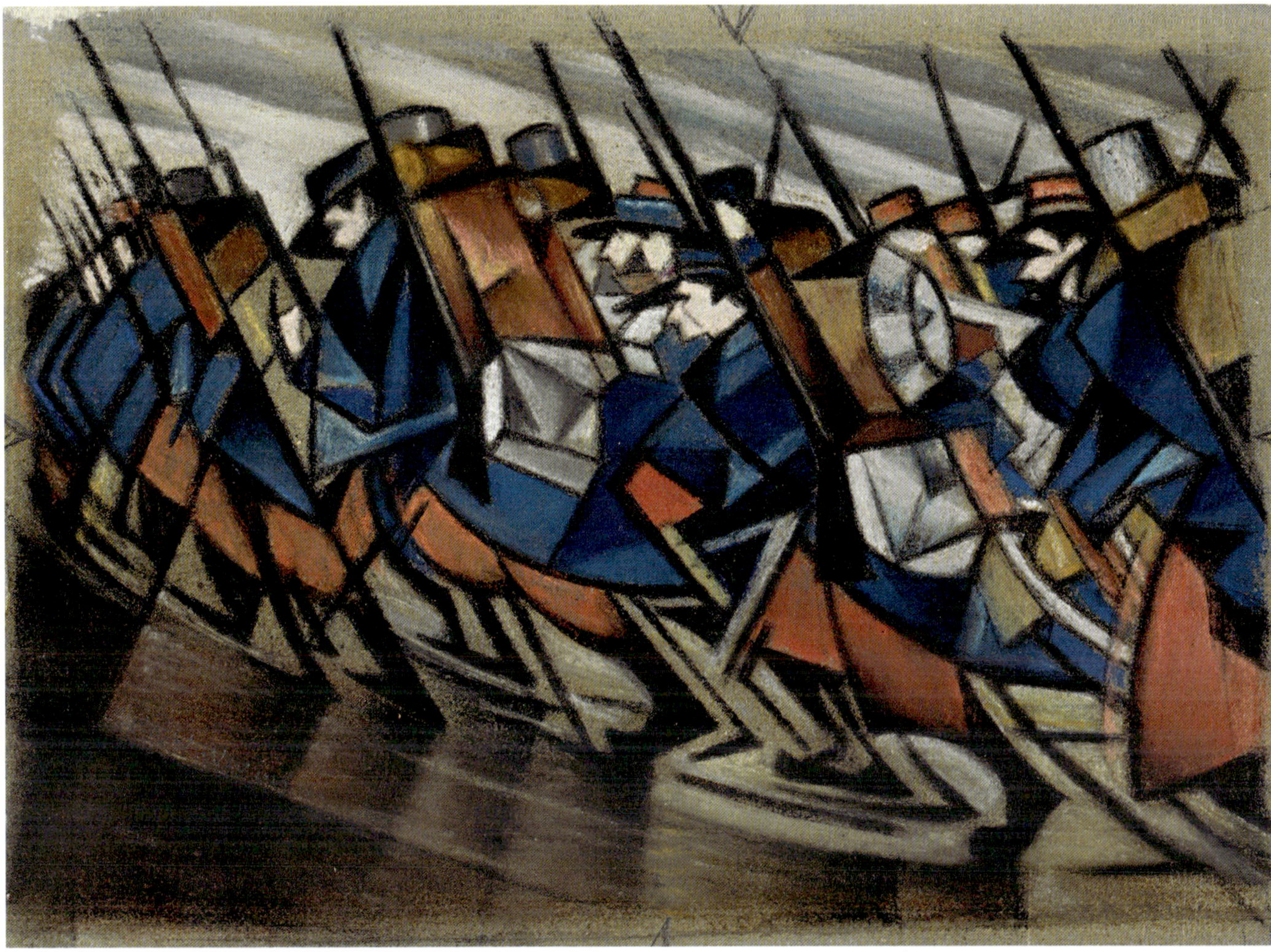

43
Christopher Nevinson
Marching Men 1916
Pastel on paper
13.9 x 20.3 cm
[B2]

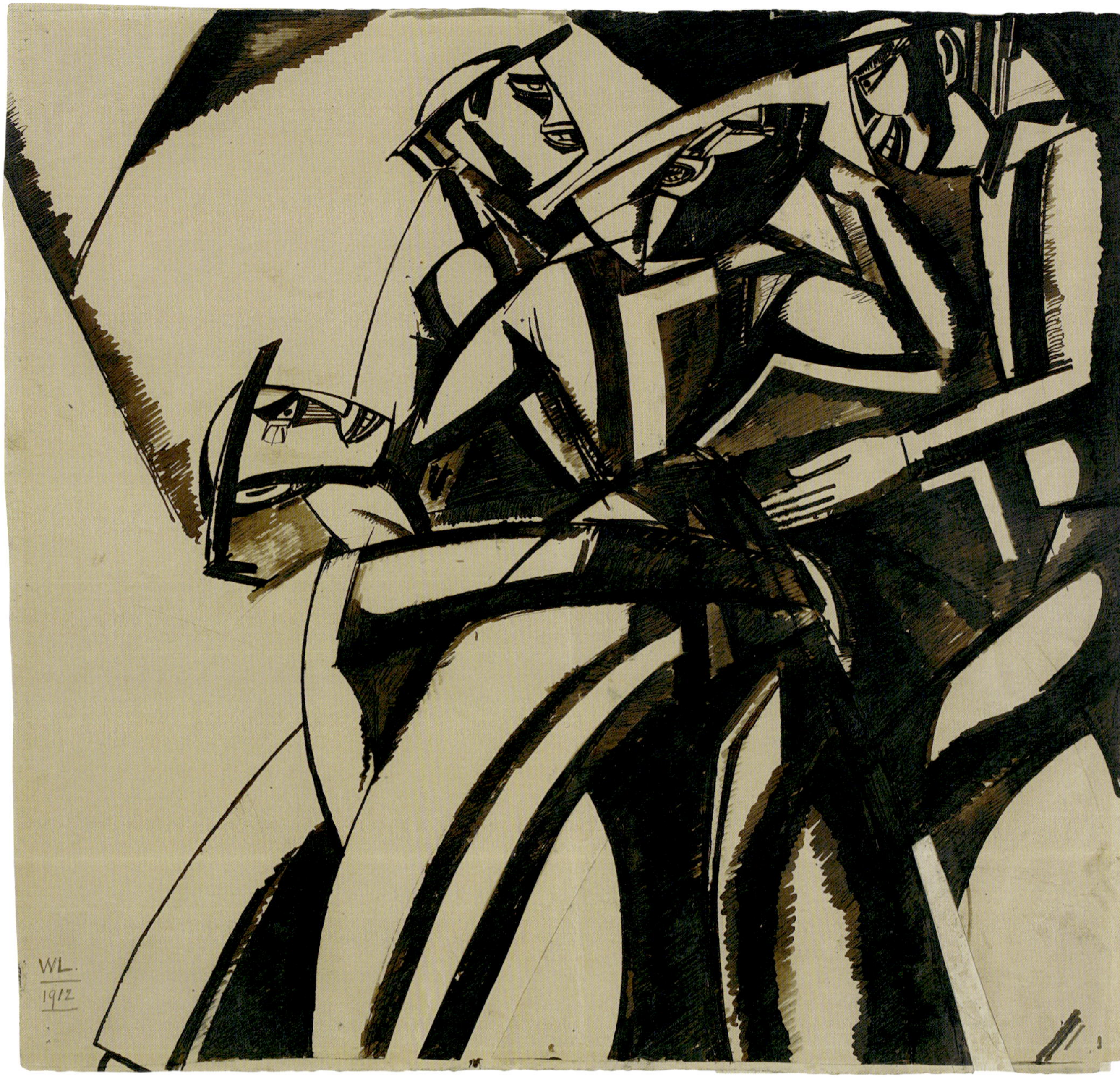

44
Wyndham Lewis
Design for Programme Cover –
Kermesse 1912
Pen and ink on paper
28.5 x 31 cm
[B2; P]

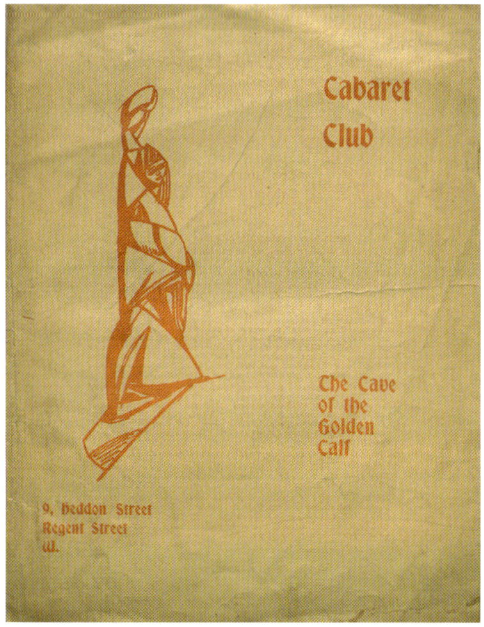

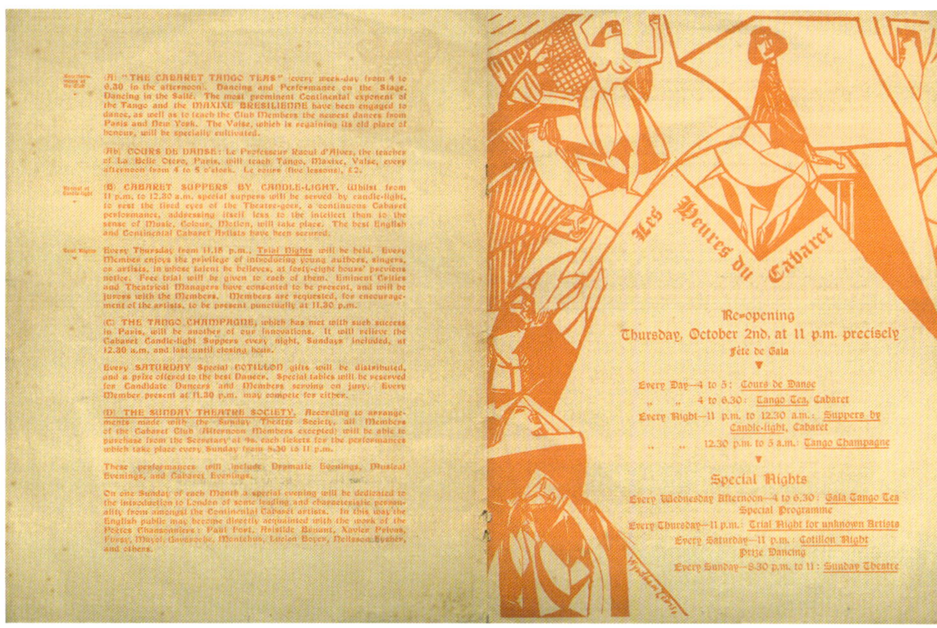

45
Booklet for 'The Cave of the Golden Calf' Cabaret Club, London, 1912
Front cover: designed by Wyndham Lewis

46
Booklet for 'The Cave of the Golden Calf' Cabaret Club, London, 1912
Designed by Wyndham Lewis

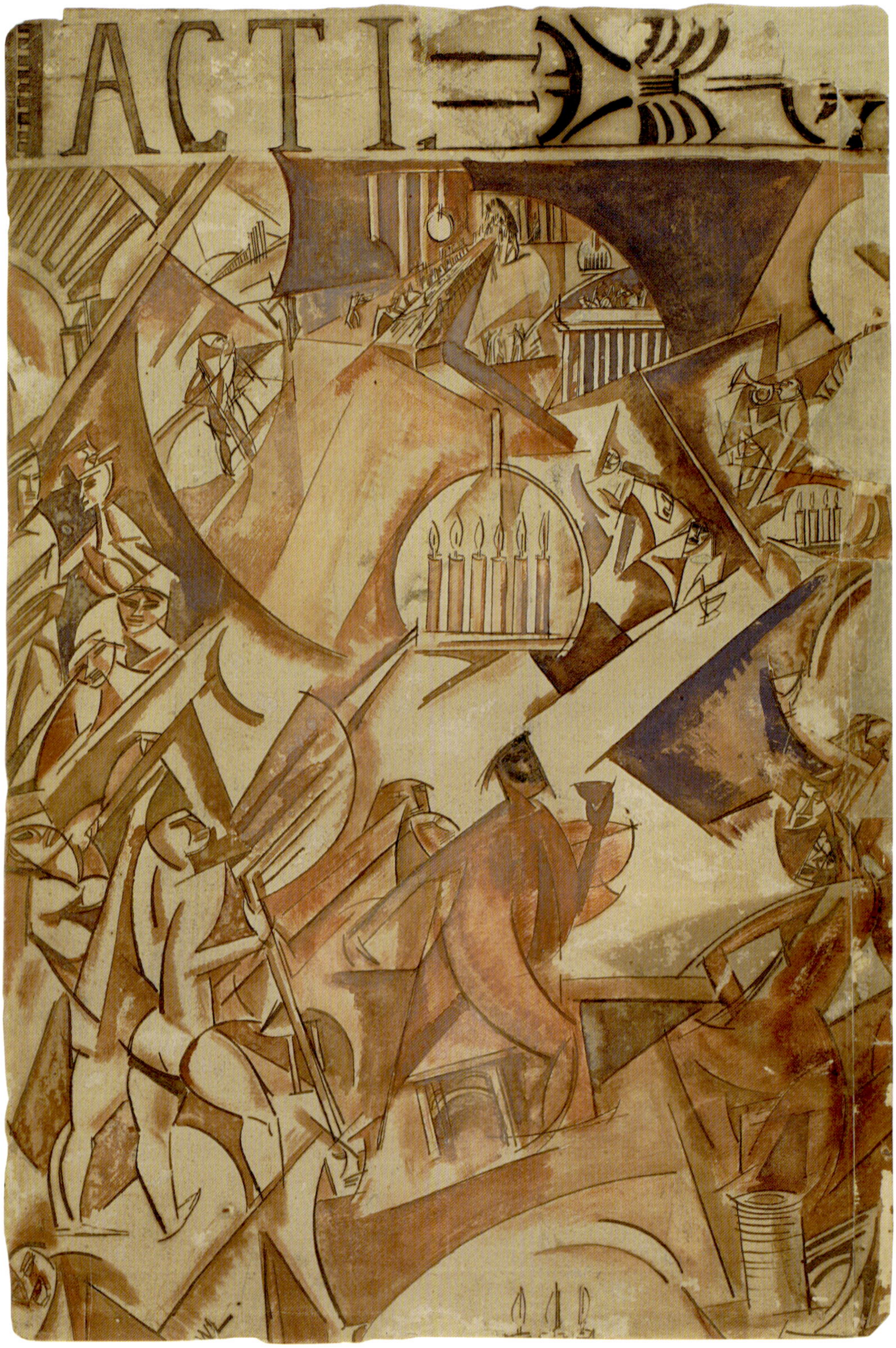

47
Wyndham Lewis
Timon of Athens, Act 1. Banquet Scene 1912
Pen, ink, and watercolour on paper
48.5 x 32.8 cm
[P]

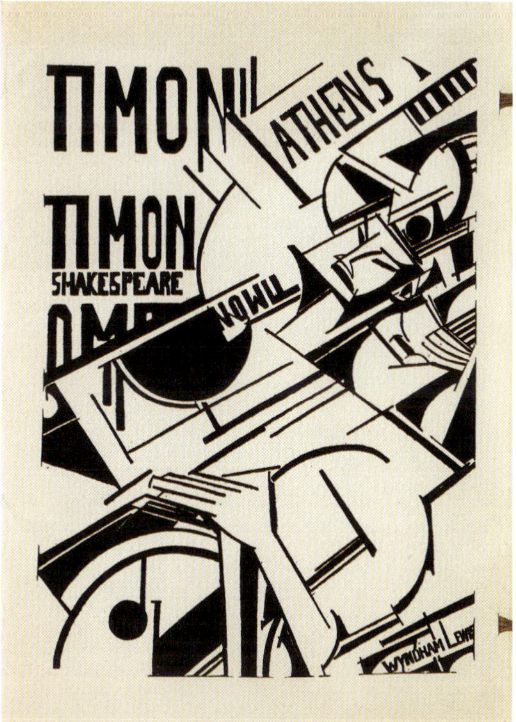

48
Wyndham Lewis
Timon of Athens 1913
Portfolio of sixteen lithographs and process engravings
40 x 27.9 cm
Front cover

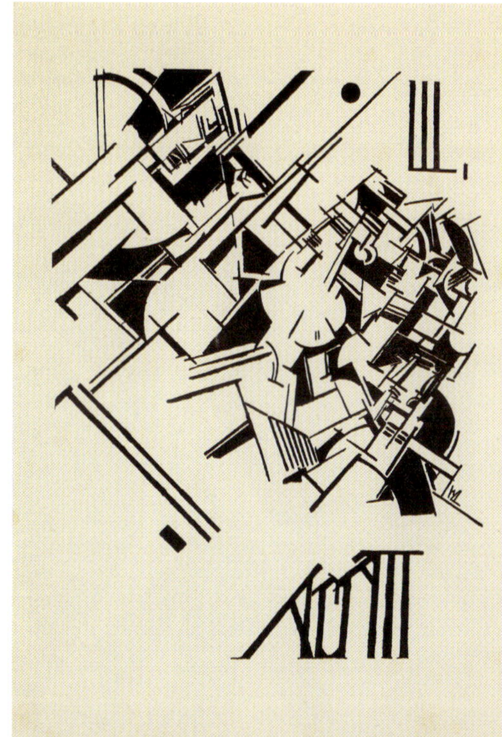

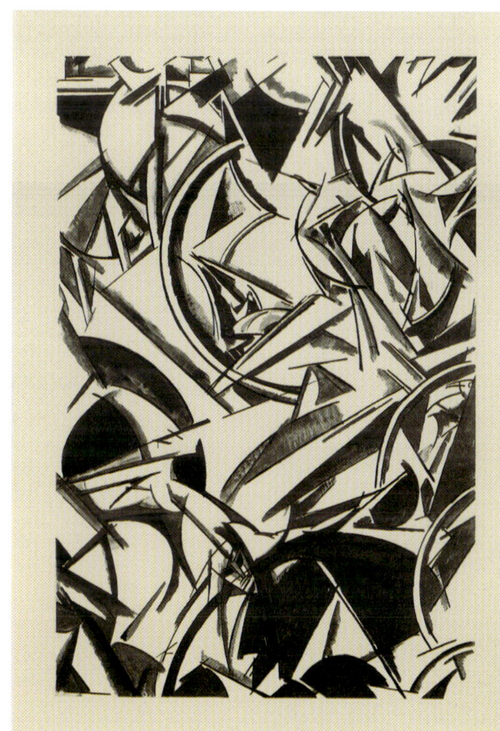

49a, b
Wyndham Lewis
Timon of Athens 1913
Two sheets from the portfolio of sixteen lithographs and process engravings
Each 39.1 x 27.3 cm

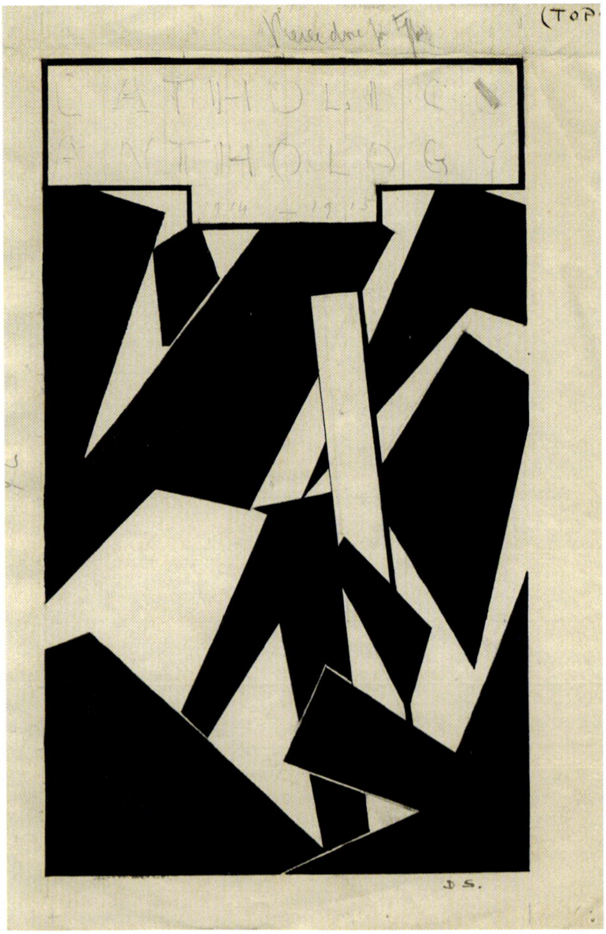

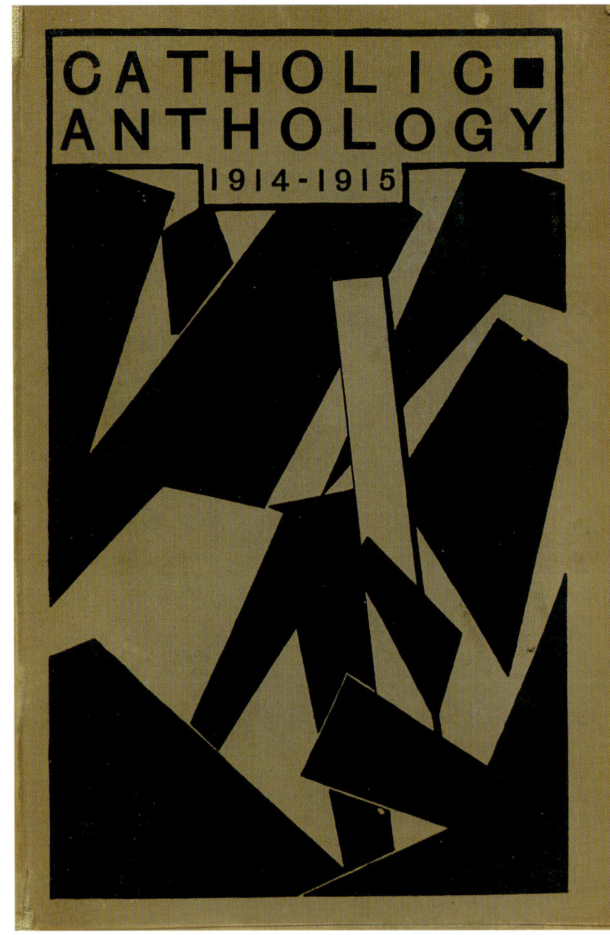

50
Dorothy Shakespear
Cover design for *Catholic Anthology* 1915
Ink and pencil on paper
26 x 16.5 cm

51
Ezra Pound (ed.)
Catholic Anthology 1915
Published by Elkin Mathews, London
Front cover

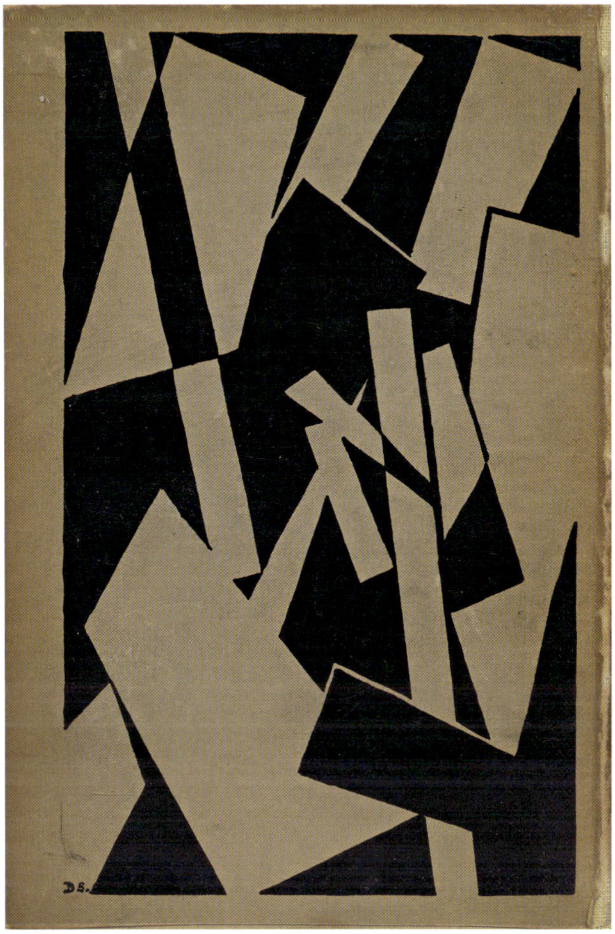

52
Ezra Pound (ed.)
Catholic Anthology 1915
Published by Elkin Mathews, London
Back cover

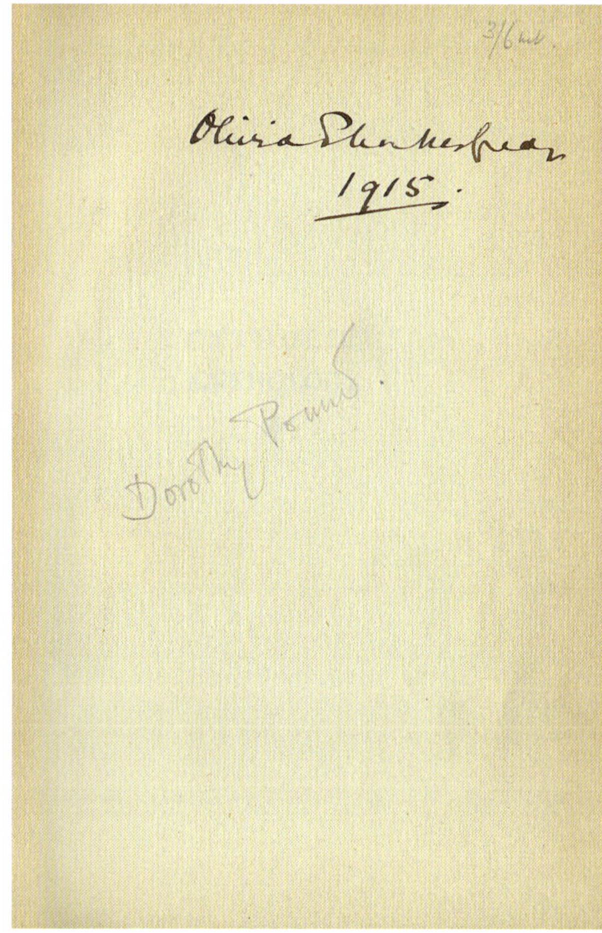

53
Inscription in Olivia Shakespear's copy of *Catholic Anthology*, signed by her in ink. Signed by her daughter Dorothy in pencil

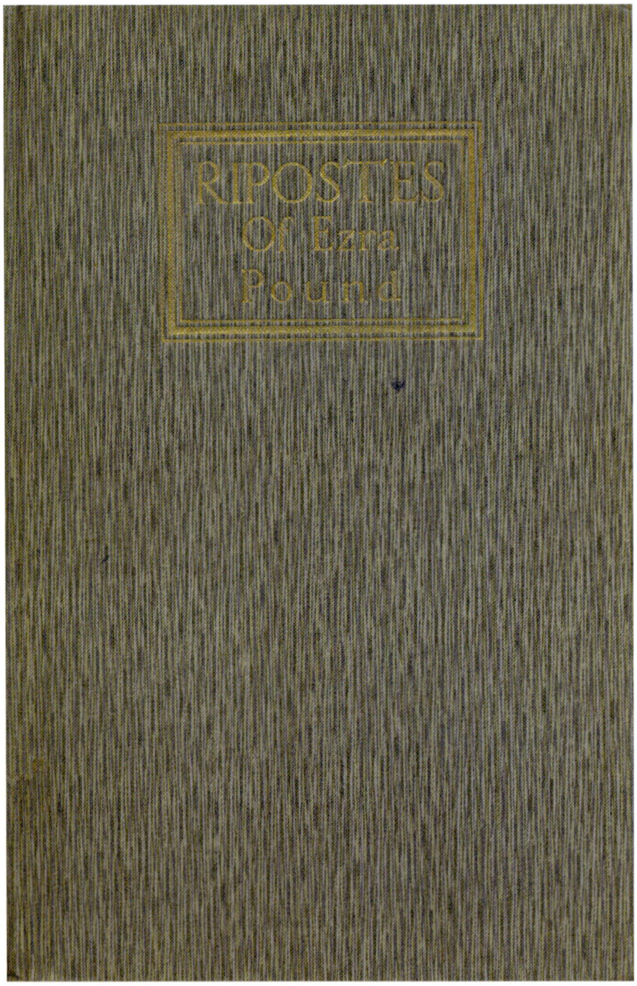

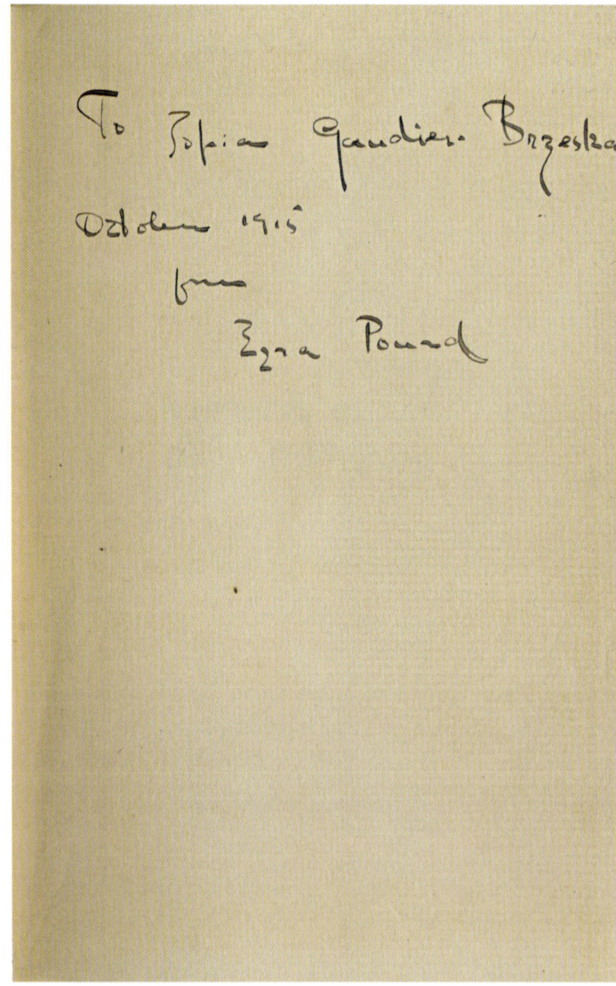

54
Ezra Pound
Ripostes 1912
Published by Stephen Swift
& Co., London

55
Inscription in Sophie Gaudier-Brzeska's copy of *Ripostes*, inscribed to her by Ezra Pound, October 1915

56
Ezra Pound
Gaudier Brzeska: A Memoir 1916
Published by John Lane, London

THE PENGUIN CLUB

The Penguin Club Exhibition of the Vorticists and Sunwise Turn

The Vorticists had their first real exposure in the United States in 1917 with the *Exhibition of the Vorticists*, on view in New York from 10 January to 1 February at the Penguin Club (an artist-run club founded by Walt Kuhn). The exhibition was organized in the midst of the First World War by two Americans, the London-based expatriate poet Ezra Pound and the New York patron and collector John Quinn. Though the latter financed the presentation, it was Pound who acted as its curator from London, inviting the artists and choosing many of the artworks. Because Pound fervently championed Wyndham Lewis, the show revolved around a notable group of his works spanning his still-brief career. Jessica Dismorr, Frederick Etchells, William Roberts, Helen Saunders, and Edward Wadsworth also each were represented with smaller selections of paintings and drawings. The exhibition was largely ignored in New York, but Quinn's enthusiasm for Vorticism led to his purchase of almost everything included in the Penguin show. What he did not acquire – some paintings, drawings, and prints by Wadsworth (the latter were not officially on exhibit according to the catalogue, but likely available for viewing), and three Dismorr drawings – he sent to the avant-garde bookstore, Sunwise Turn, run by Mary Mowbray-Clarke and Madge Jenison. These remained unsold and eventually were returned to England. Whilst the Penguin Club exhibition garnered scant notice in the United States, it was nonetheless decisive to Vorticism's fortunes and during the 1910s was the only presentation outside England to focus specifically on the movement.

57

Wyndham Lewis

Anthony 1909

Pen and gouache on paper

14.5 x 11.5 cm

[P]

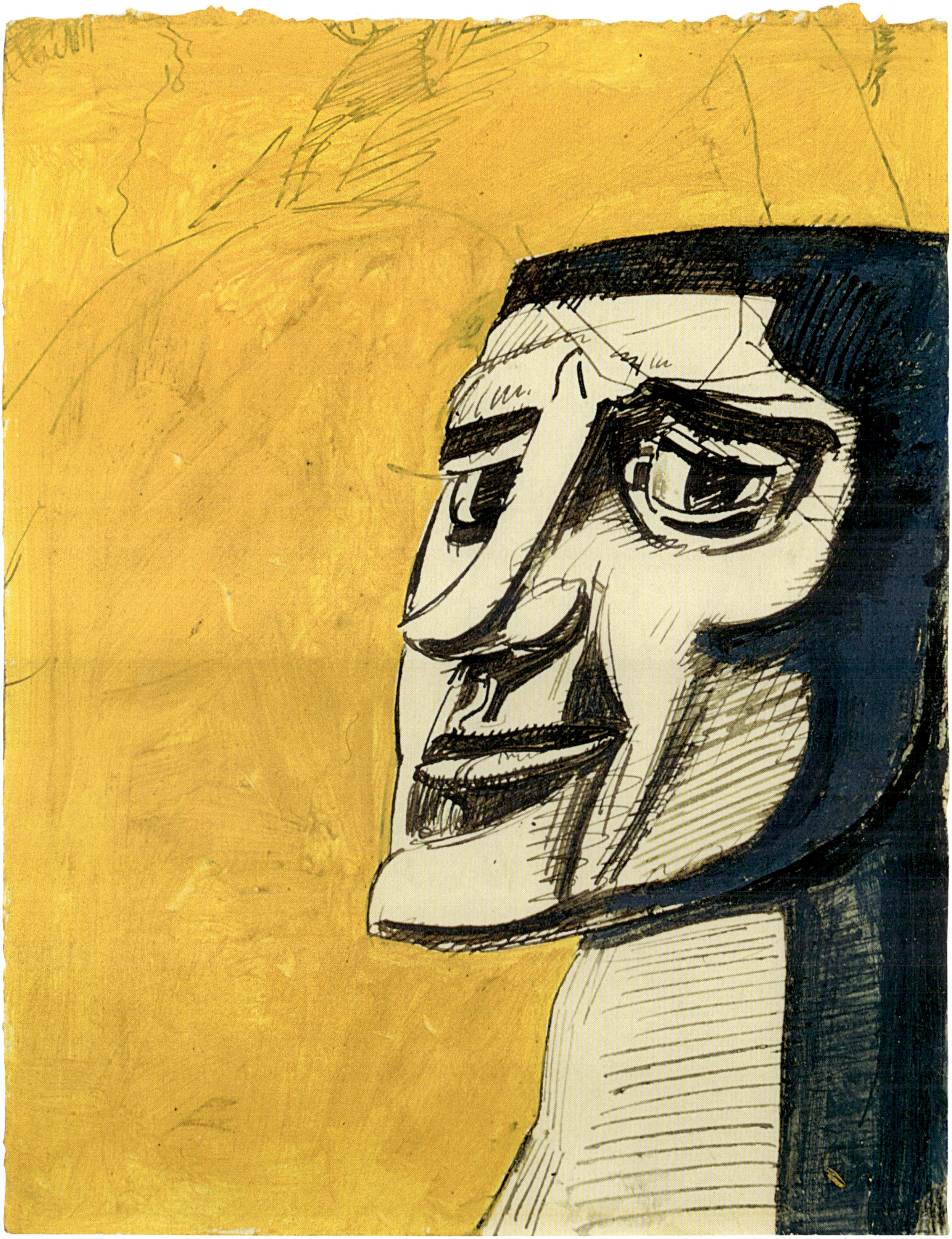

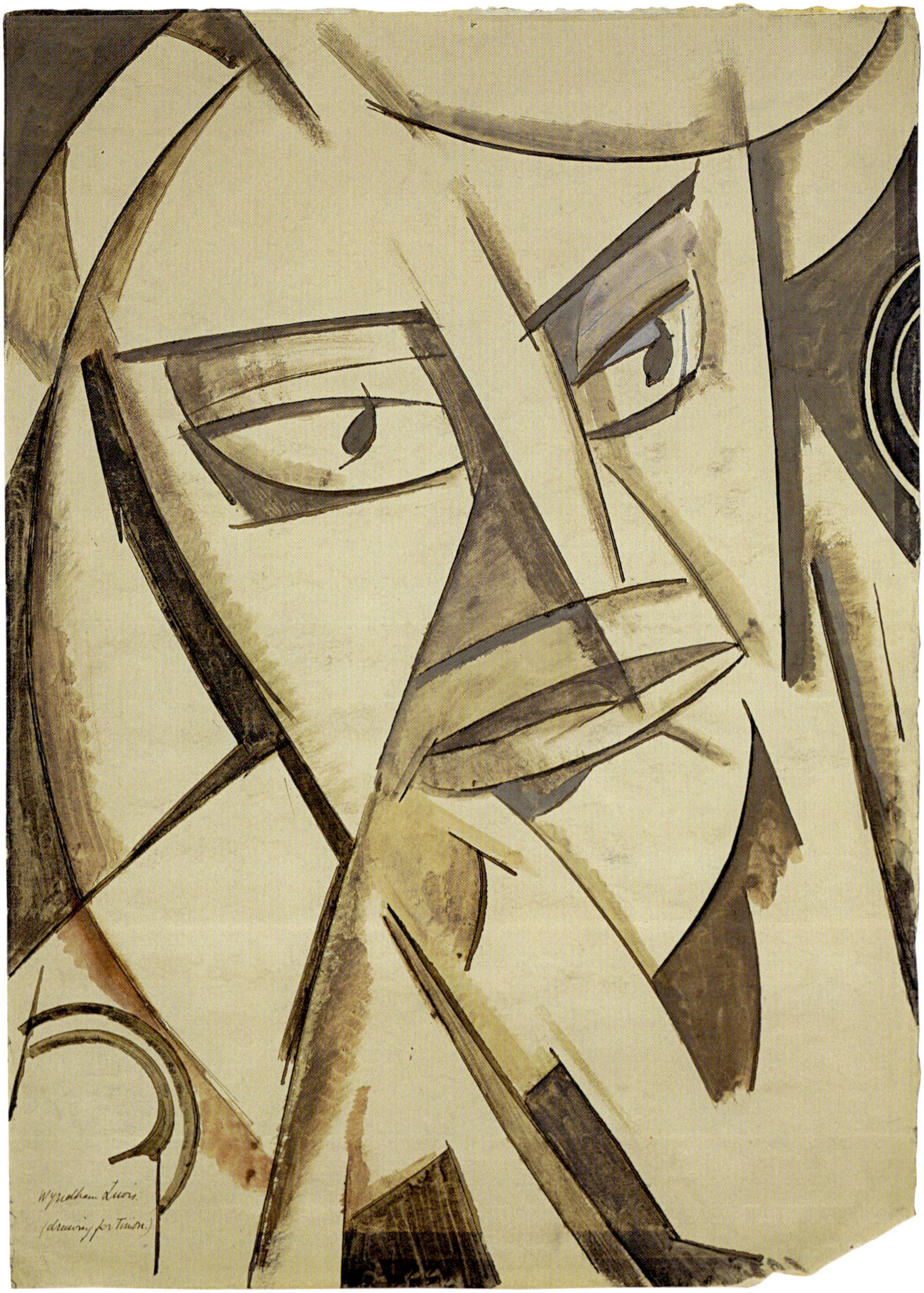

58
Wyndham Lewis
Drawing for Timon 1912
Pen, ink, and watercolour/
gouache on paper
38 x 28.5 cm

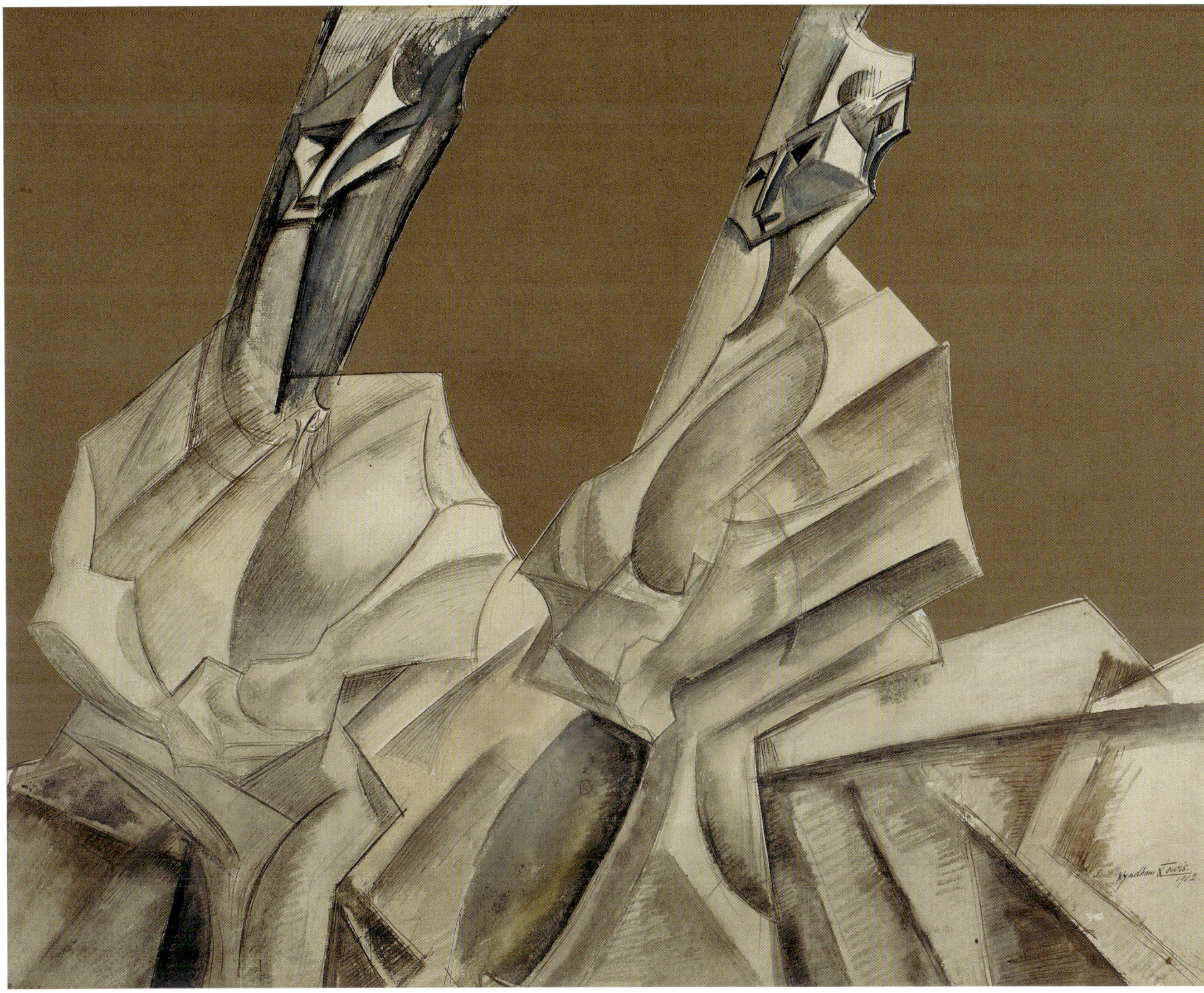

59
Wyndham Lewis
Two Women 1912
Pencil, pen, ink, gouache, and collage on paper
48 x 62.5 cm
[P]

60
Wyndham Lewis
Kermesse 1912
Gouache and watercolour with
pen and ink over pencil on
two joined sheets of paper
30.5 x 30.6 cm
[P]

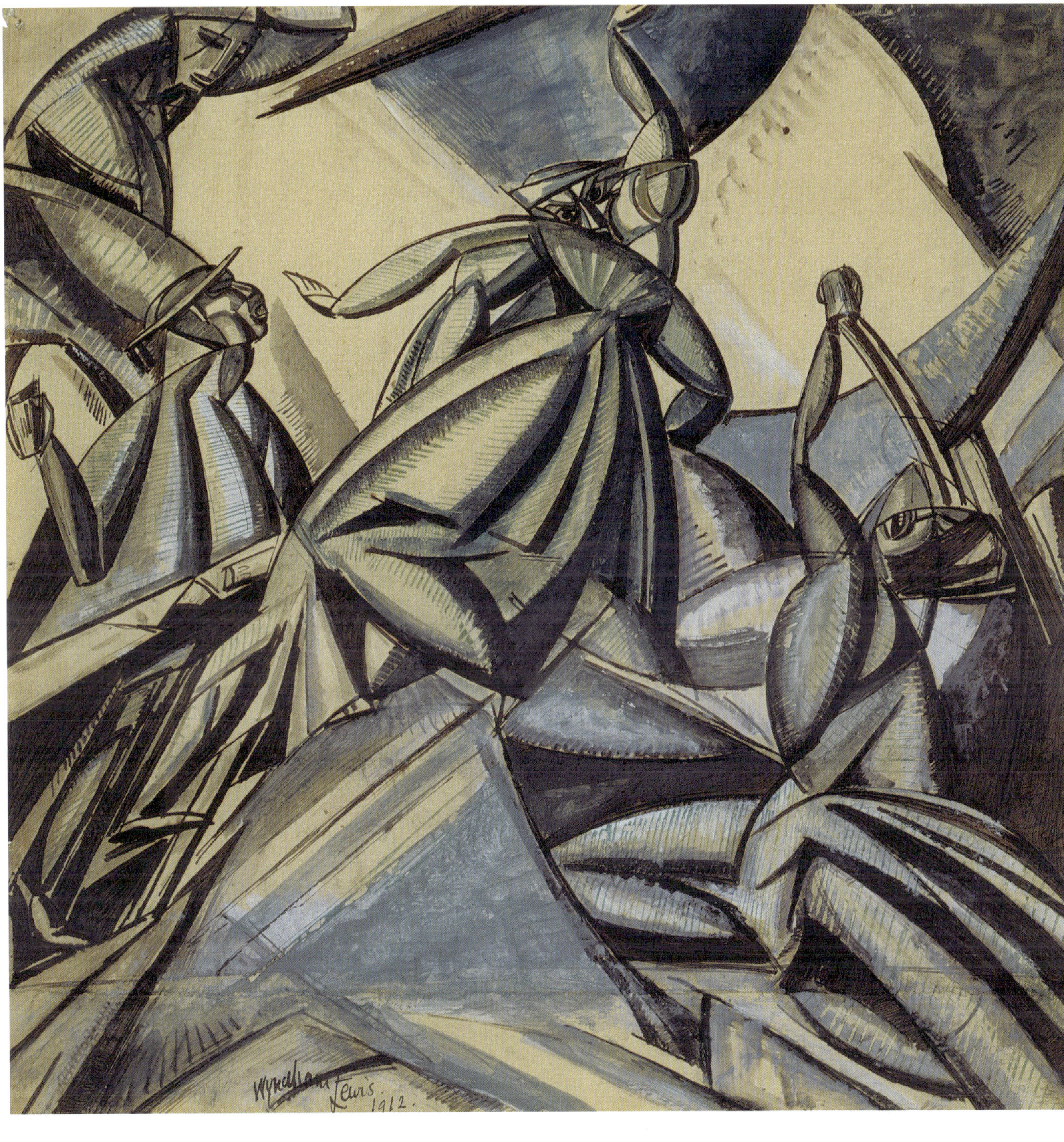
Wyndham Lewis
1912.

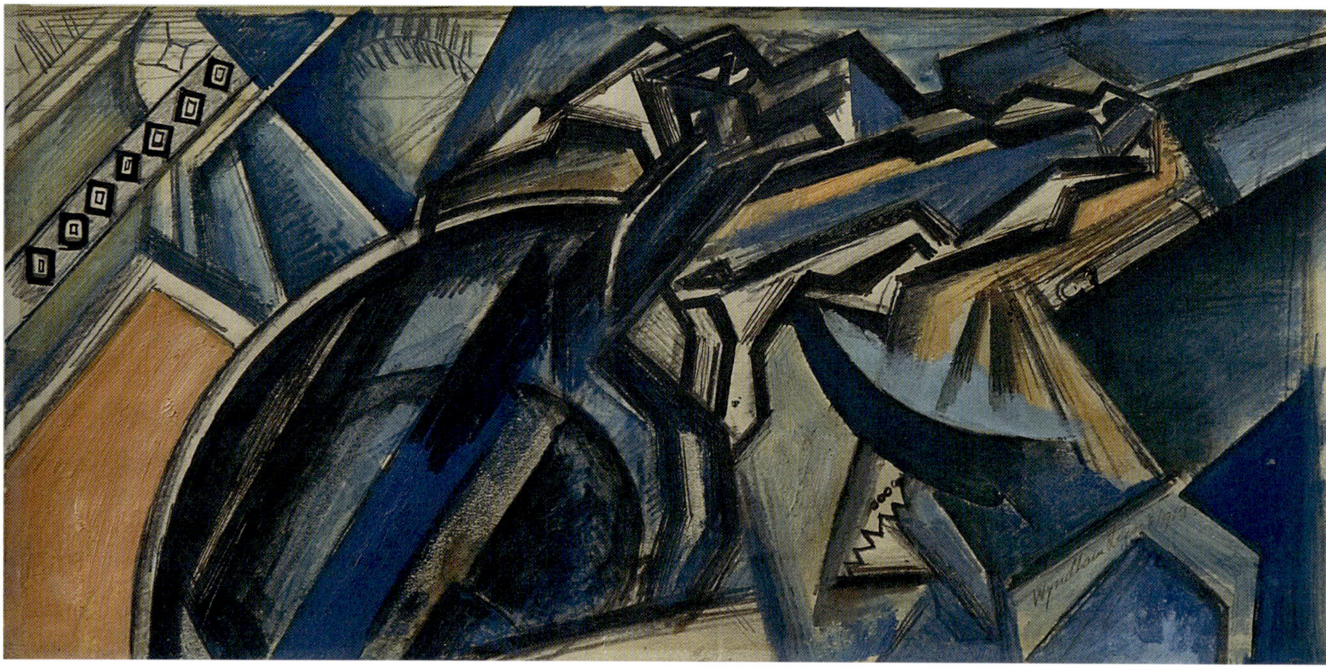

61
Wyndham Lewis
Protraction 1913
Pencil, crayon, and
watercolour on paper
15.2 x 30.5 cm
[P]

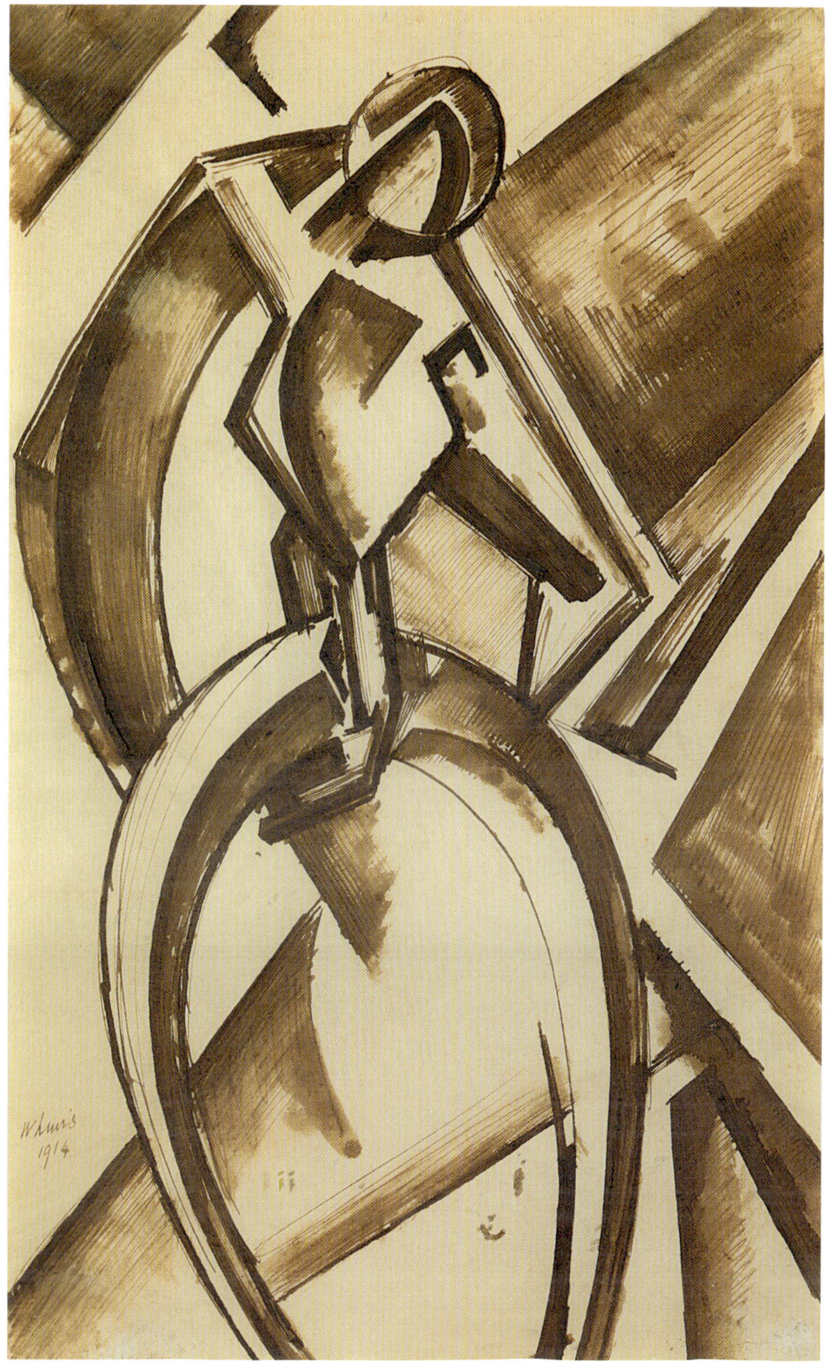

62
Wyndham Lewis
Arghol 1914
Pen, ink, and wash
on paper
33 x 20.5 cm
[P]

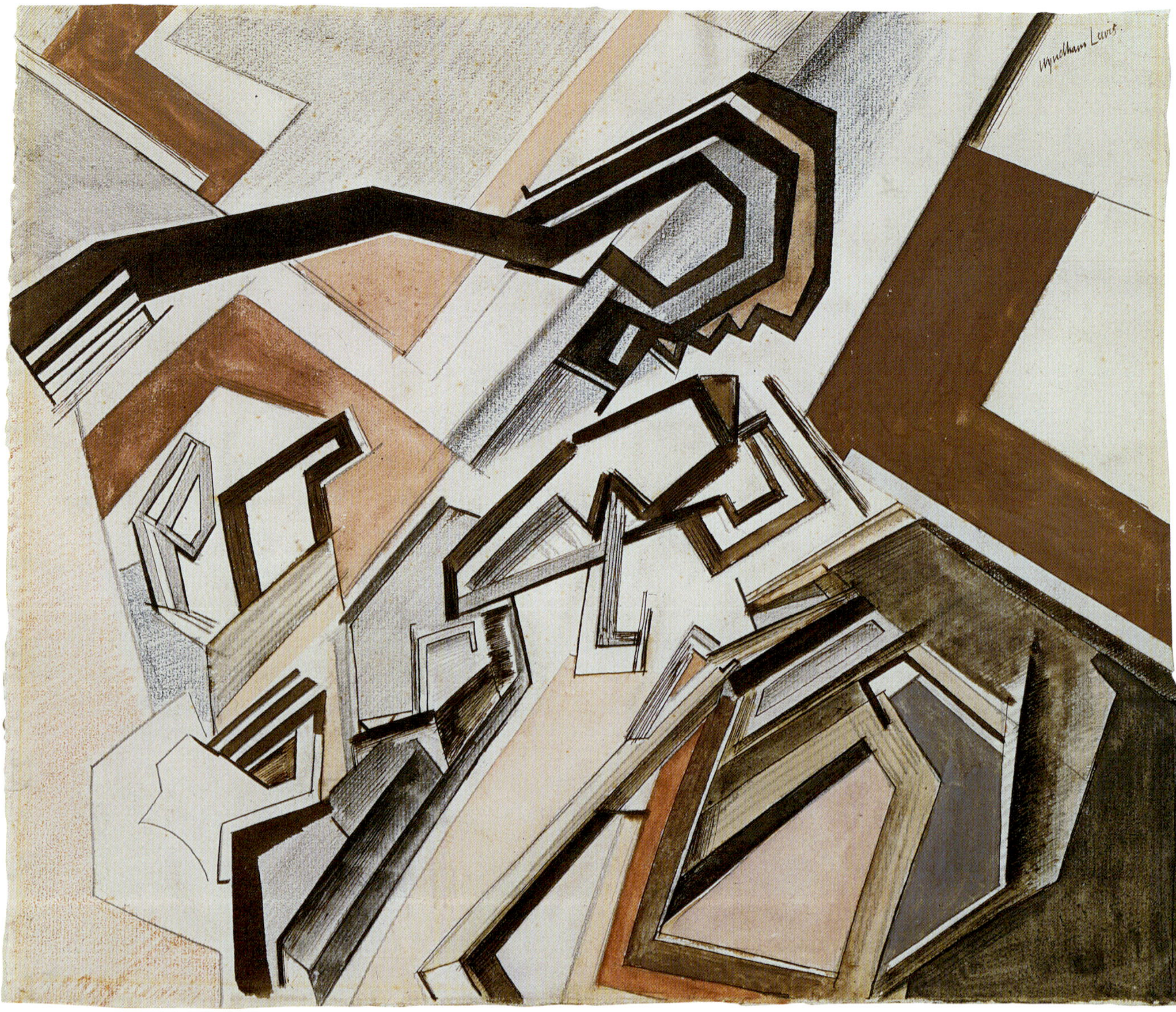

63
Wyndham Lewis
Planners: Happy Day 1912–13
Pen, gouache, and pencil on paper
31.1 x 38.1 cm
[P]

64
Wyndham Lewis
Composition 1913
Pen, watercolour,
and pencil on paper
34.3 x 26.7 cm
[P]

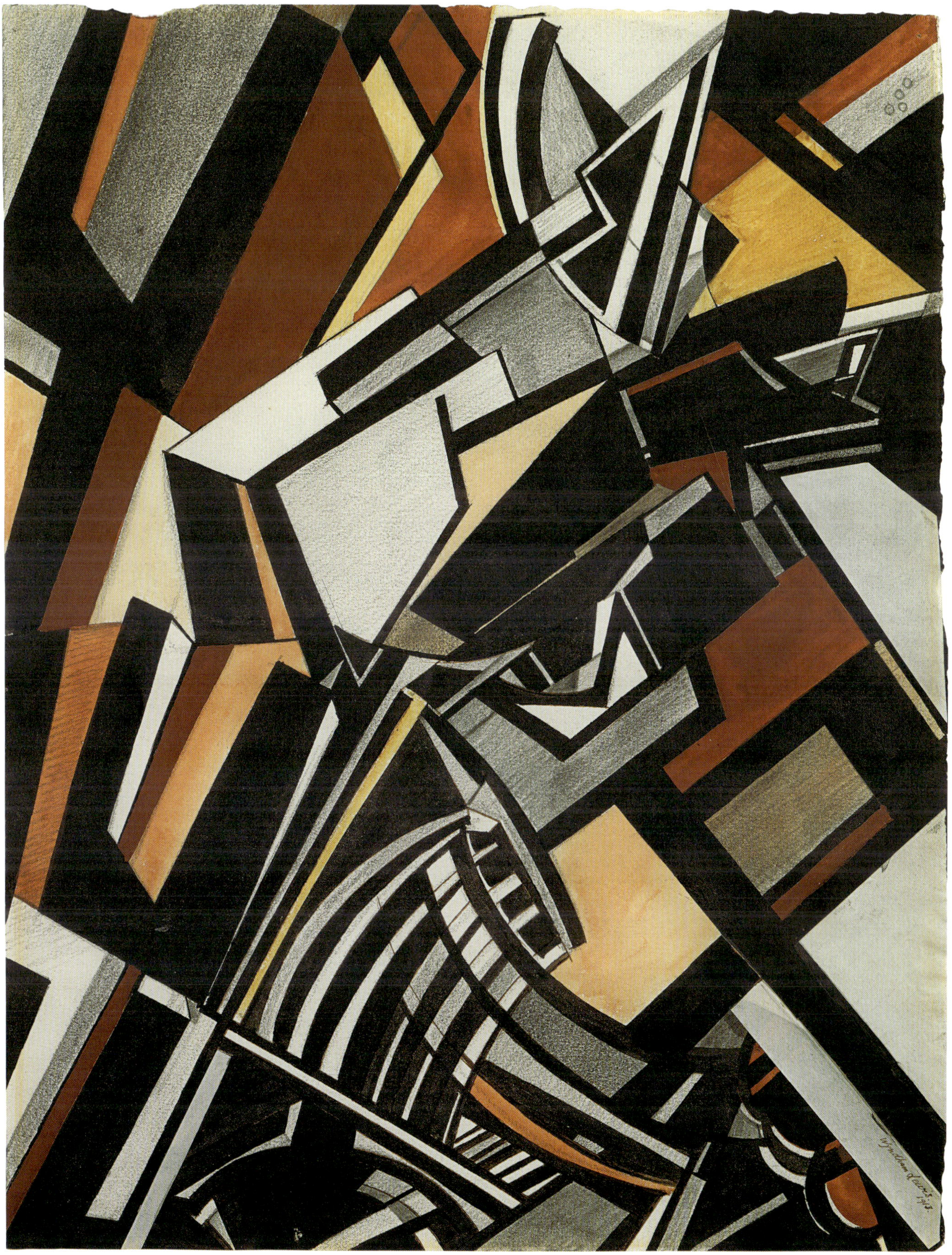

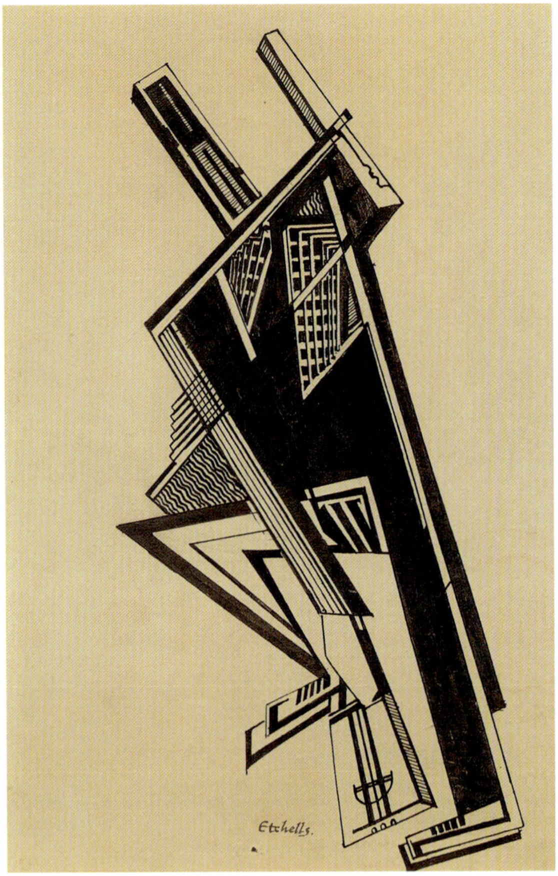

65
Frederick Etchells
The English Comedian
1914–15
Pen, brush, and ink on paper
27.5 x 18 cm
[P]

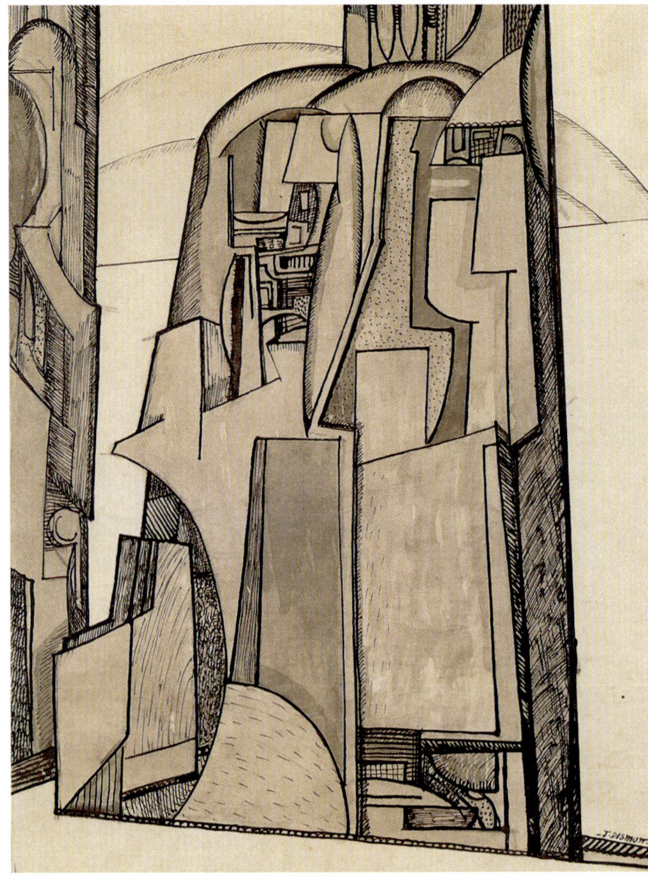

66
Jessica Dismorr
Edinburgh Castle 1914–15
Pen and watercolour on paper
24 x 19 cm
[P; S]

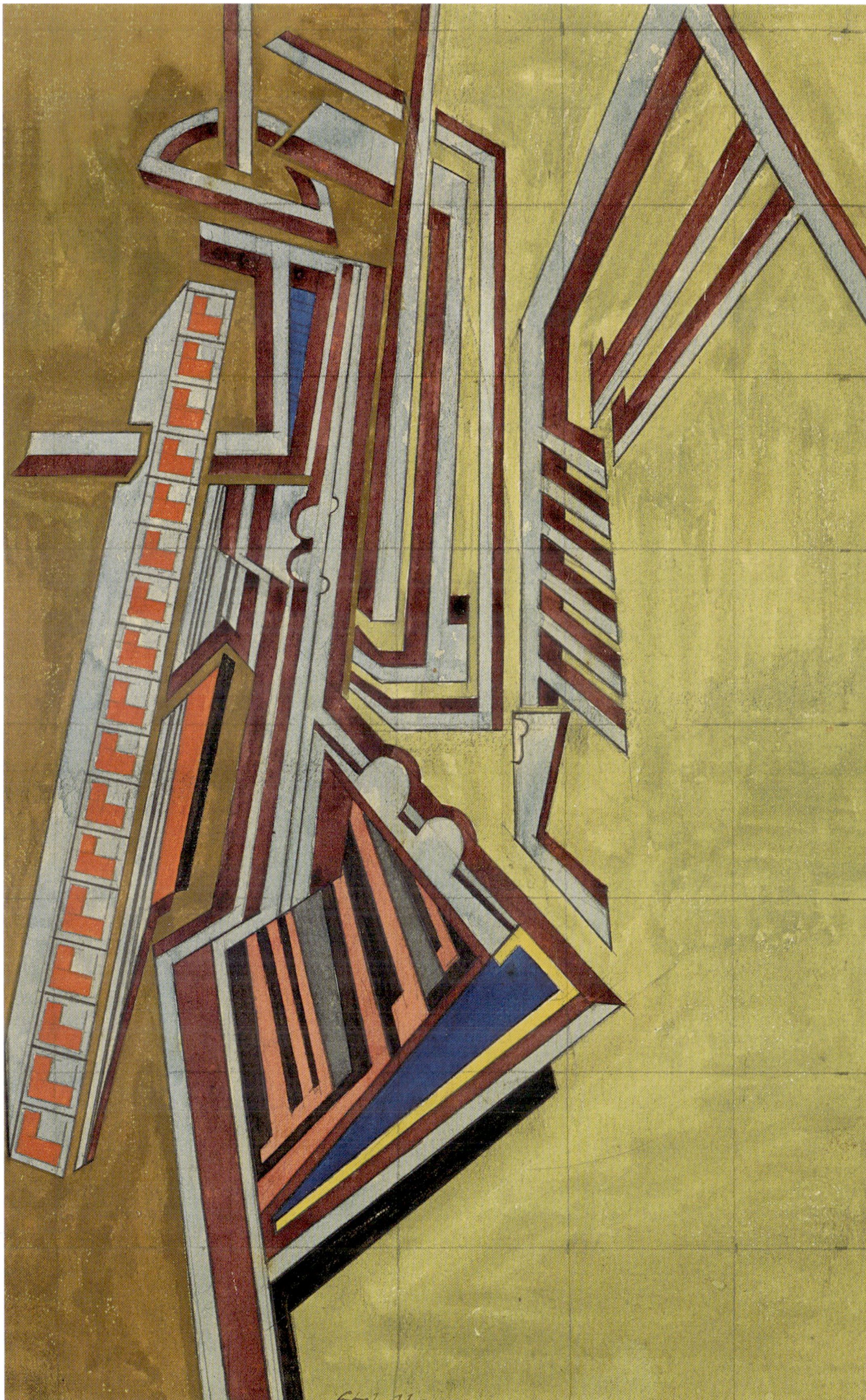

67
Frederick Etchells
Composition
[Stilts] 1914–15
Gouache and
pencil on paper
32 x 20 cm
[P]

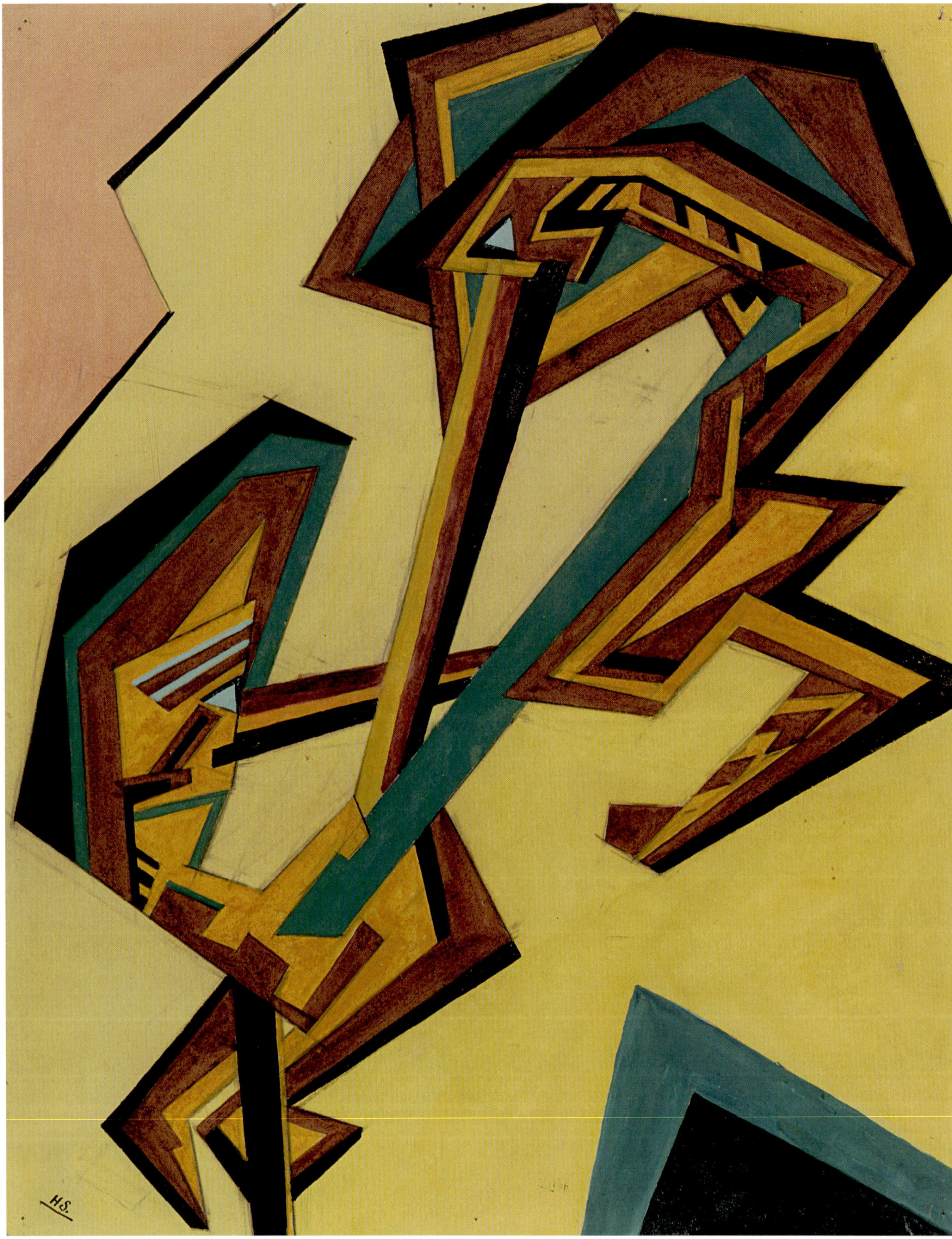
H.S.

68
Helen Saunders
Balance c.1915
Pencil and gouache on paper
36.8 x 29.8 cm
[P]

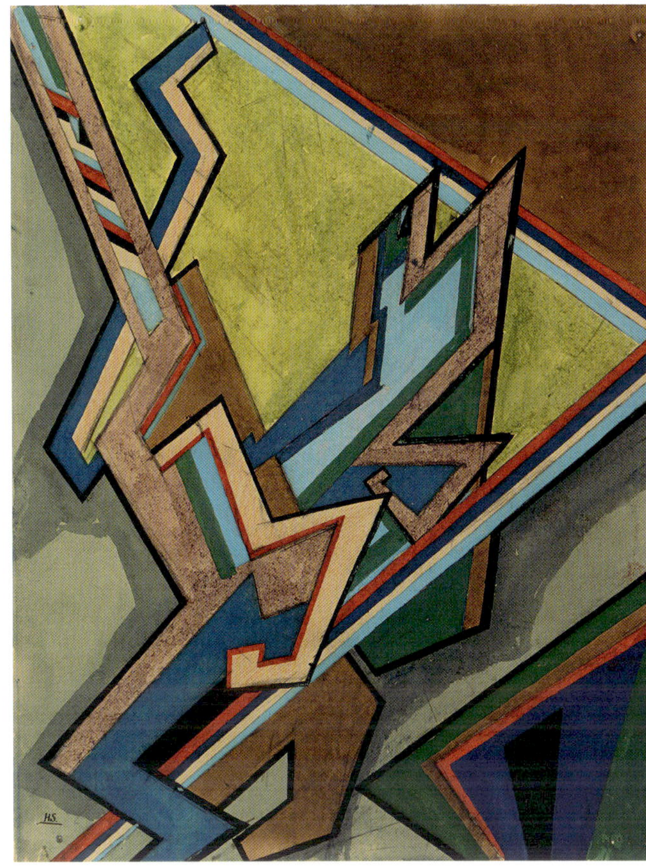

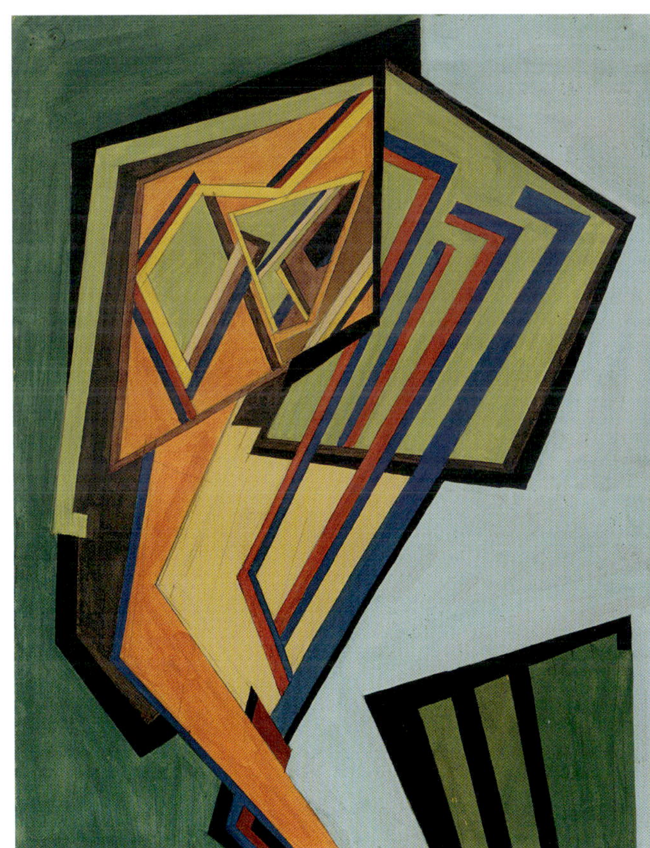

69
Helen Saunders
Dance c.1915
Pencil and gouache
on paper
37.5 x 29.2 cm
[P]

70
Helen Saunders
Canon c.1915
Pencil and gouache
on paper
36.8 x 29.8 cm
[P]

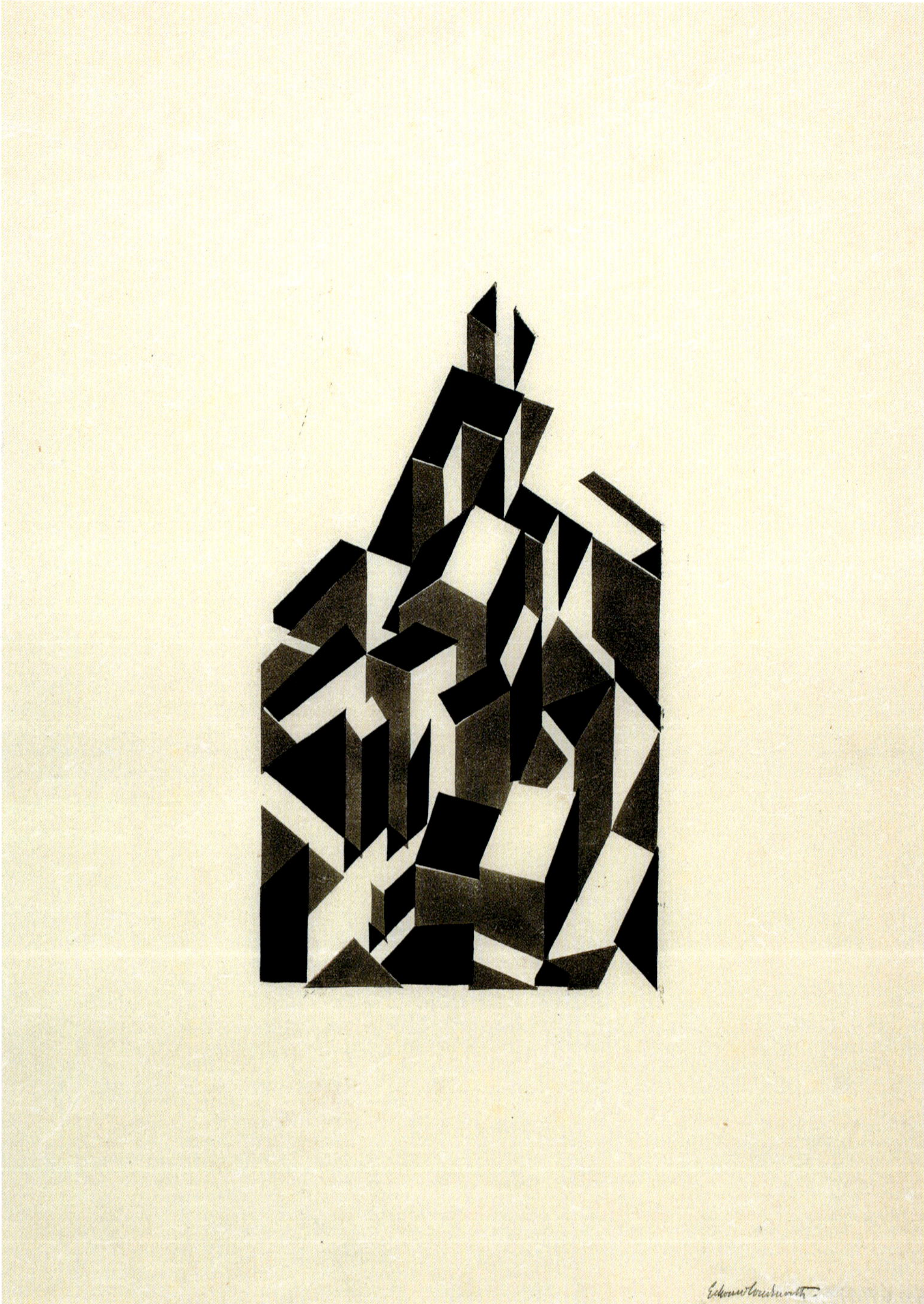

71
Edward Wadsworth
Yorkshire Village 1914
Woodcut on paper
overall: 38.2 x 28.2 cm
[S]

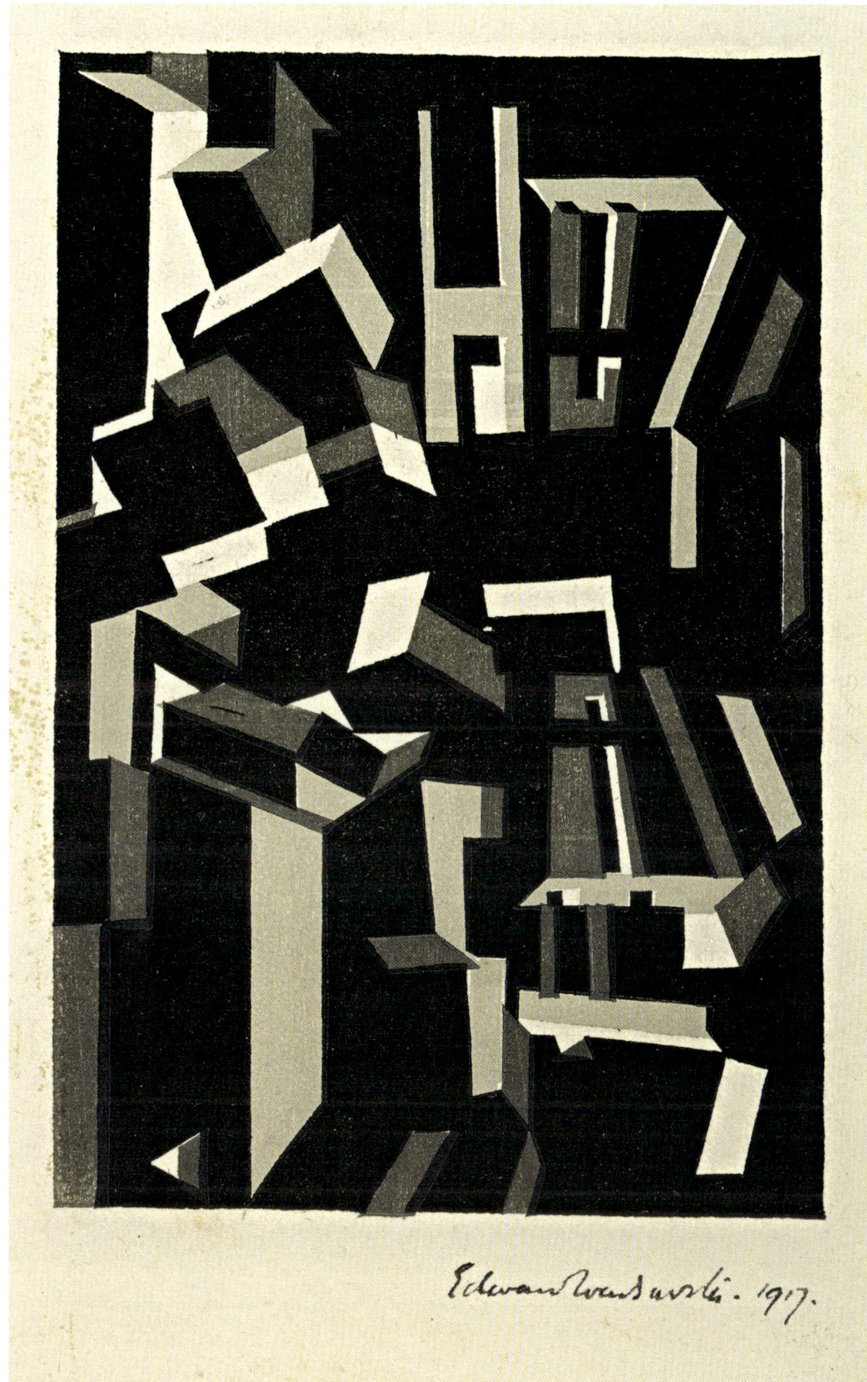

72
Edward Wadsworth
Interior 1917
Woodcut on paper
sheet: 13.3 x 8.3 cm
[S]

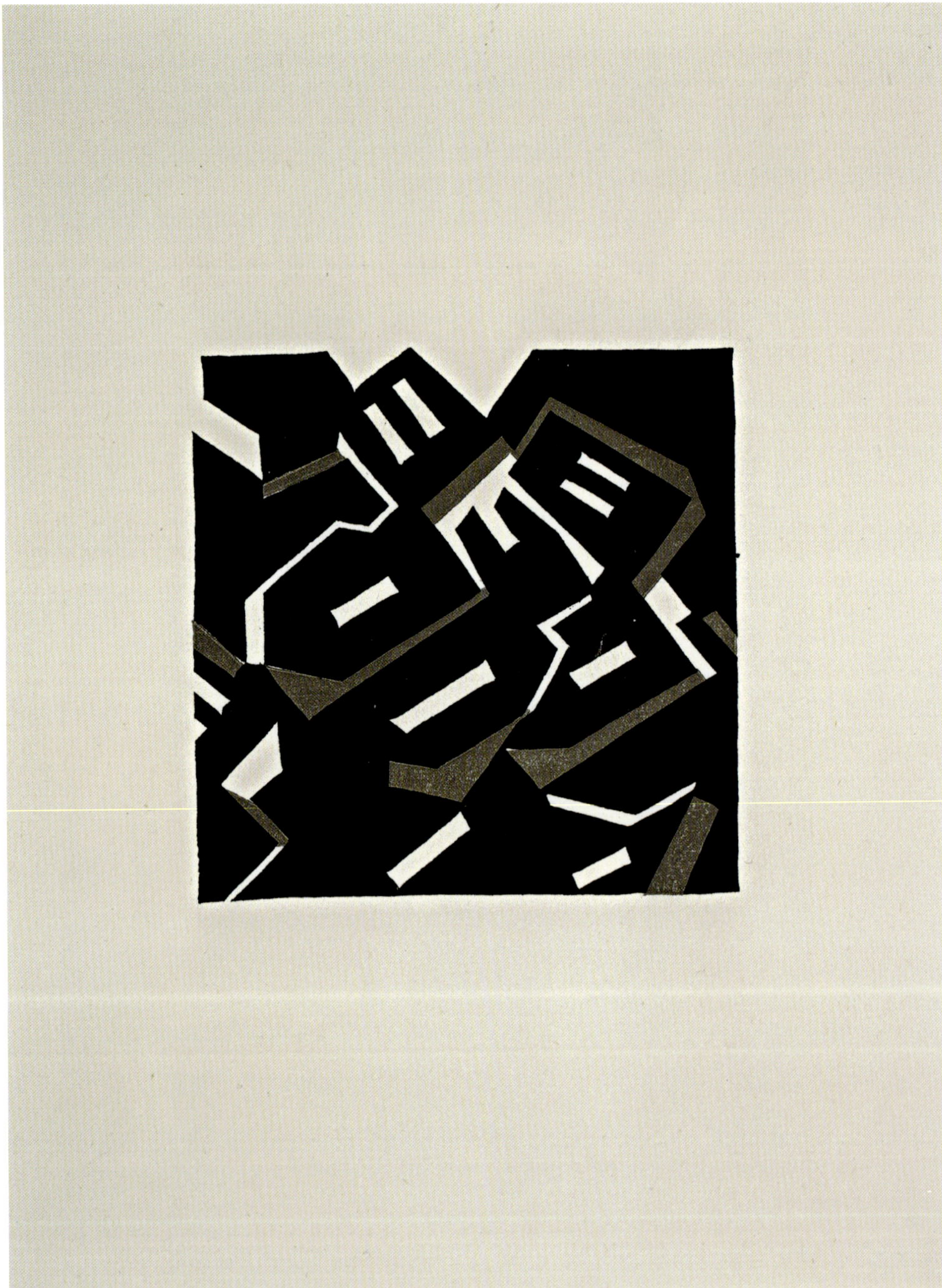

73
Edward Wadsworth
Top of the Town c.1916–17
Woodcut on paper
sheet: 17.8 x 14 cm

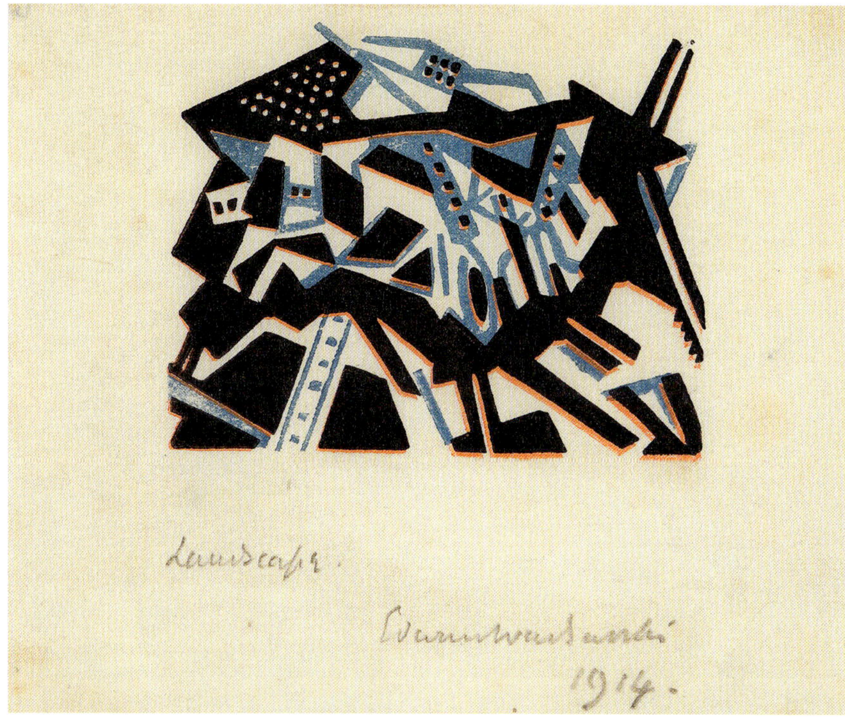

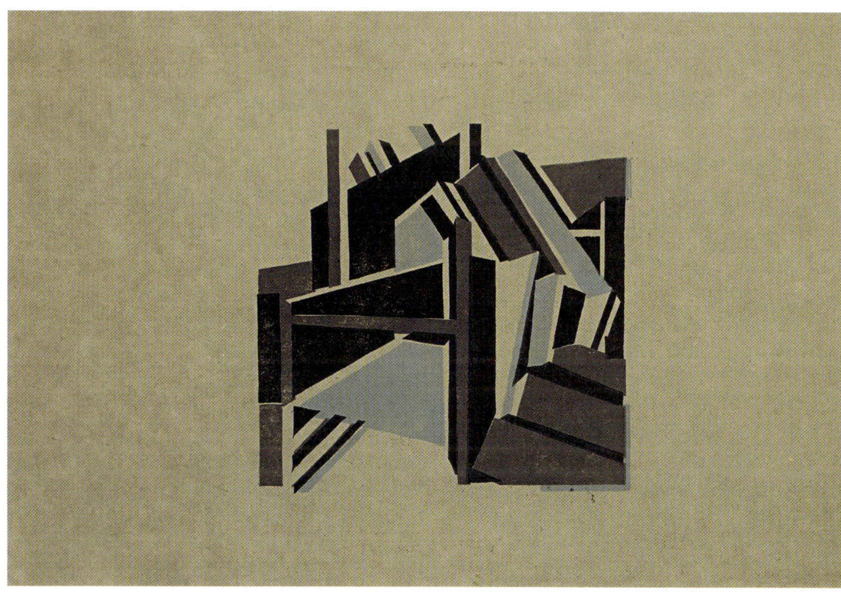

74
Edward Wadsworth
Landscape 1914
Woodcut on paper
sheet: 25.4 x 20.3 cm
image: 6.4 x 7.6 cm
[S]

75
Edward Wadsworth
View of a Town [Canal Bank] 1916
Woodcut on paper
sheet: 15.9 x 24.8 cm
[S?]

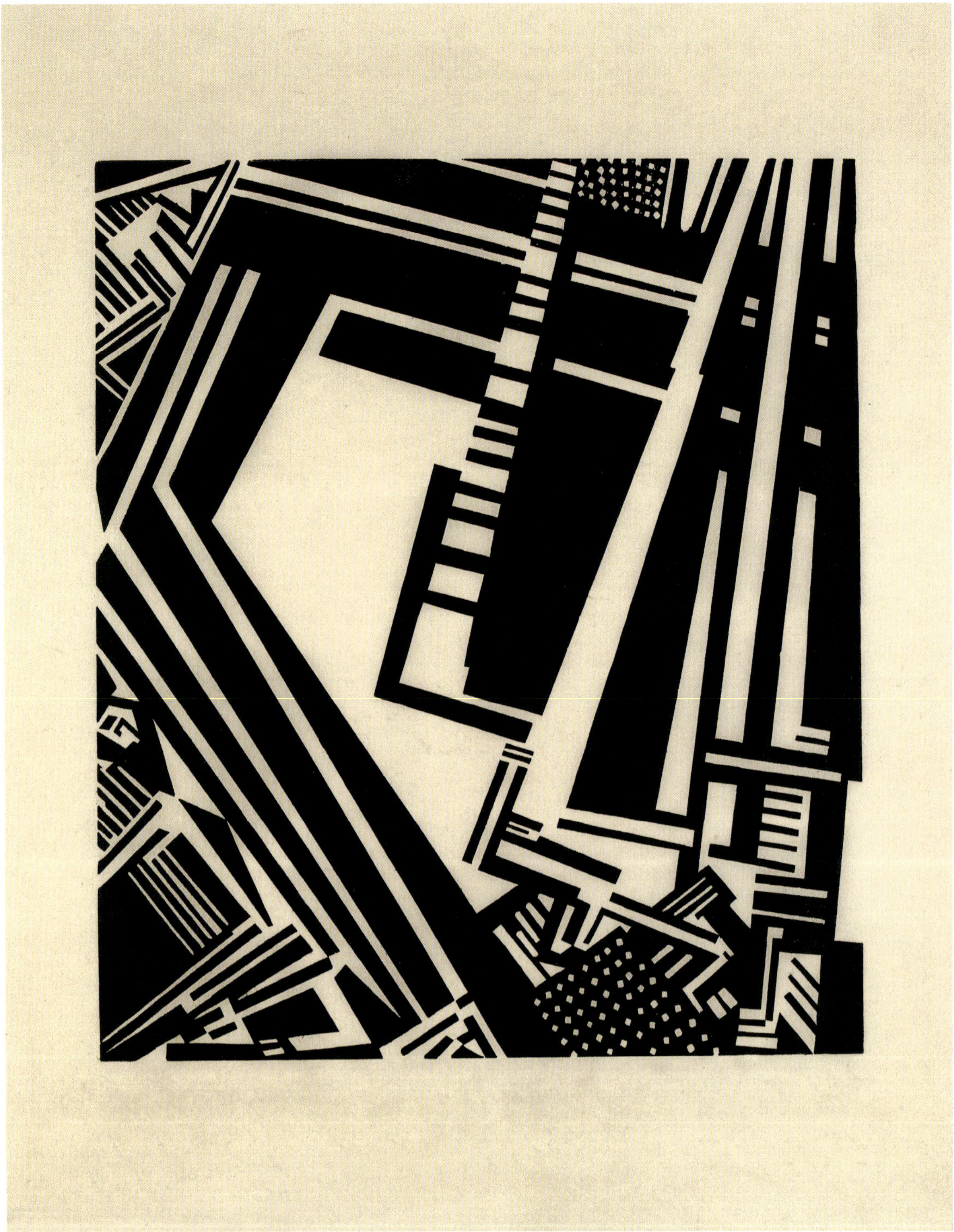

76
Edward Wadsworth
Illustration (Typhoon) 1914
Woodcut on paper
image: 28.9 x 25.3 cm

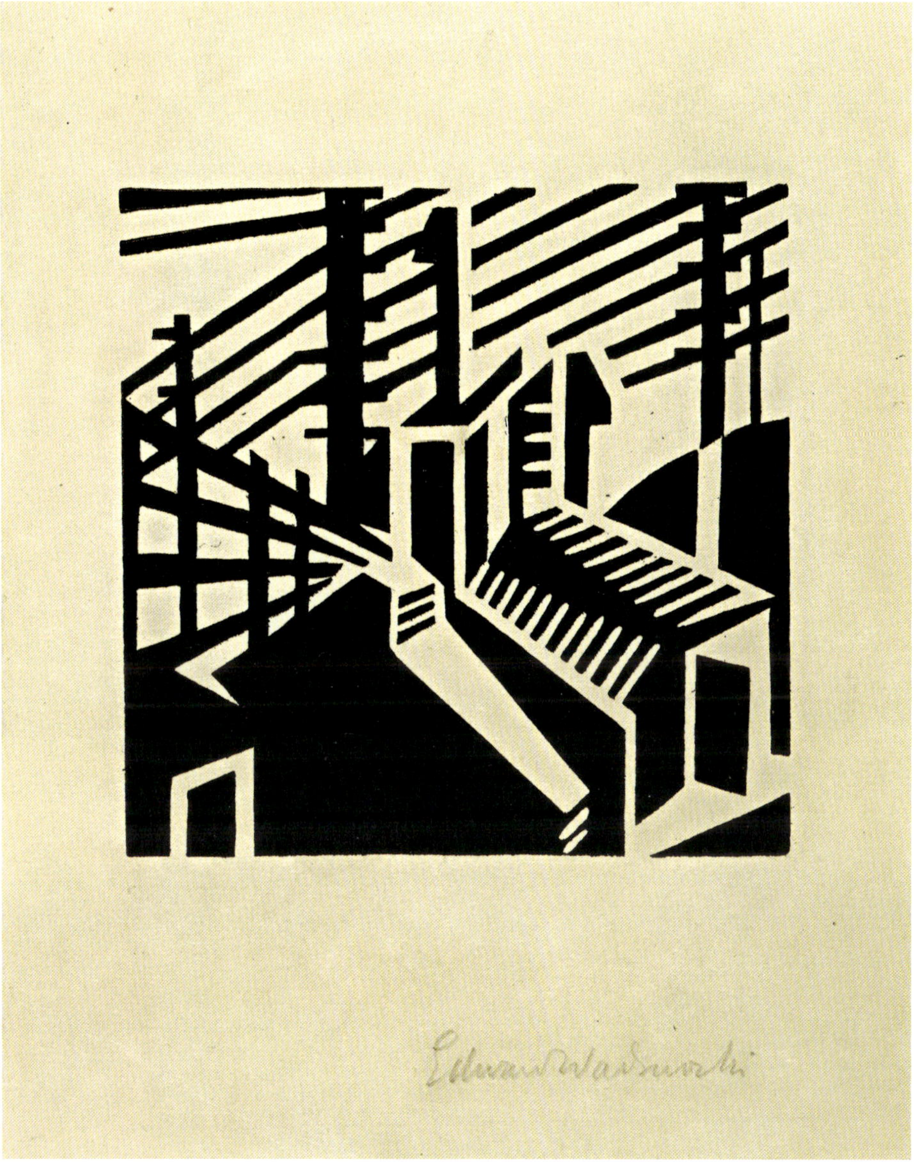

77
Edward Wadsworth
Railway Embankment [also known as Platelayers' Shed] 1914
Woodcut on paper
sheet: 13.3 x 10.8 cm
[S]

THE CAMERA CLUB

The Camera Club Vortograph Exhibition

When the celebrated photographer Alvin Langdon Coburn exhibited eighteen of his Vortographs at the London Camera Club in February 1917 he broke new ground by publicly showing the first abstract photographs in the history of art. An American expatriate, Coburn had come into contact with the Vorticists by 1913. He subsequently photographed Pound and Epstein at their homes, Lewis and Wadsworth in their studios, and acquired a number of Wadsworth's Vorticist woodblock prints. Coburn later stated that he devised the 'Vortoscope' (a kaleidoscopic instrument composed of three mirrors fastened together in the form of a triangle) in 1916 to emulate Vorticist abstraction. With his camera lens directed into this device, Coburn photographed pieces of wood and crystal on a glass table to create his non-objective Vortographs. In the late autumn he created multiple-exposure photographs of Pound that he labelled 'Cubist', and then used the Vortoscope to produce portraits of Pound with mirror effects; a group of two-dimensional profiles of Pound's silhouette; and his famous abstractions. When Coburn exhibited his Vortographs alongside his less adventurous paintings at the Camera Club, the catalogue included prefaces by both Pound and Coburn. The collaboration proved short-lived, however, owing to Pound's limited appreciation for Coburn's achievement and of the photographic medium itself. This schism, combined with hostile critical reception of his Vortographs, led Coburn to withdraw from the Vorticist movement and to a major extent from photography altogether. By 1918 Coburn had begun to frequent an artists' colony in Harlech, Wales, where he pursued a life-long interest in Freemasonry, astrology, and the occult.

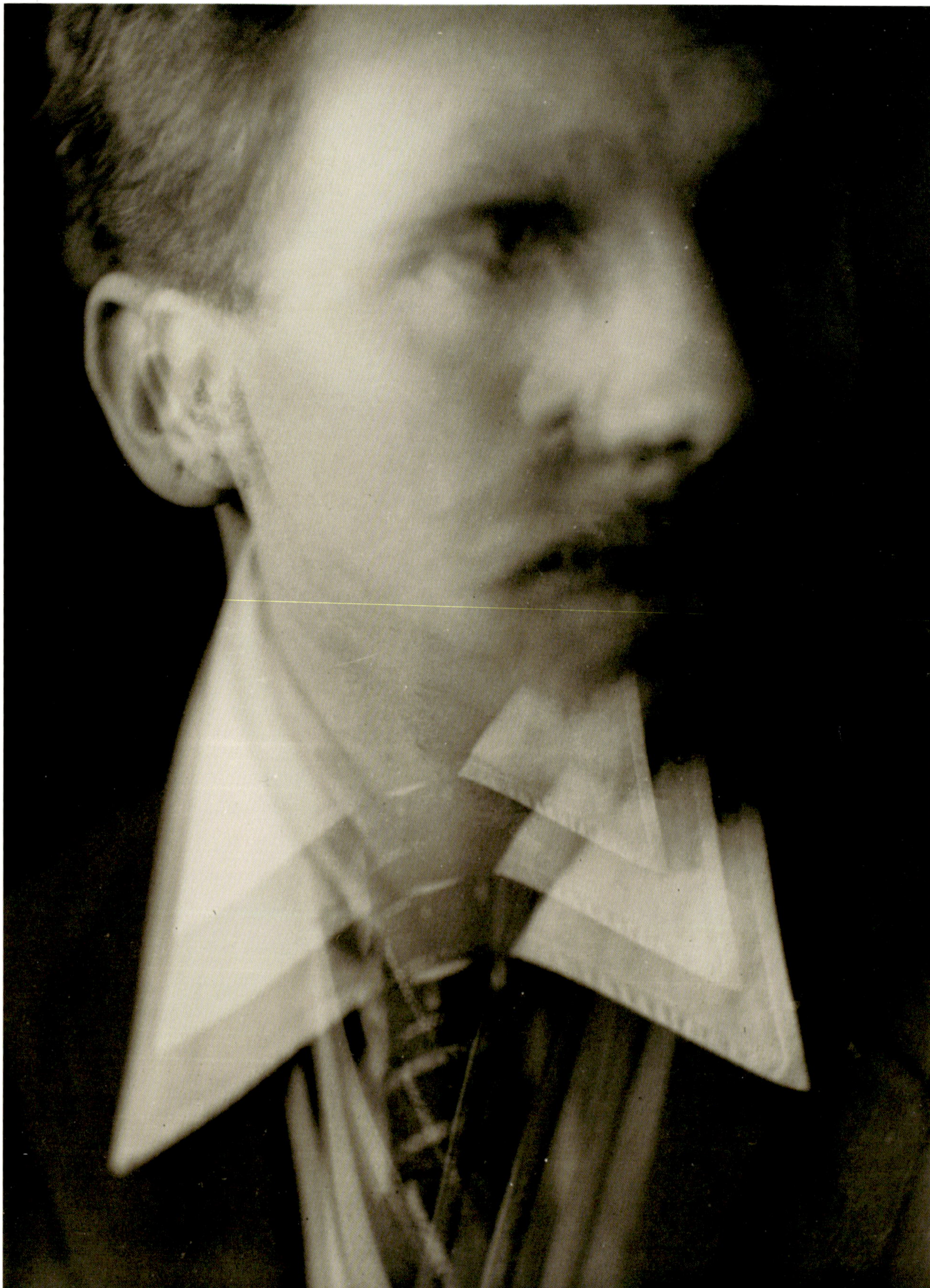

78
Alvin Langdon Coburn
Ezra Pound 1917 (printed later)
Gelatin silver print
image: 20.5 x 15.4 cm

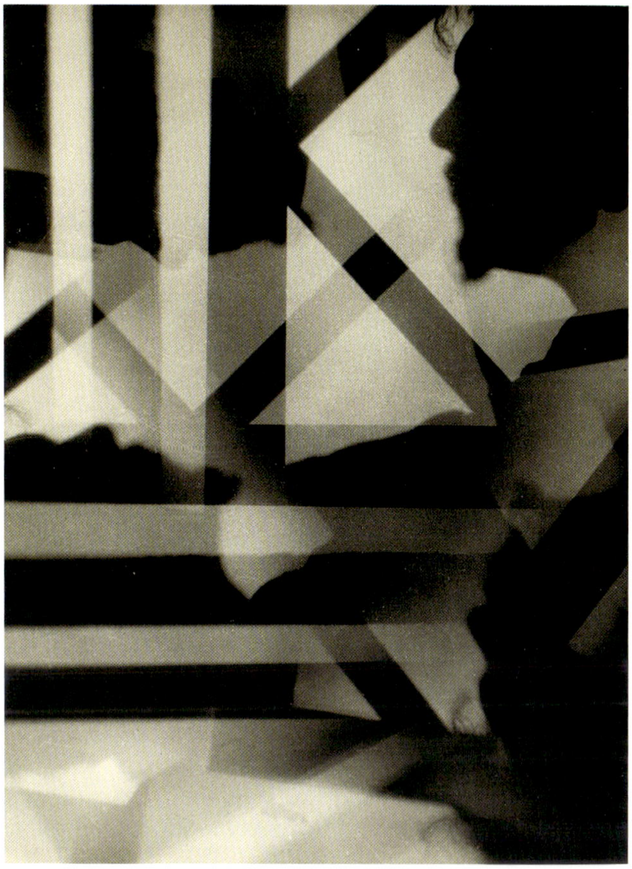

79
Alvin Langdon Coburn
Vortograph of Ezra Pound 1917 (printed later)
Gelatin silver print
image: 20.2 x 15.5 cm
[C]

80
Alvin Langdon Coburn
Vortograph of Ezra Pound 1917 (printed later)
Gelatin silver print
image: 28.4 x 19.9 cm
[C]

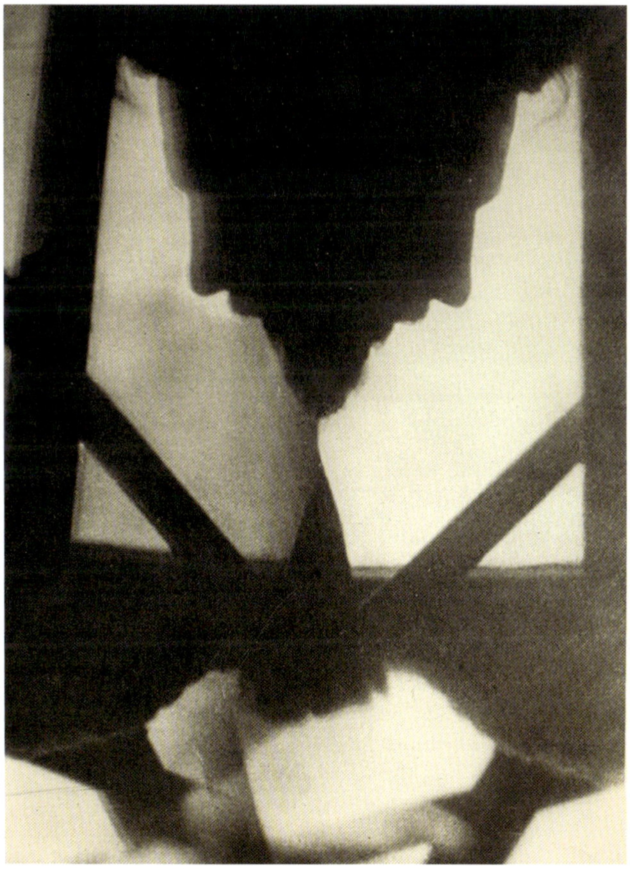

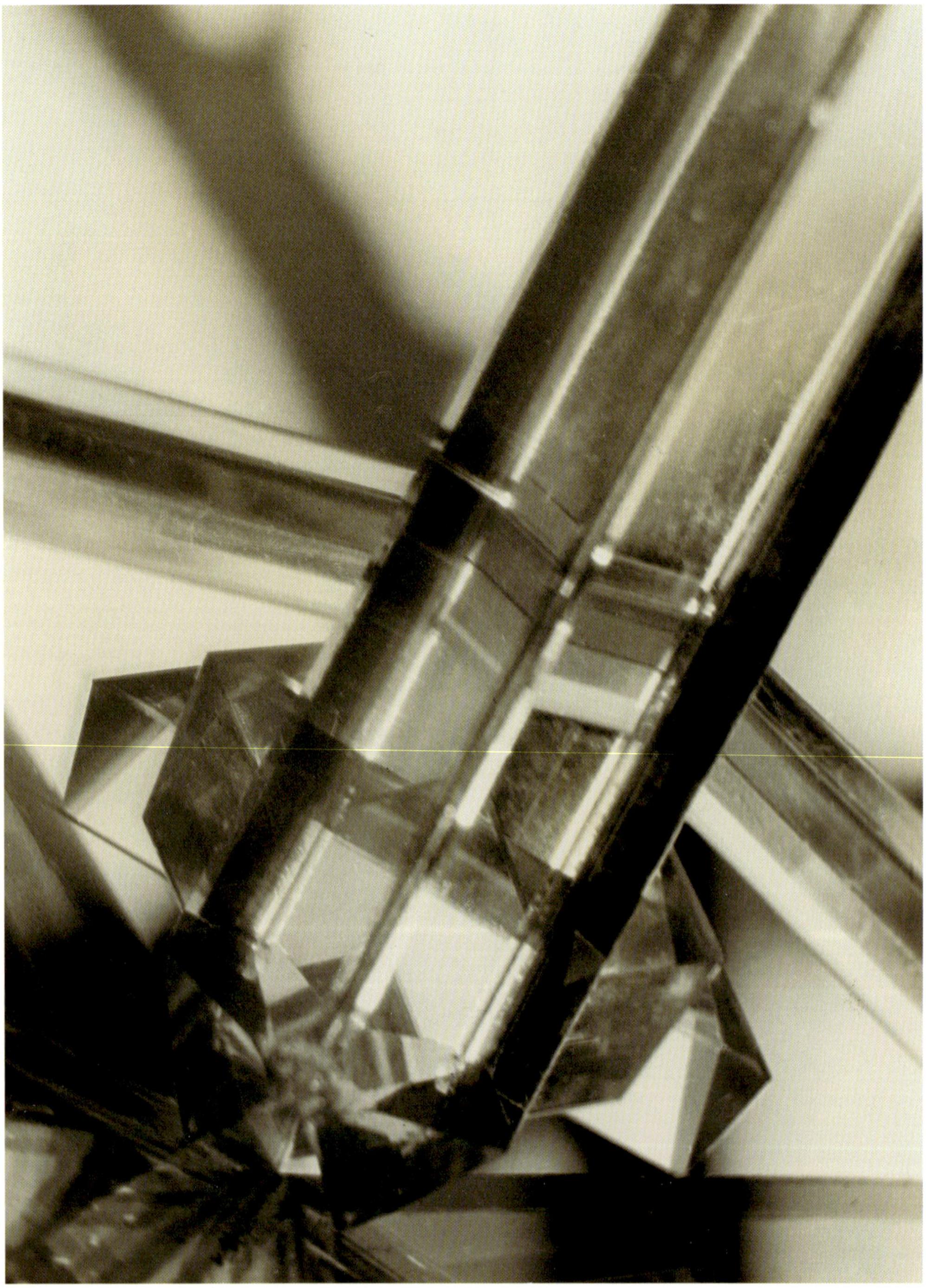

81
Alvin Langdon Coburn
Vortograph 1917
Gelatin silver print
image: 27.4 x 20.9 cm
[C]

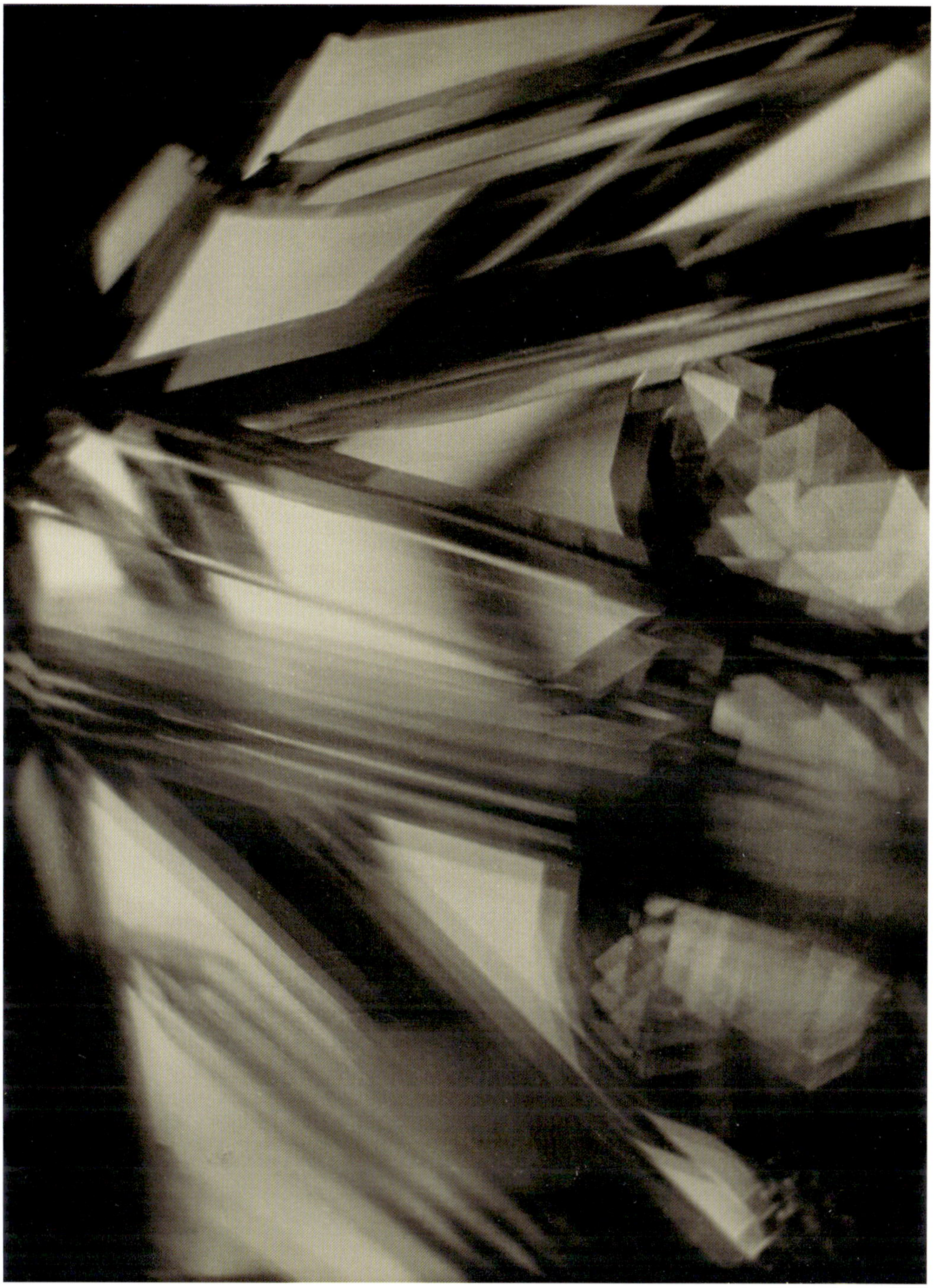

82
Alvin Langdon Coburn
Vortograph 1917
Gelatin silver print
image: 27.6 x 20.7 cm
[C]

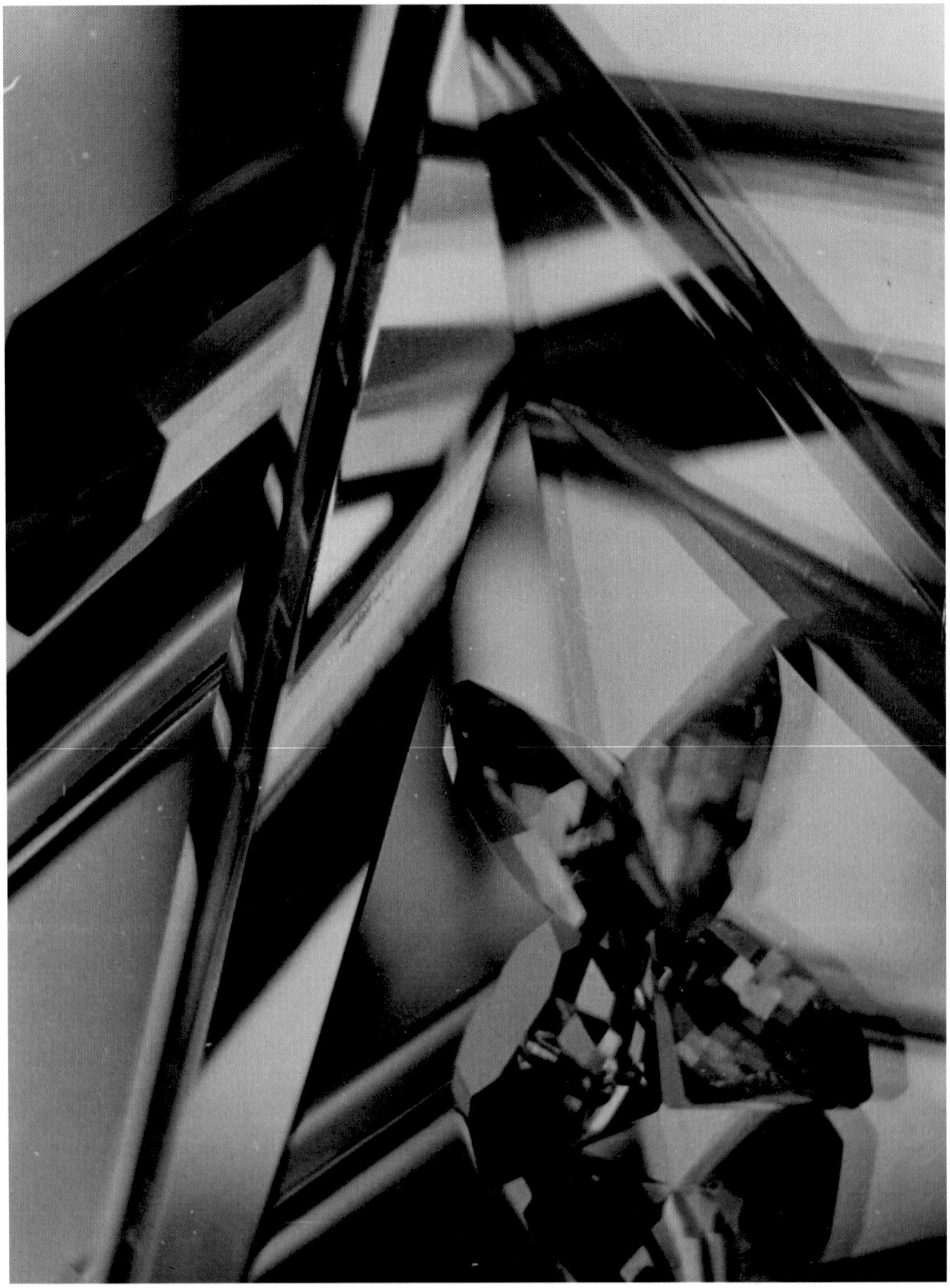

83
Alvin Langdon Coburn
Vortograph 1917
Gelatin silver print
image: 28.3 x 21.4 cm
[C]

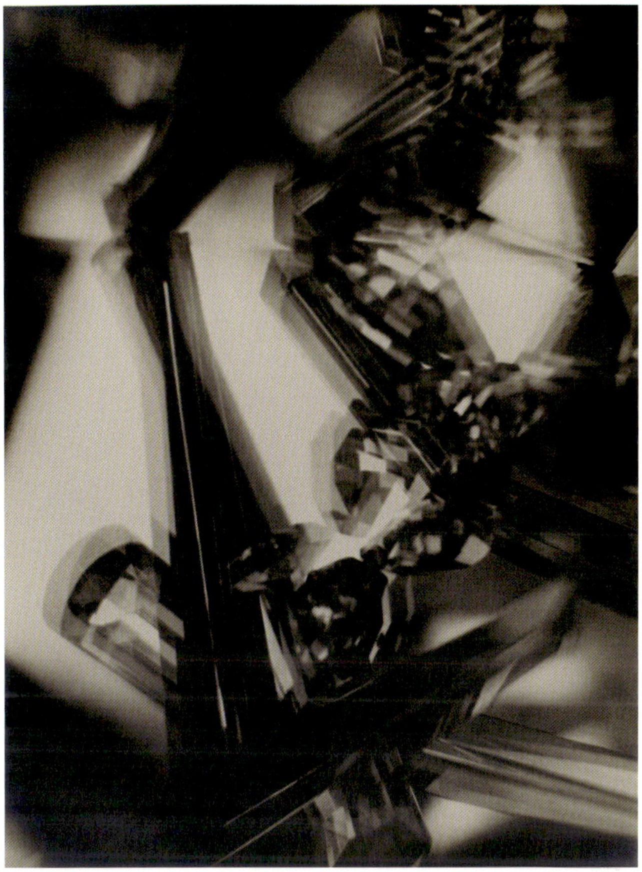

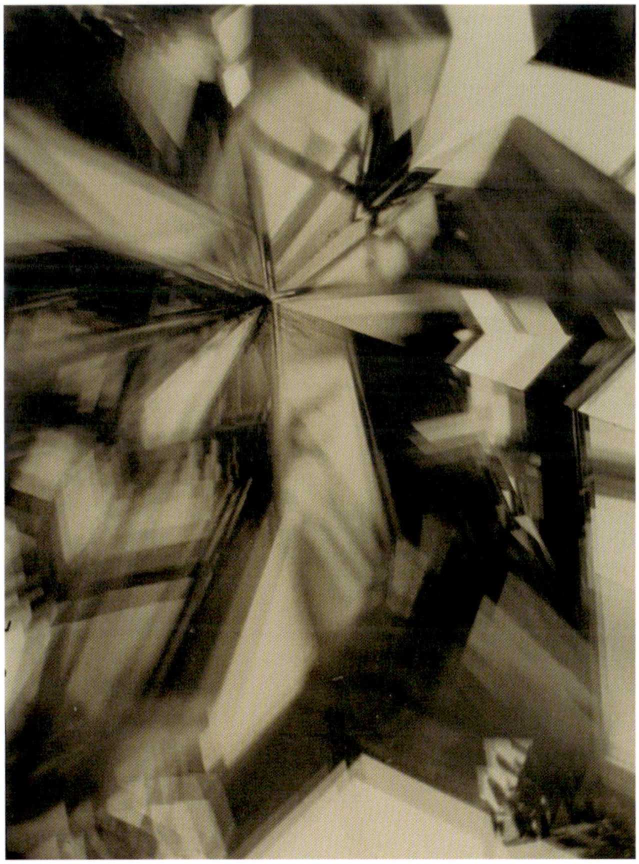

84
Alvin Langdon Coburn
Vortograph 1917
Gelatin silver print
image: 47.5 x 36.4 cm
[C]

85
Alvin Langdon Coburn
Vortograph 1917
Gelatin silver print
image: 28.2 x 21.8 cm
[C]

CHRONOLOGY
BIBLIOGRAPHY
EXHIBITED WORKS

CHRONOLOGY

1898

Percy Wyndham Lewis enters the Slade School of Fine Art, London, where he wins scholarship aged 16 (until 1901, when he is expelled).

Deaths of Edward Burne-Jones and William Ewart Gladstone.

Walter Sickert goes abroad (returning 1905), alternating between Dieppe and Venice.

1899

Cuthbert Hamilton enters the Slade (until 1903).

1900

Sigmund Freud publishes *Die Traumdeutung* (*The Interpretation of Dreams*).

April, Paris World's Fair opens.

Deaths of Oscar Wilde, Friedrich Nietzsche, and John Ruskin.

Alvin Langdon Coburn exhibits nine photographs at the London Photographic Salon (organized by the London Photographic Society).

1901

22 January, death of Queen Victoria. Edward VII succeeds to the throne.

1902

Jessica Dismorr enters the Slade (until 1903).

Summer, Augustus John becomes friends with Lewis. Lewis travels to Madrid with Frederick Spencer Gore to see the works of Goya and Velázquez.

1903

Henri Bergson publishes 'Introduction à la métaphysique' (Introduction to Metaphysics).

17 July, death of James McNeill Whistler in London.

10 October, the Pankhursts (mother Emmeline and daughters Christabel and Sylvia) found the Women's Social and Political Union (WSPU). Members soon become known as Suffragettes.

At the end of the year the American, Jacob Epstein, decides to move from Paris to London.

1905

Exhibition of French Impressionist paintings held at the Durand-Ruel Gallery, London.

1906

Edward Wadsworth studies engineering in Munich and painting at the Knirr School (returning 1907).

David Bomberg is apprenticed to the lithographer Paul Fischer and studies at the City and Guilds School, London.

Helen Saunders enters the Slade (until 1907).

1907

Bergson publishes *L'Evolution créatrice* (*Creative Evolution*).

Political theorist Georges Sorel publishes *Réflexions sur la violence* (*Reflections on Violence*).

The New Age (1907–22) appears under the editorship of A.R. Orage as a vehicle of 'Guild socialism'. Future contributors include Katherine Mansfield, T.E. Hulme, Ezra Pound, and Herbert Read.

Epstein becomes a British citizen.

Sickert forms the Fitzroy Street Group from followers who painted with him in a studio in Fitzroy Street: William Rothenstein, Albert Rutherston, Walter Russell, Gore, Harold Gilman, Nan Hudson, and Ethel Sands. In the autumn, Lucien Pissarro also joins. This group evolves into the Camden Town Group in 1911.

1908

Pound travels from the USA to Venice, where he publishes *A lume spento*, and then moves to London, where he meets Dorothy Shakespear.

Malcolm Arbuthnot exhibits photographs at the London Photographic Salon and meets Coburn.

Wadsworth enters the Slade (until 1912). Frederick Etchells enters Royal College of Art (until 1911).

April, Liberal H.H. Asquith, Chancellor of the Exchequer, succeeds Sir Henry Campbell-Bannerman as Prime Minister.

July, the first exhibition of the Allied Artists Association (AAA) at the Royal Albert Hall, London. Founded by Frank Rutter with Sickert, it is a non-juried *salon* based on the Parisian Salon des Indépendants.

Wilhelm Worringer's *Abstraktion und Einfühlung (Abstraction and Empathy)* is published in Munich.

David Lloyd George, as Chancellor of the Exchequer, passes the Old Age Pensions Act, one of the earliest steps towards the Welfare State.

November, exhibition of paintings by Georges Braque at Kahnweiler Galerie, Paris. In his review Louis Vauxcelles refers to cubes in advanced French painting, supposedly the origin of the term Cubism.

December, Lewis returns to live full time in London.

1909

January, C.R.W. Nevinson enters the Slade. Fellow students are Dora Carrington, Mark Gertler, and Stanley Spencer.

Roger Fry, aged forty-four, returns to London, having left his curatorial position at the Metropolitan Museum of Art, New York.

20 February, publication of F.T. Marinetti's 'The Founding and Manifesto of Futurism' on the front page of *Le Figaro*.

Lewis meets Ford Madox Hueffer (later Ford Madox Ford) who in May publishes the first of Lewis's stories, 'The Pole', in *The English Review* (later rewritten and published in *The Wild Body*, 1927).

Serge Diaghilev founds the Ballets Russes. Lewis and Pound meet at the Vienna Café in New Oxford Street.

William Roberts is apprenticed to a commercial art firm.

1910

January, the House of Lords rejects Lloyd George's People's Budget (which proposes to redistribute wealth to the poor). This precipitates a constitutional crisis, with a general election resulting in a hung parliament, the passing of the Irish Home Rule Act, and the curtailment of the power of the House of Lords (1911). This period of political instability lasts until the beginning of the First World War.

Henri Gaudier meets Sophie Brzeska in the Ste Geneviève Library in Paris. Clive and Vanessa Bell meet Roger Fry, drawing him into the Bloomsbury circle,which also includes E.M. Forster, Duncan Grant, Lytton Strachey, and Virginia Woolf.

April, the first of many lectures by Marinetti in London, 'Une Discours futuriste aux Anglais', is given at the Lyceum Theatre, six weeks after publication of the 'Manifesto of Futurist Painters' (11 February) and at the time of the 'Futurist Painting: Technical Manifesto' (11 April).

6 May, death of King Edward VII. George V succeeds to the throne.

Roberts enters the Slade on a scholarship (until 1913).

June–August, Robert Dell organizes the exhibition *Modern French Artists* in Brighton City Art Gallery, including French Post-Impressionist paintings.

August, Marinetti's Futurist propaganda ('Futurist Venice' and quotes from the founding manifesto) appears in *The Tramp* along with Lewis's short story 'The Breton Innkeeper'.

Dismorr studies at the Atelier de la Palette, Paris (until 1913).

Pound meets John Quinn in New York (but then loses touch with him until 1915).

8 November–15 January, Fry organizes the exhibition *Manet and the Post-Impressionists* at the Grafton Galleries, London.

18 November, Suffragettes stage an attack on the House of Commons.

December, Virginia Woolf, in her lecture 'Mr Bennett and Mrs Brown' (delivered in Cambridge, 18 May 1924), claims 'in or about December 1910, human character changed'. Marinetti speaks at the Lyceum Club for Woman on the subject of *Il futurismo e la donna* (*Futurism and the Woman*). Lewis is in the audience.

1911

Bergson's *L'Evolution créatrice* first published in English (*Creative Evolution*).

January, Gaudier-Brzeska arrives in London. Bomberg enters the Slade (until 1913); fellow students include Jakob Kramer, Paul Nash, Nevinson, Roberts, Isaac Rosenberg, Spencer, and Wadsworth.

April, Hulme hears Bergson lecture at a Philosophical Congress in Bologna.

May, Bergson lectures at Oxford University and University of Birmingham.

June, the first Camden Town Group show at Carfax Gallery, London, includes Grant, Lewis, Bevan, Charles Ginner, Gilman, Gore, and John.

While working in Paris on his Oscar Wilde tomb for Père Lachaise cemetery, Epstein meets Gaudier-Brzeska.

Summer, first issue of *Rhythm*, published by J.D. Fergusson, includes illustrations by Dismorr.

August, *Art News* publishes English translation of 'Manifesto of Futurist Painters'. First performance of Diaghilev's Ballets Russes at Covent Garden.

October, Bergson lectures at University College London.

November, in Paris, Lewis sees the Salon d'Automne, which includes large Cubist works by Fernand Léger, Albert Gleizes, and Jean Metzinger in the Salle 42.

Winter, in Berlin, Hulme hears Worringer lecture at the Berlin Aesthetic Congress.

December, Kandinsky publishes *Über das Geistige in der Kunst* (*Concerning the Spiritual in Art*), extracts of which will be published in the first issue of the Vorticist review, *Blast*, 1914.

1912

Hulme's translation of Bergson's *Introduction to Metaphysics* is published.

Coburn moves from the USA to London.

March, *Exhibition of Works by the Italian Futurist Painters* at the Sackville Gallery, London, with works by Umberto Boccioni, Carlo Carrà, Luigi Russolo, and Gino Severini.

April, the poetry group of the Imagists forms from the alliance of Richard Aldington, Hilda Doolittle (H.D.), and Pound. Pound publishes *Ripostes*, including five imagist poems by Hulme.

14–15 April, the *Titanic* sinks on its inaugural trip on the Atlantic.

May, Fry organizes the *Exposition de Quelques Artistes Indépendants Anglais*, combining Bloomsbury painters and the future Vorticists, at the Galerie Barbazanges, Paris.

June: Frida Strindberg's Cabaret Theatre Club, Cave of the Golden Calf, opens at 9 Heddon Street, London, with decorations by Lewis, Ginner, Gore, and Epstein. Lewis's *Kermesse* is exhibited in the Cave of the Golden Calf, and later shown at the AAA exhibition, Royal Albert Hall (July 1912), and in Fry's *Second Post-Impressionist Exhibition* (see below). Considered the most advanced painting of its time, it is sold in 1915 to Quinn in New York (now lost).

June–July, Arbuthnot's solo show of *Camera Portraits* held at the Goupil Gallery, London. In Paris, Epstein meets Constantin Brancusi, Amedeo Modigliani, and Pablo Picasso.

Epstein and Lewis meet Hulme through Pound.

August, Metzinger and Gleizes publish *Du Cubisme*, the first publication of Cubist theory.

11 October, Guillaume Apollinaire delivers a lecture in which he ascribes the name Orphic Cubism or 'pure painting' to Robert Delaunay, Marcel Duchamp, Léger, and Francis Picabia.

October–December, *Second Post-Impressionist Exhibition: British, French and Russian Artists*, at the Grafton Galleries includes six of Lewis's *Timon of Athens* illustrations (reopens January 1913). Lewis meets Kate Lechmere.

December, third and last Camden Town Group show at Carfax Gallery. Lewis visits Bomberg in his studio.

1913

English translation of Gleizes and Metzinger's *Cubism* published.

February, the Armory Show opens in New York.

April, Severini's solo show of paintings held at the Marlborough Gallery, London. Severini meets Nevinson. Fry takes a lease at 33 Fitzroy Square for the Omega Workshops; in May these are registered as a company; in July the official opening is held.

Wadsworth meets Lewis and Pound.

June 18, Emily Wilding Davison, suffragette, throws herself under King George V's horse at the Epsom Derby and is killed, becoming a martyr to the Votes for Women movement.

Summer, Epstein and Bomberg travel to Paris. Bomberg meets Picasso, Modigliani, André Derain, Moisé Kisling, Max Jacob, and others.

July, Pound meets Gaudier-Brzeska at the AAA.

October, the Ideal Home Exhibition in the Olympia Exhibition Hall, London, includes a 'Post-Impressionist Room' decorated by the Omega Workshops. Lewis circulates a round robin (open letter) denouncing Fry for stealing the commission. Lewis, Etchells, Hamilton, and Wadsworth abandon the Omega Workshops. The *Post-Impressionist and Futurist Exhibition* at the Doré Galleries, London, organized by Rutter, excludes Bloomsbury painters. Coburn has a solo show at the Goupil Gallery and publishes his celebrated portraits of European luminaries, *Men of Mark*. He immediately embarks on a new project titled *More Men of Mark* (published 1922) and photographs Ezra Pound on 22 October, who then introduces Coburn to his circle. The Countess of Drogheda commissions Lewis to decorate her dining room at 40 Wilton Crescent, Belgravia.

November, Lewis and Nevinson organize a dinner at the Florence Restaurant in honour of Marinetti.

Winter, Gaudier-Brzeska and Roberts join the Omega Workshops. Epstein begins work on *Rock Drill*.

December–January 1914, *Exhibition of the Work of English Post-Impressionists, Cubists and others* held at the Brighton Public Art Gallery. It includes a 'Cubist Room' organized by Lewis, with works by Bernard Adeney, Bomberg, Epstein, Jessie and Frederick Etchells, Fanny Eveleigh, Hamilton, Nevinson, and Wadsworth.

December, in his first art criticism essay, Hulme reviews Epstein's first solo show held at the Adelphi Gallery, London. The show includes drawings for the *Rock Drill*. Lewis and Pound conceive the review *Blast*, with funds provided by Lechmere. Lewis publishes his portfolio *Timon of Athens* with Cube Press. In a letter to William Carlos Williams, Pound refers to 'The Vortex'.

1914

The Egoist (1914–19) appears under the editorship of Dora Marsden. A journal championing anarcho-individualism, *The Egoist* publishes art criticism, poetry and literature by Vorticist allies Aldington, Gaudier-Brzeska, Lewis, Pound, and Rebecca West, as well as landmark publications by T.S. Eliot, James Joyce, and Williams.

The New Age publishes Hulme's series of articles on 'Modern Art' as well as 'Contemporary Drawings' by David Bomberg, Gaudier-Brzeska, and William Roberts, edited by Hulme.

January, Coburn photographs Epstein at his London flat for *More Men of Mark*. Hulme lectures on 'Modern art and its philosophy' to the Quest Society in Kensington Town Hall.

January/February, Gaudier-Brzeska begins work on his *Hieratic Head of Ezra Pound*.

February, liquidation sale held for the Cave of the Golden Calf. Clive Bell's influential book *Art* is published.

March, the first London Group exhibition at the Goupil Gallery. Gore dies of pleurisy, aged thirty-five. Lewis founds the Rebel Art Centre, with funding from Lechmere, at 38 Great Ormond Street; he is joined by Lawrence Atkinson, Etchells, Hamilton, Nevinson, Saunders, Shakespear, and Wadsworth. The centre includes decorations by Lechmere and paintings by Lewis and Wadsworth. Lewis visits Roberts for the first time. The Rebel Art Centre founders after only four months.

April, *Exhibition of the Works of the Italian Futurist Painters and Sculptors* held at the Doré Galleries includes paintings by Balla (absent from the 1912 show) and sculpture by Boccioni. Pound refers to Vorticism in a lecture at the Rebel Art Centre. *The Egoist* publishes the first advertisement for *Blast* as a vehicle for 'Cubism, Futurism, Imagism and all Vital Forms of Modern Art.' Pound marries artist Dorothy Shakespear.

May, Marinetti speaks at the Rebel Art Centre to raise funds for it.

May–June, *Twentieth Century Art: A Review of the Modern Movements* held at the Whitechapel Art Gallery, London. It is the most all-embracing exhibition of contemporary British art of its time.

Pound publishes the anthology *Des Imagistes*, with poems by Aldington, H.D., himself, as well as Skipwith Cannell, Amy Lowell, Williams, Joyce, Hueffer, Allen Upward, and John Cournos.

June, the *Observer* (7 June), and subsequently *The Times*, the *Daily Mail* and *Lacerba* publish the manifesto 'Vital English Art: Futurist Manifesto', written by Marinetti and Nevinson, using the address of the Rebel Art Centre. The *Spectator* (June 13) publishes the Rebel Art Centre's riposte, 'Manifesto of the Vorticists'. This is the first appearance in print of the term 'Vorticist'. *Blast* is announced for publication on 20 June but actually appears 2 July.

Blast is advertised in the *Spectator* as 'The Manifesto of the Vorticists – The English Parallel movement to Cubism and Expressionism – Death Blow to Impressionism and Futurism'.

28 June, Gavrilo Princip, Serbian terrorist, assassinates Archduke Franz Ferdinand and his wife Sophie in Sarajevo, the spark that ignites the First World War five weeks later.

July, Bomberg's first solo show at the Chenil Gallery, London, includes *The Mud Bath*. Publication of *Blast* (dated 20 June 1914), edited by Lewis, with a 'Manifesto' signed by Aldington, Arbuthnot, Lawrence Atkinson, Gaudier-Brzeska, Dismorr, Hamilton, Lewis, Pound, Roberts, Saunders, and Wadsworth.

4 August, First World War breaks out. Hulme joins the Royal Marine Artillery, and Nevinson the Red Cross Ambulance Corps.

September, Pound publishes 'Vorticism' in *Fortnightly Review* (1 September). Gaudier-Brezska enlists in the 129e Régiment d'Infanterie.

November, Pound publishes a 'Preliminary Announcement of the College of the Arts' in *The Egoist*, listing Coburn, Gaudier-Brzeska, Lewis, Saunders, and Wadsworth among the proposed faculty.

1915

Pound corresponds with Quinn in New York, and begins discussing an exhibition.

Shakespear designs Vorticist covers for Pound's *Catholic Anthology*.

March, Exhibition of the London Group at the Goupil Gallery includes Epstein's *Rock Drill*, with tripod.

June, Lewis, with the help of Saunders, paints three abstract panels for a Vorticist room in the Restaurant de la Tour Eiffel, London. Death of Gaudier-Brzeska, aged twenty-three, in the trenches at Neuville Saint-Vaast (5 June).

June–July, *First Vorticist Exhibition* at Doré Galleries. The Vorticists are Dismorr, Etchells, Gaudier-Brzeska, Lewis, Roberts, Saunders, and Wadsworth. 'Invited' artists are Adeney, Atkinson, Bomberg, Grant, Kramer, and Nevinson.

Shakespear designs a Vorticist cover for Pound's reissue of *Ripostes*.

July, *Blast*, no.2 (the 'war number') is published.

November, Bomberg joins the Royal Engineers.

1916

Pound publishes *Lustra* with Coburn's 1913 photograph of him as the frontispiece.

Pound publishes *Gaudier-Brzeska: A Memoir*. He encourages Quinn to start buying work.

February, Coburn photographs Lewis and Wadsworth in their studios for *More Men of Mark*.

21 February, the Battle of Verdun begins. By the end of June the French have 315,000 casualties, the Germans 281,000.

April, Roberts enlists in the Royal Field Artillery.

24–30 April, the harsh suppression of the Easter Rising in Dublin raises sympathy for Irish Republicanism (Sinn Féin), leading eventually to the Irish War of Independence (1919–21) and the formation of the Republic of Ireland (Eire).

Lewis volunteers as a gunner and bombardier, entering Cadet Artillery School, Exeter. *The Egoist* continues to publish his short stories and serializes his unpublished novel *Tarr*.

June, Epstein exhibits the *Rock Drill* in its reduced, bronze version without tripod at the fourth London Group exhibition.

Wadsworth serves with the British Naval Intelligence in the Eastern Mediterranean. Dismorr spends most of the war in France doing voluntary work.

September–October, Nevinson holds his first solo show at the Leicester Galleries.

Coburn works with Pound to devise the Vortoscope, and takes his first Vortographs, with Pound as his model.

December, Lloyd George succeeds Asquith as Prime Minister.

1917

10 January–1 February, *Exhibition of the Vorticists*, organized by Pound and Quinn, opens at the Penguin Club, New York.

February, the Camera Club, London, exhibits *Vortographs and Paintings* by Coburn.

February–March, Epstein holds a solo show at the Leicester Galleries, London.

April, Congress approves the USA's declaration of war on Germany.

May, Lewis leaves for the Western Front to serve in a siege battery. Epstein enlists in the Royal Fusiliers.

By June, Quinn arranges for those works by Wadsworth and Dismorr that he did not purchase from the Penguin Club exhibition to go to the New York avant-garde bookstore, The Sunwise Turn, and be available for sale.

31 July, almost one million Germans and one million British engage in the third battle of Ypres, also known as Passchendaele or 'the battle of the mud' (Lloyd George).

28 September, Hulme dies, hit by a German shell at Nieuwpoort in Flanders.

December, Bomberg and Lewis transfer to Canadian regiment as war artists.

1917-1918

Wadsworth, as a Lieutenant in the Royal Navy Volunteer Reserve, supervises dazzle camouflage for English warships in Bristol and Liverpool.

1918

The Representation of the People Act grants the vote to propertied women who are over the age of thirty or graduates of British universities.

Canadian War Memorials Fund commissions paintings from Etchells, Nevinson, Roberts, and Wadsworth.

Lewis publishes *Tarr*, his first novel, under the auspices of the newly founded Egoist Press.

May–June, Gaudier-Brzeska memorial show held at Leicester Galleries.

11 November, Armistice Day ends war with Germany. First World War deaths have been estimated at 16 million, of which 9.7 million were military personnel.

1919

February, Lewis holds his first solo show at the Goupil Gallery.

February–March, *The Little Review* publishes 'The Death of Vorticism' by Pound (in which Pound argues that Vorticism is still 'alive').

March, Wadsworth holds his first solo show of woodcuts and drawings at the Adelphi Gallery.

Summer, the Omega Workshops close. Publication of *Blast*, no.3 is abandoned.

Lewis publishes the pamphlet *The Caliph's Design: Architects! Where Is your Vortex?* in which he argues for a larger role of art in society.

1920

March–April, Lewis organizes the *Exhibition of Group X* at the Mansard Gallery, London, including Dismorr, Frank Dobson, Etchells, Ginner, Hamilton, E. McKnight Kauffer, Lewis, Roberts, John Turnbull, and Wadsworth. This is considered the swansong of Vorticism. Lewis's catalogue preface indicates that Vorticism is over.

Pound publishes *Hugh Selwyn Mauberley* and decides to move to France where he allies himself with the Dada movement in Paris.

BIBLIOGRAPHY

Antliff, Allan. *Anarchist Modernism: Art, Politics and the First American Avant-Garde*. Chicago: University of Chicago Press , 2001.

Antliff, Mark. 'Alvin Langdon Coburn among the Vorticists: Studio Photographs and Lost Works by Jacob Epstein, Wyndham Lewis, and Edward Wadsworth'. *Burlington Magazine* (September 2010).

___. *Gaudier-Brzeska Drawings*. New Haven: Yale Center for British Art, 1987.

___. 'Henri Gaudier-Brzeska's *Guerre sociale*: Art, Anarchism, and Anti-Militarism in Paris and London, 1910–1915'. *Modernism/Modernity*, vol.17, no.1 (January 2010), pp.135–69.

Ayers, David. *Wyndham Lewis and Western Man*. London: Macmillan, 1992.

Barassi, Sebastiano (ed.). *'WE the Moderns': Gaudier-Brzeska and the Birth of Modern Sculpture*, exh.cat. Cambridge, UK: Kettle's Yard Gallery, 2007.

Beasley, Rebecca. *Ezra Pound and the Visual Culture of Modernism*. Cambridge and New York: Cambridge University Press, 2007.

Beckett, Jane and Deborah Cherry. 'Modern Women, Modern Spaces: Women, Metropolitan Culture and Vorticism', in Katy Deepwell (ed.), *Women Artists and Modernism*. Manchester: Manchester University Press, 1998.

Bell, Quentin, and Stephen Chaplin, 'The Ideal Home Rumpus: Wyndham Lewis and Roger Fry'. *Apollo*, vol.80, no.32 (October 1964), pp.284–91.

Black, Jonathan, *Edward Wadsworth: Form, Feeling and Calculation. The Complete Paintings and Drawings*. London: Philip Wilson; New York, 2005.

Black, Jonathan, et al. *Blasting the Future! Vorticism in Britain 1910–1920*. London: Philip Wilson 2004.

Briend, Christian and Doïna Lemny et al. *Henri Gaudier-Brzeska dans les collections du Centre Pompidou, Musée national d'art* moderne, exh. cat. Paris: Centre Pompidou, 2009.

Brooker, Peter. *Bohemia in London: The Social Scene of Early Modernism*. New York: Palgrave Macmillan, 2004.

Brulé, Paul, et al. *Henri-Gaudier Brzeska Dessins*. Lyons: Fage éditions, 2009.

Cole, Roger. *Burning to Speak: The Life and Art of Henri Gaudier-Brzeska*. Oxford: Phaidon, 1978.

___. *Gaudier-Brzeska: Artist and Myth*. Bristol: Sansom & Co., 1995

Comentale, Edward P. *Modernism, Cultural Production, and the British Avant-Garde*. Cambridge: Cambridge University Press, 2004.

Comentale, Edward P., and Andrzej Gasiorek (eds.). *T.E. Hulme and the Question of Modernism*. Aldershot, England; Burlington, VT: Ashgate, 2006.

Corbett, David Peters. *Wyndham Lewis and the Art of Modern War*. Cambridge: Cambridge University Press, 1998.

Cork, Richard. *A Bitter Truth: Avant-Garde Art and the Great War*. New Haven: Yale University Press, 1994.

___. *Art beyond the Gallery in Early 20th-Century England*. New Haven: Yale University Press, 1985.

___. *David Bomberg*. New Haven: Yale University Press, 1987.

___. *David Bomberg*. London: Tate Gallery, 1988.

___. 'Edward Wadsworth's Vorticist Period'. *Print Collector's Newsletter New York*, vol.16, no.2 (1985), pp.41–4.

___. *Henri Gaudier and Ezra Pound: A Friendship*, exh. cat. London: Anthony d'Offay Gallery, 1982.

___. 'Henri Gaudier-Brzeska, Sculptor 1891–1915: York City Art Gallery'. *Burlington Magazine*, vol.126, no.971 (February 1984), pp.66, 112–14.

___. *Jacob Epstein*. London: Tate Gallery Publishing, 1999.

___. *Vorticism and Abstract Art in the First Machine Age* (2 vols.). London: Fraser; Berkeley: University of California, 1976.

___. *Vorticism and its Allies*, exh.cat. London: Arts Council of Great Britain, 1974.

___. *Wild Thing: Epstein, Gaudier-Brzeska, Gill*, exh. cat. London: Royal Academy of Arts, 2010.

C.R.W. Nevinson, 1889–1946: Retrospective Exhibition of Paintings, Drawings and Prints, exh. cat. Cambridge: Kettle's Yard Gallery, 1988.

C.R.W. Nevinson: The Twentieth Century (Imperial War Museum and Yale Center for British Art), exh. cat. London: Merrell Holberton in association with the Imperial War Museum, 1999.

Csengeri, Karen (ed.). *The Collected Writings of T.E. Hulme*. Oxford: Oxford University Press, 1994.

Dasenbrock, Reed Way. *The Literary Vorticism of Ezra Pound and Wyndham Lewis: Towards the Condition of Painting*. Baltimore: Johns Hopkins University Press, 1985.

DiFederico, Frank. 'Alvin Langdon Coburn and the Genesis of the Vortographs'. *History of Photography*, vol.11, no.4 (October–December 1987), pp.265–96.

Doherty, Charles E. 'Nevinson's Elegy: Paths of Glory'. *Art Journal*, vol.51, no.1 (Spring 1992), pp.64–71.

Ede, H.S. *Savage Messiah: A Biography of the Sculptor Henri Gaudier-Brzeska*. London: Gordon Fraser, 1971 [1931].

Edward Wadsworth: Early Woodcuts. Introduction by Richard Cork, exh. cat. London: Christopher Drake Ltd, 1973.

Edward Wadsworth 1889–1949: A Memorial Exhibition. With an essay by T.W. Earp, exh. cat. London: Tate Gallery, 1951.

Edward Wadsworth, 1889–1949: Paintings, Drawings, Prints, exh cat. London: Colnaghi, 1974.

Edwards, Paul. *Wyndham Lewis: Art and War*. London: Wyndham Lewis Memorial Trust in association with Lund Humphries, 1992.

___. 'Wyndham Lewis at the Second Post-Impressionist Exhibition: New (Old) Reproductions of Three Lost Works'. *Wyndham Lewis Annual*, vols.9–10 (2002–3), pp.73–9.

___. *Wyndham Lewis: Painter and Writer*. New Haven: Yale University Press, 2000.

___. 'Wyndham Lewis's Timon of Athens Portfolio: The Emergence of Vorticist Abstraction'. *Apollo*, vol.148, no.440 (October 1998), pp.34–40.

Edwards, Paul (ed.). *Blast: Vorticism, 1914–1918*. Aldershot, England; Burlington, VT: Ashgate, 2000.

___. *Volcanic Heaven: Essays on Wyndham Lewis's Painting and Writing*. Santa Rosa: Black Sparrow Press, 1996.

Edwards, Paul, et al. *Wyndham Lewis (1882–1957)*, exh. cat. Madrid: Fundacion Juan March, 2010

Gardiner, Stephen. *Epstein: Artist Against the Establishment*. London: Michael Joseph, 1992.

Gasiorek, Andrzej. *Wyndham Lewis and Modernism*. Tavistock: Northcote House in association with the British Council, 2004.

Gernsheim, Helmut and Alison Gernsheim (eds.). *Alvin Langdon Coburn, Photographer: An Autobiography*. London: Faber, 1966.

Getsey, David. 'Give and Take: Henri-Gaudier-Brzeska's *Coffer for Wilfred Scawen Blunt* and Ezra Pound's Homosocial Modernism in 1914'. *Sculpture Journal*, vol.16, no.2 (2007), p.39–51.

Gibbon-Williams, Andrew. *William Roberts: An English Cubist*. Aldershot, England; Burlington, VT: Lund Humphries, 2004

Greenwood, Jeremy. *The Graphic Work of Edward Wadsworth*. Woodbridge: Wood Lea Press, 2002.

Gruetzner Robins, Anna. *Modern Art in Britain, 1910–1914*, exh.cat. London: Merrell Holberton in association with Barbican Art Gallery, 1997.

Hallberg, Robert von. 'Libertarian Imagism'. *Modernism/Modernity*, vol.2, no.2 (April 1995), pp.63–79.

Heard, Andrew (ed.). *William Roberts (1895–1980)*, exh.cat. Newcastle upon Tyne: Hatton Gallery, 2004.

Henri Gaudier-Brzeska, exh. cat. Orléans: Musée des beaux-arts; Toulouse: Musée d'art moderne, 1993.

Hickman, Miranda B. *The Geometry of Modernism: The Vorticist Idiom in Lewis, Pound, H.D., and Yeats*. Austin: University of Texas Press, 2005.

Humphreys, Richard. *Pound's Artists: Ezra Pound and the Visual Arts in London, Paris and Italy*. London: Tate Gallery, 1985.

___. *Wyndham Lewis*. London: Tate Publishing, 2004.

Jameson, Fredric. *Fables of Aggression: Wyndham Lewis, the Modernist as Fascist*. London: Verso Press, 2008.

Kadlec, David. *Mosaic Modernism: Anarchism, Pragmatism, Culture*. Baltimore: Johns Hopkins University Press, 2000.

___. 'Pound, Blast, and Syndicalism', *ELH*, vol.60, no.4 (Winter 1993), pp.1015–31.

Kenner, Hugh. *The Pound Era*. Berkeley: University of California Press, 1971.

___. *Wyndham Lewis*. London: Methuen, 1954.

Klein, Scott W. *The Fictions of James Joyce and Wyndham Lewis: Monsters of Nature and Design*. Cambridge: Cambridge University Press, 2006 [1994].

Koslow, Francine A. 'The Evolution of Henri Gaudier-Brzeska's 'Wrestlers' Relief'. *MFA Bulletin*, vol.78 (1980), pp.38–49.

___. 'Gaudier-Brzeska & Ezra Pound'. *Print Collector's Newsletter* vol.16, no.5 (November-December 1985), pp.153–8.

Kush, Thomas. *Wyndham Lewis's Pictorial Integer*. Ann Arbor: UMI Research Press, 1981.

Leveridge, Michael. 'The Printing of Blast'. *Wyndham Lewis Annual*, vol.7 (2000), pp.20–31.

Lewis, Wyndham. *Tarr*, ed. Scott W. Klein. Oxford: Oxford University Press, 2010.

Lewis, Wyndham (ed.) *Blast*, no.1: *Review of the Great English Vortex*, 20 June 1914 (issued 1 July 1914). London: J. Lane, 1914.

___. *Blast*, no.2: *Review of the Great English Vortex*, July 1915. London; New York: J. Lane, 1915.

Lewison, Jeremy. 'Gaudier-Brzeska's *Weeping Woman*'. *Burlington Magazine*, vol.129, no.1009 (April 1987), pp.243–45.

___. *Henri Gaudier-Brzeska, Sculptor 1891–1915*, exh.cat. Cambridge: Kettle's Yard Gallery, 1983.

Lewison, Jeremy (ed.). *A Genius of Industrial England: Edward Wadsworth, 1889–1949*, exh cat. Bradford: Arkwright Trust and Bradford Art Galleries and Museums, 1990.

Lipke, William C. *David Bomberg: A Critical Study of his Life and Work*. London: Evelyn, Adams & MacKay, 1967.

Lipke, William C., and Bernard W. Rozran. 'Ezra Pound and Vorticism: A Polite Blast'. *Wisconsin Studies in Contemporary Literature*, vol.7, no.2 (Summer 1966), p. 201–10.

Lofthouse, Richard A. *Vitalism in Modern Art, c.1900–1950: Otto Dix, Stanley Spencer, Max Beckmann, and Jacob Epstein*. Lewiston, NY: E. Mellen Press, 2005.

Loss, Archie. '*Vile Bodies*, Vorticism, and Italian Futurism'. *Journal of Modern Literature*, vol.18, no.1 (Winter 1992), pp.155–64.

Mao, Douglas. *Solid Objects: Modernism and the Test of Production*. Princeton: Princeton University Press, 1998.

Marchio, Roberto Baronti. 'The Vortex in the Machine: Futurism in England', in Günter Berghaus (ed.). *International Futurism in Arts and Literature*. Berlin: de Gruyter, 2000, pp.100–21.

Materer, Timothy. *Vortex: Pound, Eliot, and Lewis*. Ithaca: Cornell University Press, 1979.

Materer, Timothy (ed.). *Pound/Lewis: The Letters of Ezra Pound and Wyndham Lewis, the Correspondence of Ezra Pound*. New York: New Directions, 1985.

___. *The Selected Letters of Ezra Pound to John Quinn, 1915–1924*. Durham: Duke University Press, 1991.

Meyers, Jeffrey. 'Kate Lechmere's 'Wyndham Lewis from 1912'. *Journal of Modern Literature*, vol.10, no.1 (March 1983), pp.158–66.

Michel, Walter. *Paintings and Drawings: Wyndham Lewis*. London: Thames & Hudson, 1971.

Michel, Walter, and C.J. Fox (eds). *Wyndham Lewis on Art: Collected Writings 1913–1956*. London: Thames and Hudson, 1969.

Normand, Tom. *Wyndham Lewis the Artist: Holding the Mirror up to* Politics. Cambridge; New York: Cambridge University Press, 1992.

O'Keefe, Paul. *Gaudier-Brzeska: An Absolute Case of Genius*. London: Allen Lane, 2004.

___. *Some Sort of Genius: A Life of Wyndham Lewis*. London: Jonathan Cape, 2000.

Peppin, Brigid. *Helen Saunders, 1885–1963*, exh. cat. Oxford: Ashmolean Museum; Sheffield: Oxford and Graves Art Gallery, 1996.

Peppis, Paul. *Literature, Politics, and the English Avant-Garde: Nation and Empire, 1901–1918*. Cambridge: Cambridge University Press, 2000.

Peters Corbett, David (ed.). *Wyndham Lewis and the Art of Modern War*. Cambridge: Cambridge University Press, 1998.

Pound, Ezra. *Gaudier-Brzeska: A Memoir*. New York: New Directions, 1970.

Puchner, Martin. *Poetry of the Revolution: Marx, Manifestos, and the Avant-gardes*. Princeton: Princeton University Press, 2006.

Reid, B.L. *The Man from New York: John Quinn and his Friends*. New York: Oxford University Press, 1968.

Reynolds, Paige. 'Chaos Invading Concept': Blast as a Native Theory of Promotional Culture'. *Twentieth Century Literature*, vol.46, no.2 (Summer 2000), pp.238–68.

Rose, William K. (ed.). *The Letters of Wyndham Lewis*. London: Methuen, 1963.

Sherry, Vincent. *Ezra Pound, Wyndham Lewis, and Radical Modernism*. New York: Oxford University Press, 1993.

Silber, Evelyn. *Gaudier-Brzeska: Life and Art*. New York: Thames & Hudson, 1996.

Silber, Evelyn, et al. *Jacob Epstein: Sculpture and Drawings*, exh cat. Leeds: W.S. Maney & Son, in association with the Henry Moore Centre for the Study of Sculpture, 1989.

Tickner, Lisa. 'Men's Work?: Masculinity and Modernism', in Norman Bryson, Michael Ann Holly and Keith Moxey (eds.), *Visual Culture: Images and Interpretations*. Hannover (NH): University Press of New England, 1994, pp.42–82.

___. *Modern Life and Modern Subjects: British Life in the Early Twentieth Century*. New Haven: Yale University Press, 2000.

___. 'A Lost Lewis: The *Mother and Child* of 1912'. *Wyndham Lewis Annual*, vol.2 (1995), pp.2–11.

___. 'Now and Then: The Hieratic Head of Ezra Pound,' *Oxford Art Journal*, vol.16, no.2 (Autumn 1993), pp.55–61.

Tilghman, Carolyn. 'Lewis in Contention: Identity, Anxiety, and the London Vortex'. *South Central Review*, vol.24, no.3 (Fall 2007), pp.2–22.

Tuma, Keith. 'Wyndham Lewis, Blast, and Popular Culture'. *ELH*, vol.54, no.2 (Summer 1987), pp.403–19.

Wadsworth, Barbara. *Edward Wadsworth: A Painter's Life*. Salisbury: Michael Russell, 1989.

Wagner, Geoffrey. 'Wyndham Lewis and the Vorticist Aesthetic'. *Journal of Aesthetics and Art Criticism*, vol.13, no.1 (September 1954), pp.1–17.

Walsh, Michael J.K. *C.R.W. Nevinson: This Cult of Violence*. New Haven: Yale University Press, 2002.

Walsh, Michael J.K. (ed.). *A Dilemma of English Modernism: Visual and Verbal Politics in the Life and Work of C.R.W. Nevinson (1889–1946)*. Newark: University of Delaware Press, 2007.

___. *London, Modernism and 1914*. Cambridge: Cambridge University Press, 2010.

Weaver, Mike. *Alvin Langdon Coburn: Symbolist Photographer*. New York: Aperture, 1986.

Wees, William C. 'Ezra Pound as a Vorticist', *Wisconsin Studies in Contemporary Literature*, vol.6, no.1 (Winter–Spring 1965), pp.56–72.

___. *Vorticism and the English Avant-garde*. Toronto: University of Toronto Press, 1972.

Wilhelm, James J. *Ezra Pound in London and Paris, 1908–1925*. University Park: Pennsylvania State University Press, 1990.

Wilson, Andrew (ed.). 'Vorticism', special issue. *ICSAC Cahier* (Brussels), no.8/9 (December 1988).

Wood, Jon. 'Heads and Tales: Henri Gaudier-Brzeska's *Hieratic Head of Ezra Pound* and the Making of an Avant-garde Homage', in David J. Getsy (ed.), *Sculpture and the Pursuit of a Modern Ideal in Britain, c.1880–1930*. Aldershot, England: Ashgate Publishing, 2004, pp.191–208.

Wyndham Lewis Special Issue. *Modernism/Modernity*, vol.4, no.2 (April 1997).

Zilczer, Judith. 'The Dispersal of the John Quinn Collection'. *Archives of American Art Journal*, vol.30, no.1 (1990), pp.35–40.

___. *'The Noble Buyer': John Quinn, Patron of the Avant-garde*, exh. cat. Washington, DC: Hirshhorn Museum and Sculpture Garden, Smithsonian Institution, 1978.

Zinnes, Harriet (ed.) *Ezra Pound and the Visual Arts*. New York: New Directions, 1980.

EXHIBITED WORKS

Measurements are given in centimetres, height before width.
Cross-references refer to the page on which the main illustration appears.
See p.12 for notes on abbreviations.

Lawrence Atkinson
1873–1931

Abstract Composition 1915
Ink, crayon, and watercolour on paper 33 x 21.6
Private collection
[No.22]

Abstract c.1915–20
Oil on wood 129.5 x 50.8
Arts Council Collection, Southbank Centre, London
[No.15]

David Bomberg
1890–1957

The Mud Bath 1914
Oil on canvas 152.4 x 224.2
Tate. Purchased 1964
[No.6]

Abstract Composition c.1914
Pencil and watercolour on paper 27.5 x 36.5
Private collection, California
[No.23]

Study for 'The Mud Bath' c.1914
Gouache and pencil on paper
53.4 x 70.8
Private collection, California
Exhibited at Nasher only
[Nos.4, 5]

Alvin Langdon Coburn
1882–1966

Ezra Pound 1913
Photogravure 23.5 x 17.5
Private collection
[Fig.1]

Jacob Epstein 1914
Photogravure 23.5 x 17.5
Private collection
[Fig.2]

Wyndham Lewis 1916
Photogravure 23.5 x 17.5
Archive of Documentary Arts, Rare Book, Manuscript, and Special Collections Library, Duke University Libraries
[Fig.3]

Edward Wadsworth 1916
Photogravure 23.5 x 17.5
Private collection
[Fig.4]

Cover Design for 'Vortographs and Paintings by Alvin Langdon Coburn' exhibition catalogue, The Camera Club 1917
Ink on paper 16.4 x 13.2; overall: 24.5 x 19.5
George Eastman House, Rochester, NY
[Fig.40]

Ezra Pound 1917 (printed later)
Gelatin silver print
image: 20.5 x 15.4
George Eastman House, Rochester, NY (67:098: 53)
[No.78]

Vortograph of Ezra Pound 1917 (printed later)
Gelatin silver print
image: 20.2 x 15.5
George Eastman House, Rochester, NY (67:098: 21)
[No.79]
[C]

Vortograph of Ezra Pound 1917 (printed later)
Gelatin silver print
image: 28.4 x 19.9
George Eastman House, Rochester, NY (67:098: 14)
[No.80]
[C]

Vortograph 1917
Gelatin silver print
image: 28.3 x 21.4
George Eastman House, Rochester, NY (67:098: 5A)
[No.83]
[C]

Vortograph 1917
Gelatin silver print, image: 28.2 x 21.8
George Eastman House, Rochester, NY (67:098: 24)
[No.85]
[C]

Vortograph 1917
Gelatin silver print, image: 47.5 x 36.4
George Eastman House, Rochester, NY (67:098: 29)
[No.84]
[C]

Vortograph 1917
Gelatin silver print, image: 27.4 x 20.9
George Eastman House, Rochester, NY (67:098: 40)
[No.81]
[C]

Vortograph 1917
Gelatin silver print, image: 27.6 x 20.7
George Eastman House, Rochester, NY (67:098: 42)
[No.82]
[C]

Vortograph 1917
Gelatin silver print, image: 26.6 x 20.4
George Eastman House, Rochester, NY (67:098: 45)
[Fig.42]
[C]

Jessica Dismorr
1885–1939

Edinburgh Castle 1914–15
Pen and watercolour on paper
24 x 19
Victoria and Albert Museum, London
[No.66]
[P; S]

Abstract Composition c.1915
Oil on wood 41.3 x 50.8
Tate. Purchased 1968
[No.24]

Jacob Epstein
1880–1959

Female Figure 1913
Serpentine [flenite]
61 x 16.2 x 28.9
The Minneapolis Institute of Arts. Gift of Samuel Maslon, Charles H. Bell, Francis D. Butler, John Cowles, Bruce B. Dayton and an Anonymous Donor
[No.34]

Female Figure in Flenite 1913
Serpentine [flenite]
45.7 x 9.5 x 12.1
Tate. Purchased 1972
Exhibited at PGC and Tate Britain only

Study for 'Female Figure in Flenite' c.1913
Crayon on paper
68.6 x 42.5
Private collection, California
[No.33]
[B1] Close variation of drawing reproduced in *Blast*, no.1

Studies for 'Rock Drill', 'Venus' and 'Doves' c.1913
Crayon and pencil on paper
45.7 x 58.4
Private collection, California
[No.2]

Birth 1913–14
Stone 30.6 x 26.6 x 10.2
Art Gallery of Ontario, Toronto. Purchase, 1983
[No.36]

Rock Drill 1913–15
[reconstruction by Ken Cook and Ann Christopher, after the dismantled original, 1973–4]
Polyester resin, metal, and wood
205 x 141.5
Birmingham Museums & Art Gallery. Presented by Ken Cook and Ann Christopher through the Friends of Birmingham Museums & Art Gallery, 1982
PGC and Tate Britain only
[No.3]

Torso in Metal from the 'Rock Drill' 1913–16
Bronze 70.5 x 58.4 x 44.5
Tate. Purchased 1960
[Fig.5]

Venus 1917
Marble 235.6 x 43.2 x 82.6
Yale University Art Gallery, New Haven, CT. Gift of Winston F.C. Guest, B.A. 1927
Nasher only
[No.9]

Untitled (Birth) [n.d.]
Crayon on paper 63 x 52.7
Private collection, California
Nasher only
[No.35]

Frederick Etchells
1886–1973

Composition [Stilts] 1914–15
Gouache and pencil on paper
32 x 20
The British Council
[No.67]
[P] Possibly the work bought by John Quinn titled *Stilts* 1915 listed in Penguin catalogue. Listed as a watercolour titled *Stilts*, 9 x 13 inches, in the 1926 catalogue of Quinn's collection

Progression 1914–15
Pen and ink on paper 14.3 x 22.3
Trustees of the Cecil Higgins Art Gallery, Bedford
[No.41]
[B2; P]

The English Comedian 1914–15
Pen, brush, and ink on paper
27.5 x 18
Victoria and Albert Museum, London
[No.65]
[P]

Henri Gaudier-Brzeska
1891–1915

Crouching Fawn 1913
Bath stone 30.4 x 25.3
Ivor Braka Ltd, London
[No.25]
[D] Larger variation on the work in Bath stone titled *Faun* exhibited under 'Small Objects' at the Doré exhibition

Singer 1913
Derby stone 85.1 x 21.6 x 15.9
Tate. Presented by C. Frank Stoop through the Contemporary Art Society 1930
[Fig.27]
[D]

Red Stone Dancer c.1913
Red Mansfield stone
43.2 x 22.9 x 22.9
Tate. Presented by C. Frank Stoop through the Contemporary Art Society 1930
[No.10]
[D] Listed as *Dancer* under 'Sculpture' in the Doré catalogue

Doorknocker 1914
Brass 17.8 x 8.5 x 1
Kettle's Yard, University of Cambridge
[Fig.24]

Duck 1914
Marble 6.5 x 12 x 4
Kettle's Yard, University of Cambridge
[No.27]

Fish 1914
Bronze 4.8 x 3 x 0.8
Tate. Presented by Tate Members 2010
[No.14]

Green Stone Charm 1914
Irish marble 10.8 x 8.9
Private collection
[No.26]
[D] Listed as *Charm* under 'Small Objects' in the Doré catalogue

Hieratic Head of Ezra Pound 1914
Marble 90.5 x 45.7 x 48.9
National Gallery of Art, Washington, DC. Gift from the Collection of Raymond and Patsy Nasher, 2009
Exhibited at Nasher and Tate Britain only
[No.1]
[B2]

Hieratic Head of Ezra Pound [authorized copy] 1914 (replica made in 1973)
Marble 90.5 x 45.7 x 48.9
Fondazione Giorgio Cini onlus, Venice
Exhibited at PGC only

Ornement Torpille 1914
Brass 15.9 x 3.8 x 3.2
Art Gallery of Ontario, Toronto. Purchase, 1985
[No.13]

The Imp c.1914
Alabaster 40.6 x 8.9 x 8.3
Tate. Presented by C. Frank Stoop through the Contemporary Art Society 1930
[No.28]

Portrait of Ezra Pound [n.d.]
Wood 71.1 x 7.6 x 7.6
Yale University Art Gallery, New Haven, CT. Purchase Director's Fund
Exhibited at Nasher only
[No.8]

Wyndham Lewis
1882–1957

Anthony 1909
Pen and gouache on paper
14.5 x 11.5
Victoria and Albert Museum, London
[No.57]
[P] Closely related to the work exhibited with the title *Architect* under 'Drawings' in Penguin catalogue, and quite possibly one of the two works listed as *The Architect Nos.1 and 2* in the Camden Town Group exhibition held in June 1913

Architect with Green Tie 1909
Gouache, pen, and ink on cut and pasted papers 23.5 x 13.3
The Metropolitan Museum of Art, New York. Bequest of William S. Lieberman, 2005
[Fig.35]
[P]

Design for Programme Cover – Kermesse 1912
Pen and ink on paper 28.5 x 31
Trustees of the British Museum, London
[No.44]
[B2; P] Listed as *Kermess – drawing* 1912 in Penguin catalogue

Drawing for Timon 1912
Pen, ink, and watercolour/gouache on paper 38 x 28.5
Private collection
[No.58]

Kermesse 1912
Gouache and watercolour with pen and ink over pencil on two joined sheets of paper
30.5 x 30.6
Yale Center for British Art, New Haven, CT. Paul Mellon Fund and

Gift of Neil F. and Ivan E. Phillips in memory of their mother, Mrs Rosalie Phillips
Exhibited at Nasher and PGC only
[No.60]
[P] Listed as *'Ink Drawing' – Early 'Kermess'* 1912 in Penguin catalogue

The Dancers 1912
Ink and watercolour on paper
30.1 x 29.2
Manchester City Art Galleries, Manchester
[Fig.18]
[P]

Timon of Athens, Act I. Banquet Scene 1912
Pen, ink, and watercolour on paper
48.5 x 32.8
The Wyndham Lewis Memorial Trust. On long-term loan to The Courtauld Gallery, London
Exhibited at Nasher and Tate Britain only
[No.47]
[P]

Two Women 1912
Pencil, pen, ink, wash, gouache, and collage on paper 48 x 62.5
Arts Council Collection, Southbank Centre, London
[No.59]
[P] Listed as *The Starry Sky* 1912 in Penguin catalogue

Planners: Happy Day 1912–13
Pen, gouache, and pencil on paper
31.1 x 38.1
Tate. Purchased 1956
[No.63]
[P] Listed as *A Happy Day* 1915 in Penguin catalogue

Composition 1913
Pen, watercolour, and pencil on paper 34.3 x 26.7
Tate. Purchased 1949
[No.64]
[P] Listed as *Timon* (a later drawing of the Timon series) 1913 in Penguin catalogue

Protraction 1913
Pencil, crayon, and watercolour on paper 15.2 x 30.5
Private collection
[No.61]
[P]

Timon of Athens 1913
Pencil, pen, and ink on paper
34.5 x 26.5
Private collection
Exhibited at Tate Britain only
[No.32]
[P] Possibly listed as *Drawing* (second phase of Timon) 1915 in Penguin catalogue

Timon of Athens 1913
Portfolio of sixteen lithographs and process engravings
cover: 40 x 27.9
sheets each: 39.1 x 27.3
Private collection, California
[Nos.48, 49a, 49b]

Arghol 1914
Pen, ink, and wash on paper
33 x 20.5
Ivor Braka Ltd, London
[No.62]
[P] Listed as *Argol* in Penguin catalogue

The Crowd 1914–15
Oil and pencil on canvas
200.7 x 153.7
Tate. Presented by the Friends of the Tate Gallery 1964
[No.7]
[D] Probably listed as *Democratic Composition* under 'Pictures' in Doré catalogue

Workshop c.1914–15
Oil on canvas 76.5 x 61
Tate. Purchased 1974
[No.19]
[D; P]

Christopher Nevinson
1889–1946

Marching Men 1916
Pastel on paper 13.9 x 20.3
Imperial War Museum, London. Presented by Fulham Borough Council 1961
[No.43]
[B2] Version of the work reproduced with title *On the Way to the Trenches* in *Blast*, no.2

Returning to the Trenches 1916
Etching 15.2 x 19.6
Imperial War Museum, London. Gift of Mrs May Cippico 1979

William Roberts
1895–1980

Study for 'St George and the Dragon' 1915
Pencil on paper 25.4 x 20.3
Private collection
[No.11]

Study for the lost painting 'Two-Step' 1915
Pencil, watercolour, and gouache
30 x 23
Trustees of the British Museum, London
[No.12]
[D] Study related to the work listed as *Twostep* under 'Pictures' in Doré catalogue

Helen Saunders
1885–1963

Island of Laputa 1915
Pen and ink, and collage on paper
sheet: 27 x 23.2
image: 25.4 x 21.6
The David and Alfred Smart Museum of Art, The University of Chicago. The Joel Starrels, Jr. Memorial Collection
[No.17]
[D; B2; P]

Abstract Composition in Blue and Yellow c.1915
Pencil, watercolour, and mixed media on paper 27.6 x 17.1
Tate. Presented by Miss Ethel M. Saunders in memory of her sister 1963
[No.42]

Balance c.1915
Pencil and gouache on paper
36.8 x 29.8
The David and Alfred Smart Museum of Art, The University of Chicago. Purchase, The Paul and Miriam Kirkley Fund for Acquisitions with a donation from Lorna Ferguson and Terry Clark in honour of Richard Born
[No.68]
[P]

Canon c.1915
Pencil and gouache on paper
36.8 x 29.8
The David and Alfred Smart Museum of Art, The University of Chicago. Purchase, The Paul and Miriam Kirkley Fund for Acquisitions with a donation from Lorna Ferguson and Terry Clark in honour of Richard Born
[No.70]
[P]

Dance c.1915
Pencil and gouache on paper
37.5 x 29.2
The David and Alfred Smart Museum of Art, The University of Chicago. Purchase, The Paul and Miriam Kirkley Fund for Acquisitions with a donation from Lorna Ferguson and Terry Clark in honour of Richard Born
[No.69]
[P]

Study for 'Black and Khaki' (?) c.1915
Ink and watercolour on paper
25.5 x 18
Private collection
[No.21]
[D] Probably the work listed as *Black and Khaki* under 'Drawings' in Doré catalogue

Dorothy Shakespear
1886–1973

Composition in Blue and Black 1914–15
Collage and watercolour on paper 33.7 x 46.4
Fred L. Emerson Gallery, Hamilton College, Clinton, NY. Gift of Omar S. Pound, Class of 1951
[No.18]

Untitled c.1914–15
Watercolour on paper 14 x 21
Fred L. Emerson Gallery, Hamilton College, Clinton, NY. Gift of Omar S. Pound, Class of 1951
[No.39]

Untitled (Abstract Composition) c.1914–15
Collage, watercolour, and pencil on paper 11.3 x 20.8
Fred L. Emerson Gallery, Hamilton College, Clinton, NY. Gift of Omar S. Pound, Class of 1951
[No.40]

Cover Design for 'Catholic Anthology' 1915
Ink and pencil on paper 26 x 16.5
Fred L. Emerson Gallery, Hamilton College, Clinton, NY. Gift of Omar S. Pound, Class of 1951
[No.50]

Edward Wadsworth
1889–1949

Newcastle c.1913
Woodcut on paper
sheet: 24.7 x 24.7
Johanna and Leslie Garfield Collection
[No.30]
[D; B1; S] A version of print purchased by Quinn; a version very probably among 27 Wadsworth woodcuts Quinn sent to Sunwise Turn

Cleckheaton 1914
Woodcut on paper
sheet: 45.1 x 36.8
image: 28.6 x 24.8
Private collection
[No.16]

Illustration (Typhoon) 1914
Woodcut on paper
image: 28.9 x 25.3
Trustees of the British Museum, London
[No.76]

Landscape 1914
Woodcut on paper
sheet: 25.4 x 20.3; image: 6 x 7.6
Private collection
[No.74]
[S] A version of print purchased by Quinn; a version very probably among 27 Wadsworth woodcuts Quinn sent to Sunwise Turn

Mytholmroyd 1914
Woodcut on paper
sheet: 38 x 30.4
image: 21.6 x 17.8
The Whitworth Art Gallery, University of Manchester
[Fig.37]
[S] A version of print purchased by Quinn; a version very probably among 27 Wadsworth woodcuts Quinn sent to Sunwise Turn

Railway Embankment [also known as *Platelayers' Shed*] 1914
Woodcut on paper
sheet: 13.3 x 10.8
Johanna and Leslie Garfield Collection
[No.77]
[S] A version of print purchased by Quinn; a version very probably among 27 Wadsworth woodcuts Quinn sent to Sunwise Turn

Rotterdam 1914
Woodcut on paper
image: 26.4 x 20.2
overall: 51 x 38
George Eastman House, Rochester, NY
[No.38]
[B2; D; S] This impression was owned by Coburn; another version was purchased by Quinn; and a version was very probably among 27 Wadsworth woodcuts Quinn sent to Sunwise Turn; also the basis for the painting *Rotterdam* bought by Quinn, measuring 24 x 29 inches and shown at the Penguin

Study for 'Cape of Good Hope' 1914
Ink, crayon, watercolour, and gouache on paper 33 x 25
Private collection
[No.31]
[B1] Study for painting *Cape of Good Hope* reproduced in *Blast*, no.1

Yorkshire Village 1914
Woodcut on paper
overall: 38.2 x 28.2
George Eastman House, Rochester, NY
[No.71]
[S] This impression was owned by Coburn; another version was purchased by Quinn; and a version was very probably among 27 Wadsworth woodcuts Quinn sent to Sunwise Turn

Street Singers c.1914
Woodcut on paper
sheet: 17.8 x 14
Johanna and Leslie Garfield Collection
Exhibited at Nasher only
[Fig.34]

Street Singers c.1914
Woodcut on paper
sheet: 18.5 x 13.4
image: 14.7 x 11.2
The Solomon R. Guggenheim Foundation, Peggy Guggenheim Collection, Venice. Gift, Erina Siciliani, 2007
Exhibited at PGC and Tate Britain only

Abstract Composition 1915
Gouache, pen, and pencil on paper 41.9 x 34.3
Tate. Purchased 1956
[No.20]

View of a Town [Canal Bank] 1916
Woodcut on paper
sheet: 15.9 x 24.8
Johanna and Leslie Garfield Collection
[No.75]
[S] Possibly version of *View of a Town* print purchased by Quinn; if so, very probably a version among 27 Wadsworth woodcuts Quinn sent to Sunwise Turn

Top of the Town c.1916
Woodcut on paper
sheet: 16.8 x 12.7; image 7 x 7.2
The Solomon R. Guggenheim Foundation, Peggy Guggenheim Collection, Venice. Gift, Erina Siciliani, 2009
Exhibited at PGC and Tate Britain only

Top of the Town c.1916–17
Woodcut on paper
sheet: 17.8 x 14
Johanna and Leslie Garfield Collection
Exhibited at Nasher only
[No.73]

Interior 1917
Woodcut on paper
sheet: 13.3 x 8.3
Johanna and Leslie Garfield Collection
[No.72]
[S] A version of print purchased by Quinn; a version very probably among 27 Wadsworth woodcuts Quinn sent to Sunwise Turn

Publications

Ezra Pound
Ripostes, 1912
Book, published by Stephen Swift & Co., London
Collection of Richard S. Frary
[Nos.54–5]

Ezra Pound (ed.),
Catholic Anthology, 1915
Cover design by Dorothy Shakespear
Book, published by Elkin Mathews, London
Collection of Richard S. Frary
[Nos.50–3]

Ezra Pound
Gaudier Brzeska: A Memoir, 1916
Book, published by John Lane, London
Collection of Richard S. Frary
[No.56]

Blast, no.1: *Review of the Great English Vortex*, 20 June 1914 (issued 1 July 1914)
Edited by Wyndham Lewis
Cover design by Wyndham Lewis
Magazine, published by John Lane, London
[No.29]
Four copies, lent by:

The Poetry Collection, State University of New York at Buffalo

Division of Rare and Manuscript Collections, Cornell University Library, Ithaca, NY

The Metropolitan Museum of Art, New York. The Elisha Whittelsey Collections, The Elisha Whittelsey Fund, 1967

Rare Books Collection, University of North Carolina – Chapel Hill

Blast, War Number: *Review of the Great English Vortex*, July 1915
Edited by Wyndham Lewis
Cover: Wyndham Lewis, *Before Antwerp*, 1915
Magazine, published by John Lane, London
[No.37]
Four copies, lent by:

The Poetry Collection, State University of New York at Buffalo

Division of Rare and Manuscript Collections, Cornell University Library, Ithaca, NY

The Metropolitan Museum of Art, New York. The Elisha Whittelsey Collections, The Elisha Whittelsey Fund, 1967

Rare Books Collection, University of North Carolina – Chapel Hill

Vorticist Exhibition, 1915
Introduction by Wyndham Lewis
Cover design by Wyndham Lewis
Exhibition catalogue, Doré Galleries, London
Tate Library and Archive
[Fig.28]

Exhibition of the Vorticists at the Penguin, 1917
Edited by John Quinn
Exhibition catalogue, Penguin Club, New York
Walt Kuhn, Kuhn Family Papers, and Armory Show Records, Archives of American Art, Smithsonian Institution, Washington, DC
[Fig.36]

Vortographs and Paintings by Alvin Langdon Coburn, 1917
Introductions by Coburn and Ezra Pound
Cover design by Coburn
Exhibition catalogue, the Camera Club, London
Victoria and Albert Museum, London
[Figs.38, 41]

Posters, flyers, invitations

Wyndham Lewis
Advertisement for Cabaret Theatre Club ('Cave of the Calf'), London, 1912
Poster
Division of Rare and Manuscript Collections, Cornell University Library, Ithaca, NY

Wyndham Lewis
Programme for 'The Cave of the Golden Calf' Cabaret Club, London, 1912
Booklet
The Poetry Collection, State University of New York at Buffalo
[Nos.45–6]

Wyndham Lewis
Invitation to attend Saturday gathering of members, The Rebel Art Centre, London, 1914
Flyer
The Poetry Collection, State University of New York at Buffalo

Invitation to 'Vital English Art' lecture by F.T. Marinetti and C.R.W. Nevinson, The Doré Galleries, London, 1 June 1914
Card
Division of Rare and Manuscript Collections, Cornell University Library, Ithaca, NY

Manifesto disassociating its members from Futurism, The Rebel Art Centre, London, 8 June 1914
Printed paper
Division of Rare and Manuscript Collections, Cornell University Library, Ithaca, NY

Promotional advertisement for *Blast*, no.1, 1914
Flyer
The Poetry Collection, State University of New York at Buffalo

Invitation to a 'Blast' dinner, Dieudonné Restaurant, London, 15 July 1914
Card
Division of Rare and Manuscript Collections, Cornell University Library, Ithaca, NY

Advertisement for the *First Vorticist Exhibition*, at the 'Doré Gallery', London, 1915
Poster
Division of Rare and Manuscript Collections, Cornell University Library, Ithaca, NY

Invitation to the private view of the *First Vorticist Exhibition*, The Doré Galleries, London, 10 June 1915
Card
Division of Rare and Manuscript Collections, Cornell University Library, Ithaca, NY

Wyndham Lewis
Invitation to a Vorticist evening, Restaurant La Tour Eiffel, London, 23 February 1916
Admission ticket
The Poetry Collection, State University of New York at Buffalo

LENDERS

Canada
Toronto, Art Gallery of Ontario

Italy
Venice, Fondazione Giorgio Cini onlus
Venice, Peggy Guggenheim Collection, The Solomon R. Guggenheim Foundation

United Kingdom
Bedford, Cecil Higgins Art Gallery
Birmingham, Birmingham Museums and Art Gallery
Cambridge, Kettle's Yard, University of Cambridge
London, Arts Council Collection, Southbank Centre
London, The British Council
London, Trustees of the British Museum
London, The Courtauld Gallery
London, Imperial War Museum
London, Tate
London, Victoria and Albert Museum
London, The Wyndham Lewis Memorial Trust
Manchester, Manchester City Art Galleries
Manchester, The Whitworth Art Gallery, University of Manchester

United States of America
Buffalo, Poetry Collection, State University of New York at Buffalo,
Clinton, NY, Fred L. Emerson Gallery, Hamilton College
Chapel Hill, NC, Rare Books Collection, University of North Carolina at Chapel Hill
Chicago, The David and Alfred Smart Museum of Art, The University of Chicago
Durham, NC, Archive of Documentary Arts, Rare Book, Manuscript, and Special Collections Library, Duke University Libraries
Ithaca, New York, Division of Rare Books and Manuscripts Collections, Cornell University Library
Minneapolis, The Minneapolis Institute of Arts
New Haven, CT, Yale Center for British Art
New Haven, CT, Yale University Art Gallery
New York, The Metropolitan Museum of Art
Rochester, NY, George Eastman House
Washington, DC, National Gallery of Art
Washington, DC, Walt Kuhn, Walt Kuhn family papers, and Armory Show records, Archives of American Art, Smithsonian Institution

Private collections
Ivor Braka Ltd
Richard S. Frary
Johanna and Leslie Garfield
And those lenders who wish to remain anonymous

CREDITS

Copyright credits

The publishers have made every effort to trace copyright holders but apologise for any omissions that may have inadvertantly been made.

David Bomberg: © The estate of David Bomberg, except no.6: © Tate
Alvin Langdon Coburn: works from George Eastman House © George Eastman House, International Museum of Photography and Film
Jacob Epstein: © The estate of Sir Jacob Epstein
Frederick Etchells: © The estate of Frederick Etchells
Christopher Nevinson: © The estate of Christopher Nevinson
William Roberts: © The estate of John David Roberts. By courtesy of the William Roberts Society
Helen Saunders: © The estate of Helen Saunders
Dorothy Shakespear: © Estate of Omar S. Pound
Edward Wadsworth: © Estate of Edward Wadsworth. All rights reserved, DACS 2010
Wyndham Lewis: © By kind permission of the Wyndham Lewis Memorial Trust (a registered charity)

Photo credits

Photo: Noel Allum nos.30, 72, 73, 75, 77; fig.34
Arts Council Collection, Southbank Centre, London nos.15, 59
© Birmingham Museums & Art Gallery no.3
British Council, London. Photo: Rodney Todd-White & Son no.67
© The British Library Board (*The Graphic*, 25 April 1914, p.726) fig.11
© The Trustees of the British Museum nos.12, 44, 76
The Courtauld Gallery, London. Photo: Richard Valencia no.47
International History of Photography Collection, Archive of Documentary Arts, Duke University fig.3
Courtesy George Eastman House, International Museum of Photography and Film nos.38, 71, 78, 79, 80, 81, 82, 83, 84, 85; figs.40, 42
Courtesy Fred L. Emerson Gallery, Hamilton College nos.18, 39, 40, 50
Photo: Lee Fatherree nos.2, 4, 5, 23, 33, 35, 48, 49a, 49b
The Trustees, Cecil Higgins Art Gallery, Bedford, England no.41
Imperial War Museum, London no.43
Kettle's Yard, University of Cambridge fig.24
Kettle's Yard, University of Cambridge. Photo: Peter Mennim no.27
Courtesy the Wyndham Lewis Memorial Trust fig.20
© Manchester City Galleries fig.18
Minneapolis Institute of Arts no.34
© Art Gallery of Ontario, Toronto. Photo: Ian Lefebvre nos.13, 36
Courtesy Private Collection fig.29
Prudence Cuming Associates Ltd fig.30
Image © 2010 The Metropolitan Museum of Art / Art Resource / Scala, Florence figs.35, 39
Senate House Library fig.26
© 2010 courtesy of The David and Alfred Smart Museum of Art, The University of Chicago nos.17, 68, 69, 70
Archives of American Art, Smithsonian Institution fig.36
Tate Photography nos.6, 7, 10, 19, 20, 24, 28, 42, 63, 64; figs.5, 14, 15
Tate Photography. Photo: Lucy Dawkins and Sam Drake nos.25, 62
Tate Photography. Photo: David Lambert no.14; fig.27
Tate Photography. Photo: Rodney Tidnam figs.10, 31, 32, 33; nos.16, 29, 37, 74
© V&A Images / Victoria and Albert Museum, London figs.17, 29, 38, 41, 57, 65, 66
Image © 2010 Board of Trustees, National Gallery of Art, Washington no.1; fig.25
The Whitworth Art Gallery, University of Manchester fig.37
Yale Centre for British Art no.60
Yale University Art Gallery nos.8, 9